TOWARDS
A NEW PAST

Dissenting Essays in American History

∞

TOWARDS

Dissenting Essays

 EDITED BY

VINTAGE BOOKS

A NEW PAST

in American History

BARTON J. BERNSTEIN

A Division of Random House, New York

Introduction

> A comprehension of the United States to-day,
> an understanding of the rise and progress of
> the forces which have made it what it is, de-
> mands that we should rework our history
> from the new points of view afforded by the
> present.
>
> —Frederick Jackson Turner,
> Presidential Address, American
> Historical Association (1910)

THIRTEEN YEARS after Frederick Jackson Turner's address, a young American historian, Arthur Meier Schlesinger, then thirty-five years old, chose those words for the title page of his *New Viewpoints in American History*. Writing in the heyday of progressive history and himself a progressive historian, Schlesinger aimed to "summarize . . . some of the results of the research of the present era of historical study and to show their importance to a proper understanding" of the American past. Adding his own interpretations, he presented a broadened conception of history, and in the process relied upon the impressive contributions of other progressive historians, most notably Turner and Charles A. Beard.

For Turner and Beard, for Carl L. Becker and Schlesinger, for the progressive historians in general, history was more than past politics and military battles. As they enlarged the conception of the historical enterprise, they also stressed its pragmatic function. Historical inquiry, as their "new history" emphasized, should be relevant to the present. Theirs was not a narrow conception of relevance, and their history did not express a commitment to the fleeting issues of the present. Believing that deep-rooted concerns should guide their efforts and influence their studies, they hoped that these studies would be useful in promoting liberal, democratic reform. Logically, there was no conflict between their aims of writing objective history and of influencing change. But in practice a tension developed, and their history was sometimes distorted by their commitments, provoking hostile criticism from a later generation.

Though Turner's influence may have begun to slip by the end of the twenties, the appearance in that decade of *New Viewpoints,* Beard's *The Rise of American Civilization,* and Vernon Louis Parrington's *Main Currents in American Thought* marked the triumph of the progressive synthesis. In broad outlines, it viewed much of American history as a struggle between the privileged and the less privileged: sometimes, as in the lingering influence of Turner, between sections; at other times, as in the works of Beard, Schlesinger, and Becker, between classes or economic interests. This history was marked by emphasis upon upheaval and "revolutions," upon conflicts between rival ideologies.

In the years before World War II, the volumes of Parrington and Beard were probably the most influential, and their interpretations were complementary. For Parrington, American history was generally the struggle between the forces of Jefferson and Hamilton, between liberalism and conservatism, between democracy and oligarchy, between agrarianism and capitalism. In a series of important volumes, Beard had traced the agrarian-capitalistic antagonism from the Revolution to Populism. For him the Constitution represented the triumph of personal property: the imposition upon reluctant agrarians (usually small farmers and debtors) of an economic document designed to protect and advance the interests of merchants, manufacturers, bankers, and speculators. This alignment of interests provided the economic basis of Jeffersonian Democracy: "the struggle between the agrarian masses led by slave-holding planters" and Northern capitalists. Explaining the Civil War as "the irrepressible conflict between Southern agrarianism and Northern capitalism," Beard emphasized that "the institution of slavery was not the fundamental issue." The war marked the triumph of capitalism, and, in turn, the gains of this Second American Revolution were protected by Reconstruction.

Even in its broad outlines this synthesis was unacceptable to some, and it failed to deal adequately with racism, slavery, and imperialism. Generally avoiding the problem of racism, Beard also failed to understand slavery—that it defined much of the Southern system. Only belatedly, in the thirties, did he turn to a thoughtful analysis of imperialism. Then fearing that democratic reform might be sacrificed to involvement in war for the second time in twenty years, he warned against the foreign policy of the past: it "ostensibly seeks the welfare of the United States by pushing and holding doors open in all parts of the world with all engines of government, ranging from polite coercion to the use of arms." Calling for the end of this Open Door policy, he urged the nation to halt the quest for foreign markets and to restructure the domestic economy to absorb surpluses.

Though this general analysis would later guide and inspire a prominent school of younger "left" historians (the so-called Wisconsin School associated with Professors Fred Harvey Harrington and William Appleman Williams), during the war years Beard's efforts were moving out of touch with American intellectual sentiment. His bitter attacks upon Roosevelt's foreign policy estranged many liberal historians who had admired him. His analysis of American international relations seemed profoundly wrong to them, but they still commended his earlier history and often based their own work upon the framework he had been so instrumental in establishing.

II

Actually the progressive synthesis had been under monographic attack before Pearl Harbor, and seemed to fall apart under the sustained assaults of the postwar years. In its place by the early fifties a new and more conservative view of the American past began to dominate historical writing. Though avoiding an over-arching interpretation, this new view, as Professor John Higham has explained, emphasized the homogeneity of the national past. In place of "convulsive movements" and deep economic cleavages, this new generation found consensus and continuity. With the exception of the Civil War and often the New Deal, there were, according to this school of thought, no significant discontinuities in American history.

Despite the continuing concern among some with the problems of Southern identity and a reawakened hostility to Negro slavery, the very emphases of this new history, as well as its methods and questions, tended to erode what was distinctive in the historical experience and even to blend it into catagories such as myth and paradox which minimized or embraced conflict. The renewed influence of Alexis de Tocqueville, the emphasis on social status, the quest for national character—all contributed to a neglect of classes and to a denigration or denial of ideological cleavage.

As sharers of a common ideology (presented by Professor Daniel Boorstin in a slightly different form as "givenness") and as "men on the make," Americans, according to Professors Richard Hofstadter and Louis Hartz, operated within a narrow framework in which even the dissenters usually accepted the fundamental tenets of the liberal tradition. Jacksonian Democrats, despite their nostalgia for a vanishing agrarian age, were incipient capitalists. Populists, by this interpretation, were frustrated and baffled capitalists. According to this general view, protest was understood frequently as a sour response to thwarted capitalist expectations, even as evidence of irrationality.

Believing that the nation had achieved affluence and that political power was widely distributed, American historians, along with many other intellectuals, celebrated the accomplishments of democratic capitalism. As they looked back across their national history, many affirmed the triumph of liberalism and often found in the New Deal dramatic proof of the success of nonideological reform. Rooted in the postwar decade, their history (perhaps by inadvertence) frequently supported those who proclaimed the end of ideology in the Western world and sometimes called for the defense of national values against the Communist threat. In their work, as well as in their public activities, some even came to identify the protection of freedom with the advancement of the state's interests.

Though few historians speculated publicly on the nature and function of history, most assumed that it had a relevance to the present. Some scholars, most notably Professor C. Vann Woodward and the historian-diplomat George Kennan, made clear in their analyses their commitments to change, yet sought to keep their studies free of partisan bias. But most did not openly direct their studies to the need or possibility for change. Rejecting the pragmatism of much progressive history, on the one hand, and acknowledging the impossibility of objective history, on the other, they were unwilling to make of written history "an act of faith" (as Beard had done in 1933). They usually affirmed their ability to avoid presentism and plunged on *towards* their noble dream—nearly objective history. Yet, despite these efforts, their history often reflected the needs and values of the fifties.

To emphasize the influence of the times upon their work is not to discredit them nor necessarily to invalidate their efforts. To repudiate them on this basis could be to confuse concept formation (how one gets an idea) with judgment formation (how one determines validity), and to fall victim to the genetic fallacy—the belief that the source of a theory affects its validity. It is not the *source* of a theory, but its *accuracy* which is of concern; unfortunately, however, not all historical theories can be examined for accuracy. Even those philosophers who believe that historical statements of causation and description are confirmable, recognize that much of the important work by historians cannot be proven—certainly value judgments cannot, and perhaps not even interpretations of motivation and analyses of character. Yet, these quite properly were often the subjects that concerned the historians of the fifties, and their responses, in particular, gave to that history much of its distinctive quality.

III

During the early sixties the conservative consensus began to break down. For many, the rediscovery of poverty and racism, the commitment to civil rights for Negroes, the criticism of intervention in Cuba and Vietnam, shattered many of the assumptions of the fifties and compelled intellectuals to re-examine the American past. From historians, and particularly from younger historians, there began to emerge a vigorous criticism of the historical consensus. Some, like Pro-

fessors Eugene Genovese, Jesse Lemisch, and Michael Lebowitz, were traveling along this path without the spur of
events. Others might also have independently followed a
similar path to find new perspectives on the past, and even
those who acknowledge the impact of events upon their developments are unsure of the precise influence.

In discussing this still small but apparently growing movement within the past few years, the historical profession has
come to speak of a "New Left." Though defying precise definition and lumping together those who believe in objective
history with those who do not, the term does denote a group
of various "left" views—whether they be Marxist, neo-Beard-
ian, radical, or left-liberal. In this loose sense it links some of
the more exciting young historians whose work has broken
with the earlier consensus, and understood in that way the
concept is useful and meaningful.

Unfortunately most of this new history has been restricted
to university monographs or tucked away in historical journals, usually beyond the public's reach. To make this new
revisionism more available, a number of these historians
were invited to contribute to this volume; fortunately, most
were able to accept the invitation, thus only leaving a few
fields uncovered. The mandate was general and each contributor was encouraged to develop his own interpretation
of the period or problems which he had been studying. None
was expected to cover more than he could comfortably treat
within a brief essay, and each was the final judge of emphasis
and focus.

Though some subjects obviously remain undiscussed, the
resulting essays represent the revisionism in process during
the late sixties. They express the new departures of recent
years and break with the older consensus history. While not
constituting a new synthesis but rather a series of approaches
and interpretations, they do emphasize the ideological cleavages of the past more than did the historians of the fifties.

As sophisticated Marxists, Professors Eugene Genovese
and Michael Lebowitz avoid the pitfalls of economic determinism or of treating ideology simply as a reflection of economic structure. Briskly criticizing Marxists for these errors
and Beardians for their narrow conception of slavery, Pro-

fessor Genovese emphasizes the need to understand the Slave South as a distinctive social system and to move beyond facile moral judgments in explaining the hegemony of its ruling class. By relating ideology and politics to economic conditions, Professor Lebowitz seeks to dissolve the paradox of Jacksonian Democracy—that the Jacksonian Democrats were incipient capitalists ("men on the make") moving forward, yet by their rhetoric seeking to restore the virtues of a simpler age. Declining farmers, not rising farmers, he suggests, were more likely to be Jacksonians, and they could not properly understand their problems as long as they believed in a well-ordered, self-regulating universe in which legislative interference seemed unnatural.

Reflecting the influence of Professors Fred Harvey Harrington, William Appleman Williams, and Charles Beard, Professors Lloyd Gardner and Robert F. Smith have emphasized the role of the Open Door ideology in twentieth-century American international relations. They sharply disagree with those who stress the "political" interpretation of American foreign policy, and are critical of those "realists," like George Kennan, who do not acknowledge American efforts to maintain a world order conducive to the prosperity and power of the United States.

An admirer and sympathetic critic of Beard, Professor Staughton Lynd has built upon part of the Beardian framework his explanation of the movement for the Constitution. Unlike Beard, however, he also focuses upon slavery as a source of tension leading to the creation of early sectional parties.

Moving further beyond Beard, Professor Jesse Lemisch, in his study of the American Revolution, broadens the analysis of ideology. "Some of Beard's democratic heroes turn out to be part of an antipopulist consensus," writes Lemisch. "Leaders like Jefferson and Adams may *indeed* have shared a basic agreement—on a kind of antipopulism. Thus the conflicts among those within the *merely* liberal consensus become less important than those between the 'mainstream' and those outside of it." A proper study of this latter group, he believes, requires "a revolution in historiographical attitudes, a rejection of elite history: a history 'from the bottom up' will be more nearly objectively valid than has been the attempt to understand the past through the eyes of a few at the top." Also focusing largely on the masses—the workers and migrants—in late nineteenth-century cities, Professor Stephan Thernstrom investigates the process and meaning of mobility. In the cities he finds less upward mobility than earlier historical *speculations* had allowed, and he has also uncovered a rootless population whose very movements may have impeded proletarian consciousness.

Taking issue with the Williams school and the consensus historians, Dr. Marilyn B. Young has sought to broaden the analysis of late nineteenth-century expansion. The quest for markets, she concludes, was based upon a dubious economic analysis, and both business and government, despite their rhetoric, often failed to pursue economic opportunities abroad. Expansion, she contends, must be understood in a larger framework that will accommodate flawed economic perceptions as well as the social tension of those decades—the fear of cities as "jungles," the threats of upheaval, the renewed vigor of racism.

As historians have become more troubled by American racism, they have come to focus sympathetically upon the plight of the American Negro. More than a decade ago, Professor C. Vann Woodward suggested that the abolitionists had abandoned the freedman, and more recently Professor James McPherson, his former student, has re-examined their commitments. Modifying Woodward's conclusions, he finds among these liberals and their heirs a mixed response to the challenges of racism and equality.

In my own essays on the New Deal and the later politics of the Roosevelt and Truman years, I have explored the shortcomings of liberalism in practice—the conservative achievements of the New Deal, the wartime retreat to official prejudice, the limitations of Fair Deal reforms, the mixed heritage of civil rights, and the postwar liberal assault upon civil liberties. In a closely related essay on anticommunism and contemporary liberalism, Professor Christopher Lasch, in focusing upon the Congress for Cultural Freedom, analyzes the ideology and behavior of prominent American intellectuals who for nearly two decades defined much of their purpose by their anticommunism.

It is fitting that Professor Lasch's essay* should conclude this volume, for his is a study of the very period—the Cold War—in which we came to intellectual maturity, and his is probably the most direct treatment of a theme running through most of these essays: the meaning of American liberalism. Though there has been no full-scale effort to define American liberalism nor to trace it systematically over the course of nearly two centuries, most of the contributors are concerned with aspects of this subject.

In some of these analyses, though not in all, the authors have sought explicitly to make the past speak to the present, to ask questions that have a deep-rooted moral and political relevance. In moving occasionally beyond description and causal analysis to judge significance, we have, by necessity, moved beyond objective history to the realm of values. In this venture we are following the practice, though not necessarily the prescription, of earlier generations of historians, and responding in a modest way to the call issued a few years ago to move "beyond consensus."

BARTON J. BERNSTEIN

Stanford, California
July, 1967

* His essay was first prepared for the *Nation* and later revised for this volume.

CONTENTS

TOWARDS
A NEW PAST

Dissenting Essays in American History

∽

THE AMERICAN REVOLUTION SEEN FROM THE BOTTOM UP

∽ Jesse Lemisch

Who built the seven towers of Thebes?
The books are filled with names of kings.
Was it kings who hauled the craggy blocks of stone? . . .
In the evening when the Chinese wall was finished
Where did the masons go? . . .

Young Alexander plundered India.
He alone?
Caesar beat the Gauls.
Was there not even a cook in his army?
Philip of Spain wept as his fleet
Was sunk and destroyed. Were there no other tears?
Frederick the Great triumphed in the Seven
Years War. Who
Triumphed with him? . . .

Every ten years a great man,
Who paid the piper?

So many particulars.
So many questions.

—Bertolt Brecht[1]

IN 1921 Samuel Eliot Morison used what he called a "blue-book of Boston provincial society" to demonstrate the ethnic diversity of the "Yankee race," and measured the growth of towns around Boston by the construction of mansions. Morison admired the "codfish aristocracy," and he looked at colonial Massachusetts largely from their point of view. Thus he imposed on the entire society the characteristics and values which he had discovered in an admiring examination of a part of it: the characteristics of the "Yankee race" seemed identical to those of the "middle class."[2]

In the half-century since, historians have become more sophisticated in their generalizations. In a landmark essay in the fifties one of them criticized his colleagues for their failure "to think or write as social scientists" and especially for their "reliance on leaders" as a basis for describing a "class, section, or society as a whole." But then he proceeded to urge the assembling of "the large number of career lines of different types of social *leaders* [emphasis added], essential for a picture of who succeeded in the society and how" and offered the reader a paean to the entrepreneur and a plea for more histories of business and of "important business figures." Instead of replacing elite history with a history of "average people," he had merely traded in the heroes of politics for the heroes of business.[3]

Despite our pretensions to social science, we would seem to be hardly more genuinely scientific than we were fifty years ago. Many social scientists continue to draw conclusions about entire societies on the basis of examinations of the minority at the top.[4] This approach has distorted our view and, sometimes, cut us off from past reality. Our earliest history has been seen as a period of consensus and classlessness, in part because our historians have chosen to see it that way. One of them, describing colonial Massachusetts as a "middle-class democracy," has tried to show that urban workers could qualify for the vote by offering evidence which sometimes proves only that their *employers* could do so,[5] much as one might demonstrate that slaves had it easy by describing the life of the antebellum Southern belle. Another has diluted a useful study of Loyalism and blocked our understanding of any possible class aspects of this phenomenon by presenting his data in a form which does not distinguish between employers and employees.[6] In a valuable study of legislatures before and after the Revolution, another tells us that "colonials . . . did not yet conceive that the *demos* should actually govern." *Which* colonials? Earlier in the same article he had noted that "the majority . . . were not asked, and as they were unable to speak or write on the subject, their opinions were uncertain."[7] Thus the conclusion about "colonials" indicates either that the historian has allowed the opinions of an elite to stand for those of a majority or that he has forgotten that he really does not know what the majority thought. This dilemma suggests two very different ways of writing history.

The first way, the one criticized so far, assumes the absence of conflict without demonstrating it. After consensus has been assumed, the very categories of analysis foreclose the possibility that the researcher will find evidence of conflict. History of this sort can lead, as Staughton Lynd has noted, to such grotesqueries as the claim that "equality" is at the center of American history, a claim which ignores the Negro, among others.[8] (One might with as much evidence claim that the main theme of American history has been a kind of righteous hypocrisy and point to the gap between pretension and performance indicated in our early history by slaveowners discoursing on equality and, more recently, in the newspeak of a nation which claims to value justice above all but defines justice as order and values power more than either.[9]) In a world in which many non-American movie audiences cheer every time another cowboy hits the dust we can no longer afford such obtuseness. And in our history we can no longer allow the powerful to speak for the powerless.

Those who rule may have, as Barrington Moore has put it, "the most to hide about the way society works." And these are the very people who are most favored by history and historical sources. Thus "sympathy with the victims of historical processes and skepticism about the victors' claims provide essential safeguards against being taken in by the dominant mythology."[10] (Indeed, Herbert Marcuse has suggested, in defense of Lord Acton's moralism, that a society may be most accurately judged through an examination of its worst injustices: such an approach uncovers "the deepest layer of the whole system, the structure which holds it together, the essential condition for the efficiency of its political and economic organization."[11]) This sympathy for the powerless brings us closer to objectivity; in practice, it leads the historian to describe past societies as they appeared from the bottom rather than the top, more from the point of view of the inarticulate than of the articulate. Such an approach will have two components. It will continue to examine the elite, but instead of using them as surrogates for the society beneath them, it will ask how their beliefs and conduct impinged on that society. Having determined the place of those who were ruled in the ideology of those who rule, it will study the conduct and ideology of the people on the bottom: this is nothing less than an attempt to make the inarticulate speak. This second task is perhaps more difficult than the first. But both can and indeed must be done if our generalizations about past societies are to have more than limited validity. A small part of the necessary work has been done, and a radically new view is just now becoming visible: it is hoped that some of the readers of this essay will do more. It is the purpose of this essay to suggest how we might approach the history of the inarticulate in the period of the American Revolution and to outline what such a history might look like. We begin with a critical examination of the place of the inarticulate in the political thought and practice of the colonial elite and proceed to an examination of the thought and conduct of the inarticulate themselves.

In 1955 Robert E. Brown joined the throng of social scientists who have been telling us that America is a classless society, a land of unblocked opportunity. Brown said it had always been so, or at least as far back as seventeenth-century Massachusetts, which he labeled a "middle-class democracy"; the "common man" in America "had come into his own long before the era of Jacksonian Democracy."[12] Brown argued persuasively against the idea that colonial America was "undemocratic" and especially against the idea that "property qualifications for voting eliminated a large portion of the free adult male population from participation in political affairs."[13] He showed that qualifications were often waived in practice: election officials often winked at voting by the underage or financially unqualified. At any rate, the qualifications were low enough and economic opportunity high enough so that, Brown's sampling technique indicated, most men could meet them. Of course there were a few exceptions: men whose work carried them to sea, some tenant farmers, a few town dwellers; but even these could expect, some day, to make it. Surrounded with all these blessings, Americans went to war to hold on to a good thing: the "revolution," said Brown (his quotation marks questioning the very relevance of such a term), aimed "to preserve a social order rather than to change it."[14]

Brown's methods have come under heavy fire, with Lee Benson suggesting that there may be "no basis in fact" for the Brown thesis.[15] Using statistical techniques similar to Brown's, John Cary has been able to demonstrate that 100 percent of the farmers and artisans of Massachusetts were disfranchised by the property requirements.[16] Cary attaches no particular significance to his results: for a sample to mean anything, we must have some definition of the criteria used in selecting it. Brown's reply has been a partial backdown, but he has stuck to his guns in saying that the materials which he took from deeds and wills "could be called samples only in the sense of being examples, but they were *typical examples*."[17] This is a language unknown to social science. Still, Brown has raised significant questions, and someone else might make the same points with better evidence. Certainly it is the style to try. So let us examine more closely the contention that colonial America was democratic.

In a recent study which was optimistic enough about mobility in revolutionary America to elicit a "Welcome abroad [sic]!" from Brown, Jackson Turner Main nonetheless uncovered a "proletariat" comprising "nearly 40 percent" of the population.[18] Geographical mobility was extremely high among the poor.[19] Did this translate into vertical mobility: was mobility out the same as mobility up? Main tells us that mobility is "almost impossible to study in detail," but he proceeds to equate the frontier with upward mobility. Thus, although there was a "permanent proletariat" *within* the

proletariat, it was very small.[20] How small? "Habitual drift-
ers" made up between 5 and 15 percent of the population, he
estimates.[21] He offers figures which bring the total up to between 26.9 and 30.7 percent and indicates that in the pre-
Revolutionary years 80 percent of indentured servants "died,
became landless workers, or returned to England."[22]

Main concludes that "the long-term tendency seems to
have been toward greater inequality" and a "growing number of poor."[23] Elsewhere, J. R. Pole has noted the potential
for increasing disfranchisement if suffrage is attached to
property in an area undergoing the kind of economic changes
which were taking place in eighteenth-century America.[24]
That potentiality was fast becoming actuality on Brown's
ground—Boston—where James Henretta's statistical work
reveals the existence of a propertyless proletariat comprising
14 percent of the adult males in 1687 and 29 percent in 1771.
With the population doubled, "for every man who slept in
the back of a shop, in a tavern, or in a rented room in 1687,
there were four" in 1771.[25] Increasingly, colonial Boston was
less a place of equality and opportunity, more a place of social stratification. Throughout America property qualifications excluded more and more people from voting until a
"Jacksonian Revolution" was necessary to overthrow what
had become a very limited middle-class "democracy" indeed.

What if Brown *were* right? What if every single person
could vote in the colonies? Would that prove that the common man had come into his own? The common man rarely
ran for office: the obstacles in the way of attaining office were
far greater than those in the way of voting.[26] Throughout
America, custom and law dictated the perpetuation in power
of a ruling oligarchy similar in profile to the exclusive club
which ruled England.[27] "Birth into one of the ruling families
was almost essential to the making of a political career in
18th century Virginia," says one historian.[28] The family patterns, the religious, social, and educational homogeneity of
the House of Commons were duplicated in the House of
Burgesses.[29] An examination of six pre-Revolutionary legislatures shows that the "economic elite" comprising the top
10 percent of the population held 85 percent of the seats.[30]

Even the town meeting was not in fact the hotbed of democracy of popular myth: Samuel Eliot Morison has called "political democracy" in colonial Massachusetts a "sham," and a recent study has detailed the devices which the powerful used to control the town meeting. Boston meetings were often called with whole wards unnotified, and Brown's contention that actual qualifications were less rigid than legal qualifications bears ironic fruit when the evidence is examined more closely: we find not only informal enfranchisement but also informal *dis*franchisement, all depending not on some conception of democracy but rather on how those with power thought people might vote on a particular issue.[31]

Those who might suppose that the rise of the lower houses of the colonial legislatures was equivalent to a rise in popular control of government would do well to undertake a critical examination of the laws which they wrote.[32] First of all, regardless of the extent of disfranchisement, it did not just happen: one group—the legislators—had to take deliberate steps to deprive others of the vote.[33] Sometimes legislation was a blatantly one-sided expression of class interest.[34] (And even if the laws themselves were written fairly, the poor might find themselves more harshly punished for the same offenses than were the rich.[35]) If the assemblies stood for popular control, why was there so much conflict between the people and the legislatures on questions of civil liberties? Leonard Levy has characterized the image of a colonial America "which cherished freedom of expression" as "a sentimental hallucination that ignores history."[36]

If colonial legislatures seemed in many ways like the House of Commons, this was no accident: they strove to be, and they were elected in the same way—publicly and loudly, with influential candidates on hand to note how their dependents were voting and sometimes to thank them with such remarks as "I shall treasure that vote in my memory. It will be regarded as a feather in my cap forever."[37] Although this is hardly free voting, some historians believe that many elections might not have turned out noticeably differently even if the ballot had been secret. For throughout the colonies they see a habit of *deference* on the part of the lower and middle classes disposing them to accept the upper class as their rulers.[38]

Did the people defer to their rulers? Certainly we know that their rulers expected them to defer.[39] Obedience was fully within the Lockean tradition. The *Second Treatise* is full of reassurance lest Locke's reader fear that the assertion of a right of revolution might lead to the overthrow of government "as often as it shall please a busie head, or turbulent spirit."[40] Revolution is permissible only after "a long train of Abuses" convinces the *majority* that the time has come for an "Appeal to Heaven." Until that time the stress is on "*Obedience to the Legislative*": the premature dissenter is "the common Enemy and Pest of Mankind" and deserves "ruine and perdition." Obedience is mandatory until the majority concludes that the government has broken its trust. Developing within this tradition, the political theory of the colonial elite saw the people as subordinate to their legislators. As Richard Buel, Jr. has put it: the people could apply the brakes when their rulers went off the track, but they could not dictate to them so long as they were still on the track. And when rulers went off the track—as the British did in 1776—the people were bound to obey the new governments which replaced them.[41]

A month before the Declaration of Independence, John Adams—who had earlier boasted of the subordination of the people of Massachusetts—found it necessary to preach obedience: "how much soever I may heretofore have found fault with the powers that were, I suppose I shall be well pleased to hear submission inculcated to the powers that are."[42] Adams "dreaded the Effect so popular a pamphlet" as Tom Paine's *Common Sense* "might have, among the People," and had set out to counteract Paine's plan, which he thought "so democratical, without any restraint or even an Attempt at any Equilibrium or Counterpoise, that it must produce confusion and every Evil Work."[43] In his *Thoughts on Government* Adams argued against a unicameral legislature and urged that electoral reform be delayed: "At present, it will be safest to proceed in all established modes, to which the people have been familiarized by habit."[44]

American leaders moved slowly toward independence; they had to prove, both to themselves and to the world outside, that they were not mere busy heads and unnatural rebels. They seemed to prefer "the forms to which they are accustomed"—Adams' "established modes"—and feared that it would be imprudent to change "Governments long established . . . for light and transient causes." But if "a long train of abuses" (here Jefferson's Declaration used precisely Locke's phrase) demonstrated a purpose "to reduce them under absolute Despotism," then—*only then*—it was their right, indeed their duty, to overthrow the government.[45] "Such," indeed, *had* been "the patient sufferance of these Colonies," said Jefferson the lawyer, and "To prove this" he filled more than half of the Declaration with a list of justifications for this particular rebellion.

The men who wrote and signed the Declaration of Independence were far from literal in their interpretation of the phrase "all men are created equal." Jefferson's belief that urban workingmen were "the panders of vice and the instruments by which the liberties of a country are generally overturned" suggests the narrow limits of his faith in the ability of what he unashamedly called "the swinish multitude" to govern itself.[46] And although the Congress rejected his condemnation of the slave *trade,* it did let stand his attack on the King who had excited insurrection by offering slaves their freedom if they would desert their masters.[47] It seems entirely likely that the Negro never even entered Jefferson's mind as he wrote of the equality of men: his later statements on the Negro characterize him as a definitely inferior being, and possibly inferior by nature rather than merely by condition.[48]

The meaning of Jefferson's egalitarianism in 1776 can be better understood if we examine its institutional implementation in his drafts for a constitution for Virginia. His plan resembled that presented in Adams' *Thoughts on Government:* a bicameral legislature, with only the lower house directly elected, and with senators elected for lengthy terms, possibly for life.[49] A similar antipopulism expressed itself in most of the other state constitutions: all but three provided for bicameral legislatures; property qualifications were prescribed in most; qualifications for electors and members of the upper houses were higher than for the lower houses and terms were generally longer.[50]

Some of the state constitutions went against this trend: Pennsylvania's was the most notable. Here a convention led by men who put "personal liberty and safety" ahead of "the possession and security of property"[51] drew up a constitution on the principle that "any man, even the most illiterate, is as capable of any office as a person who has had the benefit of education."[52] An early draft of a bill of rights spoke of the dangers of large concentrations of wealth in the hands of a few and saw the discouragement of such concentrations as a proper role for government.[53] The constitution as finally adopted was only slightly less populist. Its enemies called it a poor man's constitution: the people cherished their copies as they did the Bible, and they would later take up arms against its domestic opponents.[54] The Preamble and Declaration of Rights established a government "without partiallity [sic] for or prejudice against any particular class, sect or denomination of Men whatever" in which officers of government were "servants, . . . at all times accountable" to the people: "Government is or ought to be Instituted for the Common Benefit Protection and Security of the People, Nation or Community, and not for the particular Emolument or advantage of any Single man, Family, or set of Men, who are a part only of that Community." Property qualifications were abolished for both voters and officeholders.[55] Power was centered in a single legislature, annually elected, checked, and balanced by the people themselves, to whom the doors of the assembly hall were to be open and who were to participate in lawmaking through a device resembling the referendum.[56] Various officeholders were made more accountable—to meet "the danger of Establishing an inconvenient Aristocracy"—by rotation in office and limits on terms, while other provisions abolished imprisonment for debt and established the right of conscientious objection.

The Pennsylvania Constitution of 1776 shows the mark of Tom Paine's thought, if not his authorship.[57] In *Common Sense* Paine had been concerned that "the *elected* might never form to themselves an interest separate from the *electors*"; he ridiculed the idea of checks and balances in England and proposed for each colony a single-house legislature, to meet annually; elections must be held often, in order that a "frequent interchange [among electors and elected] will establish a common interest." Later, he defended the Pennsylvania Constitution, calling it good for rich and poor alike and supporting the elimination of property qualifications and the establishment of a unicameral legislature: *"bolts, bars,* and *checks"* were only an obstacle to freedom. All in all, Paine is one man whom we should not be timid about calling a "democrat": when he spoke of freedom or rights, he meant "a perfect equality of them," and he was quite literal about it. A unicameralist in an age of checks and balances, he was also an abolitionist, an internationalist, something of a feminist and anticolonialist, and one of the few leaders of the American Revolution to apply his egalitarianism to the plight of the poor.[58] He was in the tradition of the Levellers,[59] and his thought presents an alternative and a standard by which to judge the thought of the other leaders of the Revolution, for most of whom Locke went far enough.

Although Paine clearly represents a minority strain in American political thought, he was not alone in 1776. Others, many of them anonymous pamphleteers, felt that the people, who "best know their own wants and necessities," were "best able to rule themselves."[60] They tried to fight back "against the sly insinuations and proposals of those of a more arbitrary turn," and urged instead the establishment of a "well-regulated Democracy."[61] And, as if in direct response to those who would later call the Revolution conservative, these thinkers made it clear that, regardless of what *others* might seek, *they* were planning something genuinely new: "A truly popular Government has . . . never yet been tried in the world."[62] So they argued against checks and balances and for the right of "any free male of ordinary capacity" to vote and hold office, against a form of representation which gave "the man who owns six times as much as another . . . six times the power" and for such imaginative populist devices as juries of "not less than Twenty-five, a majority of which shall make a verdict."[63]

In the midst of the ferment of the year 1776 the Philadelphia Yearly Meeting of the Society of Friends decided to bar from membership those who continued to own slaves. The decision of 1776 was the outcome of over a century of anti-slavery agitation among Quakers. In 1688 the Germantown Quakers had condemned slavery as a violation of the freedom to which all men were entitled, and two decades before the Declaration of Independence the New Jersey Quaker John Woolman had applied to slavery the observation that "liberty [is] the natural right of all men equally."[64] That the Quakers thought these thoughts demonstrates that others could have, as well;[65] the range of thought among such groups as the Quakers gives us another perspective from which to examine early American values. Quakers had disobeyed unjust laws long before the American Revolution.[66] They steered clear of the American mainstream in their increasingly humane treatment of Negroes and were usually equally deviant and equally humane in their conduct toward Indians, other religious and ethnic groups, women, and the poor.[67] Few more striking alternatives to the American business ethos can be found than John Woolman, aged thirty-six, telling his customers to go elsewhere, so that he could lessen an increasingly prosperous business in order better to seek "the real substance of religion, where practice doth harmonize with principle." This absolutism, this literalism, is in a sense definitive of radicalism in a culture which has had no lack of high principles but a great deal of difficulty realizing those principles.[68]

The contradictions and limitations in the thought of Revolutionary leaders such as John Adams become evident in the light of the alternatives suggested above. Adams' exhortation to set up a representative assembly which "should be in miniature an exact portrait of the people at large" is directly contradicted by the treatment of the franchise as a "benefit" rather than a right and by the limitation of the vote—in Adams' Massachusetts Constitution—to those having "sufficient qualifications." The insistence on bicameralism and on checks and balances *within* the government is narrow when viewed from the perspective of those who attempted to make government more strictly accountable to the people: if a single assembly is, indeed, "liable to all the vices, follies, and frailties of an individual," thinkers with a broader vision than Adams would attempt to check it from below—with more democracy—rather than from above, with less. One need not question the sincerity of Adams' belief in balance to note that he is interested in balancing rich and poor and that while Paine and Woolman would agree with him that "the rich are *people* as well as the poor, . . . they have rights as well as others," it does not necessarily follow that the rich "have as clear and as *sacred* a right to their large property as others have to theirs which is smaller." While others were trying to make society over, Adams focused on the "depravity" of human nature and the inequalities among men (which he felt that he could perceive in four-day-old infants); certain that there would always be inequalities of wealth and that human nature as it will be was the same as human nature as it has been and as it is, he proceeded to erect a governmental structure which, by accepting and institutionalizing the inequalities, in a sense helped to guarantee that they *would* endure.[69]

In order to demonstrate that humane and democratic thoughts, in some ways more in tune with a later age, could be conceived in 1776, we need find only one man who thought them; in fact there were many such men. Surely the intellectual and empirical ingredients which produced the thought of a Paine or a Woolman were available to an Adams or a Jefferson. (Even if the *ingredients* of such thought were not available, the *product* was, in the form of personal conduct and published writings.) Thus we cannot explain the failure of the Revolution's leaders to choose more democratic and humane ways on grounds that the ideas' time had not yet come. The ideas were in the marketplace; the leaders' failure to buy them constitutes a choice, even if they did not conceive of it as such. Against this background, the meaning of the phrase "all men are created equal" to the men who signed the Declaration becomes clearer: they interpreted it in a limited way, and in doing so, rejected alternatives offered by their contemporaries and their predecessors. Those who have cried out for "liberty" have often sought no more than the liberty of a few, intending nothing in the way of social revolution: the liberties spoken of by Coke and Pym were primarily, as Christopher Hill has suggested, "the rights of the propertied."[70] George Rudé has seen a similar pattern in the French *parlement*'s claim that it was the guardian of the nation's "liberties" when by "liberty" it in fact often meant "privilege."[71] Thus, those who, like Daniel Boorstin,[72] have asserted that the Revolution aimed only at separation from Great Britain and not at social revolution are quite right, but only insofar as they have described the attitudes of the elite: what the common people and articulate radicals made of the Declaration of Independence may have been quite a different matter.

The evidence presented thus far suggests that in 1776 confidence in "established modes" was far from a universal sentiment. To say that Paine, Woolman, and the others mentioned above took the egalitarianism of the Declaration more literally than did those who signed the document is to say that there existed in 1776 a body of political thought which did not endorse deference. To detect such a body of thought is not necessarily to demonstrate that the people who were supposed to defer refused to do so. However, it is suggestive: people less articulate than those mentioned thus far might have developed similar ideas directly out of the actual experience of their lives. As John Woolman put it, describing the origins of war,

> Wealth is attended with power, by which bargains and proceedings contrary to universal righteousness are supported; and hence oppression, carried on with worldly policy and order, clothes itself with the name of justice and becomes like a seed of discord in the soul . . . so the seeds of war swell and sprout and grow. . . .[73]

Woolman says nothing more than this: inequalities of power produce oppression, which produces discontent. Perhaps Woolman's generalization grew in part out of his observation of discord within colonial society. Such an observation suggests that poor people in early America expressed discontent in some way against the rich.

During the period of the American Revolution there was just such an expression from below: the powerless refused to stay in the places to which a theory of deference and subordination assigned them. Among the most blatant cases are those of Negroes who petitioned for that freedom to which, "*as*

men," they claimed they had "a naturel [sic] right"; they re-
minded their masters that their struggle was merely "[In
imitat]ion of the Lawdable [sic] Example of the Good People
of these States" who were "nobly contending, in the Cause of
Liberty," and lectured them on "the inconsistancey [sic] of
acting themselves the part which they condem [sic] and oppose in others."[74] Merrill Jensen has ably described the pursuit of expanded political power by disfranchised whites and
has presented clear evidence of conflict between rich and
poor.[75] Staughton Lynd has seen "government-from-below"
in the conduct and "ideology" of New York's mechanics on
the eve of the Revolution.[76] In 1774 Gouverneur Morris observed New York's "mob" beginning "to think and to reason," debating with the rich on whether government should
henceforth be "aristocratic or democratic."[77] In 1776 much
of the impetus for the movement to overthrow Pennsylvania's old government and draw up a new constitution came
from below, in mass meetings and in the activities of privates
in the militia.[78]

Insofar as activities such as these focused on questions of
voting, they reflect a striking failure of the lower class to provide the deference which their rulers expected of them. John
Adams might boast of the respect of the Massachusetts electorate for what he later called the "natural aristocracy," and
later writers might assure us that colonials did not suppose
that they should govern: according to Tom Paine, voters too
poor to vote would borrow or lie their way up to the property
qualifications and they would do it without hesitation.[79] Let
John Adams boast about the freeness of elections in Massachusetts: in 1770 Philadelphia mechanics would refuse to
rubberstamp tickets set in advance by "leading men," while
their brothers in New York would rebel against the coercions
which *made* them vote, again and again, for the same families:

> many of the poorer People having deeply felt the Aristo-
> cratic Power or rather, the intollerable Tyranny of the
> great and opulent, who (such is the shocking Depravity of
> the Times, and their utter Contempt of all public Virtue
> and Patriotism) have openly threatened them with the Loss
> of their Employment, and to arrest them for Debt, unless

they gave their Voices as they were directed. . . . [Because of the] exorbitant Influence of the Rich over the Poor, . . . [we] need . . . a secret Method of voting.[80]

If deference ever existed, it was clearly gone when Americans began to describe the supporters of open balloting as "the great and the mighty, and the rich, and the long Wiggs and the Squaretoes, and all Manner of Wickednesses in high places."[81]

"In Pursuance of the Declaration for Independency . . .," and within less than a week, New York's debtors had been released from prison.[82] The freeing of these "oppressed"[83] indicates that some took their egalitarianism literally and extended their literalism to economics: Paine and Woolman were not alone in identifying economic subordination with lack of freedom. Ever since Thomas Morton's "partners and consocates" had rejected servitude in Virginia to "live together as equals" amidst the pleasures of Merrymount,[84] many Americans had made the same identification and chosen freedom. "*I am Flesh and Blood, as well as my Master,*" said a servant who had murdered him, "*and therefore I know no Reason, why my Master should not obey me, as well as I obey him.*"[85] Bound servants conspired to run away, to strike and to rebel, aiming "either [to] be free or dye for it," and crying out for those "*who would be for liberty and freed from bondage*" to join them.[86] Slaves, too, displayed what Cotton Mather called "a *Fondness* for *Freedom*": they revolted, ran away, and governed themselves in runaway communities from which they launched attacks against their former masters; they fought for "Liberty & Life" and marched "with Colours displayed, and . . . Drums beating"— a black Spirit of '76.[87] And long before the first trade unions, free white workers had engaged in strikes, slowdowns, and other protests, in some cases directly opposing laws which punished them for disobedience.[88] "Mutiny" is a poor word to describe those seamen who seized their ship, renamed it *Liberty,* and chose their course and a new captain by voting.[89] Many colonial laborers, white and Negro alike, expressed their refusal to defer by protests in which the economic grievance is hardly distinguishable from the social and political.[90]

"Colonials" meant many people, often people in conflict with one another: there was, from the very beginning, something of a struggle over who should rule at home. The people on the bottom of that conflict were also involved in the struggle for home rule,[91] but their activities have been made to seem an extension of the conduct of the more articulate, who have been seen as their manipulators. The inarticulate could act on their own, and often for very sound reasons. It is time that we examined the coming of the American Revolution from their perspective. What follows is an attempt to sketch some of the kinds of events and considerations which should be explored if we are to understand what opposition to the British meant to those who were to bear the burden of the fighting and dying.

Late in October of 1765 the Stamp Act Congress added its Declarations to those of the individual colonies: the Act was unconstitutional.[92] As Edmund and Helen Morgan have put it, "it would have been difficult to find an American anywhere who did not believe in them [Declarations of the Stamp Act Congress]—as far as they went."[93] The problem was that many Americans did not think that they went far enough, "did not choose that it should ever once be thought that the Enjoyment of their Rights depended merely upon the Success of these Representations or the Courtesy of those to whom they were made."[94]

The Stamp Act Congress had adjourned without answering the question, What is to be *done?* The Stamp Act riots showed that the mob had begun to think and reason. Historians have been hesitant to acknowledge it. Instead they have preferred to accept the testimony of British officials who attributed the riots to "the Wiser and better Sort," who stirred up the lower class in behalf of a cause in which that class had no real interest; thus they easily turned to plunder and violence for its own sake.[95] But gentlemen of property associated themselves with mob violence only under the most extreme conditions. Those conditions had not been achieved in 1765. British officials assumed that the lawyers and property owners were the riots' secret leaders partly because of a bias which said that leaders *had* to be people of "Consequence."[96] In addition, these officials were accustomed to confronting members of the upper class as political adversaries in the courts and in the assembly halls. But a new politics—a politics of the street—was replacing the old politics—the politics of the assembly hall. British officials failed to understand these new politics. Wherever they went—and most of them did not go very far—they saw lawyers, merchants, and men of substance. When events which displeased them took place in the streets, they understood them only in their limited frame of reference. Transferring events to that frame, they saw only their old enemies.

The upper classes may not have been pulling the strings in the Stamp Act riots. The assumption that an uninterested mob had to be artificially aroused—created—disregards the ability of the people to think for themselves; like everyone else in the colonies, they had real grievances against the British. Unlike others, they had fewer legal channels through which to express their grievances. So they took to the streets in pursuit of political goals. Within that context, their "riots" were really extremely orderly and expressed a clear purpose. Again and again, when the mob's leaders lost control, the mob went on to attack the logical political enemy, not to plunder. They were led but not manipulated: to dismantle the puppet show is not to do away with the whole concept of leadership, but instead of cynical fomentors, we find direction of the most rudimentary sort, a question of setting times, of priorities, and in the heat of the riot, of getting from one street to another in the quickest way possible.[97]

The struggle against the Stamp Act was also a struggle against colonial leadership. Declarations had not prevented the Act's taking effect. Those who had *declared* now had to *do,* but they could do no better than a boycott: the cessation of all business which required the use of stamps. This strategy put pressure on the English merchants, but it also increased the pressure on the American poor, the hungry, the prisoners in city jails who could not hope for release so long as the lawyers refused to do business.[98]

Radicals protested against the absurdity of American blustering about liberty and then refusing to do anything about it: if the law was wrong, then it was no law and business ought to go on as usual without the use of stamps. They urged disobedience. Upper-class leaders demanded legality and tried, sometimes by shady means, to suppress or distort this dissent.[99] But the radicals continued their pressure, and they were supported by the self-defeating character of the boycott strategy.[100] The more time that passed without ship sailings, the more attractive a policy of disobedience became to merchants, and they began to send their ships out without stamped papers. British officials began to cave in: they were worried about "an Insurrection of the Poor against the Rich," united action by unemployed artisans and the increasing numbers of unruly seamen who were pouring into the colonial cities and finding no way to get out. The seamen— "the . . . people . . . most dangerous on these Occasions"— especially worried customs officials; instead of waiting for them to force their captains to sail without stamps, the officials yielded, giving way before enormous pressures and allowing a radical triumph.[101] Then the Parliament itself backed down, repealing the Stamp Act.[102] The poor people of the colonies had reason to congratulate themselves: word of their actions had thrown a scare into Parliament, and they might even suspect that the economic rationale which Parliament offered for repeal covered its fear of a challenge not so much to its view of the constitution as to its actual authority in the colonies.[103] Thus the meaning of the Stamp Act crisis goes beyond the pursuit of constitutional principles.[104] The lower class had spoken out against the British, against deference, and against colonial leadership, and they had won.

The repeal of the Stamp Act left the Sugar Act of 1764 still on the books, and in 1767 Parliament added a new revenue act. Oliver M. Dickerson has described the activities of the new American Board of Customs Commissioners in enforcing these acts beginning in 1768 as "customs racketeering" and has blamed the Board for transforming "thousands of loyal British subjects into active revolutionists." Corrupt customs officers made seizures on technicalities and pocketed the proceeds. The Hancocks and the Laurenses suffered greatly, but the poor suffered more. Even the pettiest of woodboats in purely local trade were seized; even the common seaman had his chest rifled and its contents confiscated.[105] Seamen, small traders, and rich merchants all came to identify British authority with corruption and injustice.

Customs racketeering was on the wane by mid-1770. This was due in large part to popular opposition and especially to the withdrawal of troops from Boston: the Commissioners could not survive without armed support.[106] The troops left Boston after the street fight which came to be known as the Boston Massacre. The Massacre, in turn, grew out of an antagonism between the troops and the population which has been given too little attention.[107] Long-standing practice in the British army allowed off-duty soldiers to take civilian employment, and they did so at wages which undercut those given to American workingmen: soldiers in New York in 1770 worked for between 37.5 percent and 50 percent of the wages offered to Americans for the same work.[108] As might be expected, this situation led to great antagonisms, especially in hard times. In Boston, a British soldier looking for work in a ropewalk in 1770 was told by one of the employees to "go and clean my s[hi]t house."[109] The insult led to a fistfight, which led to an armed attack by more soldiers; the soldiers were defeated and humiliated and vowed to take their revenge. On the evening of March 5 one of the ropemakers who had been wounded in the earlier encounter led a mob which took on the rampaging soldiers.[110] "Come on you rascals, you bloody backs, you lobster scoundrels, fire if you dare, G[o]d damn you, fire and be damned, we know you dare not."[111] Somebody did dare: when the smoke cleared, the ropemaker was dead along with two others and several wounded (of whom two would later die).[112]

The Boston Massacre was widely and rapidly publicized throughout the colonies, but it is only the best known of several such incidents. The Battle of Golden Hill, which had arisen from similar causes, left one New Yorker dead and several cruelly injured in two days of battle with the soldiers six weeks before.[113] This was the culmination of years of antagonism. The Sons of Liberty erected Liberty Poles; the soldiers tore them down. Ostentatiously armed soldiers paraded the streets, drums and bugles assaulted the ears. The people tried to silence them, to disarm them, to run them out of town.[114] A governor noticed the "coldness and distance" between the people and the military.[115] Conflict between classes developed as antagonism directed itself at those employers who hired off-duty soldiers. The people were tired of paying a poor tax to maintain the soldiers' "Whores and Bastards." Gangs of seamen patrolled the docks with clubs and drove away soldiers, promising to take vengeance on those who hired them.[116]

Just as in the Stamp Act riots, the official theory blamed the Battle of Golden Hill on manipulation.[117] And once again, in New York as in Boston, the mob had adequate reason to act on its own. An unfriendly observer who mistakenly saw mere political opportunism in the slogans of the sixties and seventies nonetheless saw the unity of American popular grievances:

> . . . may it not from what has happened, be justly suspected, that the frequent Notices to meet at *Liberty* Poll [sic], the violent Rage and Resentment which *some* People have endeavoured generally to excite against Soldiers, pretended to proceed from a Love of Liberty, and a Regard to the *Interests* of the Poor; do all tend to the same End, although the Pretences have been so very different.—May not,—No Money to the Troops,—whoraw for [secret] Ballotting,—employ no Soldiers,—all mean the same Thing?—Liberty is the Pretext. . . .[118]

Economic and political deprivation were one and the same, and the people opposed the deprivers whether they were Englishmen or Americans.

The British Navy was as unpopular in the colonies as was the Army. One of the reasons for the Navy's unpopularity has been almost entirely missed by historians who have shown too little concern for those matters which concern the inarticulate. Impressment, previously seen as significant only in connection with the War of 1812, also played a role in bringing on the Revolution.[119] Although the poor were the press gang's peculiar victims, all classes suffered by the practice. "Kiss my arse, you dog," shouted the captain to the merchants as he made off with their men: their numbers mounted into the tens of thousands.[120] The complaints of American governmental bodies spoke for the merchant, not the seaman; they focused on the harmful effects of the practice on colonial trade and seemed almost as critical of those who violently resisted as of the Royal Navy.[121] So the seamen and poor people of the colonies were on their own. Historians have failed to see the significance of their active opposition to impressment: one seems to put blame on seamen for escaping and fighting back, much as one might blame slaves for the same offenses; another, admitting that colonial crowds became "political" in 1765, sees the innumerable impressment riots before that date as "ideologically inert."[122] But the seamen were fighting, literally, for their life, liberty, and property, and their violence was all the politics they could have. Mostly they were inarticulate, and we must read their purpose in their actions; sometimes one would leave us with words linking his thoughts to his conduct:

> I know who you are. You are the lieutenant of a man-of-war, come with a press-gang to deprive me of my liberty. You have no right to impress me. I have retreated from you as far as I can. . . I and my companions are determined to stand upon our defense. Stand off.[123]

Impressment, both at sea and ashore, brought bloodshed throughout the colonial period: how much we will never know, for it is in the nature of impressment that much of it went unrecorded both in ships' logs and in sources on shore. How do generalizations about "salutary neglect"[124] stand up when viewed thus, from the bottom? And how much more comprehensible is the violence of the urban mob in the sixties and seventies in the light of previous and continued impressment.[125] All of this bloodshed and violence was not irrelevant to the Revolution. The legalists who were to lead that Revolution were sensitive to the fact that much of this impressment was illegal under British law and inconsistent with "the Natural Rights of Mankind."[126] The men who fought in that Revolution did so, in part, because of an ancient tradition of violent resistance to British tyranny. Feelings were so deep that almost four decades later an enduring folk memory of oppression by the same "haughty, cruel, and gasconading nation"[127] would help to drive the American people to war again.

A recent account of the Boston Massacre which finds no evidence that the event was anything other than a spontaneous uprising from below nonetheless concludes that "*circumstances suggest* that there was as much purpose as spontaneity in the events leading up to the Massacre." The only circumstance which the author cites is the timing of the event: news of it arrived in London at the "fag end" rather than at the beginning of a Parliamentary session and thus came before the members when their mood was too listless for action. To the author this timing suggests the existence of manipulators behind the scenes.[128] This is no evidence at all. Are we not perhaps one-sided in our permissiveness with scholarship which alleges manipulation without demonstrating it?

Who threw the tea in Boston Harbor remains very much a mystery to this day. A merchant speculated the next day that the Tea Party was conducted so efficiently that there must have been "People of sense and more discernment than the vulgar among the Actors."[129] This is hardly evidence, but a recent account accepts it unquestioningly and consistently speculates in the direction of manipulation and elite control when evidence is unavailable.[130] But certainly there is nothing beyond the most uneducated man's capacity in the events of that December night in 1773: that the mob showed up with lanterns and hatchets, attached block and tackle to the chests, raised them from the holds, and emptied the tea in the harbor seems more nearly to suggest the skills of the lower class than to be evidence of an operation so clever as to be explicable only by upper-class manipulation. We do not know who did it, and we need to take a fresh look.

Excessive attention to *Common Sense* for its propaganda values has obscured its substantive meaning as an expression of populist democracy. Indeed, the very concept of "propaganda" has perhaps hindered us more than it has helped us to understand the causes of the American Revolution. "We know today," wrote Philip Davidson in 1941, "that large bodies of people never cooperate in any complex movement except under the guidance of a central machine operated by a comparatively few people. . . ." Davidson found a few people—men like Tom Paine and Sam Adams—managing such a campaign: " 'By their fruits ye shall know them.' "[131] The assumption here is that one can read back from the "fruits"—the Revolution—to the efforts of propagandists, that is, that Paine and Adams in some sense *caused* the Revolution. Sam Adams' biographer called his subject " 'Dictator' of Boston," "keeper" of a "trained mob," the "Pioneer in Propaganda" who "deliberately set out to provoke crises that would lead to the separation of mother country and colonies."[132] Similarly, David Hawke has seen the coming of revolution in Pennsylvania as the outcome of efforts by "a small band of men" who staged mass meetings and used propaganda and other devious methods.[133] All of this smacks of unproved conspiracy and utterly ignores the fact that Paine did speak "common sense": the Revolution has substantive causes and is rooted in genuine grievances; to explain it as the result of efficient propaganda is to belittle the reality of the grievances and to suggest that the Americans were largely content until they were aroused by a few demagogues.[134]

The final test of the agency[135] of the lower class is their conduct in the Revolution: if they had been tricked into rebellion by demagoguery and propaganda, we might expect them to have had second thoughts when the fighting became bloody. From April 19, 1775, the war was fought, on the American side, by a people in arms, understanding and interpreting their war goals in their own way. The American technique was frequently that of guerrilla warfare, depending on mobility, withdrawal, and unexpected counterattack: they fled when they could not win and turned and fought only when they had a good chance of victory. The Revolution was like modern guerrilla wars in another sense. In guerrilla warfare, according to the aphorism, the people are the water and the troops are the fish who inhabit that water. The troops must live off the people, retaining their support not by coercion but rather because the people believe in and support the cause for which the troops fight. Although the analogy with guerrilla warfare is only an analogy, it is suggestive. As long as the Americans continued to fight, it was impossible for the British to win the war. Mere military conquest was insignificant: to win, the British would have had to occupy simultaneously the entire populated area of the thirteen colonies, and even then their victory would have been unstable, a peace maintained only by force. The British could not win precisely because the Americans were fighting a popular war.

Although an analogy with guerrilla warfare can give us some suggestion as to the extent of patriotism during the Revolution, we need more specific information. One fruitful technique for evaluating the loyalties of the inarticulate is to look at them under pressure—in prison. With little chance of exchange, amidst starvation and disease, and ruled over by cruel and corrupt administrators, captured American seamen were offered a way out: they could join the Royal Navy.[136] Most remained patriots, and they were very self-conscious about it.[137] Instead of defecting, they resisted, escaping, burning their prisons, and defiantly celebrating the Fourth of July.[138] Separated from their captains and governing themselves for the first time, on their own they organized into disciplined groups with bylaws:[139] in microcosm the prisoners went through the whole process of setting up a constitution. Men from all over the colonies discovered that they were Americans, that they had common grievances and a common enemy. Studies of other men in similar situations would give our generalizations about the role of the inarticulate in the American Revolution more substance than they presently have.

If the American Revolution was a popular war, still, support for it was far from universal. John Adams later estimated that "nearly one third" of the Americans sided with the British.[140] Who were the Loyalists? Social class may have had nothing to do with the phenomenon of Loyalism, but we will never know if we foreclose research on the matter; we continue to need studies which at least pose the question. A recent study generalizes about Loyalists, including under the heading "Artisans and craftsmen" such diverse groups as an owner of salt works, managers, and manufacturers undifferentiated from laborers and waiters. Any conceivable difference between merchants and their clerks, captains and common seamen, doctors and their apprentices is obliterated by the categorization.[141] So long as our techniques of research foreclose the possibility of our finding anything but consensus the case for consensus will be unproved.

Finally, we need studies which will use Loyalism as a touchstone for a more precise definition of the Revolution. Loyalists had very little faith in man and reveled in the inequalities among men. Wealthy Massachusetts judge Peter Oliver distinguished between such "Men of Sense" as John Adams and the common people, whom he repeatedly dismissed as "Rabble."[142] Maryland clergyman Jonathan Boucher had resolved, before his twelfth birthday, not to "pass through life like the boors around me"; the people were "fickle," "false," "wrong-headed," and "ignorant."[143] The Loyalist view of the American Revolution built on their view of the nature of man. The "Mobility of all Countries," said Oliver, were "perfect Machines" which could be "wound up by any Hand who might first take the Winch." Sam Adams, he said, "understood human Nature, in low life, so well, that he could turn the Minds of the great Vulgar as well as the small into any Course that he might chuse"; the people were "duped," "deceived," and "deluded" by demagogues who were motivated by ambition and pride and aimed to satisfy "private grudges." "Nine out of ten of the people of America," wrote Boucher, "were adverse to the revolt." "Many, if not most of you," said Oliver to the rebellious people of Massachusetts, "were insensible of the ambitious views of your leaders" and would have spurned those leaders but for ignorance.[144]

There seems to be a common theme in Loyalism: a rejection of the idea that all men are created equal. If those who opposed the Revolution rejected egalitarianism, this suggests that what they rejected—the Revolution itself—might have been in some sense egalitarian. On the other hand, how much difference would one find, in regard to egalitarianism, between the views of an Oliver or a Boucher and a Hamilton? or even an Adams? When egalitarianism is the point of division, men such as Hamilton and Adams appear closer to the Loyalists than they do to Paine. Such a conclusion would strengthen the theory that the Revolution was a fight over "the true constitution of the British Empire" rather than a social movement[145]—*on the level of leadership*. Regardless of the result, studies comparing the leaders of the Revolution with the right-wing alternatives available to them would bring us much closer to the meaning of the Revolution.

In neither the French Revolution nor the American Civil War did a losing cause do so well on the battlefields of historiography as has Loyalism. While the Loyalists themselves may not have too many friends, their accents—manipulation, propaganda, and the mindlessness of the people—reign largely unchallenged, albeit in somewhat different language, in the recent historiography of the American Revolution. Perhaps underlying this remarkable congruence is a modern lack of faith in man, echoing the Loyalists' dim view of human nature. Regardless of the cause, our historiography has taken on a flavor of unintentional partisanship; this has given rise to a one-sided history which must be re-examined.

The American Revolution can best be re-examined from a point of view which assumes that all men are created equal, and rational, and that since they can think and reason they can make their own history. These assumptions are nothing more nor less than the democratic credo. All of our history needs re-examination from this perspective. The history of the powerless, the inarticulate, the poor has not yet begun to be written because they have been treated no more fairly by historians than they have been treated by their contemporaries.[146]

NOTES

1. From "A Worker Reads History" by Bertolt Brecht, in his volume, *Selected Poems,* translated by H. R. Hays, copyright 1947, by Bertolt Brecht and H. R. Hays. Reprinted by permission of Harcourt, Brace & World. Inc.

2. Samuel Eliot Morison, *The Maritime History of Massachusetts, 1783–1860* (Boston, 1921), pp. 21–26. For further comments on Morison's approach, see Jesse Lemisch, "Jack Tar in the Streets: Merchant Seamen in the Politics of Revolutionary America," *William and Mary Quarterly* (in press).

3. Thomas C. Cochran, "The Social Sciences and the Problem of Historical Synthesis," *The Social Sciences in Historical Study,* Social Science Research Council Bulletin No. 64 (New York, 1954), pp. 159, 162–68. For the centrality of business history in Cochran's thinking see also pp. 158, 169. Well over half the titles cited by

Cochran—including three of his own—are clearly in business history.

4. Stephan Thernstrom, *Poverty and Progress: Social Mobility in a Nineteenth Century City* (Cambridge, Mass., 1964), p. 241, cites many of the studies of the business elite favorably cited by Cochran but criticizes them as dealing with "social advances which were, if often dramatic, necessarily atypical" (p. 2). Gabriel Kolko, *Wealth and Power in America: An Analysis of Social Class and Income Distribution* (New York, 1962), pp. 5, 24–29, makes a similar point in criticizing those who have drawn conclusions about the income of the entire population on the basis of Simon Kuznets' study of the top 5 percent.

5. Robert E. Brown, *Middle-Class Democracy and the Revolution in Massachusetts, 1691–1780* (Ithaca, N.Y., 1955), pp. 28–29 ("Table 2. Estates of Town Workers or Artisans"), lists five "mariners" who could qualify for the vote. John Cary's excellent "Statistical Method and the Brown Thesis on Colonial Democracy," *William and Mary Quarterly*, 3rd Ser., XX (April 1963), 257, notes that two of the five were definitely captains, and some or all of the remainder might have been. For Brown's response, see his "Rebuttal," *ibid.*, p. 272.

6. Wallace Brown, *The King's Friends: The Composition and Motives of The American Loyalist Claimants* (Providence, R.I., 1965). See below, p. 27.

7. Jackson Turner Main, "Government by the People: The American Revolution and the Democratization of the Legislatures," *William and Mary Quarterly*, 3rd Ser., XXIII (July 1966), 392, 397. Main goes on to claim that "the voters themselves seem to have adhered, in practice at least, to the traditional view, for when the people were asked to choose their representatives they seldom elected common farmers and artisans. Instead they put their trust in men of the upper class" (pp. 392–93). But the opinions of voters are not necessarily synonymous with those of "the people"; nor does the election of men of the upper class necessarily indicate that the people—or even the voters—"put their trust" in them.

8. Staughton Lynd, "On Turner, Beard and Slavery," *Journal of Negro History*, XLVIII (October 1963), 250. Francis P. Jennings, "The Indian Trade of the Susquehanna Valley," *Proceedings of the American Philosophical Society*, CX (December 1966), 424, notes that discussions of the relationship between democracy and the frontier are generally grounded on "the customary unspoken assumption . . . that democracy is a process in which Indians don't count."

9. For an account which concludes that Americans have made "real progress toward fulfillment" of their "chosen destiny" but nonetheless notes that "We have betrayed our tradition and our heritage," see John W. Caughey, "Our Chosen Destiny," *Journal of American History*, LII (September 1965), 239–51.

10. Barrington Moore, Jr., *Social Origins of Dictatorship and Democracy: Lord and Peasant in the Making of the Modern World* (Boston, 1966), pp. 522, 523. It should be noted that Moore is not arguing that historians should "serve the underdog"; he calls that kind of history "just cheating" and deals with it as harshly as he does with the "celebration of the virtues of our own society which leaves out its ugly and cruel features" (p. 522).

11. Marcuse's remarks (in a review in *American Historical Review*, LIV [April 1949], 558) were called to my attention by Norman Pollack of Wayne State University. In his *The Populist Response to Industrial America: Midwestern Populist Thought* (Cambridge, Mass., 1962), pp. 32, 153, Pollack sees Clarence Darrow enunciating a similar standard.

12. Brown, *Massachusetts*, p. 408. A partial list of other historians who have stressed equality, mobility, and consensus would include Louis Hartz, *The Liberal Tradition in America: An Interpretation of American Political Thought since the Revolution* (New York, 1955); Daniel J. Boorstin, *The Americans: The Colonial Experience* (New York, 1958), and *The Americans: The National Experience* (New York, 1965), and Richard Hofstadter, *The Age of Reform: From Bryan to F.D.R.* (New York, 1965). For suggestive discussions of this trend and a fuller biblography, see John Higham, "Beyond Consensus: The Historian as Moral Critic," *American Historical Review*, LXVII (April 1962), 609–25 and Norman Pollack, "Fear of Man: Populism, Authoritarianism, and the Historian," *Agricultural History*, XXXIX (1965), 59–67. For one consensus historian's effort to relate his history to the politics of the fifties, see Daniel J. Boorstin's statement that one form of his "opposition [to the Communist party] has been an attempt to discover and explain to students in my teaching and in my writing, the unique virtues of American democracy. I have done this partly in my Jefferson book [*The Lost World of Thomas Jefferson* (New York, 1948)] . . . and in . . . *The Genius of American Politics* [Chicago, 1953]. . . ." U.S. House of Representatives, Committee on Un-American Activities, 83rd Cong., 1st Sess., *Communist Methods of Infiltration (Education)*, Part I, pp. 51–52.

    Studies by nonhistorians along similar lines include Daniel Bell, *The End of Ideology: On the Exhaustion of Political Ideas in the Fifties* (New York, 1960); Seymour Martin Lipset, *Political Man: The Social Basis of Politics* (Garden City, N.Y., 1960) and *The First New Nation: The United States in Historical and Comparative Perspective* (New York, 1963). For a discussion of the role of some of these "New Conservatives" in a contemporary political conflict, see James F. Petras and Michael Shute, "Berkeley 65," *Partisan Review*, XXXII (Spring 1965), 314–23.

13. Brown, *Massachusetts*, p. v. Brown was arguing, of course, against the work of such men as Carl Becker and Charles A. Beard; for a summary of their influence on textbooks, see p. 2n.

14. *Ibid.,* pp. 27–30, 401. Robert E. and B. Katherine Brown have stressed many of the same themes in *Virginia, 1705–1786: Democracy or Aristocracy?* (East Lansing, Mich., 1964). Although slavery, "of course, ruled out the possibility of democracy as far as the Negro was concerned" (p. 63), pre-Revolutionary Virginia had "what now passes in this country as middle-class, representative democracy" (p. 308). Like the possession of property in Massachusetts, slave ownership was "an ambition that was fulfilled for a large number of men" (p. 308) and thus "Protection of slave property was of constant and vital concern to all classes of the white population" (p. 77).

15. Lee Benson, in *Turner and Beard: American Historical Writing Reconsidered* (New York, 1960), pp. 183–84, contests Brown's methods in *Charles Beard and the Constitution, a Critical Analysis of "An Economic Interpretation of the Constitution"* (Princeton, 1956) and concludes that Brown's thesis about middle-class democracy is fictitious "If the distribution of property in other states even loosely resembled that in New York."

16. Cary, *William and Mary Quarterly,* XX, 257–58.

17. Brown, "Rebuttal," *ibid.,* p. 271. Emphasis added. Nonetheless, here Brown implies that his techniques were more rigorous in his work on Virginia (p. 271). Many reviewers have disagreed, noting in the later work a "tendency to omit contrary evidence" (*Virginia Quarterly Review,* XL [Summer 1964], cxviii–cxix; see also Carl Bridenbaugh in *American Historical Review,* LXX [January 1965], 473) and a failure to offer evidence supporting contentions about broad suffrage: David Alan Williams in *William and Mary Quarterly,* 3rd Ser., XXII (January 1965), 150.

18. Jackson Turner Main, *The Social Structure of Revolutionary America* (Princeton, 1965); review by Robert E. Brown, *Journal of American History,* LIII (June 1966), 112–13. Brown shows discomfort with the term "proletariat"—which Main uses repeatedly, along with "poor" (e.g., pp. 37, 49, 66, 156)—commenting, "Perhaps our difference lies in my ignorance of the meaning of the word 'proletariat.'"

Main's 40 percent figure includes Negroes (p. 156); about one fifth of the whites were poor, although in some areas the proportion went as high as 61 percent (p. 37). Both the 40 percent and the 20 percent figures are probably low, since Main acknowledges that probate records, which he calls his "most valuable" source (p. 288), largely excluded "the bottom 10 per cent or more of the white population" (p. 291). Although such a comparison is of limited value, it should be noted that what was called a "War on Poverty" began in the 1960s after estimates that "somewhere between 20 and 25 percent of the American people are poor": Michael Harrington, *The Other America: Poverty in the United States* (New York, 1963), p. 194.

Pessimistic conclusions about social mobility in early America are supported by Staughton Lynd, "Who Should Rule at Home? Dutchess County, New York, in the American Revolution," *William and Mary Quarterly*, 3rd Ser., XVIII (July 1961), 332, describing pre-Revolutionary Dutchess County as "a harsh, hierarchical community," a place of rigid class division. Aubrey C. Land, "Economic Base and Social Structure: The Northern Chesapeake in the Eighteenth Century," *Journal of Economic History*, XXV (December 1965), 639–54, describes the social advance of most poor people as "glacial" and detects a group of poor farmers comprising 54.7 percent of the population (1730–1739) living at a level of "rude sufficiency" (pp. 642, 653).

19. Main, *Social Structure*, pp. 175, 193. James A. Henretta, "Economic Development and Social Structure in Colonial Boston," *William and Mary Quarterly*, 3rd ser., XXII (January 1965), 77, finds that the lower the economic standing, the greater was the individual's impermanence: 65 percent of the bottom 14 percent were no longer inhabitants of Boston eight years after 1687. Thernstrom, p. 85, finds the same phenomenon and similar percentages in nineteenth-century Newburyport: "The first generalization to make about the 'typical' Newburyport laborer of this period, it appears, is that he did not live in Newburyport very long!"

20. Main, *Social Structure*, pp. 156, 164–65, 193, 196, 271, 287.

21. Main offers no evidence for this estimate (*ibid.*, pp. 193–94). For a discussion of Morison's claim (*Maritime History*, p. 106) that Massachusetts "has never had a native deep-sea proletariat" see Lemisch, "Jack Tar in the Streets."

22. The percentages are computed on the basis of Main's statements that one or two out of twenty whites "remained permanently poor" (*Social Structure*, p. 271; partially contradicted p. 194) and that Negroes made up 23 percent of the total population in 1760. It is assumed that all but an insignificant number of the Negroes remained permanently poor. For indentured servants, see p. 165. Main's contention that "In Philadelphia the chance to rise was indeed a good one" seems to be directly contradicted by the figures which he offers. Cf. p. 194 and table, p. 195n, indicating that those nontaxpayers who rose economically were far fewer than those who did not rise; in addition it seems reasonable to assume that a higher proportion of those who "disappeared" from the records did not rise than did (p. 195).

The optimistic assumptions and computations in Main's study noted in this paragraph are perhaps a small price to pay for the most informative work yet produced on the subject of its title.

23. *Ibid.*, pp. 286, 287.

24. J. R. Pole, "Historians and the Problem of Early American Democracy," *American Historical Review*, LXVII (April 1962), 643.

25. Henretta, *William and Mary Quarterly*, XXII, 85.

26. See, e.g., Charles S. Sydnor, *Gentleman Freeholders: Political Practices in Washington's Virginia* (Chapel Hill, N.C., 1952), p. 73.

27. See Gerrit P. Judd, IV, *Members of Parliament: 1734–1832* (New Haven, Conn., 1955), an exemplary statistical analysis which supplies ample data for an indictment which its author does not choose to make.

28. Sydnor, p. 78.

29. Jack P. Greene, "Foundations of Political Power in the Virginia House of Burgesses, 1720–1776," *William and Mary Quarterly,* 3rd Ser., XVI (October 1959), 485–506.

30. Main, *William and Mary Quarterly,* XXIII, 397.

31. Morison, p. 23; David Syrett, "Town Meeting Politics in Massachusetts, 1776–1786," *William and Mary Quarterly,* 3rd Ser., XXI (July 1964), 352–66. For a critical view of the Newburyport town meeting, stressing merchant domination, see Benjamin W. Labaree, *Patriots and Partisans: The Merchants of Newburyport, 1764–1815* (Cambridge, Mass., 1962), pp. 12–15. Labaree disagrees directly with Robert E. Brown, concluding that "True political democracy had not yet come to [pre-Revolutionary] Newburyport" (p. 15).

32. As Pole, *American Historical Review,* LXVII, 633–34, notes, the contemporary claims of British officials that there was an excess of "democracy" in the colonies reduce to the claim that the lower house—the "democratic" element of a mixed constitution—was disproportionately powerful. But if the lower houses were too powerful, this can hardly be equated with democracy: the lower houses were no more strongholds of democracy than was the House of Commons. See also Roy N. Lokken, "The Concept of Democracy in Colonial Political Thought," *William and Mary Quarterly,* 3rd Ser., XVI (October 1959), 568–80.

33. Pole, *American Historical Review,* LXVII, 643, notes the same deliberateness later on in the new constitutions of the Revolutionary era.

34. Colonial laws regarding maritime labor, for instance, were made for the benefit of merchants and masters—who voted—aiming at assuring a ready supply of docile seamen—who did not vote. The record is consistently one-sided, starting with the New Netherland law of 1638 which provided that seamen who disobeyed orders would be punished as "turbulent and seditious persons": Edmund Bailey O'Callaghan, ed., *Laws and Ordinances of New Netherland, 1638–1674* (Albany, N.Y., 1868), p. 12. This sort of legislation was common in all the colonies: see Richard B. Morris, *Government and Labor in Early America* (New York, 1946), p. 230n; for a fuller discussion, see Lemisch, "Jack Tar in the Streets." See also below, note 88.

35. Jules Zanger, "Crime and Punishment in Early Massachusetts," *William and Mary Quarterly,* 3rd Ser., XXII (July 1965), 471–77.

36. Leonard W. Levy, "Did the Zenger Case Really Matter? Freedom of the Press in Colonial New York," *ibid., XVII* (January 1960), 35. See also the same author's *Freedom of Speech and Press in Early American History: Legacy of Suppression* (New York, 1963).

37. Quoted in Sydnor, pp. 21–22 (this particular dialogue occurred in a 1799 Congressional election but is not untypical of earlier elections). Cf. Lewis Namier, *The Structure of Politics at the Accession of George III*, 2nd ed. (London, 1957), pp. 64–73.

38. E.g., Main, *William and Mary Quarterly*, XXIII, 392–93, 396–97; Pole, *American Historical Review*, LXVIII, 629, 645–46; David Hawke, *In the Midst of a Revolution* (Philadelphia, 1961), pp. 83, 187. Walter Bagehot coined the term and described the "happy state" in which "the numerous unwiser part . . . —whether by custom or by choice is immaterial—is ready, is eager to delegate its power of choosing its ruler to a certain select minority." Forrest Morgan, ed., *The Works of Walter Bagehot . . . Now first Published in Full by the Travelers [sic] Insurance Company of Hartford Connecticut* (Hartford, 1891), IV, 267.

39. The best recent discussion of the political thought of the colonial elite is Richard Buel, Jr., "Democracy and the American Revolution: A Frame of Reference," *William and Mary Quarterly*, 3rd Ser., XXI (April 1964), 165–90.

40. Peter Laslett, ed., John Locke, *Two Treatises of Government* (Cambridge, 1960), p. 435. Subsequent quotations from *Second Treatise* are from *ibid.*, pp. 374, 398, 433, 435, 436. For an illuminating brief discussion of this aspect of Locke, see William Appleman Williams, *The Contours of American History* (Cleveland, O., 1961), pp. 64–65.

41. Buel, *William and Mary Quarterly*, XXI, 179, 188.

42. Charles Francis Adams, ed., *The Works of John Adams* (Boston, 1850–56), IV, 68; IX, 391.

43. L. H. Butterfield *et al.*, eds., *Diary and Autobiography of John Adams* (New York, 1964), III, 331, 333. Paine's conduct in the thirty years following hardly softened Adams, who described him in 1805 as "a mongrel between Pigg and Puppy, begotten by a wild boar on a Bitch Wolf": Worthington Chauncey Ford, ed., *Statesman and Friend: Correspondence of John Adams With Benjamin Waterhouse, 1784–1822* (Boston, 1927), p. 31.

44. Adams, IV, 193–200.

45. Cf. Carl L. Becker, *The Declaration of Independence: A Study in the History of Political Ideas* (New York, 1958), pp. 186–87, and Laslett, p. 433.

46. Julian P. Boyd *et al.*, eds., *The Papers of Thomas Jefferson* (Princeton, 1950–   ), VIII, 426; Andrew A. Lipscomb and Albert Ellery Bergh, eds., *The Writings of Thomas Jefferson* (Washington, 1905), IX, 307. Cf. William Peden, ed., *Notes on the State of Virginia by Thomas Jefferson* (Chapel Hill, N.C., 1955), p. 165: "The mobs of great cities add just so much to the support of pure government, as sores do to the strength of the human body." For Edmund Burke's earlier use of the phrase "swinish multitude" (Jefferson used it in 1795) see *Reflections on the Revolution in France* (1790) in *The*

Works of the Right Honorable Edmund Burke (Boston, 1866–67), III, 335.

47. Becker, *Declaration,* pp. 166–67, 171–72, 190. It should be noted that Jefferson was attacking the *trade* more than slavery itself; to urge the abolition of the first is not necessarily to urge the abolition of the latter.

48. See Peden, pp. 138–43. Jefferson wrote: "I advance it . . . as a suspicion only, that the blacks, whether originally a distinct race, or made distinct by time and circumstances, are inferior to the whites. . . . It is not against experience to suppose, that different species of the same genus, or varieties of the same species, may possess different qualifications" (p. 143). Jefferson came under attack from the clergy in the election of 1800 for having seemed to suggest that both Indians and Negroes were separately created, a suggestion which the Reverend William Linn called "contrary to the sacred history that all mankind have descended from a single pair." To Jefferson's suspicion that the Negroes might have been "originally a distinct race," Linn replied, "Would a man who believes in divine revelation even hint a suspicion of this kind? . . . You have degraded the blacks from the rank which God hath given them . . . ! You have advanced the strongest argument for their state of slavery! . . . we exclude you, in your present belief, from any department among Christians!": [William Linn], *Serious Considerations on the Election of a President: Addressed to the Citizens of the United States* (Trenton, N.J., 1800), pp. 8, 10, 11. Daniel J. Boorstin argues convincingly that Jefferson did not intend to claim that Negroes were separately created (*Lost World of Thomas Jefferson,* pp. 68–98, esp. 93–94) and, while noting that Jefferson was uncertain, "tentative [and] ambiguous," contends that his position on the equality of the Negro was one of "qualified assurance" (pp. 94, 89).

49. For an interesting contribution to a definition of "Jeffersonian democracy" as it is illuminated by an examination of his drafts for a constitution for Virginia and his reform bills of 1776–1780, see Elisha P. Douglass, *Rebels and Democrats: The Struggle for Equal Political Rights and Majority Rule During the American Revolution* (Chicago, 1965), pp. 287–316. Jefferson justified the indirect election of senators because "a choice by the people themselves is not generally distinguished for its wisdom" (Boyd, I, 503). His first-draft provision for life terms for senators (*ibid.,* I, 341) was revised to a nine-year term, although Jefferson still contended that he "could submit, tho' not so willingly to an appointment for life, or to anything rather than a mere creation by and dependence on the people" (*ibid.,* I, 504).

50. William Clarence Webster, "Comparative Study of the State Constitutions of the American Revolution," *Annals of the American Academy of Political and Social Science,* IX (May 1897), 390–93.

51. Timothy Matlack, quoted in Theodore Thayer, *Pennsylvania Poli-*

tics and the Growth of Democracy, 1740–1776 (Harrisburg, Pa., 1953), p. 189.

52. An unfriendly comment by Thomas Smith, quoted in Douglass, p. 265.

53. *Ibid.*, p. 266.

54. Philip S. Foner, ed., *The Complete Writings of Thomas Paine* (New York, 1945), II, 282; I, 378. For the "Fort Wilson" Riot (October 4, 1779), see J. Thomas Scharf and Thompson Westcott, *History of Philadelphia, 1609–1884* (Philadelphia, 1884), I, 401–2; Ellis Paxson Oberholtzer, *Philadelphia: A History of the City and Its People* (Philadelphia, 1912), I, 290. For complete text of Constitution, see Thayer, pp. 211–27.

55. An indirect financial requirement for the franchise was that the voter be a taxpayer; in practice this meant the payment of a poll tax; "the only free males who could not vote were sons of non-freeholders living with their parents" (Douglass, p. 268n). J. Paul Selsam, *The Pennsylvania Constitution of 1776: A Study in Revolutionary Democracy* (Philadelphia, 1936), p. 188, comments: "The essentially democratic feature of the Constitution was the complete abolition of all property or financial qualifications, not only for the electorate but also for the elected."

56. An opponent of the Constitution described it as a system which gave "a part of the people, particularly those who frequent public houses where the laws are always posted up for consideration, a negative upon the proceedings of the whole state" (quoted in Douglass, p. 274).

57. John Adams was one of the many who assumed that Paine was one of the authors (Butterfield, II, 391), but Paine claimed that he had "no hand in forming any part of it." (Foner, II, 270). Thayer, p. 197, describes Paine as the authors' "mentor."

58. For the quotations from Thomas Paine in this paragraph, see Foner, I, 6, 7, 28; II, 282–83, 284, 286, 288. For Paine as abolitionist, see II, 15–22; internationalist and anticolonialist: II, 20, 23–27, 552; feminist (as editor of *Pennsylvania Magazine*): II, 34–38; egalitarian in regard to the poor: I, 398–454.

59. Christopher Hill, *Puritanism and Revolution: Studies in Interpretation of the English Revolution of the 17th Century* (New York, 1964), pp. 100–102; E. P. Thompson, *The Making of the English Working Class* (New York, 1964), pp. 23–24.

60. *The People the Best Governors: or a Plan of Government Founded on the Just Principles of Natural Freedom* (1776) in Frederick Chase, *A History of Dartmouth College and the Town of Hanover, New Hampshire* (Cambridge, Mass., 1891), I, 654.

61. *Ibid.*, I, 663; *The Interest of America* (1776) in Peter Force, ed., *American Archives* (Washington, 1837–53), 4th Ser., VI, 841.

62. *Force*, 4th Ser., VI, 841.

63. *Ibid.*, VI, 842; Chase, I, 656–57, 662, 658; *Four Letters on Interest-*

ing Subjects (Philadelphia, 1776) in Clifford K. Shipton, ed., *Early American Imprints, 1639–1800* (microcard edition published by American Antiquarian Society; Worcester, Mass., 1955–   ), pp. p. 12).

64. Thomas E. Drake, *Quakers and Slavery in America* (New Haven, Conn., 1950), pp. 5ff., 11–12, 72; John Woolman, *Journal and A Plea for the Poor* (New York, 1961), p. 53.

65. Some did. For the rejection of slavery by the "Dixie-Dutch" (and their later adoption of it, as part of the process of "Americanization"), see Richard H. Shryock, "British Versus German Traditions in Colonial Agriculture," *Mississippi Valley Historical Review,* XXVI (June 1939), 39–54.

66. Woolman, pp. 57, 69, 80; Staughton Lynd, ed., *Nonviolence in America: A Documentary History* (Indianapolis, 1966), pp. xvii–xxiii.

67. See Woolman, *passim;* Frederick B. Tolles, *Quakers and the Atlantic Culture* (New York, 1960); Rayner Wickersham Kelsey, *Friends and the Indians, 1655–1917* (Philadelphia, 1917), pp. 1–88; Mary Sumner Benson, *Women in Eighteenth-Century America: A Study of Opinion and Social Usage* (New York, 1935), pp. 119–20, 248, 263–67. In many of these areas the Quakers' conduct, although better than that of other Americans, was far from perfect. The struggle against slavery was, to begin with, a struggle against slave ownership *within* the Society of Friends. For the negative side of Quaker treatment of the Indians, see, e.g., Francis P. Jennings, "The Delaware Interregnum," *Pennsylvania Magazine of History and Biography,* LXXXIX (April 1965), 174–98 and the same author's "Indian Trade of the Susquehanna Valley," *Proceedings of the American Philosophical Society,* CX, 406–24.

68. Woolman, pp. 41, 79. For a critique of Quaker absolutism, see Boorstin, *Americans: Colonial Experience,* pp. 33–69; for a reply, stressing the richness of Penn's "Holy Experiment," see Tolles, *passim* and esp. pp. 114–15. For a discussion of the conflict between American principles and their realization, see Caughey, *Journal of American History,* LII, 239–51.

69. Adams, IV, 195, 225; VI, 62, 65, 115, 279–80, 452, 516. It is illuminating to contrast Adams' constitutional principles with his provisions for implementing them. Many provisions in the Massachusetts Constitution clearly contradict the statement in the Declaration of Rights that officers of government are "at all times accountable" to the people (IV, 225). Adams' endorsement of the principle of rotation in office in his *Thoughts on Government* (IV, 197–98) is contradicted by his later assertion that "No people in the world will bear to be deprived, at the end of one year, of the service of their best men, and to be obliged to confer their suffrages, from year to year, on the next best, until the rotation brings them to the worst" (VI, 68). These contradictions should be further contrasted with

the literalism of the Pennsylvania Constitution of 1776 (see above, p. 12).

70. Hill, p. 68.

71. George Rudé, *The Crowd in History: A Study of Popular Disturbances in France and England, 1730–1848* (New York, 1964), pp. 49–50.

72. *Genius of American Politics* pp. 66–98.

73. Woolman, p. 241.

74. Herbert Aptheker, ed., *A Documentary History of the Negro People in the United States* (New York, 1965), I, 8, 10, 11. For a 1772 poem by a Negro likening British "tyranny" to slavery, see Julian D. Mason, ed., *The Poems of Phillis Wheatley* (Chapel Hill, N.C., 1966), pp. 33–35.

75. Merrill Jensen, "Democracy and the American Revolution," *Huntington Library Quarterly*, XX (August 1957), 321–41.

76. Staughton Lynd, "The Mechanics and New York City Politics, 1774–1788," *Labor History*, V (Fall 1964), 232. Lynd and Alfred Young speak of a "distinctive mechanic ideology" in "After Carl Becker: The Mechanics and New York City Politics, 1774–1801," *ibid.*, p. 217.

77. Force, 4th Ser., I, 342–43.

78. For the role of the Associators in Pennsylvania politics, see Selsam, pp. 74–129. See also above, note 54, for the "Fort Wilson" Riot. For some other instances of democratic movements from below during the Revolutionary period, see Philip Davidson, *Propaganda and the American Revolution, 1763–1783* (Chapel Hill, N.C., 1941), pp. 65–82; Richard Walsh, *Charleston's Sons of Liberty: A Study of the Artisans, 1763–1789* (Columbia, S.C., 1959). But note that these "mechanics" and "artisans" are never clearly defined; they are certainly not all lower class. (Carl Bridenbaugh, *The Colonial Craftsman* [Chicago, 1961], p. 156, says that mechanics "constituted a vertical, not a horizontal, section of colonial population"). I have attempted to restrict my examples to those who were clearly lower class.

79. Adams, IV, 68, 397 (John R. Howe, Jr., *The Changing Political Thought of John Adams* [Princeton, 1966], p. 137, identifies the concept of "natural aristocracy"—although not the term—in Adams' thought as early as "around 1760"); Main, *William and Mary Quarterly*, XXIII, 397; Foner, II, 287–88; for the efforts of the Pennsylvania Associators to broaden the franchise, see Selsam, pp. 86, 138. Hawke, p. 34n., interprets the voters' disobedience of property qualifications optimistically: "Paine's remarks suggest that the property qualification was not so restrictive as has been generally believed." Paine's remarks also seem to belie Hawke's contention (pp. 20–21) that "at no time did an outraged populace try to improve their political position."

80. Adams, IV, 393; Lynd and Young, *Labor History*, V, 224; *New-York Gazette; or, the Weekly Post-Boy*, January 8, 1770.

81. *Ibid.*

82. *New-York Gazette: and Weekly Mercury,* July 15, 1776.

83. *New York Packet,* July 11, 1776. For a report of a petition by debtors in the Philadelphia jail in January 1776 "praying that the several Colony Assemblies may be directed to devise Methods to free all prisoners for Debt," see "Diary of Richard Smith in the Continental Congress, 1775–1776," *American Historical Review,* I (April 1896), 496.

84. William Bradford, *Of Plymouth Plantation, 1620–1647,* ed. Samuel Eliot Morison (New York, 1953), p. 205.

85. Quoted in Lawrence W. Towner, " 'A Fondness for Freedom': Servant Protest in Puritan Society," *William and Mary Quarterly,* 3rd Ser., XIX (April 1962), 210–11.

86. Morris, pp. 167–82.

87. Towner, *William and Mary Quarterly,* XIX, 201; Herbert Aptheker, *American Negro Slave Revolts* (New York, 1943), pp. 162–208. See Aptheker, *ibid,* pp. 169–70, 178–79, for participation in similar activities by Indian slaves. For a suggestion that Indians within the jurisdiction of Puritan Massachusetts called religion "a politicke divise to keepe ignorant men in awe" see Nathaniel B. Shurtleff, ed., *Records of the Governor and Company of the Massachusetts Bay in New England* (Boston, 1853–54), III, 98.

88. Morris, pp. 193–207. In 1647 two seamen were convicted of tearing off their vessel's mainmast a copy of the New Netherland law of 1638 against seamen's disobedience (see above, note 34 and I. N. P. Stokes, *The Iconography of Manhattan Island, 1498–1909* [New York, 1895–1928], IV, 87).

89. Deposition of Thos. Austin, December 10, 1769, in Hutchinson to Hillsborough, December 20, 1769: Great Britain, Public Record Office, CO 5/759, part 2 (Library of Congress transcript).

90. It is fruitful to consider the nondeferential conduct of whites and Negroes together. Might not the "infantilism" which Stanley M. Elkins, *Slavery: A Problem in American Institutional and Intellectual Life* (New York, 1963), sees in the Negro's acceptance of an inferior role be seen as well in whites who defer: is not *any man* who believes that others are better qualified to make his decisions for him in some sense infantilized? This suggests that some of the same challenges which can be made against the idea of Negro infantilization might be equally suitable as a critique of deference among whites. First, how widespread was nondeferential conduct: do not historians and historical sources tend to minimize it? Second, when we find deferential conduct, how much does it reflect deferential attitudes and how much the necessary pose of the powerless ("putting Whitey on")? Third, if people are found to be genuinely deferential in both conduct and attitude, how permanent is the malady: might they not become less deferential when the coercive factors which made them defer were removed or lessened? In any case, we cannot with any validity conclude anything about the

inarticulate—neither that they have been rebellious nor that they have been deferential—until we actually study them. For further remarks on accommodation and rebelliousness as themes in the history of the powerless, see Jesse Lemisch, "New Left Elitism," *Radical America*, I (September–October, 1967), 43–53.

91. The terms are those of Carl L. Becker, *The History of Political Parties in the Province of New York*, 2nd ed. (Madison, Wis., 1960), p. 22.

92. For all the colonial resolves, see Edmund S. Morgan, ed., *Prologue to Revolution: Sources and Documents on the Stamp Act Crisis, 1764–1766* (Chapel Hill, N.C., 1959), pp. 44–69.

93. Edmund S. Morgan and Helen M. Morgan, *The Stamp Act Crisis: Prologue to Revolution* (Chapel Hill, N.C., 1953), p. 107.

94. *New-York Gazette; or, the Weekly Post-Boy*, November 7, 1765.

95. General Gage to Secretary Conway, January 16, 1766: Clarence Edwin Carter, ed., *The Correspondence of General Thomas Gage with the Secretaries of State, 1763–1775* (New Haven, Conn., 1931), I, 81. For three accounts of the Stamp Act riots which stress manipulation see Morgans, *Stamp Act Crisis*, pp. 180–81, 187; Douglass Adair and John A. Schultz, eds., *Peter Oliver's Origin and Progress of the American Rebellion: A Tory View* (San Marino, Cal., 1963). pp. 46–59; John C. Miller, *Sam Adams: Pioneer in Propaganda* (Stanford, Cal., 1960), pp. 48–81. Unless otherwise noted, the following account of the Stamp Act is based on Jesse Lemisch, "Jack Tar vs. John Bull: The Role of New York's Seamen in Precipitating the Revolution" (unpublished Ph.D. dissertation, Yale University, 1962), pp. 76–128.

96. See, e.g., William Johnson to Lords of Trade, November 22, 1765: Edmund Bailey O'Callaghan, ed., *Documents Relative to the Colonial History of the State of New York* (Albany, N.Y., 1865–87), VII, 790.

97. *New-York Gazette; or, the Weekly Post-Boy*, November 7, 1765; *New-York Mercury*, November 4, 1765. European crowds have also been described as fickle, irrational, criminal, and as acting only in response to a "hidden hand." In *The Crowd in History* and in other writings, George Rudé has shown that in fact the crowd was purposeful, disciplined, and discriminating, that "in the eighteenth century the typical and ever recurring form of social protest was the riot" (p. 66). Rudé has shown that the negative view of the crowd is a partisan view, and that party is conservative. The extent to which the historiography of the Stamp Act riots—and indeed of American mob action in general—is conservative is revealed by an examination of Rudé's work, and our understanding of crowds in eighteenth-century America is further increased if we see such action as part of an old English tradition. For a collection of relevant psychological studies, see Duane P. Schultz, *Panic Behavior: Discussion and Readings* (New York, 1964). See also below, pages 24–26.

98. *New-York Gazette; or, the Weekly Post-Boy*, December 19, 1765.

99. *Ibid.*, December 27, 1765. Cf. the Rhode Island resolves, discussed in Jesse Lemisch, "New York's Petitions and Resolves of December, 1765: Liberals vs. Radicals," *New-York Historical Society Quarterly*, XLIX (October 1965), 324–25. See *ibid.*, pp. 316–24, for a description of the successful effort to seize control of a mass meeting in New York on November 26, 1765, in order to prevent it from resolving on a policy of disobedience.

100. *New-York Gazette; or, the Weekly Post-Boy*, November 25, 1765; Governor Henry Moore to Lord Dartmouth, December 27, 1765: O'Callaghan, VII, 802.

101. Morgans, *Stamp Act Crisis*, pp. 130, 133–39, 159–68.

102. Morgan, *Prologue to Revolution*, pp. 155–56.

103. Indeed, a reading of notes on Parliament's secret debates on repeal indicates that although merchant pressure was effective, it was fear of the possible development out of the violent resistance in America of a war involving France and Spain which swayed the members. Lawrence Henry Gipson, "The Great Debate in the Committee of the Whole House of Commons on the Stamp Act, 1766, as Reported by Nathaniel Ryder," *Pennsylvania Magazine of History and Biography*, LXXXVI (January 1962), 10–41, notes that merchant pressure was only the "ostensible" cause of the ministry's decision to seek repeal (p. 11) and concludes that "certain members not only saw the serious threat to their mercantile system but, what is even more important, they also foresaw the seriousness of a potential military involvement" (p. 40). I am indebted to Edmund Morgan for calling these notes to my attention.

104. This is the Morgans' view in *Stamp Act Crisis* (e.g., p. 295); I think their own evidence indicates that that search ended very rapidly and the time quickly arrived when the assertion of constitutional rights became consensual and thus a bar to action.

105. Oliver M. Dickerson, *The Navigation Acts and the American Revolution* (Philadelphia, 1951), pp. 208, 212–19, 224–50.

106. *Ibid.*, pp. 254–55.

107. For a brief account which stresses competition for work, see Morris, pp. 190–92.

108. *Ibid.*, p. 190n.; Broadside, "The Times," New-York Historical Society Broadsides, 1770–21.

109. Frederick Kidder, ed., *History of the Boston Massacre* (Albany, N.Y., 1870), p. 56.

110. Captain Thomas Rich to the Admiralty, March 11, 1770: Great Britain, Public Record Office, Adm 1/2388.

111. Captain Thomas Preston, quoted in Merrill Jensen, ed., *English Historical Documents: American Colonial Documents to 1776* (New York, 1955), p. 751.

112. Morris, p. 191; Edmund S. Morgan, *The Birth of the Republic, 1763–1789* (Chicago, 1956), p. 48.

113. *New-York Gazette; or, the Weekly Post-Boy*, February 5, 1770; Lemisch, "Jack Tar vs. John Bull," pp. 154–61.

114. *Ibid.*, pp. 132–61; *New-York Gazette; or the Weekly Post-Boy*, August 14, 1766; Stokes, IV, 806; *The Montresor Journals*, New-York Historical Society, *Collections*, 1881 (New York, 1882), pp. 383–84; General Gage to Duke of Richmond, August 26, 1766: Carter, I, 104.

115. Governor Moore to Lord Hillsborough, August 19, 1768: O'Callaghan, VIII, 99.

116. *New-York Gazette; or, the Weekly Post-Boy*, February 5, 1770; Broadside, The Times," New-York Historical Society Broadsides, 1770–21.

117. Cadwallader Colden to Lord Hillsborough, February 21, 1770: *The Colden Letter Books, 1760–1775*, New-York Historical Society, *Collections*, 1876–1877 (New York, 1877–78), II, 211.

118. Broadside, "The Times," New-York Historical Society Broadsides, 1770–21.

119. James Fulton Zimmerman, *Impressment of American Seamen*, Columbia University *Studies in History, Economics and Public Law*, CXVIII, No. 1 (1925), begins by stating that "The impressment of American seamen by the British navy began shortly after the Revolutionary War" (pp. 11–12). Better accounts are Dora Mae Clark, "The Impressment of Seamen in the American Colonies" in *Essays in Colonial History Presented to Charles McLean Andrews by His Students* (New Haven, Conn., 1931), pp. 198–224; R. Pares, "The Manning of the Navy in the West Indies, 1702–63," *Transactions of the Royal Historical Society*, 4th Ser., XX (1937), 31–60; Neil R. Stout, "Manning the Royal Navy in North America, 1763–1775," *The American Neptune*, XXIII (July 1963), 174–85. See Lemisch, "Jack Tar in the Streets."

120. Deposition of Nathaniel Holmes, July 18, 1702: PRO CO 5/862; James Otis, *The Rights of the British Colonies Asserted and Proved* (1764) in Bernard Bailyn and J. N. Garrett, eds., *Pamphlets of the American Revolution, 1750–1776* (Cambridge, Mass., 1965–   ) I, 464.

121. See e.g., *Journals of the House of Representatives of Massachusetts, 1715–1749* (Boston, 1919–1950), XX, 98–99; XXIV, 212.

122. Stout, *American Neptune*, XXIII, 176–77, 180, 181; Bailyn and Garrett, I, 582–83.

123. Adams, IX, 318.

124. The phrase is Edmund Burke's, in his "Speech on Moving His Resolutions for Conciliation with the Colonies" (March 22, 1775) in Burke, II, 117.

125. See, e.g., impressment during the Stamp Act Crisis (log of *Guarland*, April 22, 1766: PRO Adm 51/386); impressment at the time of the *Liberty* Riot (log of *Romney*, June 10, 1768: PRO Adm 51/793).

126. *New-York Gazette; or, the Weekly Post-Boy*, August 12, 1754.

127. William M. Willett, *A Narrative of the Military Actions of Colonel Marinus Willett, Taken Chiefly from his own Manuscript* (New York, 1831), pp. 149–51.

128. John Shy, *Toward Lexington: The Role of the British Army in the Coming of the American Revolution* (Princeton, 1965) pp. 318–19. Emphasis added.

129. Quoted in Benjamin Woods Labaree, *The Boston Tea Party* (New York, 1964), p. 144.

130. See, e.g., "Possibly Sam Adams realized he could better manipulate such a gathering" (*ibid.*, p. 124); "Other patriot leaders . . . apparently did not go on board any of the tea-ships that night. Their work was already done" (p. 144); the "probably's," "may have," "seems to" in the paragraph on pp. 141–42. For a description of the Tea Party as Sam Adams' "masterpiece," see Miller, pp. 276–96.

131. Davidson, pp. xv–xvi.

132. Miller, pp. 8, 53, 69, 276.

133. Hawke, p. 13. Such treatments often lead to the contention that Revolutionary leaders were in some sense maladjusted or neurotic. Ralph Volney Harlow, *Samuel Adams, Promoter of the American Revolution: A Study in Psychology and Politics* (New York, 1923), described a "nervously unstable" Adams—with shaky hands and shaky voice—"compensating" for an "inferiority complex" with a politics of "psychopathic effusions"—all in all, together with Mohammed, Savonarola, and Joan of Arc, "an interesting 'case' for the psychoanalyst" (pp. 37–39, 64, 190). More recently, Hawke, p. 103, has quoted Eric Hoffer approvingly—"The sick in soul insist that it is humanity that is sick, and they are the surgeons to operate on it"—and applied the quotation to the "small band of men" who were hounded by family troubles and business failures and were bitter, ambitious, and frustrated (pp. 103–6).

134. In describing the actual effect of *Common Sense,* John Adams offered a view which challenges manipulative assumptions: "The Temper and Wishes of the People, supplied every thing at that time . . ." (Butterfield, III, 333). Two years before Adams had denied "the power of popular leaders . . . to persuade a large people, any length of time together, to think themselves wronged, injured, and oppressed, unless they really were, and saw and felt it to be so" (Adams, IV, 14; quoted in Gordon S. Wood, "Rhetoric and Reality in the American Revolution," *William and Mary Quarterly,* 3rd Ser., XXIII [January 1966], 31).

135. I use the term as it is used by Thompson, p. 12: "the degree to which they ["working people"] contributed, by conscious efforts, to the making of history."

136. See Lemisch, "Jack Tar in the Streets." Two representative accounts of American seamen in prison during the Revolution are Albert Greene, *Recollections of the Jersey Prison Ship from the Manuscript of Capt. Thomas Dring* (New York, 1961), a patriotic

memoir, and James Lenox Banks, *David Sproat and Naval Prisoners in the War of the Revolution with Mention of William Lenox, of Charleston* (New York, 1909), a favorable account of the British Commissary of Naval Prisoners at New York.

137. A defection rate of 7.7 percent of the seamen in one English prison is reported in an American source (*Boston Gazette,* June 24, July 1, 8, 1782) and confirmed by the records of the British Commissioners for Sick and Hurt Seamen, which indicate a defection rate for all English prisons of 7.4 percent (PRO Adm 98/11–14).

138. Greene, pp. 97–116; *New-York Gazette and Weekly Mercury,* February 12, 1781; *Boston Gazette,* June 24, July 1, 8, 1782.

139. Greene, pp. 25, 84–89.

140. Quoted in Herbert Aptheker, *The American Revolution, 1763–1783* (New York, 1960), p. 54; for a discussion of "Dividing the Population into Thirds," see pp. 52–56.

141. W. Brown, *King's Friends,* pp. 295, 296n, 308n, 313n, 318n, 326n, 330n, 334n. I am not contending that Loyalism was necessarily an upper-class movement, only that in many situations class may have been a factor in determining loyalties *one way or another.* We have evidence for this contention in recent studies of groups at the bottom of society which saw freedom in an alliance with the British rather than the Americans: see e.g., Staughton Lynd, "The Tenant Rising at Livingston Manor, May 1777," *New-York Historical Society Quarterly,* XLVIII (April 1964), 163–177; Benjamin Quarles, *The Negro in the American Revolution* (Chapel Hill, N.C., 1961), pp. 19–32, 111–33.

142. Oliver, pp. 43, 65, 83, 94, 95.

143. Jonathan Boucher, ed., *Reminiscences of an American Loyalist, 1738–1789: Being the Autobiography of the Revd. Jonathan Boucher* (Boston, 1925), pp. 12, 119, 136.

144. Oliver, pp. 39, 48, 65, 145, 158, 162, 165; Boucher, pp. 68–69, 95–96, 121.

145. Boorstin, *Genius,* p. 76.

146. For a theoretical discussion which attempts to demonstrate the necessity of an approach from the bottom up if written history is to have more than limited validity, and which concludes that "both humanity and science dictate sympathy with history's victims," see Lemisch, *Radical America,* I (no. 2), 43–53.

BEYOND BEARD

∽ Staughton Lynd

FOR MORE THAN half a century now, historians have been engaged in dubious battle with Charles Beard's *An Economic Interpretation of the Constitution of the United States* (1913) and *Economic Origins of Jeffersonian Democracy* (1915).

Beard's theory of the formation of the Constitution and of the opposition to Secretary Hamilton has been repeatedly attacked, and, like the dragon teeth sown by Jason, has repeatedly sprung up again to confront its destroyers. One reason for this is that those who have sought to revise Beard have not agreed on a coherent alternative way of telling the story.

Thus among Beard's principal critics, one—Robert Brown—believes that "the really fundamental conflict in American society at the time" was not between classes but between slaveholding and nonslaveholding sections of the country.[1] Another critic—Forrest McDonald—concludes that from the beginning of the Revolution through the adoption of the Constitution the leading patriots were divided into two groups, "hard-shelled republicans" from Virginia and New England, and realistic nationalists from South Carolina, Pennsylvania, and New York.[2]

Among the scholars who, without directly attacking Beard, have provided new versions of the same events, there is similar disagreement.[3] Argument persists as to whether or not, and if so in what sense, a "depression" took place in the mid-1780s. There is no consensus as to why Madison broke with Hamilton. Students of Merrill Jensen, such as E. James Ferguson and Jackson Main, document the undemocratic character of the United States Constitution; equally predictably, Clinton Rossiter finds the Convention "a case-study in the political process of constitutional democracy."[4] Biographers of Hamilton, Jefferson, and Madison champion their respective protagonists' roles in the events of the early 1790s.[5] A debate so unimaginative and results so eclectic necessarily compare unfavorably with the bold simplicity of the Beard thesis.

What has been at stake in this debate is much more than an appraisal of the formation of the Constitution and the early Republic. To begin with, in *The Rise of American Civilization* (1927) Beard and his wife extended his hypothesis to include the origins of the Civil War. In that work the "conflict between capitalistic and agrarian interests"[6] previously presented as the basis of both the conflict of Federalists and Antifederalists in 1787–1788 and the conflict of Hamiltonians and Jeffersonians in the 1790s, was held to be also the root of the "Second American Revolution" of 1861–1865. Hence the controversy over Beard involves our assessment of the entire period between the Revolution and the Civil War.

Moreover, Beard offers the most substantial American version to date of an economic approach to history in general. The specter of Marx has haunted historians' response to Beard. Although Beard was careful (as he observed in introducing a 1935 reprinting) to call his 1913 work *an* economic interpretation, not " 'the' economic interpretation, or " 'the only' interpretation possible to thought,"[7] one of Beard's prominent critics asserted in his rebuttal that "economic interpretation of the Constitution does not work."[8]

These overtones are the more obvious when it is recalled that sustained criticism of Beard's work is largely a product of the Cold War years. At a time when the politics of dead center and an apparent end to ideology prevailed in American society at large, historians rather suddenly discovered that Americans had always shared a consensus about fundamentals which enabled them to muddle through. Robert

Brown, for example, repeatedly cites John Adams in contending that New England society was democratic even before the Revolution; but Brown does not quote John Adams'
statement that

> the state of Connecticut has always been governed by an
> aristocracy, more decisively than the empire of Great Brit-
> ain is. Half a dozen, or, at most a dozen families, have con-
> trolled that country when a colony, as well as since it has
> been a state.[9]

Cecilia Kenyon, who has effectively criticized Beard's assumption that Antifederalism was democratic, reveals her
own assumptions in an essay called "Where Paine Went
Wrong." Paine (she says) was "incurable naive"; he espoused
an "idealized conception" rather than observing "historical
actuality"; he failed to recognize that the proper task of the
Founding Fathers was to achieve "at least a moderate measure of justice in a society ruled by men who would always
and unavoidably be influenced by private and sometimes
selfish interests"; in a word he was "essentially alien."[10] The
process of reading Paine and Paine's ideas out of the American tradition culminated in Forrest McDonald's treatment
of the period in *E Pluribus Unum*:

> Sometimes in the course of human events, as the Declara-
> tion of Independence had proclaimed, it becomes necessary
> for people to dissolve political bonds. . . . The American
> Revolution was only a beginning in teaching men the pro-
> cess, but once it was done—once the vulgar overstepped the
> bonds of propriety and got away with it—there was no
> logical stopping place. *Common Sense* led unerringly to
> Valmy, and Valmy to Napoleon, and Napoleon to the
> Revolution of 1830, and that to the Revolutions of 1848,
> and those to the Paris Commune of 1871, and that to the
> Bolshevik Revolution, and that to the African and Asian
> Revolutions in Expectations, and those to eternity.[11]

But lucky America, McDonald concluded, had Founding
Fathers who were able to check the forces they had unleashed.
    Now to be sure, the influence of Populism on Beard and
on his mentor, Frederick Jackson Turner, is as evident as

the influence of the affluent society on their critics. Turner, in an introduction to Orin G. Libby's study of the vote on the United States Constitution, commented that

> the present Populistic agitation finds its stronghold in those western and southern regions whose social and economic conditions are in many respects strikingly like those existing in 1787 in the areas that opposed the ratification of the Constitution.[12]

"We may trace the contest between the capitalist and the democratic pioneer from the earliest colonial days," Turner wrote later; and Beard echoed him in placing this phrase at the beginning of his *Economic Origins,* in asserting (in his *Economic Interpretation*) that "the democratic party was the agrarian element," in giving the title "Populism and Reaction" to the chapter in *The Rise of American Civilization* which dealt with the 1780s.[13]

The point is not that Beard was scientific and his critics biased, but that his critics as much as he have reflected their social environment. Nor need one dismiss the contributions of either school for this reason. *Wie es eigentlich gewesen* is an elephant with many sides, and if a scholar grasps that leg which is closest to him he nevertheless lays hold of something that is really there. To say our preconceptions constitute the inevitable point of departure for our conceptions does not destroy a vision of history as a cumulative enterprise in which more and more truth is discovered. In fact, it holds out hope that more truth will be discovered as changing current circumstances suggest new points of view.

The picture presented in this essay is subject to qualification and justification in precisely the same way. It has been stimulated by two upheavals in recent history: the American civil rights movement, which suggested a fresh look at the importance of slavery in the Revolutionary era; and the worldwide colonial independence movement, which seemed to offer a new model for conceptualizing the Revolution and its relation to the Civil War. The resulting hypothesis seeks to incorporate what both the Beardian and the anti-Beardian arguments have solidly established, while attempting to surmount what each argument has been unable to explain.

Personalty and Realty

Beard posited an essentially unchanging conflict through-out American history between capitalists and farmers. But the evidence is overwhelming that internal conflict was a secondary aspect of the revolution of 1776, which in fact was primarily a war for national independence. On the other hand, Beard's critics have generally maintained that the national unity they correctly perceive in the American Revolution continued to characterize the rest of American history. For them, then, the Civil War must be conceptualized as a tragic accident produced by a blundering generation: a model at variance with the very substantial body of evidence supporting Beard's thesis of the Civil War as a "Second American Revolution."[14] The way out of the dilemma is to synthesize Beard's view of the Civil War and the view of the American Revolution insisted on by Beard's critics.

Such a synthesis, so it seems to me, should embody the following elements:

1. The American Revolution (like most colonial independence movements) was waged by a coalition of diverse social groups, united in the desire for American independence but with various additional aims that were in conflict.

2. The popular elements in this coalition—small farmers and city artisans—often clashed with their upper-class leaders, and fear of what the Declaration of Independence calls "convulsions within" and "domestic insurrections amongst us" was a principal motive for the formation of the United States Constitution.

3. The upper-class leaders of the Revolution were themselves divided into two basic groups, Northern capitalists and Southern plantation owners, and the Constitution represented not a victory of one over the other but a compromise between them.

4. Serious conflict between North and South preceded the compromise of 1787, and in the 1790s—not in 1820 or 1850—the coalition of sectional leaders which had directed the Revolution and the movement for the Constitution almost at once broke down.

5. Thus (as in most colonial independence movements) a first revolution for national independence was followed by a second revolution which determined what kind of society the independent nation would become.

6. America therefore did have a bourgeois revolution comparable to the French Revolution, but it was directed not against England but against slavery and took place not in 1776 but in 1861.

These formulations retain Beard's emphasis on "personalty" (i.e., mobile capital, represented by investments in securities, commerce, manufacturing, bank loans, land speculation) while rejecting his conception of "realty" (i.e., capital invested in agricultural production). The Beardian category of "realty" obscures what really happened in the American Revolution and in the Civil War by blurring distinctions between different kinds of farmers, and most importantly, between freehold farmers of the North and West on the one hand, and Southern plantation owners on the other. The model presented here proposes that the Revolution and the formation of the Constitution expressed an alliance between Northern "personalty" and the particular form of "realty" which dominated the South; while in the eighteenth century as in the mid-nineteenth, the political role of other forms of "realty"—for example, of Midwestern wheat growers during the Civil War—requires separate analysis.

As applied to the Civil War, the distinction between "personalty" and "realty," capitalist and agrarian, emerges from the obvious facts: hence Beard's portrait of the Second American Revolution remains far more convincing than his analysis of the first. But here too, Beard's neglect of slavery as a force in American history seriously damaged his results. Thus Barrington Moore, Jr., for example, sees the Civil War as "the last revolutionary offensive on the part of what one may legitimately call urban or bourgeois capitalist democracy." Moore differs from Beard in refusing to eliminate the issue of slavery. This is not because Moore believes that Southern slavery obstructed Northern industrial development. On the contrary, slavery may have been a stimulant. But "striking down slavery was a decisive step, an act at least as important as the striking down of absolute monarchy in the English Civil War and the French Revolution," for in the absence of emancipation American capitalism might have come to maturity in an undemocratic political context, as was the case in Germany and Japan.[15] In contrast, Beard was led by his concept of "agrarianism" and "realty" to a view of the Civil War which came very close to that of the rural Southerners who fought in it.

As applied to the formation of the Constitution, Beard's distinction between "personalty" and "realty" was doubly unfortunate because it overlaid Orin Libby's more useful distinction between groups more and less involved in a commercial economy. Beard acknowledged Libby handsomely, and built his discussion of ratification on Libby's maps. But Libby, like Jackson Main more recently, did not draw the line between Federalist and Antifederalist at the boundary between city and country. For Libby as for Main, the "commercial farmer" located on some large river which allowed him to export for distant markets naturally inclined to Federalism. As Main says: "the struggle over the ratification of the Constitution was primarily a contest between the commercial and the non-commercial elements in the population. This is the most significant fact, to which all else is elaboration, amplification, or exception." He specifies as to the division among farmers that

> the commercial interest was not just urban. The commercial centers were supported by nearby rural areas which depended upon the towns as markets and as agencies through which their produce was exported overseas. That is to say, the commercial interest also embraced large numbers of farmers, . . . permeated the rich river valleys and bound the great planters and other large landowners in the commercial nexus.[16]

The city artisan, too, was involved in the commercial economy although not himself an owner of large capital, and the artisans' overwhelming support for the Constitution is more readily explained à la Main and Libby than à la Beard.[17]

Thus the distinction (to use Libby's terminology) between "commercial" and "interior" farmers makes understandable what Beard's distinction between "personalty" and "realty" altogether fails to explain: how the Constitution could have been ratified by a society in which more than nine out of every ten adult white males were farmers. Above all the Southern slaveholder stands forth in the Libby-Main framework, not (as Beard was forced to cast him) as an investor in land and government securities, but as the most substantial commercial farmer in the new nation's economy. The mere presence of so many large plantation owners at the Constitutional Convention suggests to common sense that there is something wrong with Beard's dichotomy. Beard was obliged to say: "The south had many men who were rich in personalty, other than slaves, and it was this type, rather than the slaveholding planter as such, which was represented in the Convention that framed the Constitution"; and to make his analysis fit ratification of the Constitution by that heartland of "realty," Virginia, accepted Libby's assertion that Tidewater Virginia—of all places—was "the region of the large towns, and where commercial interests were predominant."[18]

As I see it, the United States Constitution represented, not the triumph of capitalism over a landed aristocracy (like the French Revolution and the American Civil War), but a compromise or coalition between men of wealth in the cities and men of wealth on the land. Robert Brown is absolutely right when he states that "if Beard had based his thesis on *property* and not *personalty,* he would have been on much safer ground."[19]

Where Beard's analysis of the formation of the Constitution remains valid is in its stress on the initiating role of "personalty." Forrest McDonald himself concedes that Beard's portrait of the Middle State capitalists grouped around Robert Morris of Philadelphia as "a consolidated group whose interests knew no state boundaries and were truly national in their scope," who (in McDonald's words) were "the greediest, most ruthless, and most insistent in demanding political action in their behalf," is a "perfectly accurate" description as of 1783.[20] But McDonald is right in maintaining that the movement which produced and ratified the Constitution in 1787–1788 was more broad than this. Well-to-do leaders both in New England and the South—especially in Virginia—had in the interim decided to throw their weight behind a movement for stronger national government. If personalty and Shays' Rebellion explain the former, they do not explain the latter. The dichotomy of "personalty" and "realty" fails to describe either the men who wrote the Constitution or the men who voted to ratify it.[21]

Jeffersonian Democracy and Slavery

The emergence of sectional parties in 1789–1792 constitutes the connecting link between analysis of the formation of the Constitution and analysis of the origins of the Civil War.

Beard believed that the party struggle of the 1790s simply extrapolated the conflict between capitalists and farmers over the Constitution. When compared to the earlier *Economic Interpretation,* the *Economic Origins* shows more awareness of the role of slavery and therefore less naiveté about agrarian democracy. Yet Beard, while insisting that "Jeffersonian Democracy" did not seek suffrage extension or any other "devices for a more immediate and direct control of the voters over the instrumentalities of government," and "simply meant the possession of the federal government by the agrarian masses led by an aristocracy of slave-owning planters," nevertheless failed to emphasize sufficiently the extent to which Jeffersonian Democracy was essentially Southern. Manning Dauer has shown that in the late 1790s noncommercial farmers in the Middle and Northern states deserted the Federalist party.[22] But the original opposition to Hamilton, which played the same role in the genesis of Jeffersonian Democracy as had "personalty" in instigating the movement for the Constitution, was overwhelmingly sectional.

The key evidence for this contention is the votes of the Congresses of 1789–92 which followed the Constitution's ratification. I think what they show is the intricate interaction of interest and ideology in the following three ways:

1) although the South—and subsequently Charles Beard—
conceptualized the planter as a "farmer" and the regional
interest of the South as a "landed interest," in fact the opposition which crystallized by 1792 did not include all farmers
and was restricted almost exclusively to the South; 2) although the upper and lower South had quite different dis-
crete interests, the tendency was toward the subordination of
immediate pocketbook interests and increasing concern with
the broader struggle for sectional dominance; 3) although in
general the influence of slavery was in differentiating the
entire institutional fabric of the South from that of the rest
of the nation, still there was in this early period explicit anxiety about Federal interference with slavery which intensified resistance to expansion of Federal power in other areas.

Upper and lower South, Virginia and South Carolina, dif-
fered in 1789–1790 over tariff discrimination against British
shipping, Federal assumption of state debts, and slavery.[23]
Nevertheless, in the spring of 1790 the various concrete differences between the interests of upper and lower South
began to be overshadowed by broader sectional concerns.
Georgia split from South Carolina on assumption, voting
solidly against it. North Carolina, as its representatives
trickled into Congress during March and April 1790, aligned
itself with Virginia on the issue of both tariff discrimination and assumption. And while the alignment of congressmen in voting on the Bank in 1791 was essentially similar to
the pattern of voting on assumption in 1790, there is the important difference that for the first time a majority of every
Southern state delegation voted against Hamilton on a major
measure.[24] Not only were nineteen of the Bank's twenty
opponents in the House Southerners; not only did Southern
congressmen vote nineteen to five against the Bank; but two
of the three South Carolina delegates who voted joined their
fellow Southerners to form for the first time a solid South. In
the debate before the vote Jackson of Georgia, Stone of Maryland, Smith of South Carolina, and Giles of Virginia all said
that, consistent with Madison's observation in 1787, the votes
of Congress were divided by the geographical line which
separated North and South.[25]

The philosophy of Antifederalists, North and South, in

1787 had special charms for Southerners in 1790 because the issue of Federal interference with slavery had already appeared. Jackson of Georgia expressed a common Southern response to the antislavery petitions of 1790 intermittently debated in the midst of the funding and assumption drama, stating that

> the people of the Southern states will resist tyranny as soon as another. The other parts of the continent may bear them down by force of arms, but they will never suffer themselves to be divested of their property without a struggle. The gentleman says, if he was a Federal Judge, he does not know to what length he would go in emancipating these people; but I believe his judgment would be of short duration in Georgia, perhaps even the existence of such a judge might be in danger.[26]

Senator William Maclay wrote at the time of the excitement in the House over the Quaker memorial. Under date of March 22, 1790, Maclay said: "I know not what may come of it, but there seems to be a general discontent among the members, and many of them do not hesitate to declare that the Union must fall to pieces at the rate we go on. Indeed, many seem to wish it."[27] The same thing was true in the Senate. Two days later Maclay's entry recorded: "Izard and Butler both manifested a most insulting spirit this day, when there was not the least occasion for it nor the smallest affront offered. These men have a most settled antipathy to Pennsylvania, owing to the doctrines in that State on the subject of slavery."[28] Thus the senators from South Carolina, the Southern state hitherto strongly Hamiltonian, were sensitized to the dangers of loose construction; and in the House, similarly, South Carolina's staunchest Federalist congressman, William Smith, made a long speech on March 17 which began and ended on the theme of Federal interference and in the middle developed every argument for slavery as a positive good which Calhoun would bring forward half a century later.[29] The episode must have been in the minds of Southern congressmen as they haggled about the constitutionality of the Bank for a week the following February.

What Southerners counted on in 1787, what they still hoped for in 1790, was that—to use Madison's words—in-only a few years "the Western and S. Western population may enter more into the estimate" so that the South would have a majority in the House.[30] But the results of the 1790 Census were not encouraging. The Northern majority of seven created by the Constitutional Convention's apportionment in 1787 would become a majority of nine even if, as Southerners hoped, Congress apportioned one congressman for every 30,000 persons. If, as Northerners consistently voted, apportionment were on the basis of one congressman to every 33,000 persons, then the Southern situation would be still worse. One or two votes were not trifling matters in a Congress where a switch of two or three votes had determined the fate of assumption. In the long debates on apportionment between October 1791 and April 1792 the discussion, as at the Constitutional Convention, began with abstract political theory, moved on to the interests of small and large states, and ended on the conflict between North and South. Never had sectionalism been so forcefully articulated. Williamson of North Carolina said the South "had suffered so much under the harrow of speculation" that he hoped it would not be denied the proportion of representation to which it was entitled. Murray of Maryland noted that the long debate had been "entirely constructed on the tenets of Northern and Southern interests and influence." Sedgwick of Massachusetts said still more sweepingly that "there existed an opinion of an opposition of interests between the Northern and Southern states. The influence of this opinion had been felt in the discussion of every important question which had come under the consideration of the Legislature." Summing up, William Branch Giles argued that a larger Congress would be more sympathetic to "the landed interest" and that "he felt a conviction that the agricultural or equalizing interest was nearly the same throughout all parts of the United States." He was wrong: 31 of the 34 votes for a smaller House came from the North; 25 of their 30 opponents were Southerners.[31]

Thus while one theme of these first Federalist years is Hamilton's promotion of his closely coordinated measures to enhance public credit, a second theme is the resurrection of that chronic sectional antagonism which had plagued both

the Continental Congress and the Constitutional Convention. If from the first standpoint we can view these years as
the completion of the Union, from the second we must see
them as prefiguring its dissolution. Joseph Charles says of
congressional response to Hamilton's financial bills: "A
sharp sectional division appeared in the voting upon the
measures of that program, a division which foreshadowed the
first phase in the growth of national parties."[32] John C. Miller's summary states explicitly:

> The gravest weakness of the Federalists was that their
> power was based upon a coalition of northern businessmen
> and southern planters. In all probability, this uneasy alli-
> ance would have succumbed sooner or later to the strains
> and stresses generated by the divergent economic interests
> and social and political attitudes of Northerners and South-
> erners. As might be expected, victory—in this case, the
> adoption of the Constitution—hastened the dissolution of
> the coalition, but the event was not ensured until 1790,
> when Hamilton launched his fiscal and economic programs.

Consensus had given way to conflict in which, as Miller puts
it, the "parties were divided by economic and ideological
differences greater than those which have generally existed
between major American political parties."[33]

Beyond Beard

To reject an interpretation of the formation of the Constitution and the early Republic built on the antithesis between "personalty" and "realty" does not require abandoning an economic approach to the period. Beard's drama for
villainous capitalist and virtuous farmer must make room
for a more complex scenario which preserves his sense of the
role of economic power.[34]

The slave, though he spoke few lines, should be moved
front and center. If as Beard said there was a "large propertyless mass" which the Constitution "excluded at the outset,"
the one fifth of the population in hereditary bondage better
deserves that description than any group of whites; for few
whites who began life without property failed to acquire it.[35]
To whatever extent the Constitution betrayed the promise

of the Declaration of Independence, it did so most of all for the Negro; surely John Alden says justly: "Had human slavery in the United States disappeared promptly as a result of the social ferment which was stimulated by the Anglo-American conflict, it would indeed be proper to think in terms of an Internal Revolution."[36]

Madison, from whose tenth Federalist Paper Beard claimed to derive his economic interpretation of history, put far more stress on slavery than Beard himself did. He told the Constitutional Convention that "the States were divided into different interests not by their difference of size, but by other circumstances; the most material of which resulted partly from climate, but principally from the effects of their having or not having slaves."[37] Madison insisted that "the institution of slavery & its consequences formed the line of discrimination" between the contending states.[38]

But this was not the only conflict stressed by Madison. Rather than refuting a thesis of struggle between those with wealth and those without, what Madison did was to point out an additional division among men of wealth, based on slavery.

This becomes clear if one considers the earlier versions of Federalist Paper No. 10 which Madison wrote for the more intimate audience of his colleagues at the Convention. Douglass Adair has argued that Beard, in citing Federalist No. 10, simply omitted that part of Madison's essay which described noneconomic motives.[39] However, in the unpublished fragment on "Vices of the Political System of the United States" written just before the Convention, Madison himself paid relatively little attention to them:

> All civilized societies are divided into different interests and factions, as they happen to creditors or debtors—rich or poor—husbandmen, merchants or manufacturers—members of different religious sects—followers of different political leaders—inhabitants of different districts—owners of different kinds of property etc. etc.[40]

The next version of the argument, in a speech at the Convention on June 26, emphasized even more the economic basis of politics:

> In all civilized Countries the people fall into different
> classes havg. a real or supposed difference of interests.
> There will be creditors & debtors, farmers, merchts. & manu-
> facturers. There will be particularly the distinction of rich
> & poor.

Madison's concern in this speech was to urge the creation of
constitutional checks against "levelling" tendencies which
might lead to an "agrarian law."[41] Here he expressed the tension between the Convention as a whole and the small farmers unrepresented there, just as in other speeches he articulated the tension within the Convention between slave states
and free.

Beard's fundamental plea for a "removal of the Constitution from the realm of pure political ethics and its establishment in the dusty way of earthly strife and common economic
endeavor"[42] remains valid. But Beard's version of the nature
of that strife requires revision. Northern capitalist and
Southern planter joined hands in 1776 to win independence
from England; united again in 1787 to create the United
States Constitution; then drifted, almost immediately, into
sectional cold war. A showdown could be postponed, however, because each sectional society expected to augment its
power from new states to be formed in the West. What Turner's frontier thesis explains is why Beard's second American
revolution was so late in coming, and why the Jeffersonian
ideology which rationalized slavery as "agrarianism" lin-
gered so long.

NOTES

1. Robert E. Brown, *Reinterpretation of the Formation of the American Constitution* (Boston, 1963), p. 48.
2. Forrest McDonald, *E Pluribus Unum: The Formation of the American Republic 1776–1790* (Boston, 1965), pp. 1 ff. *et passim.*
3. The most notable recent effort at synthesis, *The American Revolu-
   lution Reconsidered* by Richard B. Morris (New York, 1967), does
   not altogether succeed in reconciling a concern to demonstrate
   more social conflict than conceded by Beard's critics (Ch. 2) with a
   desire to refute "the thesis that the group that started the war were
   libertarians and democrats and were supplanted by a conservative
   authoritarian party" (Ch. 4).

4. Clinton Rossiter, *1787: The Grand Convention* (New York and London, 1966), p. 14.
5. This generalization would appear to apply not only to biographers such as Broadus Mitchell, Dumas Malone, and Irving Brant, but to the editors of papers, such as Julian P. Boyd.
6. The phrase is taken from Beard's summary of the "general conclusions" of both the 1913 and the 1915 book in *Economic Origins of Jeffersonian Democracy* (New York, 1915), pp. 464–67.

The following pages focus on these general conclusions rather than on the detailed argument of each of Beard's two books.

"It is established upon a statistical basis [Beard concluded] that the Constitution of the United States was the product of a conflict between capitalistic and agrarian interests. The support for the adoption of the Constitution came principally from the cities and regions where the commercial, financial, manufacturing, and speculative interests were concentrated, and the bulk of the opposition came from the small farming and debtor classes, particularly those back from the seaboard. . . ."

The general conclusions then asserted that the same conflict was the basis of party strife in the 1790s:

"The men who framed the Constitution and were instrumental in securing its ratification constituted the dominant group in the new government formed under it, and their material measures were all directed to the benefit of the capitalistic interests—*i.e.*, were conciously designed to augment the fluid capital in the hands of security holders and bank stock owners and thus to increase manufacturing, commerce, building, and land values, the last incidentally, except for speculative purposes in the West. The bulk of the party which supported these measures was drawn from the former advocates of the Constitution.

The spokesmen of the Federalist and Republican parties, Hamilton and Jefferson, were respectively the spokesmen of capitalistic and agrarian interests. . . ."

The general conclusions characterized Jeffersonian Democracy as "the possession of the federal government by the agrarian masses led by an aristocracy of slave-owning planters." They did not resolve Beard's lack of clarity as to whether the slave-owning planters had supported the Constitution or, together with the "backwoods agrarians," had opposed it.

7. Charles Beard, *An Economic Interpretation of the Constitution of the United States* (New York, 1935), p. viii.
8. Forrest McDonald, *We the People: The Economic Origins of the Constitution* (Chicago, 1958), p. vii.

9. Quoted by S. Hugh Brockunier, forward to Richard J. Purcell, *Connecticut in Transition: 1775–1818,* 2nd. ed. (Middletown, Conn., 1963), p. x.

10. Cecilia Kenyon, "Where Paine Went Wrong," *American Political Science Review,* XLV (1951), 1094, 1095, 1098; and "Men of Little Faith: The Anti-Federalists On The Nature Of Representative Government," *William and Mary Quarterly,* 3rd Ser., XII (1955), pp. 3–43.

11. McDonald, *E Pluribus Unum,* pp. 235–36.

12. Frederick Jackson Turner, introduction to Orin G. Libby, *The Geographical Distribution of the Vote of the Thirteen States on the Federal Constitution. 1787–1788* (Madison, Wis., 1894), pp. vi-vii.

13. Turner, "Social Forces in American History," *The Frontier in American History* (New York, 1920), p. 325; Beard, *Economic Interpretation,* p. 258.

14. Thus Daniel Boorstin terms the Civil War one of the "most inexplicable . . . events of the modern era" (*The Genius of American Politics* [Chicago, 1953], p. 99), and Louis Hartz, while insisting that the Civil War was "unique to America," concedes that it disrupted the liberal consensus which he considers the central theme of American history (*The Liberal Tradition in America: An Interpretation of American Political Thought Since the Revolution* [New York, 1955], pp. 18–19, 43, 148, 172). Recent specialized studies accept Beard's theory of the Civil War in fundamentals while criticizing it in detail. For example, Robert F. Sharkey criticizes the Beards for picturing Northern capitalism as a "conceptual monolith" but adds, "with the overall dimensions of this interpretation I have no quarrel" (*Money, Class and Party: An Economic Study of Civil War and Reconstruction* [Baltimore, 1959], pp. 290–92, 299–306). Again, W. R. Brock rejects the contention that Northern businessmen had a unified economic program which they wished to promote but does not reject economic interpretation or the "overall" conception of the Civil War as a revolution (*An American Crisis: Congress and Reconstruction 1865–1867* [London, 1963], esp. pp. 239–40).

15. Barrington Moore, Jr., *Social Origins of Dictatorship and Democracy: Lord And Peasant in the Making of the Modern World* (Boston, 1966), Ch. 3, esp. pp. 112, 153.

16. Jackson Maine, *The Antifederalists: Critics of the Constitution 1781–1788* (Chapel Hill, N.C., 1961), pp. 271, 280.

17. See Main's comment at *ibid.,* p. 266: "the most serious of all objections to an interpretation based exclusively on an alignment along class lines is the complete absence of a division of opinion in the towns." Also Staughton Lynd and Alfred Young, "After Carl Becker: The Mechanics And New York City Politics, 1774–1801," *Labor History,* V (1964). 215–76.

18. Beard, *Economic Interpretation,* pp. 30, 285.

19. Robert E. Brown, *Charles Beard and the Constitution: A Critical Analysis of "An Economic Interpretation of the Constitution of the United States* (Princeton, 1956), p. 131.

20. McDonald, *E Pluribus Unum,* pp. 34, 247.

21. Lee Benson, in *Turner and Beard: American Historical Writing Reconsidered* (Chicago, 1960), pp. 160–74, suggests that Beard and his principal critics all make the mistake of concentrating their attention on delegates to the Constitutional Convention and to the state ratifying conventions, as if those representatives were the electorate in microcosm. In reality, Benson insists, if Antifederalist delegates were almost as wealthy as their Federalist counterparts it would not disprove Libby's demonstration that a clear economic pattern appears in their constituencies. However, Beard is as much in error in overlooking the many poor men (commercial farmers and artisans) who *voted* for the Constitution, as he is in overlooking the rich "farmers" who helped to *draft* it.

22. Manning Dauer, *The Adams Federalists* (Baltimore, 1953), *passim.*

23. The evidence for the argument which follows is presented in more detail in my "Beard, Jefferson, and the Tree of Liberty," *Class Conflict, Slavery, and the United States Constitution,* essay 10.

24. *Annals of Congress* (Washington, 1834), II, 2012.

25. *Ibid.,* pp. 1970, 1979, 1981–82, 1989.

26. *Ibid.,* I, 1242.

27. *The Journal of William Maclay, United States Senator from Pennsylvania, 1789–1791* (New York, 1927), p. 216.

28. *Ibid.,* p. 217.

29. *Annals of Congress,* II, 1503–14.

30. The South's hope in 1787–1788 that it was "growing more rapidly than the North" and Jefferson's hope in 1792 "that census returns would . . . strengthen the South," are described in John Alden, *The First South* (Baton Rouge, La., 1961), pp. 75, 131.

31. *Debates and Proceedings . . . Second Congress* (Washington, 1855), I, 244, 269, 272, 546, and (final vote in the House) 548.

32. Joseph Charles, *The Origins of the American Party System* (Williamsburg, Va., 1956), p. 23.

33. John C. Miller, *The Federalist Era 1789–1801* (New York, 1960), pp. 100–101.

34. E. James Ferguson sharply rejects Beard's distinction between "personalty" and "realty" while upholding the general validity of economic interpretation of formation of the Constitution. In an exchange with Stuart Bruchey, Ferguson asserts that Beard's work "incorporates the idea that there were differences in attitude and interests between commerce and agriculture, between big property and small property, and among social classes, which led to political divisions, and that the classes of the nation possessing higher status and property were the driving force behind the movement for the Constitution. My initial reply to Mr. Bruchey would be that these

concepts are not Beard's alone; that his work is not the sole test of their validity; that they infuse the sources for the period and constitute the operative hypotheses of a good many historical studies of it old and new; and that subscribing to them does not necessarily make one a Beardian, unless indeed the name is given to anyone who deals with social and economic divisions as major causal factors." ("The Forces Behind the Constitution," *William and Mary Quarterly,* 3rd Ser., XIX [1962], 434).

35. "Out of twenty whites only one or two remained permanently poor" (Jackson Main, *The Social Structure of Revolutionary America* [Princeton, 1965], p. 271).

36. John Alden, *The South in the Revolution 1763–1789* (Baton Rouge, La., 1957), p. 348.

37. *The Records of the Federal Convention of 1789,* ed. Max Farrand, rev. ed. (New Haven, Conn., 1937), I, 486.

38. *Ibid.,* II, 10

39. Douglass Adair, "The Tenth Federalist Revisited," *William and Mary Quarterly,* 3rd Ser., VIII (1951), 60, and note.

40. *The Writings of James Madison,* ed. Gaillard Hunt (New York, 1901), II, 366–67.

41. *Records of Federal Convention,* I, 422–23 (Madison's notes), 431 (Yates's notes).

42. Beard, *Economic Origins,* p. 3.

THE

JACKSONIANS: PARADOX

LOST?

∽ Michael A. Lebowitz

> O gigantic paradox, too utterly monstrous for
> solution!
>
> —E. A. Poe, "William Wilson"

WHILE CONFLICTING EVIDENCE and interpretations may produce truth, they may also generate anxiety. And those who survey the Jacksonians will find in the gaggle of contradictory interpretations, in the parade of urban proletariat, rising middle classes, agrarian goodfolk, classical economists, and others, ample reason for anxiety. It is possible, of course, to react to this dilemma by suppressing contradictory evidence or, alternatively, by solomonly declaring all interpretations correct *in part* and then proceeding about one's own business. Yet the most satisfactory method of reducing anxiety is by reconciling the discordant themes, and this impulse may account for the attractiveness of the device of paradox as applied to the Jacksonians. In the limbo of paradox, all is possible. Notwithstanding its therapeutic value, however, the employment of a paradox interpretation may be no more than a mechanism by which the confusion of present historians is projected back to the actors of the period. It all bears looking into.

Although the contrary position often is argued implicitly,

an interpretation of the Jacksonian movement should begin at the beginning. Here we have Jackson, the hero of New Orleans, a man who projects himself back into the public eye with his resolute actions in the Seminole Campaign and who receives from congressional criticism and ultimate acquittal an extension of public attention. The "Old Hero," man of action and defender of America against its enemies, triumphantly tours the Eastern cities in 1819 as the country enters a new crisis. The country next discovers Jackson, the proposed presidential candidate, as a local conservative Tennessee political faction advances his name in order to regain advantages on a state level.[1] Support spreads rapidly—despite the limited objectives of his local backers. Jacksonian sentiment emerges in Alabama, Mississippi, North Carolina, and in Northern cities.

In the locus of that initial support is its essence. A Calhoun lieutenant attributes Jackson's popularity early in 1823 in Pennsylvania to "the grog shop politicians of villages and the rabble of Philadelphia and Pittsburgh."[2] At a Cincinnati Clinton meeting, an attempt is made to reverse the organizers' proposal and to support Jackson for President and Clinton for Vice-President. William Green, who jumped into the Clay camp after the derailment of Clinton's candidacy, describes that meeting (a meeting presumably swelled because of unemployment resulting from a fire at the large steam mill):

> A powerful excitement in favour of Jackson among some men and more boys, seemed to threaten a dissolution of the meeting. . . . the noise on the occasion referred was characteristic of the cause it was attempted to promote. The cries of "The Hero of New Orleans," "Hurra for the 8th of January," were calculated to inflame the passions of an ignorant multitude, and did so. . . . Better that N. Orleans had been lost. . . .[3]

Elsewhere, the early Jackson support is described simply as "the people." The people, the rabble, the ignorant multitude declare themselves early for the Old Hero, the man of action and defender of America against its enemies. Who could compare with him?

Yet the "people" were soon joined by politicians and political factions with ears to the ground and ends to be served. In Ohio, local political leaders and a rural political organization shifted to Jackson as the Clinton campaign dissolved. In Pennsylvania, opposing parties vied to lead the fight for Jackson, and in the process the Calhoun campaign was shelved. In Maryland and New Jersey, displaced Federalist and disappointed Calhoun politicians chose Jackson as the man to lead them to their deserved rewards. The election of 1824 gave Jackson a plurality of electoral votes; yet the forbidding John Quincy Adams was selected to be President in the House of Representatives. The Jackson movement now had at its head the man of action, the choice of the people and the victim of the corrupt bargain of base and dishonest politicians.

Once in office, the Adams administration displayed the strong nationalistic tendencies of its President and Secretary of State and generated, in the process, a congressional opposition which consisted of Jackson and Calhoun men and the Old Republican supporters of Crawford. The Calhoun men, united by ties of ambition and then by opposition to the national policies, were the first to merge with the Jackson cause; subsequently, the Crawford men led by Van Buren came over, convinced that Jackson was more likely than Adams to support a Jeffersonian program of limited central government. Jackson was not the first choice of politicians, with or without programs, but he was available.

Now the Jackson coalition prepared for the next election. Newspapers were established around the country to spread the party line. Correspondence and vigilance committees emerged to guide and coordinate local activities. Legislative bills were tailored to increase support from doubtful regions. And the people were provided with songs, slogans, and talismans to reinforce their faith. Jackson was the candidate of the people, and the people were urged to support him against their enemies. It was a successful campaign, with Jackson receiving an overwhelming majority of electoral votes. The Jackson machine had elected a president, and the people gloried in their triumph.[4]

The Hero in office, believing himself to be the champion

of the people, did not disappoint his most enthusiastic followers. He defeated in battle nationalizing tendencies in his Maysville Road Veto, defended the integrity of the nation in the nullification controversy, and entered into conflict with the greatest of all monsters and enemies of the Republic, the Second Bank of the United States. In return, the people re-elected Jackson and then gave support to his chosen successor. Van Buren, in his turn, punctured the little monsters, the state banks, which had puffed themselves up and feasted at the leavings of their old master.

Not all of Jackson's original backers, however, were pleased. There were defections. Advocates of national public works and protective tariffs, upholders of Southern states' rights, supporters of the national bank and then of the state banks in turn left the Democratic party. Men of wealth, alarmed at what they considered a spirit of anarchy, shifted into the opposition—though they left behind some who were not prepared to move.[5] The Whig party, a party composed of old opponents of the Jackson men plus recent defectors, a party blatantly united only in its opposition to the Democratic party, took the field against a party which itself had been united largely only in its opposition to the Adams administration. In 1840 the Whigs, with a Western military hero, a well-organized campaign of ballyhoo, and a depression on their side, were given their turn—by the people.

From scattered support to semiorganized movement to machine to victory, one dominant theme comes through, and that is coalition—coalition for power, coalition for political and social ends, coalition against common enemies. In particular, the extent to which the "presidential issue" was used, on a state and national level, by ambitious politicians justifies the description of the Jackson machine as a "loose, opportunistic, all-inclusive and eclectic" coalition.[6] It similarly devaluates those analyses of the Jacksonians which concentrate on the cross-sectional characteristics of the politicians. For when the Jacksonian movement is considered as an unfolding process, it becomes clear that the movement must be traced to the earlier periods, to the original support for Jackson which surprised and discomforted the state politicians. The shock of Jackson's own Tennessee backers, the dismay of Calhoun and Crawford men—all this was the product of a movement which caught fire without the manipulations of established politicians. Once the support for the Old Hero had been demonstrated, only the blind, the entrenched, or the unambitious among politicians could ignore it. The politicians followed the "people"; unfortunately, many historians have followed the politicians.

But, then, who were the "people"? In the 1828 election when Jackson received 178 electoral votes to 83 for Adams, he carried only 56 percent of the popular vote. (Nor did the proportion change significantly in subsequent elections.) And since it is doubtful that the "enemies of the people" constituted almost half of the population, it is apparent that many of "the humble members of society—the farmers, mechanics, and laborers" did not vote for Jackson. Nevertheless, neither the closeness of votes nor the employment of leaders drawn from a common stock implies the identity of the two parties. For the Jacksonians deployed a unique rhetoric, a rhetoric chosen for a purpose—and people believed it.

In states where the Jacksonians campaigned actively and called upon the people "to come forth in their own strength and majesty," they came. Voting participation rates climbed —with special gains in those Middle and Western states which had been the main target of the Jackson campaign.[7] This was a rhetoric consistent both with the early appeal of Jackson and with Old Republican dogma: a call against aristocracy, privilege, and government interference with a providential order; a call for the simple, the natural, the just. These were clever appeals, but that in no way detracts from the fact that they struck a responsive chord. It was easy enough to call the people out against their enemies, but what determined their enemies? Clearly, both the appeals and the nature of those to whom the appeals were directed must be central in an examination of the Jacksonians.

In *Andrew Jackson: Symbol for an Age,* John W. Ward explored the symbolic use of Jackson by contemporaries as a way of revealing the values of the period.[8] It was an age, he found, which emphasized the role of nature, which rested its faith in a providential order, which stressed the role of man's will. It was an age which believed that the man who strove, who exerted his will to conquer nature, would receive his just rewards. An age in which Nature and Providence united to provide the man of will with the opportunity to create his own destiny, it was an age in which every success was further proof of the beneficence of the order. And for a time which stressed such values, Andrew Jackson, orphan and self-made man, man of action and man of iron will, was a fitting vessel.

Many of the same themes appear in Marvin Meyers' examination of Jacksonian values.[9] Here again the emphasis is upon steady work, upon an industry honest and simple. It is the view of an order in which industry, economy, and useful toil are certain to be rewarded in an ideal world; a world in which the industrious stand in opposition to the idle and speculative. In such a scheme, where the artificial and unnatural were equated with evil, the place of government was a logical one: the ideal government was one which removed itself from interference with the natural order. In a world of bliss, there was no place for the legislation of bliss.[10]

In this context, the main Jacksonian policies—opposition to special corporate charters, hostility toward paper money, suspicion of public enterprise and public debt—fall into place; all involve resistance to an interference with a natural and just order. Meyers interprets these policies and the accompanying appeals as reflecting the desire of Jacksonians to maintain or restore the virtues of an earlier and simpler age. They were, he argues, appeals to a generation which sought a return to an old agrarian republic, to a paradise lost.

Yet Meyers is obsessed by facts. He knows that this was a period of rapid economic change, and he is familiar with Hofstadter's treatment of the age as one of emerging liberal capitalism and of acquisitiveness.[11] Thus Meyers takes his Old Republican man, blends him with the New Acquisitive man, and discovers the schizophrenic Jacksonian, the man who looks backward while plunging forward. And with this dualistic man, Meyers explains the Jacksonian paradox, that a movement which idealized the past cleared the way for the future. He explains the paradox by personifying it.

It is difficult to avoid the suspicion that paradox, irony, and hybrid interpretations of the Jacksonians are the result of the tendency to think in terms of an archetypical Jacksonian. If we recall the coalitional aspects of the Jackson movement, if we move away from a composite Jacksonian, can we understand better to whom this imagery and rhetoric appealed?[12]

Clearly, the men whose values and status should be examined first (both in order and in importance) were the farmers. They were, after all, a significant majority of the population. However, despite their numbers, despite the description of Jacksonian rhetoric as agrarian rhetoric, despite speculations that the Jacksonians wished to return to an earlier agrarian republic, farmers get little attention from historians of the Jacksonians. The lack of emphasis is striking. There are analyses of party workers, bankers, manufacturers, trade union activists—of any individuals who succeeded in detaching themselves from the mass. Yet the farmers, unorganized, anonymous, and collectively most important, are largely ignored.

When the farmer's political behavior is considered, it becomes readily apparent that although much Jacksonian rhetoric was directed toward the farmer, the most noble of all men, he did not direct all of his collective favor toward the Jacksonian party. Why? Was the type of appeal made by the Democrats more attractive to a particular type of farmer? Can one, in fact, talk accurately about *the* farmer or were differences among farmers great enough to make this a misleading category? Were the differences within the category of farmers greater than differences between farmers and other categories?

The picture of the farmer during this period is generally that of a new settler taking land, either clearing it himself or purchasing it from a person who cleared it. With the aid of the major transportation changes of the period, he finds he is able to produce for distant markets. His land value rises; he invests in more land or improves his land. Often he becomes more interested in the speculative value of his land than in production. He is the rising entrepreneur in farming; he is the expectant agricultural capitalist. For him, transportation changes, banks, and other advances are tools which provide the opportunity for higher returns.

Yet this is not the only farmer of the period. The very changes benefitting the first farmer tend to add to another farmer's problems. While improved river transport and new canals aided both the Western farmer and the consumers, "western wheat demoralized farmers in the older communities, who were already struggling with declining fertility, low yields, parasitic infestations, increasing costs, and declining prices."[13] These latter farmers, the victims of regional specialization effects of transport changes, might tend to center in the older regions of the Middle States, in New England, in parts of the South. Some might respond simply by moving, others by shifting into different agricultural products in which they had a comparative advantage, and others by working their land even harder. There were two farmers in this period, and one had good reason to be discontent.

But how could nature's nobleman, the hardy farmer, the member of the steady honest class, reconcile the disappointment of his goals with his vision of a world in which men received just returns for honest labor? His vision provided him with an answer: one could expect to receive one's reward only if self-seeking men had not upset the natural balance by obtaining special privileges and other obstructions to justice from government. Here, then, was a farmer to whom the Democratic party could appeal—an embattled farmer, a disappointed farmer, a declining farmer.[14]

Of course, if the embattled and declining farmers were the Democratic farmers, the Jacksonian paradox as applied to farmers would be somewhat weakened. One would not be able to argue that these farmers were looking back to a simple old republic while advancing in a new order. Those Democratic farmers who feared the new order would be those who were *injured* by it, those for whom a solid old world was crumbling. In their efforts to find reasons, rather than questioning a providential design or focusing upon the real causes, they tended to emphasize the most obvious artificial aspects of the new order: banks, bank paper, and the paper aristocracy. It was banking which altered the normal relationship between prices and costs; it was banking, both in expansion and contraction, which "disturbed the equality of society," which was "a two-edged sword in the hands of the enemy."[15] And theirs could not be a negative concept of government, for government action was necessary to undo the evil which had been done. The "independent silence of the farmer, who ask[ed] nothing from his government but equal laws, and nothing of heaven, but rain and sunshine" was replaced by the demand, "Get out of my sunlight."[16]

By combining, then, our knowledge of the nature of Jacksonian appeals and of the changes in the fortunes of farmers in the period, it is possible to suggest the hypothesis that farmers in relatively declining regions were more likely to vote for the Democrats than those in relatively rising regions. It should be emphasized that we are not arguing that all Western farmers were rising farmers or that rising farmers had no reason to vote Democratic. Rather our suggestion is twofold: that declining farmers were more likely to vote Democratic than were rising farmers in any region (because of the nature of Jacksonian appeals), and that the proportion of declining farmers was likely to be higher in the older or bypassed areas than in the emerging ones.[17]

One of the most significant attempts to examine a hypothesis of this nature and to employ the type of information required for a test occurs in Lee Benson's *The Concept of Jacksonian Democracy*. Utilizing county and township data for New York State, Benson examines the argument that the Whigs were "the prosperous farmers living on better soils or along good transportation routes" and the Democrats, "the poor or less-well-to-do farmers."[18] He concludes, after looking at figures on voting and housing assessments, that there is no basis for this traditional claim; on the contrary, "the Democrats tended to find their strongest support in eastern New York among groups living in long-settled areas and enjoying considerable prosperity."[19]

Benson's conclusions may appear to disprove the hypothesis we have suggested above; but if so, it is only because he is not entirely precise in the interpretation of his observations. Whereas the hypothesis relating declining farmers to the Democrats is a dynamic statement which requires information on *changes* in economic status, Benson examines a static proposition relating wealth to voting affinity. In his hypothesis and in the variables considered, there is no place for change or for the responses to change. And, as Jacksonian appeals reveal, it was change which was central to the period.

A conclusion that the Democrats received their strongest support from farmers in the wealthiest regions is not necessarily inconsistent with the suggestion that the Democrats were supported by farmers in declining regions. A relatively wealthy Eastern farmer *could* be the farmer whose economic position was declining. Yet would it be his wealth or his declining status which attracted him to the Democratic position? In several places, Benson indicates that the prosperity of Eastern farmers was due not to their enterprise but primarily to their "headstart." "Yorker families," he notes, "had decades, often centuries to pick out the best sites, accumulate wealth (and status) and pass it on to their descendants."[20] Of course, the best sites of decades and centuries ago were obviously not the best sites of this period—and accumulated wealth and status were not necessarily *accumulating* wealth and status. In this light, what did it mean to be "enjoying considerable prosperity"?

Actually, it is even questionable whether Benson correctly identifies "prosperous" economic units. His variable for wealth, the average value of dwelling unit per family, tells us more about previous investment in housing than it does about prosperous *farming* units, and it is supported only by "impressionistic" evidence about the relative position of towns within counties.[21] The image of grand old houses constructed in the bloom of eastern New York and now presiding over declining and marginal farmland is a powerful one.

The significant sectional differences and the identification of older ("wealthier") regions with rural Democratic strength in New York revealed in Benson's study are entirely consistent with the argument relating declining farmers to the Jacksonian persuasion. And as Benson notes in his own discussion, New York may not be an exceptional case. (The correspondence between areas of *long-time* Democratic support and areas of low land value has often been noted.) The hypothesis is not challenged; neither, though, has it been properly tested.[22]

Were there any other groups (or segments of groups) besides farmers which had reason to resent the economic changes of the Jacksonian period? Among the other "humble members of society," mechanics and laborers, employment and price fluctuations or economic dislocation could easily be a source of discontent. The same transportation improvements, for example, which aided Western farmers and demoralized Eastern farmers were logically such as to disrupt the activities of those Western mechanics who had previously functioned behind the natural tariff wall of high transportation costs; and if these mechanics searched, they could certainly find a scapegoat in the presence of a bank which facilitated the import of Eastern merchandise.[23] Yet there were more far-reaching changes than these, which increased the insecurity of many members of the remaining two humble classes.

The Jacksonian period was one in which master mechanics found themselves threatened by the emergence of the merchant-capitalists. "With easy access to credit," this new group "began to invade the mechanical trades and to establish small-scale factories."[24] For masters who found themselves undersold by quantity production, an obvious response was an attack on what they considered the source of their problem: the banks, which made possible the engrossing activities of their favored competitors and which thus increased the difficulties of those who earned their living by labor. Another response for a master, though, was the attempt to emulate the merchant-capitalist by shifting to a greater use of apprentices as a source of cheap labor in place of more costly journeymen. This reaction, shifting the pressure to the journeymen, produced trade union activity on the part of the journeymen with the intent of preventing the downgrading of craft skills and status. Innovations in the organization of industry during this period clearly were the cause of discontent for some mechanics.

Overriding all concerns in the 1830s, though, for the journeyman and the master (and other small businessmen) was the enormous price increase from 1834 to 1837. For the small businessman, the contractor, the grocer, price changes upset the normal relations between costs and prices; for the wage earner, both journeyman mechanic and unskilled laborer, gains in money wages lagged significantly behind price rises.

"Wage-workers, already concerned over their loss in status, became desperately alarmed over money-earnings, which exchanged for less and less food and shelter."[25]

For those injured by declining real wages, there were two resorts: an attempt to increase money wages at least proportionately to price rises, and/or an attack on the source of inflationary tendencies. Generally, that source was identified as the banking system—and in particular, the small notes generated by the banks. In the Loco Foco claim "as the currency expands, the loaf contracts" was typified the belief that bank notes operated as a tax upon the laboring people.[26] Therefore, the participation of wage earners in trade union activity to raise money wages and in political coalition to attack the banking system were in no way inconsistent.[27]

Both in trade union activity and in the struggle against the inflationary tendencies of the banking system, there was a common assumption that wage earners suffered from a weak position relative to the power of other groups within the society. And central to this weakness was their inability to combine—both for legal reasons and also because of the nature of their productive activity. In relationship to trade union activity, this issue was often raised; unions were defended as a countervailing force against the combinations of others. Thus Frederick Robinson argued: "the capitalists, monopolists, judges, lawyers, doctors and priests . . . know that the secret of their own power and wealth consists in the strictest concert of action. . . . Unions among themselves have always enabled the few to rule and ride the people."[28] Or, as John Greenleaf Whittier complained:

> The merchants may agree upon their prices; the lawyers upon their fees; the physicians upon their charges; the manufacturers upon the wages given to their operatives; but the *laborer* shall not consult his interest and fix the price of his toil and skill. If this be the *law,* it is unjust, oppressive and wicked.[29]

Although it was less obvious, the same weakness characterized the position of wage earners in respect to rising prices. "The laboring part of the community (farmers and laborers) are the last in society who can bring up their services to the standard of a depreciated currency," noted William Carroll in 1823.[30] "Wages are the first to be affected by a depreciated medium, and the last to adapt themselves to it. The poor are therefore the first victims of overissues," argued Theodore Sedgewick, Jr., in 1835.[31] The vulnerability of wage earners, however, was not the result of chance factors; it too had its roots in their relative weakness, in their relationship to the productive process. Rhetorically asking if wages rose proportionately to prices, the *Weekly Ohio Statesman* replied:

> *They do not,* and from the circumstances of the case, *they can not.* And the reason is obvious.—The bankers who cause the expansion, and consequent depreciation of paper, (or *increase* of prices, just as you choose—the meaning is the same) are incorporated—connected—concentrated. They act simultaneously and immediately. But mechanics and laborers are simply individuals—unincorporated—unconnected—pursuing different occupations, and frequently waging opposite pursuits.[32]

Nor was it only the bankers who were able to swim with the tide of bank money. "There is a privity of interest and feeling between these banks and the merchants and speculators dependent upon them. The latter *anticipate* the expansion. They expand with it. They govern their dealings by it. But the mechanic and the laborer are only aware of it when everything they consume is cracked up 100 or 200 per cent. upon their hands." A belief in their relative weakness (attributed often to unequal legislation), an acceptance of the quantity theory of money, and the experience of falling real wages: all of this made logical an attack by wage earners upon the banks, which gave artificial and fictitious value to all things, which disturbed the equality of society, which were a two-edged sword in the hands of the enemies of the people.[33]

Rather than simply the cupidity of expectant capitalists, among urban mechanics and laborers there were attitudes and reactions identifiable as those of people *injured* by change—as opposed to those of people impatient with it. The expectant capitalist argument is an attractive one; but before concluding that it was a dominant attitude among wage earners, it is necessary to show that wage earners acted and supported positions during this period which were not

in their interest *as wage earners* to take. While on many issues the interests of wage earners were not inconsistent with
those of small businessmen, for some wage earners this coin-
cidence was probably no more than that. Unskilled laborers,
for example, were the least well off of all workingmen, the
most subject to seasonal and cyclical unemployment and the
most helpless in dealing with uncurrent paper money; they
were probably also the least likely to allow illusions of expectant capitalism to dominate their concern over their immediate position.[34]

If the hypothesis relating the relatively declining farmers
to the Democrats has an urban counterpart, it is that the laborers and mechanics least subject to illusions of expectant
capitalism, most helpless in the face of movements of an
economy which they did not understand, were more likely to
vote Democratic. (Once again, this is a statement of a general
tendency—not all rising mechanics would be Whigs.) In
this light, Benson's identification of New York lumbering
towns as generally Democratic is worthy of note. Unable to
find any "economic" reason for this pattern, Benson suggests
that lumbering may have generated antipuritanical behavior
and that antipuritans may have tended to vote Democratic.[35]
However, before concluding that frequenters of grog shops
were more likely to vote Democratic (and confusing a symp-
tom with a cause), it may be suggested that Jacksonian positions on paper money and privilege were particularly attractive to low-skill and unskilled workers with limited horizons.
And this same attraction may go a long way towards explaining the initial adherence of unskilled immigrant Irish Catho-
lics to the Democratic party.[36]

The opposition of workingmen's parties to Democratic
candidates has often been cited as an indication of a gap between the Jacksonians and labor.[37] Yet the dominant tone
of that opposition (where it in fact occurred) was that of the
vehemence of reformers to betrayers of the faith. Workies
and Loco Focos, "methodists of democracy," sought to bring
the Democrats back from where they had been led astray by
entrepreneurial elements in the party; and when the Democrats responded by absorbing parts of the workingmen's program, support for the latter groups dwindled. In this sense,

the workingmen's parties may be viewed as a wing of a general movement which centered in the Democratic party. As Pessen concluded, the existence of workingmen's parties reveals that "an important minority in the Jacksonian Era were disenchanted with their society and its institutions."[38] And much of this disenchantment was the disenchantment of the injured and declining rather than that of the rising.

Thus, consideration of economic changes during the Jacksonian era indicates that not all groups within the society had reason to praise the changes which were occurring. Some in this period found their positions and status under attack or deteriorating; and they were likely to respond to Jacksonian (or more extreme) attacks on government—granted privileges, public spending, and paper money. In this sense, it may be argued that the Jacksonians represented, partly, declining groups. An association of the Jacksonian persuasion with declining groups is a natural one; Meyers himself notes that the political analysis of Jacksonian Democracy would be simpler and clearer "if the Jacksonians could in fact be taken for innocent—still better, struggling—victims of external social changes."[39] Impressed, though, by the economic changes of the period and the apparent role of Jacksonians in creating them, Meyers rejects this possibility and creates in its stead the paradoxical Jacksonian, the man who backed into the future. The Jacksonians need not be viewed as only the losers of the period; it is sufficient to suggest that a significant portion of them, however, were.

Where does this leave the expectant capitalists, the rising merchants and manufacturers, the frontier achievers who have generally been identified with the Jackson party? And what of programs in Jacksonian and workingmen's platforms which were designed to appeal to men on the make, men who supported reforms in order to rise? Obviously, there were many of these men among the Jacksonians—more than can be accounted for by the availability of patronage and favors from a successful party. The Jacksonians were a coalition of rising and declining men; but on what basis were they able to unite?

For people unsatisfied with the status quo, the belief in a beneficent natural order provided an obvious scapegoat to explain the failure of goals—man-made disasters. The un-happy rising master mechanic and the declining farmer could easily agree that it was the existence of artificial privileges which was the bane of all. Thus, the attack on artificial inter-ferences with the natural order was a logical recourse for those who failed to receive their just rewards (as defined by themselves). This was clearly the argument of men on the rise, who found themselves confronted by special privileges; yet it was similarly the cry of injured men. Whereas histo-rians have heard in the Jacksonian appeals the voice of the rising middle classes, they have largely turned a deaf ear to the supporting chorus from men who were the victims of eco-nomic change.[40]

As the discussion has developed, the issue which has come increasingly to the fore is that of banking. And this is as it should be. The battle over privilege in the Jacksonian period was primarily one over the privilege of banking. Banking dominated both national and state politics in all regions, and it is not unimportant that both parties attempted to pin the "bank party" label on the other. For banks were the mon-sters, the unnatural things, and those associated with the banks were the enemies of the people. Thus, it is both neces-sary and appropriate that the peculiar Jacksonian coalition be examined in relation to banking.

In political and economic life, banking occupied a posi-tion more central than it was subsequently to hold. Banks had two essential functions: as providers of currency at a time when the demand for money for transaction purposes was rapidly increasing, and as providers of credit facilities at a time when the opportunities for investment were outrun-ning the resources of private accumulation.[41] Individuals, ac-cordingly, confronted banks in two roles: as credit seekers and as currency takers. Often one role was dominant.

On the credit side, access to banking facilities meant an ability to command resources. Yet since only banks chartered by governments were able to function freely under normal circumstances (and charters were limited), the holders of ex-isting bank charters were in a position to dominate and to exclude. The merchant or manufacturer from a distant (de-prived) town or region suffered from discrimination when he sought accommodation from a bank; the small, unestablished merchant or mechanic found the limited resources of existing banks in his own town channeled to his more respectable competitors; and boosters and entrepreneurs in new industries saw older, more traditional callings favored by banks dominated by representatives of the latter. Limitation of bank charters meant that established groups, established industries, established regions were in a position to gain and maintain undue influence and power.

For the excluded credit seekers, the further extension of banks, in both newer regions and older regions, was a first demand. Where efforts to achieve this were unsuccessful, however, the solution was either a removal of *all* privileges or a removal of all controls over the extension of these privileges. Eliminate artificial privileges which produce injustice and unnatural power or extend these privileges sufficiently to remove any suggestion of power and monopoly: this was the program of rising men, of rising sections, of rising industries.[42] The dominant tone was that of men who expected to rise once unnatural and discriminatory constructs were removed. And there appears to be no reason to associate such men more with the Democrats than with the Whigs. While Democrats (particularly in older regions) often fell into this category, Whig supporters, especially of the Anti-Masonic variety, were as likely to attack monopoly and privilege from this perspective.

For those individuals whose primary relationship to banks was that of currency takers, banking was also the central issue of the period. Both because of the bank notes which circulated below face value and because of rising prices (which contemporaries attributed to bank-note issues), the power of banking was judged by such men as the power to tax. It was a power to tax which was condemned by men who received uncurrent money or who found their returns rising less rapidly than their costs, by men who were struggling or declining.[43] And such men were hard-money Democrats.

Clearly, an entrepreneurial demand for more banks or for the removal of legislative control over banks and a currency taker's demand either for *no* banks or for the removal of bank control over the currency were inconsistent—once the issues were drawn distinctly. *As long, however, as the conflict was one between defenders of existing banks and those disturbed by the status quo, rising and declining groups could unite under the same banner.* All could agree: the banks were a source of power for a selected few, were the product of discriminatory legislation which upset the natural balance, and were the enemy of the people. What was uncertain, though, was whether banks per se were all these things.[44]

One way of examining the differences between those Democrats who represented declining elements and those who fit the stereotype of rising men may be to investigate the distinction between hard-money Democrats and those more "moderate" on the bank issue. It should be possible to study state legislative debates on the question and to explore the economic characteristics of the sections represented on each side of the debate. From legislative votes, there is some indication that on this issue the difference between the two types of Democrats was greater than that between "moderate" Democrats and Whigs.[45] If subsequent study does reveal such a pattern, then one suggested conclusion is that the rising man, the man on the make, the expectant capitalist was in no way uniquely related to the Jacksonians; rather, the declining or embattled man who struggled against change would appear the more unique Jacksonian.[46] And this conclusion would conform not only to the image appropriate to the Jacksonian persuasion, but also to the identities discovered by those historians who have studied the rising men in each party.

However, if the Jacksonians included both rising men and declining men, with the declining men representing the unique element in the party, then why have the Jacksonians been identified as rising men? In part, it may be due to the tendencies to study dominant and emerging individuals or to ignore declining elements in the period.[47] Yet a more deceptive tendency may be operative. Since there have been no systematic studies of the characteristics of the Jacksonians, one is inclined to conclude that the identification of the Jacksonians as rising men has been made because the period of Jacksonian national political dominance coincided with a period of rapid economic growth—and that, implicitly, historians have assumed that the policies pursued by the Jacksonians produced (and were intended to produce) the economic changes of the period.

But why assume that Jacksonian policies had anything (significant) to do with the economic growth of the Jacksonian Era? The Jacksonians had little to do with the flow of capital from Europe (which also made its way to Canada and Australia). In fact, the Whigs were often more enthusiastic advocates of public projects, which generated the securities for foreign investors. Nor does the argument emphasizing the assault on the Bank of the United States and the subsequent flood of state banks provide much support for the view that the Jacksonians changed the course of development. Even assuming that the expansion in the number of state banks had a positive effect on economic growth, it began *before* Jackson's veto. In New York State, for example, the expansion followed the passage of the Safety Fund Act in 1829, which broke a long impasse over the chartering of banks. And in Ohio, banks which had failed were re-established and banks previously authorized were placed in operation—beginning in early 1831. The expansion of state banks occurred as the demand for banks rose; and this was a function of the expansion in general economic activity. It was an expansion in the number of banks which occurred via specific state charters—not via laissez-faire policies. Here, too, contemporary records suggest that a large proportion of state bankers were Whigs.

The Jacksonian paradox, the idea that Jacksonians, though opposing economic progress, in fact cleared the path for it, has as its base the assumption that the Jacksonians actually *did* foster economic change. This is an unsubstantiated assumption, and without it the paradox disappears. Attempts to explain the paradox by arguing from the general to the particular, by creating hybrid, Janus-like, confused, paradoxical Jacksonians, are marred by the neglect of injured and declining men in this age of rising men, by the failure to recognize that not everyone benefits, in the short run, from economic advance. The suggestion here has been that it was these "victims," these farmers, laborers, and mechanics, who gave Jacksonian Democracy its dominant tone.[48] But this would imply that the "campaign claptrap" meant something, that studies of leading men in each party are misleading, and that speculations based upon a consideration of rhetoric and ideology may be a better guide than an implicit vulgar economic determinism which substitutes, for the study of economic problems, genuflection to indices of past economic growth.

NOTES

1. Charles G. Sellers, Jr., "Jackson Men with Feet of Clay," *American Historical Review* (April 1957).
2. George McDuffie to Charles Fisher, January 13, 1823, cited by Sellers, *ibid.*
3. Harry Stevens, *The Early Jackson Party in Ohio* (Durham, N.C., 1957), p. 87.
4. See Robert Remini, *The Election of Andrew Jackson* (Philadelphia, 1963) for a fine discussion of events from 1824 to 1828 and the creation of the Democratic election machine. By beginning his account in 1824, however, Remini de-emphasizes the origins and appeal of the early Jacksonian movement and thus may place undue emphasis on the activities of politicians in his chosen period.
5. In his paper "Money and Party in Jacksonian America" (presented to the American Historical Association in December 1966), Frank Gatell notes both that 84 percent of the men of wealth in New York City were Whigs in 1844 and that one third of the original wealthy Democrats bolted the party.
6. Edward Pessen, "The Working Men's Party Revisited," *Labor History* (Fall 1963), p. 220.
7. Statistics on voting participation rates, a significant additional tool for analysis, are the work of Richard P. McCormick in his "New Perspectives on Jacksonian Politics," *American Historical Review* (January 1960) and later, his *The Second American Party System: Party Formation in the Jacksonian Era* (Chapel Hill, N.C., 1966). McCormick uses decennial federal census data, and then, by "interpolation," estimates the number eligible to vote at the time of national elections. Unfortunately, he does not explain his interpolation procedure—nor does he justify adequately his restriction to federal data. Thus, his voting participation rates for Ohio in the elections of 1824 and 1828 are 35 percent and 76 percent respectively. Calculation of voting participation, however, from Ohio's official count of eligible voters (collected on a county basis and published in the official state newspaper) indicates voting participation of 40 percent and 90 percent respectively. McCormick, by his method, overstates the number of eligible voters by 15 percent in

1824 and 19 percent in 1828. (McCormick's Ohio 1840 estimate of
84.5 percent is less impressive when compared with earlier official
estimates.) Several questions are in order: To what extent did Mc-
Cormick's method for interpolation take into account business cy-
cles? Are waves of migration considered and was there a lag between
migration and eligibility? (*Any* lag!) To what extent does an 1840
voting participation rate (calculated from actual population and
coming at a point when westward migration and immigration are
lessened) contain less of a downward bias than those for preceding
elections? McCormick explains that he avoided the available state
data in order to maintain consistency. Was this data used, however, to improve his method of extrapolation and his estimates of
the number eligible to vote? These questions, which are important,
should not have to be asked. For McCormick's methodology, see
ibid., p. 379. For figures on eligible Ohio voters, see *Ohio State
Journal,* January 9, 1828; for figures on voting, see *Ohio State
Journal,* November 11, 1828.

8. John W. Ward, *Andrew Jackson: Symbol for an Age* (New York,
    1962).

9. Marvin Meyers, *The Jacksonian Persuasion: Politics and Belief*
    (New York, 1960).

10. John Kenneth Galbraith, *American Capitalism: The Concept of
    Countervailing Power* (Boston, 1956), p. 28: "In a state of bliss,
    there is no need for a Ministry of Bliss."

11. Richard Hofstadter, "Andrew Jackson and the Rise of Liberal
    Capitalism," in *The American Political Tradition* (New York,
    1961).

12. As Lynn Marshall noted in his discussion of Jackson's Bank Veto
    message, it is necessary to move beyond talk of the Jacksonian ap-
    peal and to an "investigation of the general values and aspirations
    of the people to whom it was addressed." "The Authorship of Jack-
    son's Bank Veto Message," *Mississippi Valley Historical Review*
    (1963–64), p. 466.

13. Paul W. Gates, *The Farmer's Age: Agriculture, 1815–1860* (New
    York, 1960), p. 160.

14. Charles G. Sellers' description of ferment in Tennessee as that of
    the "disquietude of an agrarian people, nurtured on Jeffersonian
    precepts" is quite consistent with the general argument here:
    "Banking and Politics in Jackson's Tennessee," *Mississippi Valley
    Historical Review* (June 1954).

15. Joseph L. Blau, ed., *Social Theories of Jacksonian Democracy:
    Representative Writings of the Period, 1825–1850* (Indianapolis,
    1954), p. 333.

16. James Kirke Paulding, *Letters from the South* (New York, 1817),
    p. 73.

    It is significant to note the similarity of Jacksonian themes to the
    arguments of Adam Smith (all quotations are from the Modern Li-
    brary edition of *Wealth of Nations*):

"Projectors disturb nature in the course of her operations in human affairs; and it requires no more than to let her alone, and give her fair play in the pursuit of her ends that she may establish her own designs." (p. xliii)

"All systems either of preference or of restraint, therefore, being thus completely taken away, the obvious and simple system of natural liberty establishes itself of its own accord." (p. 651)

"In the political body, however, the wisdom of nature has fortunately made ample provision for remedying many of the bad effects of the folly and injustice of man." (p. 638)

17. The existence of the Anti-Masonic party, initially organized on noneconomic issues, and strong in rural areas, introduces definite complications. In particular, Anti-Masonic opposition to the Democrats in New England appears contrary to the suggested hypothesis. However, in New England rank-and-file members of the Anti-Masonic parties did not generally follow their leaders into the Whig coalition—unlike the experience in the Middle States. Was differing behavior due to the characteristics of the various areas? Were declining farmers less likely to follow their Anti-Masonic leaders into the Whigs? For purposes of testing the hypothesis, areas in which Anti-Masonic support shifted to the Democrats could be classified as Democratic regions. For Anti-Masonic shifts, see McCormick, *Second American Party System,* p. 49, p. 75, p. 84, p. 121, p. 146.

18. Lee Benson, *The Concept of Jacksonian Democracy: New York as a Test Case* (New York, 1961), p. 140.

19. *Ibid.*, p. 156. Benson, as his readers know, does not himself adopt the inverse of this "traditional claim." Instead, he argues that there was "no significant relationship between *wealth* and voting in 1844" and suggests that any relationship which *appears* to exist is, in fact, the product of ethnic and behavioral variables. Yet Benson's methods in this case (as in others) are quite dubious. He is descriptive rather than analytical and uses this license to slip from examination of county voting behavior to examination of deviant town behavior within counties. In both cases, too, he fails to distinguish between ethnic and sectional conflict—a distinction crucial because of the tendency of ethnic immigrant groups to settle closely together. Despite Benson's interest in the behavior of Germans, Dutch, Old British, and the like, his failure to explain Yankee voting behavior gives the game away. Yankees, an estimated 65 percent of New York's population, tended to vote Whig in western New York and Democratic in eastern New York; in large sections of eastern New York, adjoining rural counties voted Democratic— whether they were Yankee or Dutch. So, rather than attributing Democratic votes in predominantly Dutch countries to piety, tra-

dition, and the belief in witchcraft, the regional variation in Yankee voting should act as a control against an erroneous conclusion. For a discussion of some other errors, see the writer's review essay, "The Significance of Claptrap in American History," *Studies on the Left* Vol. III, No. 2 (1963).

20. Benson, *Concept of Jacksonian Democracy*, p. 181.
21. *Ibid.*, p. 340.
22. Materials for such a test are available from state and federal records. Data which might be used are, with all their faults, real property assessments per improved acre, assessed personal property per capita, *changes* in the above variables over a given period, the proportion of gainfully employed men in agriculture, and material on product mix and yield per acre. Such information might be employed to attempt to explain voting behavior or changes in voting behavior for counties or townships on a national or state level, respectively. And ethnic variables could be subsequently introduced to see if they add significant explanatory power. A serious test of the determinants of voting behavior requires the use of multiple correlation procedures. The promised land cannot be reached by selecting high and low units in each county—despite the economy of such an approach. (See the supplementary note on method for the paperback edition of *The Concept of Jacksonian Democracy*.)
23. "In 1826 Drake and Mansfield noticed that Cincinnatians were complaining of the influx of foreign manufactured goods. This complaint was joined with a criticism of the Bank of the United States which mobilized eastern credit to encourage the sale of eastern manufactures in the West" Harold E. Davis, "The Economic Basis of Ohio Politics, 1820–1840," *Ohio State Archaeological and Historical Quarterly*, XLVII (1938), 288.
24. Walter Hugins, *Jacksonian Democracy and the Working Class* (Stanford, Cal., 1960), p. 53.
25. George Rogers Taylor, *The Transportation Revolution, 1815–1860* (New York, 1964), p. 253.
26. F. Byrdsall, *The History of the Loco-Foco or Equal Rights Party* (New York, 1842), p. 100.
27. Obviously, there was far more involved in the struggle over banks than simply the desire "to create better business conditions and remove panics." See Joseph Dorfman, "The Jackson Wage-Earner Thesis," reprinted in *The Economic Mind in American Civilization* (New York, 1966), Vol. II.
28. Blau, *Social Theories of Jacksonian Democracy*, p. 330.
29. Philip Foner, *History of the Labor Movement in the United States* (New York, 1962), I, 156.
30. Sellers, "Banking and Politics in Jackson's Tennessee," p. 73.
31. Blau, *Social Theories*, p. 230.
32. *Weekly Ohio Statesman*, September 12, 1838.
33. It is interesting to note the argument in the *Ohio Statesman* begins with the initial assumption that "the scale prices for mechanic labor

is exactly proportioned to the ordinary cost of provision, rent, fuel, *etc.*" Disaster follows a decision made "in the secret councils of the Banks."

34. Taylor, *Transportation Revolution,* pp. 288 ff.

35. Benson estimates that 75 percent of men engaged in lumbering in New York State voted Democratic. *Concept of Jacksonian Democracy,* p. 205.

36. Benson estimates that 95 percent of the Catholic Irish in New York State voted Democratic in 1844. *Ibid.,* p. 171, p. 185.

37. The workingmen's parties, of course, included among the leaders and members many who were neither mechanics nor laborers. They too were coalitions, and even the mechanics among them may not have been a representative sample of labor. Mechanics, for example, as a group were more likely to respond favorably to the tariff issue than common laborers.

38. Pessen, "Working Men's Party Revisited," p. 226.

39. Meyers, *Jacksonian Persuasion,* p. 140.

40. See, for example, Hofstadter: "This is the philosophy of a rising middle class; its aim is not to throttle but to liberate business, to open every possible pathway for the creative enterprise of the people." *American Political Tradition,* p. 62. Much of the confusion over the battle against privilege in this period has been the result of a failure to distinguish clearly between those in the coalition who opposed the existence of specific privileges and those who were opposed only to their exclusiveness.

41. The Turner-Hammond conflict over the frontier demand for banks rests on this dual function. For a discussion emphasizing the importance of the growing public demand for banknotes, see the writer's "The Role of Banks in Developing Regions . . ." presented to the Canadian Political Science Association in June, 1967.

42. Specific evidence concerning New York State supporting many of these general points appears in the writer's "In the Absence of Free Banks, What?" in the *Bulletin* of the Canadian Association for American Studies, Winter, 1967.

43. This "tax" was not one which fell only upon labor: "Banks are, in fact, legally authorized banditti, levying contributions and indirect taxation from every honest business." Byrdsall, *History of the Loco-Foco,* p. 111.

44. A definite effort has been made to avoid the particular issue of the Second Bank of the United States and to concentrate instead on the general issue of banking. On one level, the Second Bank may be viewed as a Philadelphia bank, attempting to control a hinterland that was slipping away from it, as a bank equipped with a capital and an institutional form which were inflexible and which came into conflict with a national (Western) bourgeoisie and competing (imperial) metropoli. However, most of those who cheered and voted for Jackson in the Great Struggle fought the symbol rather than the reality of the Bank.

45. In Ohio Assembly debates in 1837, for example, a series of proposals aimed at curbing banks received the consistent, support of
over 20 Democrats (out of 36) and a handful of Whigs (out of 30).
"Moderate" Democrats and Whigs combined to defeat these measures.

46. Apropos, Meyers notes at one point that there is some evidence that
"the Jacksonians were relatively weak among the most successful,
ambitious, enterprising groups." He finds the evidence inconclusive
—it is most damaging to his thesis—and returns to his split Jacksonian. It may be suggested that not only were the Jacksonians
relatively weak among such groups, but that the Jacksonians of this
ilk were, as a group, the major source of defectors to the Whigs.
Meyers, *Jacksonian Persuasion,* p. 138.

47. Although Meyers summarizes Taylor's discussion of economic
changes (in the above-cited work) and at several points notes the
effect of transportation innovation upon the "intersectional division of labor," he does not appear to recognize that the "sequence
of economic adaptations of the largest consequence" meant disappointment and decline for some. Adaptation is not the hope of
every man, and "a view of economic processes" which sees only the
good side of adaptation is perhaps not the best one with which to
understand the Jacksonians (many of whom saw only the bad side).
Ibid., pp. 116–20.

48. The generalization that the Whigs spoke to the hopes of Americans,
and the Jacksonians to their fears and resentments, would appear
not only to be true but also to be logical. Cf. Meyers, *ibid.,* p. 13,
and Glydon G. Van Deusen, "Some Aspects of Whig Thought and
Theory in the Jacksonian Period," *American Historical Review*
(Jan. 1958).

MARXIAN

INTERPRETATIONS OF THE

SLAVE SOUTH[*]

∞ Eugene D. Genovese

A science that hesitates to forget its founders
is lost.

—Alfred North Whitehead

Je ne suis pas un marxiste. —Karl Marx

AMERICAN MARXISM has had a curious history; in
a sense, it has not so much had a history as a series of aborted
births. In the political realm the experience of the last half-
century has been unpleasant: the large and promising Socialist party of the World War I era went to pieces and the
impressive stirrings of the Communist party during the 1930s
has culminated in the pathetic exhortations of a beleaguered
sect kept alive by government persecution and a franchise
from the slight remains of a world movement. The political
record, however disappointing, constitutes a history; the
same could only be said for the intellectual record if one
were determined to display Christian charity. In the early
period Marxian thought, typified perhaps in the historical
writing of Algie M. Simons, rarely rose above the level of economic determinism. In the 1930s the economic determinism
remained but was encased in the romanticization of the lower
classes. The workers, farmers, and Negroes increasingly be-

came the objects of affection and adulation. In both periods the political movement was on the upswing, and the prime function of theory, and especially of the interpretation of history, was assumed to be to provide a justification for the revolutionary cause by uncovering roots in American experience and to give the intellectuals and the masses a sense of a common and inevitably victorious destiny.

Most American Marxian historians of any reputation came out of the generation of the 1930s. The depression helped forge them as Communists, but the advance of fascism and the threat to the survival of the world's only socialist state in some ways had a more profound impact. The racist doctrines of the German fascists led Marxists, as well as others, to reaffirm their commitment to racial equality and to view with intense hostility any critical comment on Jews, Negroes, or other peoples. The possibility of a fascist victory led them to seek allies in a defensive Popular Front, which despite rhetoric and appearance generally produced ideological as well as political capitulation to New Deal liberalism. The Communist party's search for an alliance with liberals, from Roosevelt to the Kennedys, has stressed the possibilities of working with the "progressive" sections of the bourgeoisie against the "reactionary" sections. In practice this policy has meant support for those who have been willing to accede to a modus vivendi with the USSR in return for the sterilization of the revolutionary forces in the world generally and the underdeveloped countries in particular. For American Marxian historiography it has meant a lack of concern with class forces and the process of capitalist development in favor of the pseudo-radical division of historical categories into "progressive" and "reactionary," which has generally been translated into the glorification of the Jefferson-Jackson-Roosevelt liberal tradition and the denigration of the evil men of the Right. This parlor game, so reminiscent of liberals like Parrington and Josephson, spiced with leftist jargon and a few words about the masses and the revolutionary heritage, has passed for Marxism.

Popular Front Liberalism has by no means been merely a product of the political exigencies of the 1930s; it has deep roots in the history of the American working class. From the beginning the working class has held full political rights within a bourgeois-democratic republic that has been one of the modern world's great success stories. Presided over by a powerful, confident bourgeoisie, which has had to face serious internal opposition only once in its life and which crushed that opposition during the war of 1861–1865, American capitalism has generally been able to divert, placate, and buy the potentially troublesome sections of its working class. Without much possibility of building a revolutionary working-class movement in the near future, more and more Marxists have turned in despair to an illusory "people's movement" against entrenched privilege and have taken this alleged movement to be the principal manifestation of the class struggle in America. For the specific subject at hand— the Slave South—the results were predictable. The slave-holders naturally and wonderfully qualify as reactionaries and defenders of an entrenched privilege, which of course they were, and important sections of the bourgeoisie qualify as candidates for membership in a progressive coalition, which they, in the same sense, also were. All that is missing from this viewpoint is an awareness of the process of capitalist development and of the metamorphosis of the bourgeoisie —that is, all that is missing is the essence of a Marxian analysis.

For Popular Front Marxists—that is, for liberals with radical pretensions—the Slave South constitutes a nightmare. It is not so much that it conjures up the full horror of white supremacy and chattel slavery, although the emotional reaction to these has been both genuine and understandable; it is rather that the slaveholders presented the only politically powerful challenge to liberal capitalism to emanate from within the United States. It was they, especially in the brilliant polemics of George Fitzhugh but also in the writings of Calhoun, Holmes, Hughes, Hammond, Ruffin, and others, who questioned the assumptions of liberal society, denounced the hypocrisy and barbarism of the marketplace, and advanced a vision of an organic society and a collective community. That their critique was self-serving and their alternative reactionary need not detain us. As in the European tradition of feudal socialism, the self-serving and reactionary can prove illuminating and, in the most profound sense, critical. The commitment of American Marxists to Popular Front liberalism has prevented them from taking the ideology of the Slave South seriously. As a result, they have been unable to reconstruct the historical reality and have been unwilling to admit that certain elements of the slaveholders' ideology deserve the attention and respect of those who would build a socialist order. It is no accident that the one American socialist historian to glimpse these possibilities, William Appleman Williams, is more of a Christian than a Marxist.

Even the strongest proponents of Marxism must admit that Marxian historical writing in the United States has been something less than a cause for rejoicing and that it has not approached the level attained by such English Marxists as Christopher Hill, Eric J. Hobsbawm, and E. P. Thompson. Marxian writing on the Slave South and the origins of the secession crisis looks especially weak when ranked alongside work done on Brazilian slave society by such Marxists as Caio Prado Junior, Octavio Ianni, and Fernando Henrique Cardoso.[1] The record is so poor that we would be justified in ignoring it, if it had not become so curiously influential in traditional circles and if Marxism did not have so much to contribute to the interpretation of American history.

The paradoxical juxtaposition of ostensible Marxian influence and the low level of Marxian performance arises in part out of the widespread confusion of Marxism with economic determinism. American historians, especially the most harshly anti-Marxian, generally confuse the two and then, since economic determinism is easy to refute, dismiss Marxism as being of no value. This game would prove entertaining, were it not that these same historians so often retreat into banal economic explanations to suit their convenience. How often does one find discussions of the profitability of slavery embracing the assumption that one or another accounting result would explain the course of political events? Or that the idea of an irrepressible conflict between North and South has to stand on proof of an unnegotiable economic antagonism? Or that proof of natural limits to slavery expansion would constitute proof that the slave system, left to itself, would evolve into something else? These and even cruder notions run through the literature, and their equivalents infect much of American history. The fountainhead of this tendency has been the work of Charles Beard. When his line of thought has proven useful for conservative or liberal purposes, his arguments have been appropriated and his name more often than not dropped; when it has proven an obstacle, his name has been remembered and linked with Marxism in order to discredit him. Yet, a concern for "economics," and more to the point, for "classes," has been irresistible even for his most caustic critics. Marxism has both fed the stream of economic interpretation and been contaminated by it.

Of greater importance is what Marxism, shorn of its romanticism and superficial economic determinist trappings, might offer. That it has not accomplished more has been due to many things, not the least of which have been the periodic purges of Marxists from our universities and the venal treatment meted out by professional associations and learned journals. (It would be wonderful fun to list the respected and influential historians who have protected their jobs and their families by eschewing the Marxist label while writing from a Marxian viewpoint and even greater fun to recount the multitude of ways in which the profession has misunderstood what they are in fact doing and saying.) More fundamental, however, has been the misrepresentation of Marxism by our official Marxist historians—that is, by those who have written with the blessings of the more important, if also the most morally discredited, political organizations. These blessings have proven a double joy: to the writers in question, generally although by no means always men of little talent, they have provided high status in a limited but adoring circle; to the profession as a whole, ever anxious to identify Marxism with imbecility, they have provided the perfect straw men. They have converged—I almost said conspired—to present Marxism on the general level as economic determinism and on the level of specific analysis as some variation of moralistic fatalism. We may properly suspect that Herbert Aptheker's grand pronouncement would simultaneously have convulsed Marx with laughter and raised his temper to the boiling point: "There is an immutable justice in history, and the law of dialectical development works its inexorable way."[2] For the liberals statements such as this prove Marxism's uselessness; for the illiterates among the political faithful of the Left they offer consolation in a period of defeat. All they fail to do is to present Marxian thought seriously and therefore to provide the slightest genuine utility for a political movement that seeks to alter the existing order.

Perhaps the strongest indication of the power of Marxian analysis, even its more vulgar forms, has been the extent to which class analysis has intruded itself into American history despite the contempt poured out on "Marxian economic determinism." For this reason alone a careful review of Marxian interpretations of a defined portion of American history has its uses. If vulgar Marxism and simplistic economic interpretations have, as is generally conceded, somehow illuminated the subject, Marxism, purged of its adolescent cravings for neat packages and the easy way, ought to be able to do much more. The first task is to see clearly and specifically what has gone wrong.

Would it not be incongruous for Marxists to believe in original sin, we might trace our embarrassment to our fathers, for in truth they are guilty, but it is incumbent upon us to be charitable, for their guilt is less than that of their descendants. Marx and Engels restricted themselves to journalistic pieces on the secession crisis and never attempted that kind of analysis of class dynamics which we have come to call Marxian. As political journalism their writings are of a high order and ought to give their admirers no cause to blush.[3] As Professor Runkle, hardly a friendly critic, has shown, their writings display remarkable insight into a wide variety of political and military problems and still repay careful reading.[4] It is not their fault that later generations of epigoni have canonized them and insisted on the value of every word, have mistaken political commitment for historical analysis, and have done violence to Marxism by defending positions taken by Marx and Engels on matters to which they devoted little study. Marx and Engels probably had not read much more than Olmsted's travel accounts and J. E. Cairnes's *The Slave Power,* which is hardly unimpeachable even as a secondary source; their writings show little special acquaintanceship with Southern life and history. Political journalism, even at its best, often breathes passionate commitment, which rarely facilitates sober historical analysis. We need not side with those who would transform Marx into a nonpartisan sociologist—those who would draw his revolutionary teeth in the manner of the European Social Democrats—to recognize that his burning hatred of slavery and commitment to the Union cause interfered with his judgment. It need not have been so, for as Karl Kautsky observes, if the socialist movement genuinely believes that history is on its side, it can profit only from the truth, no matter how disadvantageous in the short run, and can only lose by politically expedient fabrications.[5] It was proper for Marx to hate slavery and to throw his efforts into organizing the European proletariat against it; it was neither proper nor necessary for him to permit his partisanship to lead to a gross underestimation of the slaveholding class and to an ambiguous assessment of the origins of the war.

It would be comfortable to account for the weaknesses in the performance of Marx and Engels wholly by reference to their political engagement and thereby, in a sense, to acquit them at the expense of their successors. There is, however, a deeper difficulty. The Marxian interpretation of history contains an undeniable ambiguity, which creates a dangerous tendency toward economic determinism—that vulgar and useless historical dogma. Even Marx's Preface to *The Critique of Political Economy,* which remains the best brief statement of the Marxian viewpoint, may be reduced to economic determinism, not to mention such politically serviceable if historically simplistic notions as the unilinear theory of history.[6] As a general and preliminary statement, the Preface[7] leaves little to be desired, but it does, by its necessarily schematic form, lend itself to economic, unilinear, and other deterministic interpretations. To be understood properly—I refer not to what Marx "really meant" but to what is meaningful in his thought—passages such as this must be understood in the context of his life's work. The Hegelian

and dialectical side of Marx's thought cannot be introduced
and dropped at will; it constitutes an integral part of its core
and renders, on principle, all forms of mechanism foreign to
its nature.

Marx and Engels tell us that ideas grow out of social existence, but have a life of their own. A particular base
(mode of production) will generate a corresponding superstructure (political system, complex of ideologies, culture,
etc.), but that superstructure will develop according to its
own logic as well as in response to the development of the
base. If, for example, the crisis of ancient slave society produced the Christian religion, the development of its theology
would still depend—and in fact has depended—significantly
on its own internal logic and structure as well as on social
changes. The staying power of such a religion would depend,
therefore, on the flexibility of its leaders in overcoming un-
avoidable contradictions between internal and external lines
of development.[8]

If ideas, once called into being as a social force, have a life
of their own, then it follows that no analysis of the base is possible without consideration of the superstructure it engen-
ders since the development of that superstructure only partially is determined by its origins, and since any changes in
the superstructure, including those generated by its inner
logic, must modify the base itself. If, from the Marxian point
of view, classes and class struggles are at the center of historical transformations,[9] then economic determinism, in any of
its forms, can have no place in Marxism. The confusion between Marxism and economic determinism arises from the
Marxian definition of classes as groups the members of which
stand in a particular relationship to the means of production.
This definition is essentially "economic" but only in the
broadest sense. Broad or narrow, there is no excuse for identifying the economic origins of a social class with the developing nature of that class, which necessarily embraces the full
range of its human experience in its manifold political, social, economic, and cultural manifestations. That the economic interests of a particular class will necessarily prove
more important to its specific behavior than, say, its religious
values, is an ahistorical and therefore un-Marxian assump-

tion. Since those values are conditioned only originally and broadly by the economy, and since they develop according to their own inner logic and in conflict with other such values, as well as according to social changes, an economic interpretation of religion can at best serve as a first approximation and might even prove largely useless.

On a more general level the distinction between "objective" and "subjective" forces in history, which so persistently fascinates dogmatic Marxists, ends by making a mockery of dialectical analysis. As the great Italian Marxist, Antonio Gramsci, observes after noting Marx's more sophisticated statements on the role of ideas: "The analysis of these statements, I believe, reinforces the notion of 'historical bloc,' in which the material forces are the content and ideologies the form—merely an analytical distinction since material forces would be historically inconceivable without form and since ideologies would have to be considered individual dabbling without material forces."[10] The decisive element in historical development, from a Marxian point of view, is class struggle, an understanding of which presupposes a specific historical analysis of the constituent classes. Such an analysis must recognize the sociological uniqueness of every social class as the product of a configuration of economic interests, a semiautonomous culture, and a particular world outlook; and it must recognize the historical uniqueness of these classes as the product of the evolution of that culture and world outlook in relation to, but not wholly subordinate to, those economic interests. If certain kinds of economic threats sometimes shake a society more severely than do other kinds of threats, it is only because they ordinarily strike more closely at the existence of the ruling class. Most ruling classes have been wise enough to know, however, that particular ideological challenges can be quite as dangerous as economic ones and that no challenge need be taken seriously unless it presents itself, at least potentially, on the terrain of politics.

If Marxism is misrepresented as economic determinism by friends as well as foes, Marx and Engels are partly responsible. As Gramsci observes, Karl Marx, "the writer of *concrete* historical works," was not guilty of such naiveté,[11] but as the statement implies, Karl Marx, the journalist and essayist, cannot always be acquitted. With a tendency toward economic interpretation and an intellectually undisciplined political passion, Marx and Engels left us nothing close to a coherent and comprehensive critique of the Slave South. In view of how hard our official Marxists have been working to conceal this fact, one would suppose they think Marxism too fragile to withstand the revelation.

Nowhere do Marx or Engels examine systematically the origins, history, ideology, or character of the slaveholding class; yet without such an examination no "Marxian" analysis is possible. Instead, they resort to ridicule and charge hypocrisy and cynicism. At times their writings come close to demagogy. "The Confederate Congress," writes Marx, "boasted that its new-fangled Constitution, as distinguished from the Constitution of the Washingtons, Jeffersons, and Adamses, had recognized for the first time slavery as a thing good in itself, a bulwark of civilization, and a divine institution."[12] These sentiments he branded as "cynical confessions." He cheered signs that the North was ready to deal with these upstarts and to return the Union "to the true principles of its development."[13] Marx and Engels denied the legitimacy of Southern claims. North and South, they wrote, form one country. "The South, however, is neither a territory strictly detached from the North geographically, nor a moral unity. It is not a country at all, but a battle cry."[14] These assertions could do very well to rally support to the Union, which is what they were supposed to do, but they go down hard as serious assessment.

In a more sober moment they wrote: "The present struggle between the South and North is, therefore, nothing but a struggle between two social systems, the system of slavery and the system of free labor."[15] If we are to admit of two social systems in the country and if, as we must, we recognize that they occupied substantially different territory, what are we to make of the contemptuous rejections of Southern claims to legitimacy? When the Confederates proudly proclaimed the defense of slavery, they were being neither cynical nor hypocritical but honest. The corresponding values, ethos, and standards of civilization represented their social system as properly as those of the bourgeoisie represented

Northern capitalism. Between the Revolution and the War
for Southern Independence the slaveholders took long strides
toward the perfection of a world view of their own. In their
political, social, and economic thought they steadily sloughed
off those liberal-bourgeois elements of the Virginia Tidewater tradition, which had, in any case, never struck deep
social roots. Even in the early national period John Taylor
of Caroline and John Randolph of Roanoke, not to mention
the lesser lights of Virginia and South Carolina, advanced, in
however a contradictory way, essential ideas for a conservative Southern philosophy. Step by step, from Thomas Cooper
to Thomas Roderick Dew to John C. Calhoun to George
Fitzhugh, we may trace the formation of a political and social
philosophy singularly appropriate to the defense of the plantation regime. On another level, several forces combined to
generate a peculiar ethos among the slaveholders. With the
closing of the African slave trade in 1808 slave prices rose
sharply, and slaveholders had to depend on the natural increase of their labor force or on purchases in the older areas,
which was the same thing once removed. Improvement in
the material conditions of slave life became the order of the
day and with it a growing rationale of paternalistic responsibility. At the same time these very conditions slowly generated an almost wholly American-born slave force and
narrowed the cultural gap between master and slave and
between white and black. When the abolitionist onslaught
began, the slaveholders, reigning as resident lords over dependent human beings, had only to look about them and
into their own souls to discover that they held values and social attitudes at variance with those of their Northern contemporaries and that they and the abolitionists did not speak
the same language or live in the same world. The slaveholders, in short, matured as a ruling class and with increasing
self-consciousness came to stand for a social system of a distinct type. If the legitimacy of their ideology is not understood, it will not be possible to estimate the strength of their
system and its peculiar forms of class rule. Marx and Engels
badly misjudged these men and their society, but then so have
virtually all the liberal historians and not a few conservatives. So appalling is the idea of slavery to our historians, as

to Marx and Engels, that they vigorously resist crediting it
with the formation of a respectable and authentic ideology
and way of life. In their insistence on treating the slaveholders' ideology as a rationalization for plunder, as something
unworthy of attention and analysis except as mere apolo-
getics, Marx and Engels assume a liberal stance. The correspondence between their view and the view of the liberals
and vulgar-Marxists on this question stems less from the positive influence of Marxism over our liberal historians than
from the retreat of Marx, Engels, and too many Marxists into
liberalism. To criticize Marx and Engels on this particular
question, as on some others, ironically means to criticize
certain features of American liberal dogma. Marxism, however, necessarily brings into historical analysis a central concern with the process by which ruling classes arise and establish their hegemony and offers an indispensable framework
for the study of the civilization of the Slave South.

The denial of Southern legitimacy had a more serious
effect than an underestimation of the slaveholders; it introduced a curious ambiguity into the notion of "social systems"
itself. Rather than admit the territoriality of these systems,
with everything it implies, they interpret the struggle strictly
as a class struggle within the Union as a whole.[16] The concentration of the slave system in one part of the country is
not considered of great importance. Most subsequent Marxists, as well as the Beards and their followers, insist on the
same point and thereby sacrifice historical reality to the need
to fit the conflict into a unilinear model of world development. Marx and Engels, followed somewhat more cautiously
by the Beards, argue that the South desired not an independent existence but the reorganization of the Union on a slaveholding basis. A Confederate victory, they insist, would have
eventually detached the Northwest from the Union: "In the
Northern states, where Negro slavery is in practice unwork-
able, the white working class would gradually be forced down
to the level of helotry."[17] In more strident terms Marx wrote
Lincoln on behalf of the International Workingmen's Association:

> Counter-revolution, with systematic thoroughness, gloried
> in rescinding "the ideas entertained at the time of the Old

Constitution," and maintained "slavery to be a beneficent institution, indeed the only solution of the great problem of the relation of labor to capital," and cynically proclaimed property in man "the cornerstone of the new edifice"; then the working classes of Europe understood at once, even before the fanatical partisanship of the upper classes for the Confederate gentry had given its dismal warning, that the slaveholders' rebellion was to sound the tocsin for a general holy crusade of property against labor. . . .[18]

That a Confederate victory would have strengthened reaction internationally and confronted the working classes with new dangers cannot be denied, but Marx's exaggerations open the way for a series of dubious assertions. The fear that the South might conquer the Union for slavery deserves to be taken only slightly more seriously than Marx's charge in 1863 that Union military reverses suggested treason. Certainly, the Confederates would have liked to take Chicago and New York—why not?—but few thought it remotely possible. Confederate imperialist ambitions extended to the south and southwest. Yet, so bound are Marx and Engels to this notion that without a shred of evidence they proceeded to this astounding appraisal of the outbreak of hostilities: "The secessionists resolved to force the Union government out of its passive attitude by a sensational act of war, and *solely for this reason* proceeded to the bombardment of Fort Sumter. . . ."[19]

The worst feature of this nightmare is its negation of an excellent insight on the role of the Northwest. Marx and Engels were among the first to realize that the agrarian Northwest, contrary to all simplistic notions of an irreconcilable struggle between agrarianism and industrialism, would stand with the Northeast against the South and would be much more militant about it. They write, in terms economic determinists are not likely to appreciate, that the Northwest was "a power that was not inclined by tradition, temperament, or mode of life to let itself be dragged from compromise to compromise in the manner of the Northern states."[20] This judgment, based on newspaper and other ordinary sources of information, flows from their profound grasp of the process of capitalist development; it is neither mere guesswork nor hasty but lucky extrapolation. Their study of the history and economic theory of capitalism enables them in this case to project their data legitimately and to excellent effect. Their analysis of the course of American development corresponds to their brilliant treatment of the agrarian origins of capitalism in Europe and of the revolutionary role of the small producers.[21] It is, therefore, discouraging to watch them tremble at the danger that the Confederates would win the Northwest by threatening to close the Mississippi.[22] This retreat into economic interpretation might have been a politically useful gambit, but does not reflect well on their analysis. Apart from its dismissal of those traditions and sentiments which ought to have led the Northwestern classes to other solutions, it overlooks the central economic point. The Northwest, as Marx and Engels say, formed part of a developing national economy; hence, theoretically and in fact, its economic ties with the Northeast were steadily tightening at the expense of those with the South. Railroads east to west, not the Mississippi River north to south, proved decisive, and if they had not already been built, no economic law or Southern economic aggression could have prevented their being built. The argument of Marx and Engels makes sense only on the crude economic-determinist assumptions that they so contemptuously and rightfully toss aside.

The discussion of slavery expansionism, for which they owe a considerable debt to the liberal economist J. E. Cairnes's influential book *The Slave Power,* constituted the most impressive part of their historical analysis, if we put aside their acute observations on military and international affairs:

> By force of circumstances South Carolina is already transformed in part into a slave-raising state, since it already sells slaves to the states of the extreme South and Southwest for four million dollars yearly. As soon as this point is reached, the acquisition of new Territories becomes necessary in order that one section of the slaveholders may equip new, fertile landed estates with slaves and in order that by this means a new market for slave-raising, therefore for the sale

of slaves, may be created for the section left behind it. It is, for example, indubitable that without the acquisition of Louisiana, Missouri and Arkansas by the United States, slavery would long ago have been wiped out. In the secessionist Congress at Montgomery, Senator Toombs, one of the spokesmen of the South, has strikingly formulated the economic law that commands the constant expansion of the territory of slavery. "In fifteen years more," said he, "without a great increase in slave territory, either the slaves must be permitted to flee from the whites, or the whites must flee from the slaves."[23]

This passage contains a clause that sets it apart from many contemporary ideas and from such well-known theses as those of Weber, Ramsdell, and Phillips: that in Virginia and Maryland ". . . slavery would long ago have been wiped out." For Marx and Engels the political, not the economic, side of the process would have been decisive, the implication being that acute economic distress in the midst of a society with warring ideologies would have generated a new relationship of class forces. They ridicule the idea that economic laws would lead to the extinction of slavery. As Marx observes, those economic laws were understood perfectly by the slaveholders, who were using their political and military power to stay them. In discussing the origins of slavery expansionism they stress three things: economic pressure, the balance of political power in the Union, and the exigencies created by an uneasy rule over the nonslaveholders. Each of these represents an aspect of the class rule of the slaveholders. What is most clearly missing is an adequate treatment of the ideological side and therefore of the problem of hegemony.[24] The omission in part results from and in part causes their exaggeration of the place of the yeomanry in the strategy and tactics of the ruling class.[25]

The hegemony of the slaveholders extended over urban and rural classes but has been little studied. In particular, we need to examine the specific economic, political, social, and psychological relationships between each of these quite distinct classes and strata and the ruling slaveholders. If we take the industrialists as a case in point, their supine loyalty to the regime becomes no mystery when they are studied as a specific historical class rather than as a historical abstraction of such classes. Much of their capital came from surpluses accumulated by the planters; many of the industrialists themselves were planters or from planter families; their corporate charters and political existence were dependent on planter-dominated legislatures; and much of their market consisted of the plantations. These and other ties bound the industrialists, as individuals and even as an economic stratum, narrowly considered, to the regime, although their class interests, which might hypothetically be constructed as a program for the expansion of the South's industrial base and of the power of its industrialists, clearly required the overthrow of slavery. Marxian economic historians, notably Maurice Dobb in his groundbreaking *Studies in the Development of Capitalism,* explore the reasons for and mechanisms by which the commercial bourgeoisie normally serves the existing order instead of trying to overthrow it. As a class that profits from existing arrangements and stands to lose everything by social disruption, their prime ambition normally is to expand their share of the profits being siphoned from the productive mechanism. Any abrupt change in that mechanism threatens them with disaster. Dobb demonstrates, in particular, the conservative and at times reactionary role played by the commercial bourgeoisie during the revolutionary upheavals that accompanied capitalism's rise as a social system. Eric Hobsbawm, in his work on the seventeenth century, questions the rigid dichotomy that Dobb, following Marx, makes between industrial and commercial capitalists, and suggests the need for closer analysis of particular strata within these classes. Thus, he argues, important entrenched sections of industrial capital can, and during the seventeenth century did, play a similarly reactionary role. So, we may add, did the industrialists of the Slave South. These questions, which concern the notion of class and class rule, ought to be at the center of all Marxian historical analysis, but like most liberals who write on slavery and the Negro, American Marxists have generally been preoccupied with narrow economic analysis or, worse, with the romanticization of the submerged classes.

Marx and Engels themselves exaggerate the degree of class

conflict in the South. Secession, they argue, was a *coup d'état* against the nonslaveholders. In particular they insist that the masses of the border states were pro-Union and held down only by their political inexperience. Their discussion is marred by contradictory judgments and ignorance. Nowhere do they analyze the class structure to distinguish among such groups as self-sufficient upcountry farmers, black-belt yeomen, agricultural laborers, and poor whites. When convenient, they are "poor white trash," good only for brigandage and for frightening the slaveholders by their nihilism. In general, we are offered a two-class white South.[26] The potentially revolutionary masses of 1861 become the white trash of 1865. Thus, Engels to Marx on July 15, 1865: "The mean whites, I think, will gradually die out. With this stock there is nothing to be done; what is left after two generations will merge with the migrants into a stock entirely different.[27] We need not inquire into the accuracy of such judgments, based as they are on little more than a few tendentious books, but we cannot ignore the total failure to confront the problem of hegemony—to try to discover the economic, political, social, cultural, and psychological bonds binding the masses to the ruling class.[28]

The other side of their misunderstanding, or lack of curiosity, about the essentials of the slaveholding rule is their assessment of Northern society. It all depends on mood and the vicissitudes of battle. Thus, "The manner in which the North wages war," writes Marx to Engels, "is only to be expected from a *bourgeois* republic, where fraud has so long reigned supreme."[29] Thus, Engels to Marx: "I must say that I cannot work up much enthusiasm for a people which on such a colossal issue allows itself to be continually beaten by a fourth of its own population and which has achieved nothing more than the discovery that all its generals are idiots and all its officials rascals and traitors. After all, the thing must happen differently, even in a bourgeois republic, if it is not to end in utter failure.[30] Marx replies ten days later that Northern corruption and stupidity serve some purpose, for at least "the bourgeois republic exposes itself in thoroughgoing fashion, so that in future it can never again be preached on its own merits but solely as a means and a form of transition to the social revolution. . . ."[31] And again in 1864, when predicting Lincoln's re-election, Marx writes to Engels, "In the model country of the democratic swindle this election time is full of contingencies. . . ."[32] In the light of these hard but not unfair judgments, what are we to make of some other pronouncements, except to suspect a combination of wishful thinking and political opportunism?

In the "Address to the International Workingmen's Association to Abraham Lincoln" Marx refers to the Northern workers as "the true political power of the North."[33] Not content with this excursion into fantasy, he adds that the international workers' movement considers "it an earnest omen of the epoch to come that it fell to the lot of Abraham Lincoln, the single-minded son of the working class, to lead his country through the matchless struggle for the rescue of an enchained race and the reconstruction of a social world."[34] This would seem quite a feat to expect from the leader of a bourgeois republic in which fraud reigns supreme and which has thoroughly exposed itself. Yet, this obviously self-serving cant is taken at face value even by so sober a Marxian historian as Philip S. Foner, who labors to save the "proletarian" character of the struggle. Marx puts himself in a box. If the South represented the counterrevolution of property, why should the Northern bourgeoisie be its most determined adversary? It is, accordingly, necessary to invent a labor-based antislavery movement and then to attribute to it a major share of regional power or at least a decisive role in pushing a reluctant bourgeoisie to the left.[35] Foner, who did excellent work on the New York merchants, comes close to judging the Northern bourgeoisie by its most vacillating and Southern-oriented section.[36] Most Marxists continue to write in this way, although William Z. Foster, in his superficial but occasionally shrewd *Outline Political History of the Americas,* after a verbal bow to the heroism of the Northern workers, places the leadership in the hands of the industrial bourgeoisie.[37] Foner flirts with improper extrapolations from his conscientious but limited study and does not attempt a full analysis of the Southern regime. In his *History of the Labor Movement in the United States,* the first volume of which has much to say about the conditions and attitudes of labor, he does not discuss the nature of the war itself. In *Business & Slavery* he explicitly presents a modified Beardian thesis. Marx and Engels, for their part, limit themselves to political exhortations when publicly discussing some of the most important questions.[38]

In the end Marx and Engels regain their balance. During the early phase of Reconstruction Marx writes: "The American Civil War brought in its train a colossal national debt, and with it the pressure of taxes, the rise of the vilest financial aristocracy, the squandering of a huge part of the public land on speculative companies for the exploitation of railways, mines, etc., in brief, the most rapid centralization of capital. The great republic has, therefore, ceased to be the promised land for emigrant laborers."[39] Gone is the working class that supposedly constituted the real power. Marx and Engels normally do not idealize the working classes or exaggerate their virtues, although their claims, and those of their successors, that the British working class prevented intervention are unwarranted. As Royden Harrison convincingly demonstrates, the British workers did not mobilize in defense of the Union until other forces had already compelled the government to abandon any idea of intervening on the Confederate side.[40]

The opportunism is more disturbing. On February 2, 1862, writing in *Die Presse,* they praise the workers' "obstinacy" in resisting, by silence or open hostility, efforts to panic them into interventionism.[41] Later in the same year, Marx writes to Engels: "During this recent period England has disgraced herself more than any other country, the workers by their christian slave nature, the bourgeois and aristocrats by their enthusiasm for slavery in its most direct form. But the two manifestations supplement one another."[42] Between the mechanistic tendencies in their thought and these opportunistic and uninformed assertions they badly cluttered the legacy they left their successors, but there is no excuse for surrendering the class analysis of history, which was the highest product of their genius, in order to embrace what is tangential and superficial in their remarkable life's work.[43]

The response of avowed Marxists to these writings of Marx and Engels is drearily revealing. Somehow, there is not a critical word in sight; the masters' writings apparently contain no mistakes. We shall consider only Herbert Aptheker's review and Richard Enmale's introduction to *The Civil War in the United States*. Aptheker, writing in *New Masses*, insists that Marx and Engels were right about everything, including the details of the role of Northern wheat in the British economy, the central contribution of the British working class in preventing intervention, and various other judgments that no longer seem flawless to everyone. Finally, Aptheker asks how Marx and Engels could have seen so much and predicted so well: "Marx and Engels brought into their analysis of the present their historical materialism—their theory of the fundamental significance of the forces of production in explaining human events, and the shaping of these events in the cauldron of class struggle. . . . This book is one more evidence of the scientific nature of Marxism, for it passes the ultimate test of science—accuracy of prediction, and significance for the future."[44] Of such is the Kingdom of Heaven.

Enmale presents the official Marxist version which, despite years of professional advances and the development of Marxian thought, still somehow survives as the only version acceptable in party circles. It is a version that shares everything essential with the liberals while it berates them for ignoring the workers and Negroes. As such, it constitutes a perfect illustration of how the notion of Popular Front can and generally does end in ideological as well as political capitulation to those being courted. Since more and more liberals in this field are coming to study the Negroes with an attention and sympathy equal to those of the Marxists, the gap between the two groups of historians is steadily narrowing, and we may soon look forward to open concubinage—the liberals, of course, would never hear of marriage.

Enmale praises Charles Beard—it is astonishing how easily poor Mary disappears—and Arthur C. Cole for recognizing the war as a conflict of two social systems, but adds:

> The work of Beard and Cole, though containing much useful material, suffers from certain limitations inherent in the liberal bourgeois approach. . . . Failing to appreciate

fully the dynamics of historical development, liberal bourgeois historians do not clearly distinguish between the class forces at work. This leads them to ignore some of the most significant revolutionary phenomena of the period. Not least is the part played by the American working class in bringing the Civil War to a successful conclusion.[45]

We have seen how Marx and Engels treat the working class. As for the Negroes, to whom Enmale subsequently refers in a similar way, Marx and Engels say little or nothing beyond suggesting the psychological, as well as military, need to use Negro troops against the Confederacy. Despite attempts to make them say other than what they do say, they recognize significant passivity in the slaves: "Thanks to the slaves, who perform all productive labors, the entire manhood of the South that is fit to fight can be led into the field."[46] Their tendency to view the slaves more as objects than subjects— that is, to see them as a potential weapon in the hands of the North rather than as an independent force—is consistent with the realistic view of slave classes in evidence in their scattered writings on the ancient world. In this instance they set an example their followers might have profited from, had not short-run political considerations influenced them.

Like Marx and Engels, the early American socialist Algie M. Simons is ambiguous about the origins of the war because he is ambiguous about the quality of the Slave South. For Simons the war grew out of a clash between two expansive social systems—a Northern capitalism and a Southern "semi-feudal" slavery. Each enonomic system (the shift from "social" to "economic" comes easy to Simons, as it does to Beard) needed control of the federal government to advance and protect its interests; since they both needed the same territory to exploit, a clash was inevitable. Simons is never clear about the reasons for the inability of the two systems to compromise their differences, even at someone else's expense. Yet, if only economic interests were at stake, joint imperialist projects ought to have appeared as a solution. Simons's Marxism here and in general was never more than simplistic economic determinism. Yet, in some ways his analysis is superior to the fuller, more knowledgeable treatment of the period by the Beards, who stress Southern opposition to homesteads, tariffs, and bounties, and minimize the territorial question. For them, the rapid and disorderly growth of divergent economic systems and the interests they created generated the war. They come close to a Marxian standpoint when writing that slavery provided the basis for the Southern aristocracy and merged its economic interests and ethical standards, but the burden of their treatment centers on the clash of economic interests, narrowly defined. They are well behind Marx, who properly dismissed the tariff question as a matter of little substance.[47]

The Beards, for all their apparent concern with class forces, see little more than economic interests. Like some Marxists after them, they write:

> Merely by the accidents of climate, soil, and geography was it a sectional struggle. If the planting interest had been scattered evenly throughout the industrial region . . . the irrepressible conflict would have been resolved by other methods and accompanied by other logical defense mechanisms. [48]

Thus are the world outlooks of ruling classes reduced to "logical defense mechanisms"—that is, to the rationalization of particular interests. Despite occasional general statements, the Beards never see ideology as something partially autonomous and capable of affecting material interests profoundly. Their insistence that a scattered slaveocracy would behave no differently from a geographically compact one substitutes a consideration of ostensible economic interests for an analysis of a specific social class and thereby reduces itself to idealism, for it becomes a concern for abstract economic models instead of for the actual historical process within which all class interests develop their own content.

As a result the Beards are unable to deal adequately with many other questions, especially those raised by the notion of a "Second American Revolution." In their terms the Northern farmers and capitalists grew stronger during the war and shaped events in their own interests. They badly underestimate the capitalist quality of the farmers and have great difficulty explaining their subsequent defeat at the hands of their former capitalist allies. Rather than examine the problems associated with the developing hegemony of the bourgeoisie, they remain, as usual, narrowly tied to an analysis of economic interests and therefore end by seeing conspiracies everywhere.[49]

Many Marxists, as well as non-Marxists, extricate themselves from difficulty only to plunge into greater ones by treating the Slave South as a "feudal" society. The definitions of feudalism used by non-Marxists make little sense here, for the medieval European political and juridical arrangements that loom large in such definitions clearly did not exist in the South. Consciously or unconsciously, some variation of Marxian categories has come to be applied. For Marxists the term feudal refers to a mode of production within which property is privately owned, the laborer retains claims to the means of production, and the laborer owes the lord an economic yield, whether in money, kind, or service.[50] Definitions being tools, not religious tenets, they must be judged by their usefulness; at issue here is not the usefulness of the definition, with which I have no quarrel, but its applicability to the Slave South. If the Marxian notion of mode of production is as valuable as the steady retreat into its framework by ostensibly anti-Marxist historians would suggest, there is all the more reason to avoid blurring lines. In Marxian terms the Slave South was prebourgeois in essential respects, but it was far from being feudal. That is, the South rested on a distinct mode of production that was as different from the feudal as from the capitalist. At the same time the slave mode of production arose anachronistically and as a hybrid during the epoch of capitalism's world conquest. As such, the full autonomy of the slave mode of production could never be achieved; it functioned as part of the capitalist world and could not separate itself from the bourgeois economy or ideology. It was a system perpetually at war with itself, struggling to perfect its own spirit and simultaneously to remain part of a world foreign to that spirit. It helps not at all to label it feudal and then to think that by doing so some problem has been solved.

That the world market bent the slave economy to its own ends is incontrovertible. In this sense capitalism certainly did make its appearance in Southern agriculture; in this sense the South certainly was part of the capitalistic world. Slavery did something else, which those who would write Southern and nineteenth-century American history cannot avoid: it raised to regional power a prebourgeois ruling class of formidable political strength and military potential. Capitalism may be able to absorb and use prebourgeois economies, but it cannot readily digest prebourgeois ruling classes that are proud and strong enough to reject the roles of comprador and retainer.

There have been two obstacles to the development of the Marxian viewpoint along these lines. First, the obsession of Marxists with the unilinear theory of history has compelled them to view Southern slavery as a form of feudalism—a formulation that plays loose with the principal categories of the Marxian interpretation of history—and to treat it as a general American rather than a sectional question. In these terms the problem of "two social systems" reduces itself to one of internal class struggle between anachronistic and modern formations. Unilinear Marxists find incomprehensible the notion that social stages may be reversed or that archaic modes of production may reappear in modern forms with considerable political independence. History, it seems, may not go backwards.

Second, most Marxists suffer from their passionate commitment to the cause of Negro liberation and from their hatred of slavery.[51] They identify politically and morally with abolitionism and sacrifice much of their historical sense and even their political acumen. Marxists understand morality as a class question; they reject absolute values. They see process in history and class struggles at the center of that process. Accordingly, they judge slavery, in its modern phases, to be immoral and to represent a fetter on the development of human freedom, which during the seventeenth and eighteenth centuries, and even to some extent the nineteenth, cannot be separated from the development of bourgeois social relations. Their class morality is proletarian and insists that the secular interests of the working class, and the cause of its liberation, requires the abolition of bourgeois social relations. From this point of view it is possible to read history in such a way as to separate "progressive" from "retrogressive" forces: the former are those which revolutionize the economic base of society and create conditions for the advancement of human freedom. This viewpoint has its problems. The rise of ancient slavery, for example, must be interpreted as progressive and revolutionary since the enslavement of one portion of mankind made possible the development of the productive forces, of civilization, and therefore of a much more extensive and meaningful freedom.[52] Modern slavery presents an easier problem because it provides valuable support for the rise of capitalism but was far from indispensable. The main problem concerning modern slavery arises from the duality inherent in a class approach to morality. It is at least one-sided to judge Judah P. Benjamin, Jefferson Davis, and J. H. Hammond by the standards of bourgeois society or by the standards of a projected socialist society. These men were class conscious, socially responsible, and personally honorable; they selflessly fulfilled their duties and did what their class and society required of them. It is rather hard to assert that class responsibility is the highest test of morality and then to condemn as immoral those who behave responsibly toward their class instead of someone else's. There is no reason, unless we count as reason the indignation flowing from a passionate hatred for oppression, to withhold from such people full respect and even admiration; nor is there any reason to permit such respect and admiration to prevent their being treated harshly if the liberation of oppressed peoples demands it. The issue transcends considerations of abstract justice or a desire to be fair to one's enemies; it involves political judgment. If we blind ourselves to everything noble, virtuous, honorable, decent, and selfless in a ruling class, how do we account for its hegemony? The people cannot long be held down by force alone, especially since so much of this force must be recruited from the lower orders of society, nor are the people so cowardly as to accept arbitrary dictation forever. Ruling classes must develop a comprehensive world outlook that transcends its immediate and particular interests and that, however partially, identifies itself with the values and aspirations of the people as a whole. Such hegemony could never be maintained without some leaders whose individual qualities are intrinsically admirable. There is a firm link between the doctrinaire inability of many Marxists to appreciate the positive qualities of the best elements of the slaveholding class, and their common tendency to underestimate the hegemony of the bourgeoisie in our own day by seeing in it merely the deception or corruption of the working class.

On another level, Marxists avoid the embarrassment of analyzing the Southern world outlook because it is so patently antibourgeois. It would be difficult for a Marxist not to agree with much of George Fitzhugh's criticism of bourgeois society. Rather than admit as much, and proceed to delineate the differences between reactionary and socialist criticism, they usually charge hypocrisy. We may doubt that a ruling class could stand a year with an ideology based on nothing more than hypocrisy and deception.

The one Marxian writer who tries to take the South on its own terms, with the partial exception of Du Bois, is William Appleman Williams. That Williams is a Marxist in any meaningful sense is open to question, but he speaks as one, and it would be unjust, to say the least, to quarrel over his credentials. As a Socialist whose views have been influenced by Marx he offers many fruitful suggestions that might profitably be integrated into a Marxian analysis.[53]

In its weaker manifestation Williams' argument recapitulates that of the Beards, although with greater sophistication. Here again we have a conflict that might have been avoided had America's economic growth been less disorderly. Here again is an expansive North aiming primarily at the containment of a South that presents itself essentially as an economic rival. Here again we find the South largely as victim.[54] This side of Williams' analysis displays little originality and is not even especially suggestive. The other side displays a good deal more.

For Williams, American history has been a struggle between "mercantilism" and "laissez faire," with the former to be understood as an effort "to retain and adapt an original Christian morality during the dynamic secularization of a religious outlook as an agrarian society was transformed into a life of commerce and industry."[55] Within this struggle Williams sees the South as offering much to the "mercantilist" (i.e., socially responsible) tradition he admires. He speaks well of the planters, especially those of the early national period, and admires their style of life, their architecture, and their sense of community. At the same time he assumes a critical stance toward what he calls the "physiocratic" tendency in their thought (the attempt to build a feudal utopia within the context of a laissez-faire world), which he regards as a defense of purely agricultural and local interests against the common good. Before long he must defend Calhoun, the "mercantilist," against John Taylor, the "physiocrat." What begins as a suggestive dissection of the conflict in Southern thought between bourgeois and anti-bourgeois values, albeit a conflict translated into a strange language, ends back with Beard as an account of alternative economic policies.

Williams comes to grief over the question of slavery. For him, the best representatives of the Southern school during the early national period were antislavery or at least moving in an antislavery direction. So far does he press this dubious notion that he declares the three-fifths clause of the Constitution to have antislavery implications. He insists, contrary to all fact and reason, that the provision shows the Southerners to be intent on effecting the eventual freedom of the slaves. The disorderly onrush of laissez-faire capitalism generated new economic pressures for the preservation of slavery, and the attacks of the abolitionists convinced Southerners that the defense of slavery was the defense of their community values against the ideology of the marketplace. "Perhaps the greatest, if unplanned, strategic triumph of the laissez-faire antislavery campaign was its making the slave system a hero in the eyes of Southerners."[56] Williams misses the essential thrust of Southern development: the rising self-consciousness of the planters and their growing knowledge that Southern community values rested wholly on the plantation-slave nature of their regime. Williams' idealism misleads him at the very moment of his keenest insight, for he fails to ask the main question: On what kind of material base did the slaveholders' ideology arise? His dichotomy between "mercantilist" and "physiocratic" tendencies is beside the point. The particularism he laments went hand in hand with the sense of community, for each reflected conditions of locally rooted lordship.

Williams' treatment of the abolitionists is unfair and wrong on principle. Since he sees only one national society, with the South a particular set of local interests, he is appalled at abolitionist fanaticism and narrow-mindedness. In his view they ought to have concentrated on ameliorating the conditions of bondage and thereby setting the institution on the road to extinction. He does not appreciate the conflict of worlds, not just interests, underlying the conflict of ideologies. Were he to see the slave system as a social system in itself, he might be able to see that amelioration and reform would have strengthened it, much as liberal reformism has strengthened capitalism.[57] His view is unjust both to the slaveholders and to the abolitionists. It is unjust to the slaveholders because it implicitly makes their ideology a defensive afterthought, instead of appreciating its legitimacy—in Williams' terms, its place at the center of Southern "mercantilism." It is unjust to the abolitionists because it denies their fundamental insight—that no compromise was either possible or desirable. By glossing over the problem of divergent social systems Williams retreats even from the Beards, but it is in part a useful retreat, capable of preparing for new advances, for it reopens in a serious way the question of rival world outlooks.

The most successful attempt at a Marxian analysis of the South and the coming of the war is Barrington Moore's "The American Civil War: The Last Capitalist Revolution."[58] Since Moore discusses a great number of European and Asian societies, a critique of his chapter on the United States in isolation risks some distortion, and since he makes no pretense to specialized knowledge, and relies on a relatively slim literature, some allowance needs to be made for a confessed tendency to generalize beyond the data presented. His analysis is nonetheless impressive and unintentionally reveals how banal most Marxian interpretations have been.

Moore sees the war as the last revolutionary offensive on the part of the urban or bourgeois democracy. He rejects simplistic economic interpretations but insists on the ultimate importance of the economic impulse which generated slavery and therefore provided the basis for a divergent social order in the South. In this way Moore develops a two-civilizations thesis without surrendering an "economic" interpretation. As he observes, the numerical balance between free and slave states could be understood as "something that mattered . . . only if the difference between a society with slavery and one without mattered."[59]

Moore's rejection of the thesis of economic rivalry reveals the fundamental weakness in his discussion. Plantation slavery did not rival industry capitalism, he argues, but arose as an integral part of it. Slavery was a spur, not a fetter, to industrial growth. In this form the argument is unexceptionable, but it does obscure the class issue. Slavery simultaneously extruded a ruling class with strong prebourgeois qualities and economic interests that did conflict with Northern capitalism. Moore himself notes the probability of an expansionist tendency in the Southern economy and society, but he pays insufficient attention to it and to the extraordinary expansionism of Northern capitalism, and thereby minimizes the economic aspect of the collision. (If it is not presumptuous to suggest it, I think he would have benefitted from careful concern with Williams' work here.) Moore is so anxious to repel crude economic interpretation that he concedes far more ground than is necessary or safe. The development of national capitalism, he says, transformed the Western farmers into petty capitalists and tied them to the East. The existence of free land muted the class struggle in the Eastern cities. Without a major threat from the Left, the bourgeoisie had no need of Southern "Junkerism" and every need for a democratic alliance with Western farmers in order to expand and deepen its home market and to strengthen its position in the world market. With slavery's generating an antidemocratic ethos in the South, the two sections pulled further and further apart. Slavery, in Moore's view, did not inhibit industrial capitalism but did inhibit the democratic, competitive capitalism from which the bourgeoisie stood to profit most and to which it was increasingly committed ideologically.

Moore returns, in this manner, to the question of two civilizations and to the nature of Southern society. He begins weakly by drawing a parellel between the slaveholders and the Junkers in whom he sees a class of "not quite slavehold-ers." In the end, however, he surrenders this part of the argu-ment by noting that the Northern bourgeoisie could only absorb the planters into a conservative coalition when slavery was gone and Northern capital was conquering the South. In general, he exaggerates the prebourgeois quality of the post-Napoleonic Junkers and underestimates the prebourgeois quality of the slaveholders.

Moore pays little attention to Southern ideology and weakens his two-civilizations argument. His notion that slaveholders were too "ashamed" to justify slavery on eco-nomic grounds and sought elaborate rationales does him no credit. He does recognize certain genuinely prebourgeois and aristocratic features in the Southern world outlook but insists, on balance, that they were largely a fraud. After all, did not the Southern social system rest on commercial profits? He does not consider the possibility of a social system and ethos at war with itself, much less one in which the old was prevailing over the new—the prebourgeois over the bourgeois—because nowhere does he analyze the plantation as community and way of life. Despite a framework that places social classes at the center, he never analyzes the slave-holders as a class; he merely describes certain of their features and interests in a tangential way. Finally, he settles for the extraordinary formulation: "The South had a capitalist civilization, then, but not a bourgeois one. Certainly it was not based on town life."[60]

Thus, with much greater skill and subtlety than can be apparent in this short account, Moore tries to bridge the gap between the notion of the South as agrarian-capitalist and the notion of it as aristocratic or prebourgeois. The implica-tions of this point of view are beyond the scope of this paper, but they clearly represent the beginnings of a serious class analysis and of a viable Marxian interpretation. I have else-where presented, somewhat schematically and one-sidedly, the case for the prebourgeois thesis,[61] but no one would argue that a strong dose of capitalism did not exist in the South. The argument turns on the proportions and their significance. Ultimately, the task of Marxian interpretation is the analysis of the constituent social classes, their interests and ideology, and especially of the ruling slaveholders. The advantages of Moore's model or some other can only be definitively established in a broader context, such as the one Moore offers in his remarkable book. Unable to pursue this subject here, we may welcome Moore's effort as a new departure, which, if taken seriously by the developing generation of American Marxists, may finally bring us out of the wilderness of dogmatism, romanticism, and humbug.

The suggestions of Moore and Williams will hopefully constitute a beginning; that neither is part of the orthodox Marxian movements is its own comment on those movements. This beginning means, above all, a break with naive determinism, economic interpretation, and the insipid glorification of the lower classes, all of which ends as some form of fatalism. There are at least three reasons for retreating into fatalism—cowardice, laziness, and simple-mindedness—and probably many more for resorting to political formulas instead of proceeding with honest research. Marxism and the socialist movement have no need for fatalism or formulas. Marxism has already contributed much to the history of the Slave South by bringing a class focus to a subject that historians increasingly recognize as a special case of class rule. Freed of dogmatism and special pleading, it has infinitely more to bring to an empirical analysis of the rise, course, and fall of the slaveholding class and of its relationship to other classes in society. The advance of such an analysis should help practical socialist work, no matter how many treasured theories and prejudices fall away, for it should tell us a great deal about the way in which a ruling class rules. Marxists have only begun to study the hegemonic mechanisms of bourgeois society. Without suggesting easy and probably false analogies to contemporary problems, we might expect that a study of such mechanisms in a society displaying so many typically American and Western European political and institutional forms ought to illuminate some features of present problems. At least it ought to serve as a check against oversimplification and the exaggeration of the place of purely economic and material forces. In view of this promise and potential those who would defend Marxian socialism by protecting its founder from just criticism do an immeasurable disservice. They would do well to recall Marx's Preface to the First German edition of *Capital:* "Every opinion based on scientific criticism I welcome. As to the prejudices of so-called public opinion, to which I have never made concessions, now as aforetime the maxim of the great Florentine is mine: '*Segui il tuo corso, e lascia dir le genti.*' "[62]

NOTES

* I shall not define "Marxian" too closely here. The works considered are those by professed Marxists, by certain writers like Beard who acknowledge a strong influence from Marx, and by those whose analysis centers on essential Marxian categories. I received a copy of Raimondo Luraghi's *Storia della guerra civile americana* (Turin, 1966), too late for inclusion in this discussion. Luraghi's analysis of the origins of the war and his treatment of the South are important contributions toward the development of a class analysis of American history and will hopefully secure the attention they deserve from Marxists and non-Marxists alike.

1. *Cf.*, Caio Prado, Junior, *Formação do Brasil Contemporâneo: Colônia,* 7th ed. (São Paulo, n.d.); Fernando Henrique Cardoso, *Capitalismo e Escravidão no Brasil Meridional* (São Paulo, 1962); Octavio Ianni, *As Metamorfoses do Escravo* (São Paulo, 1962) and *Raças e Classes Sociais no Brasil* (Rio de Janeiro, 1966), esp. Part 2.
2. Herbert Aptheker, *American Foreign Policy and the Cold War* (New York, 1962), p. 291. This book is a leading illustration of the uses to which Popular Frontism can be put in trying to effect "an opening to the right." Cf. my critique "Dr. Herbert Aptheker's Retreat from Marxism," *Science & Society,* XXVII (Spring, 1963), 212–26.
3. Marx's articles for the *New York Daily Tribune* and those of Marx and Engels for the Vienna *Die Presse,* together with relevant correspondence, have been collected and translated as *The Civil War in the United States,* first published in 1937 and edited by Richard Enmale and reprinted in 1961. In the latter paperback edition, to which all page references here refer, the editor's name is dropped; obviously it was a pseudonym. For convenience, however, I shall use the name Enmale when referring to the editor's own remarks in his introduction.
4. Gerald Runkle, "Karl Marx and the American Civil War," *Comparative Studies in Society and History,* VI, No. 1 (1963–64), 117–41.
5. Karl Kautsky, *The Foundations of Christianity* (New York, 1953), Foreword.

6. For an illuminating discussion of some phases of this pseudo-revolutionary juggling see Eric J. Hobsbawm's Introduction to Karl Marx, *Pre-Capitalist Economic Formations* (New York, 1965), which traces the fate of Marx's pregnant notion of an "Asiatic mode of production" in later Marxist writing.

7. Karl Marx, *A Contribution to the Critique of Political Economy* (Chicago, 1904), pp. 11–13.

8. In the history of science Marxists have generally stressed the social impulses to theoretical advance, whereas others have stressed the theoretical impulses internal to the science. But as S. Lilley says: "Any scientific development, I suggest, becomes possible only when both internal and external conditions are ripe. So much can be demonstrated by considering conspicuous cases in which, for a considerable period, one set of conditions, *either* external *or* internal, was favorable to an advance, but the other was not." "Cause and Effect in the History of Science," *Essays in the Social History of Science,* ed. S. Lilley (Copenhagen, 1953), p. 59.

9. I mean fundamental transformations in the way in which human beings face each other in society. To trace all historical events and changes to class structure and class struggles is to convert Marxian analysis into a childish formula worthy of a particularly fanatic and simple-minded religious cult.

10. Antonio Gramsci, *Il Materialismo storico e la filosofia di Benedetto Croce, Opere* (Turin, 1949), II, 49.

11. Quoted by John M. Cammett, *Antonio Gramsci and the Origins of Italian Communism* (Stanford, Cal., 1967), p. 191. This book is an invaluable introduction to Gramsci's political and intellectual work.

12. Marx and Engels, *Civil War,* p. 4.

13. *Ibid.,* p. 7.

14. *Ibid.,* p. 72.

15. *Ibid.,* p. 81.

16. Runkle is therefore wrong to accuse them of inconsistency. He argues that if their historical viewpoint were valid, the main struggle would have been within the South itself. In their terms, however, the Union as a whole was the relevant entity. Beyond this formal matter, Runkle's distinction between internal and external contradictions ignores the first principle of dialectics—the interrelatedness of all phenonema—and is a false problem. See Runkle, *Comparative Studies in Society and History,* VI, No. 1 (1963–64), 117–41.

17. Marx and Engels, *Civil War,* p. 81. Cf. Charles and Mary Beard, *The Rise of American Civilization* (2 vols. in 1; New York, 1944), II, 33 and esp. 56.

18. Marx and Engels, *Civil War,* p. 280.

19. *Ibid.,* p. 60; original emphasis.

20. *Ibid.,* p. 70.

21. In addition to Marx, *Capital* (3 vols.; Moscow, n.d.) see Maurice

Dobb, *Studies in the Development of Capitalism* (New York, 1947), esp. Chaps. I and II, and Dobb, ed., *The Transition from Feudalism to Capitalism* (New York, 1963), esp. the essay by H. K. Takahashi.

22. Marx and Engels, *Civil War*, p. 80.

23. *Ibid.*, pp. 67–68.

24. I use the term hegemony in its Gramscian sense—the seemingly spontaneous loyalty that a ruling class evokes from the masses through its cultural position and its ability to promote its own world view as the general will. For an introduction to Gramsci's ideas see Cammett, *Antonio Gramsci*, Ch. 10, and Gwynn A. Williams, "Gramsci's Concept of *Egemonia*," *Journal of the History of Ideas*, XXI (October-December 1960), 586–99.

25. For an alternative view of Southern expansionism, which nonetheless owes much to their lines of inquiry, see my *The Political Economy of Slavery* (New York, 1965), Ch. 10. For the discussion that follows, Part 3 of this book examines the position of the industrialists and tries to account for their conservatism.

26. See, e.g., *Civil War*, p. 190.

27. *Ibid.*, p. 277.

28. No Marxist writer has yet dealt adequately with this question. For some it is not even a question since the lower-class whites were ostensibly moving not only into opposition to slavery but toward an alliance with Negroes. Those wishing to pursue these fairy tales may consult Herbert Aptheker, "Class Conflicts in the South, 1850–1860," *Toward Negro Freedom* (New York, 1956), pp. 44–67.

29. Marx and Engels, *Civil War*, p. 255.

30. *Ibid.*, p. 259.

31. *Ibid.*, p. 259.

32. *Ibid.*, p. 271.

33. *Ibid.*, p. 281.

34. *Ibid.*, p. 281.

35. Philip S. Foner, *Business & Slavery* (Chapel Hill, N.C.), 1941. For an alternative view see Bernard Mandel, *Labor: Free and Slave* New York, 1955).

36. Foner, *Business & Slavery*, *passim*.

37. William Z. Foster, *Outline Political History of the Americas* (New York, 1951), Ch. 17.

38. The worst illustration is the "Address of the International Workingmen's Association to President Johnson," *Civil War*, pp. 283–85, which is embarrassing in its pompous rhetoric and sentimentality.

39. Marx, *Capital*, I, 773.

40. Royden Harrison, "British Labor and American Slavery," *Science & Society*, XXV (December 1961), 291–319.

41. Marx and Engels, *Civil War*, p. 141.

42. *Ibid.* pp. 261–62.

43. In view of the foregoing the reader may judge for himself the review of my *Political Economy of Slavery* that the *William and*

Mary Quarterly chose to publish. Written by one Melvin Drimmer, it informed the readers of that distinguished journal that I had applied and updated Marx on the Civil War. But this judgment looks almost like responsible scholarship alongside the silly statements that Drimmer attributed to me, such as that slavery was unprofitable and could not survive, that all the available land in the South had been used up by 1860, and that the planters became what they were through a "will to power"!

44. Herbert Aptheker, *Toward Negro Freedom,* pp. 84–85.

45. Richard Enmale in Marx and Engels, *Civil War,* pp. xviii–xix. Aptheker makes the same points.

46. Marx and Engels, *Civil War,* pp. 199–200, 252. The recent work of Brazil's outstanding Marxists is refreshingly free from the dogmatism and romanticism of American Marxian writing on the Negro. Octavio Ianni, especially, is ruthlessly objective and places the Negro contribution to the abolition of Brazilian slavery in realistic perspective without the slightest tendency to exaggerate, Cf. *As Metamorfoses do escravo,* pp. 232–35.

47. Beard and Beard, *Rise,* II, Ch. 17–18. For another example of essentially economic interpretation by a Marxist see Herman Schlüter, *Lincoln, Labor and Slavery: A Chapter from the Social History of America* (New York, 1913), Ch. 1. Thomas J. Pressly, *Americans Interpret their Civil War* (New York, 1962), pp. 238 ff., does a good job in showing just how narrowly economic the Beardian viewpoint is. Pressly does, however, exaggerate the critical side of Marxian writings in an apparent attempt to show how far the Beards are from Marxism. He does not seem to appreciate how close most of these Marxists are to being Beardians.

48. Beard and Beard, *Rise,* II, 53.

49. *Ibid.,* II, 99, 106. Among the Marxists who follow Beardian lines is George Novak, but some of his generalizations are well balanced and suggestive: see esp. his discussion of the stages of the development of American slavery. *Marxist Essays in American History* (New York, 1966), pp. 10, 34.

50. Cf. Dobb, *Studies in the Development of Capitalism,* pp. 35–36.

51. The closest any avowed Marxist has come to an appreciation of the strength and quality of the slaveholding class is W. E. B. Du Bois, *Black Reconstruction in America* (New York, 1935), Ch. 3, but even he retreats into moralizing and mystification.

52. Many Marxists nevertheless gag and try to interpret the rise of ancient slavery as a reactionary phenomenon. See, e.g., Kautsky, *Foundations of Christianity.*

53. Williams' understanding of Marxism comes out most sharply in his book, *The Great Evasion: An Essay on the Contemporary Relevance of Karl Marx and on the Wisdom of Admitting the Heretic into the Dialogue about America's Future* (Chicago, 1964). I have criticized this book and its interpretation of Marxism at length. See

"William Appleman Williams on Marx and America," *Studies on the Left,* VI, No. 1 (1966), 70–86.

54. William Appleman Williams, *The Contours of American History* (Cleveland, O., 1961), see esp. pp. 285–99.

55. *Ibid.,* p. 33. Williams' categories are his own and owe nothing to Marx. For a discussion of mercantilism from a Marxian viewpoint see the relevant chapter in Dobb, *Studies in the Development of Capitalism.*

56. *Ibid.,* p. 299.

57. Barrington Moore, Jr., on the other hand, sees the point clearly and criticizes Stanley M. Elkins on just this point: "These [reform] measures seem to me highly reactionary, a form of tokenism within the framework of slavery." *Social Origins of Dictatorship and Democracy: Lord and Peasant in the Making of the Modern World* (Boston, 1966), p. 132. n. 47.

58. *Ibid.,* Ch. III, pp. 110–55. Moore's categories are basically Marxian, and I shall treat his work as such. He writes, nevertheless, in a manner calculated to divorce himself from Marxism. At times he descends to something close to red-baiting. Thus, on Philip S. Foner: "The author is a well-known Marxist but in this study seems quite undogmatic" (p. 125, n. 29). That a scholar of Moore's quality should pander to prejudices in this way is a sad commentary on how far into the Cold War gutter even some of our best intellectuals have gone.

59. *Ibid.,* p. 120.

60. *Ibid.,* p. 121.

61. Genovese, *Political Economy,* esp. Ch. I, "The Slave South: An Interpretation." For an incisive critique by a conservative who shares some important ideas with Moore see Stanley M. Elkins' review in *Commentary,* July 1966, pp. 73–75. I would not deny having exaggerated my case and having opened the way to Elkins' strictures, but I would insist on the main lines of the argument, which will have to be developed in future efforts. Elkins' thoughtful attempt to come to terms with the argument demonstrates that a mutually useful dialogue between Marxists and anti-Marxists is possible even in Cold War America.

62. ["Follow your course, and let people say what they please."] Marx, *Capital,* I, 11.

THE

ANTISLAVERY LEGACY:

FROM RECONSTRUCTION

TO THE NAACP

∽ James M. McPherson

THE WHITE LIBERAL has become one of the most forlorn figures in the civil rights movement. Tormented by self-doubt and a guilty conscience, denounced by the radical right and disparaged by the militant left, bewildered by the kaleidoscopic forms of racial change, he has been cast adrift in an uncharted sea of baffling disesteem. His motives doubted, his naiveté ridiculed, his equalitarianism questioned, he has withdrawn in confusion and disorder from the vanguard of the civil rights movement.

It is too soon to assess the impact upon the racial scene of the white liberal's fade-out. But the historian recalls that the retreat of Northern liberals from full commitment to the goals of racial equality in the 1870s played a part in the failure of the First Reconstruction, and he wonders if history is repeating itself. Several scholars have commented on the abandonment of the Negro's cause by white liberals of antislavery background during and after Reconstruction. A Negro historian has written that "Northern liberalism, which had over-extended itself in the abolitionist crusade, began a precipitate retreat from reality in the Reconstruction era. Frederick Douglass made a valiant effort to rally his old colleagues . . . but they were busy, indifferent, or otherwise engaged."[1] C. Vann Woodward asserted that it was "quite common" after Reconstruction to find "Northern liberals and former abolitionists mouthing the shibboleths of white supremacy regarding the Negro's innate inferiority, shift-lessness, and hopeless unfitness for full participation in the white man's civilization."[2] August Meier wrote that in the 1870s "many of the abolitionists" became "disillusioned with reconstruction" and "deserted and betrayed the southern Negroes. . . . This was even true of many who had once been enthusiastic about guaranteeing Negroes their citizenship rights."[3]

Whether or not white liberals are disappearing from the current scene, it appears that their antislavery counterparts of a century ago abandoned *their* struggle. Yet a perusal of the activities of many abolitionists during Reconstruction calls the traditional interpretation into question. Most of these reformers were active in behalf of equal civil and political rights for Negroes and worked to bring education and economic assistance to the freedmen in the 1860s. Even in the 1870s a majority of former abolitionists continued to insist on strict and expanded enforcement of the Fourteenth and Fifteenth Amendments.[4] There has been no thorough study of the post-Reconstruction attitudes of former white abolitionists and their descendants toward the race problem. Such a study might revise some ideas about the follow-through of the antislavery crusade, help explain the role of an earlier generation of Northern liberals, and shed new light on the evolution of race relations during a crucial period of the Negro's history in America.

This essay, which is based on an investigation of approximately 125 white abolitionists and their descendants, will set forth some tentative generalizations about the racial attitudes and activities of these people from 1870 to 1910.[5] It will be wise to concede at the outset that the thesis concerning their "abandonment" of the Negro is partly correct. Nearly half of the abolitionists alive in the 1870s did become disillusioned to some degree with radical Reconstruction and approved or accepted the withdrawal of federal troops from the South in 1877. But their subsequent behavior cannot be summed up in the simple concepts of indifference or abandonment. Many of them remained committed to the equalitarian ideals of Reconstruction and active in efforts (chiefly educational) to fulfill these ideals. More than half of the old abolitionists opposed the cessation of Reconstruction and continued to demand federal enforcement of the Fourteenth and Fifteenth Amendments. And in the years after 1890, as disfranchisement and segregation rendered these amendments nugatory, some abolitionists and their descendants played key roles in a movement that led to the founding of the NAACP in 1909–1910.

I

Historians are familiar with the revulsion of Northern opinion toward Reconstruction in the 1870s. Widely publicized stories about the corruption and incompetence of "Negro-Carpetbag" governments produced a growing disgust that helped the Democrats win control of the House in the 1874 congressional elections. By the middle of the decade there were multiplying signs that influential Republicans were prepared to jettison the party's Southern policy as a political liability.

Many veterans of the antislavery crusade were alarmed by these developments. Vice-President Henry Wilson told William Lloyd Garrison in 1874: "I fear a Counter-Revolution. Men are beginning to hint at changing the condition of the negro." The old abolitionists, said Wilson, "must call the battle roll anew, and arrest the reactionary movements."[6] Garrison admonished a reunion convention of abolitionists to "beware of the siren-cry of 'conciliation' when it means humoring the old dragon spirit of slavery and perpetuating caste distinctions by law. . . . We shall still show ourselves to be the truest friends [of the South] by refusing to compromise any of the principles of justice as pertaining to her colored population."[7]

In 1875 a group of Boston citizens held a meeting in Faneuil Hall to denounce the use of federal troops to uphold Republican control of Louisiana. Wendell Phillips appeared at the meeting and spoke in defense of the Grant administration. He declared that the freedmen would be abandoned to the fury of unreconstructed whites if federal protection was withdrawn. "When the negro looks around on the State government about him and sees no protection," said Phillips, "has he not a full right, an emphatic right, to say to the National Government at Washington, 'Find a way to protect me, for I am a citizen of the United States'?" Phillips would consider himself "wanting in my duty as an old Abolitionist [loud hissing and applause] if I did not do everything in my power . . . to prevent a word going out from this hall that will make a negro or a white Republican more exposed to danger and more defenseless."[8]

In 1877 President Rutherford B. Hayes withdrew the last federal troops from the South. Phillips, Garrison, and many of their old abolitionist allies protested against what they considered this betrayal of the freedmen. Phillips had little faith in the pledges of Wade Hampton and other Southern leaders to respect and uphold the equal rights of Negroes. "To trust a Southern promise would be fair evidence of insanity," said Phillips in a bitter denunciation of Hayes's Southern policy. "What the South needs to-day is the element which Charlemagne, William the Conqueror and Cromwell contributed to their times—the heavy hand and fearless grasp which holds disorderly and struggling forces quiet—until peace tempts and wins to action the elements which mold our modern civilization."[9]

Hayes and his supporters defended the administration's policy on the grounds that disorder and violence had ceased in the South since the troops were withdrawn. "We are complacently told that this wonderful 'policy' has brought quietude to South Carolina and Louisiana, the shot-gun is laid aside, and blood no longer flows," wrote Garrison caustically in 1878. "Well, 'order reigns in Warsaw,' but where is Poland? . . . The colored people of those States have, by this process, been thoroughly 'bull-dozed'; their spirits are broken, their hopes blasted, their means of defense wrested from them: what need of killing or hunting them any longer? And is this awful state of things to be held up as something worthy of congratulation?"[10] Garrison never changed his mind about Hayes's policy, and shortly before his death he uttered a final rallying cry to the dwindling antislavery hosts: "While the freedmen at the South are, on 'the Mississippi plan,' ruthlessly deprived of their rights as American citizens, and no protection is extended them by the Federal Government . . . the old anti-slavery issue is still the paramount issue before the country."[11]

But the country wanted nothing more to do with "the old anti-slavery issue." The *New York Times* commented that "Wendell Phillips and William Lloyd Garrison are not exactly extinct forces in American politics, but they represent ideas in regard to the South which the great majority of the Republican party have outgrown."[12] Approximately 55 to 60 percent of the one-time abolitionists still alive joined Phillips and Garrison in deploring the abandonment of Reconstruction,[13] but their voices fell on increasingly deaf ears.

Garrison died in 1879 and Phillips in 1884, but a handful of their followers tried to carry on the old traditions. In 1886 Norwood P. Hallowell, an abolitionist who had commanded Negro soldiers during the war, spoke to a reunion gathering of his regiment. Hallowell praised John Brown and Robert Gould Shaw, another commander of black troops, who had died at the head of his regiment, as the greatest men of the Civil War era. "They did not die in vain," he told the colored veterans. "See to it that we whose good fortune it has been . . . to survive the casualties of war, do not live in vain." Negroes were still the victims of injustice in both North and South, said Hallowell, and so long as this was true "there is work to be done by those who revere the lives of John Brown and of Colonel Shaw."[14] Two years later Norwood's brother, Richard P. Hallowell, said that "protection of the colored people in their political rights as guaranteed by the Constitution" should be the most important issue before the country.[15]

At times it appeared that the Republican party agreed with Hallowell. Republican orators often waved the bloody shirt in the 1880s, and talked with seeming conviction about the necessity to protect Negro rights in the South. But the bloody shirt was little more than a rhetorical device. The federal government made no real effort to intervene in "Southern affairs" after 1877.[16]

II

Nearly three fifths of the old antislavery crusaders and their descendants still alive in the 1870s and 1880s resisted the retreat from Reconstruction. Some, at least, of the Northern liberals did not desert the cause of Negro rights. But what of the 40 to 45 percent who did sanction the withdrawal of troops? Did their attitude constitute a desertion of the Negro? What were the reasons for their apparent change of mind toward the race problem in the South? The answers to these questions are complex, and they can perhaps best be approached by examining the statements of some of the most prominent antislavery spokesmen for Hayes's policy. These people were more influential than the former abolitionists who denounced the abandonment of Reconstruction, partly because their ideas were in closer accord with Northern opinion by the mid-1870s, and partly because several of them were editors of powerful periodicals or newspapers.

The *Nation*, founded in 1865, effectively supported radical Reconstruction in its early years, but by 1870 this famous weekly had become an outspoken critic of Republican policies in the South. The *Nation* was largely abolitionist in its origins. George L. Stearns, Richard P. Hallowell, and J. Miller McKim raised most of the capital to launch the paper, which they hoped to make an organ for the cause of Negro rights and freedmen's education. When the first issue appeared in July 1865, Garrison gave his blessing to the *Nation* as the successor of the *Liberator*. One of Garrison's own sons, Wendell Phillips Garrison, was assistant editor of the *Nation* from 1865 to 1881 and editor from 1881 to 1906. The British-born Edwin L. Godkin, who had come to America in 1856, was selected as editor. Godkin had not been an abolitionist, but during the Civil War he was a staunch advocate of emancipation and the Republican party, and he was accepted as editor by George L. Stearns and Wendell Phillips after they had quizzed him at length about his attitudes toward Reconstruction and the Negro.[17]

Although Godkin may have appeared liberal on racial and social issues in 1865, his underlying conservatism and elitism soon emerged. He molded the *Nation* into an influential mouthpiece for the Brahmin elite of the Northeast, men of Mugwump outlook who were disgusted by the materialistic, get-rich-quick climate of the postwar period and its accompanying political corruption and crass ethics. Godkin quickly revealed an antipathy also to social reformers, including some abolitionists, whom he occasionally derided as "sentimentalists" (analogous to today's "bleeding heart liberals"). Almost the only "reform" he approved of was civil service reform, which would take the administration of public affairs out of politics and put it in the hands of intelligent people like himself.

This framework of attitudes soon produced disillusionment with Republican state governments in the South. In the early 1870s the *Nation* declared that some Southern governments were "an offence against civilization" run by "vulgar and rapacious rogues who rob and rule a people helpless and utterly exhausted."[18] At first Godkin directed most of his venom against the "carpetbaggers" and "scalawags," but increasingly he placed the blame for Southern misgovernment on the freedmen. In 1873 the *Nation* said of Negro voters in South Carolina that "as regards the right performance of a voter's duty [they] are as ignorant as a horse or a sheep." Godkin began to hint that the enactment of universal Negro suffrage had been a mistake: "After [seven] years' experience of the working of negro suffrage at the South," he wrote in 1874, "we . . . regret . . . that the admission of the negroes to the franchise was not made gradual, and through an educational test."[19] In 1876 the *Nation* concluded that Reconstruction was a failure because it had undertaken "the insane task of making newly-emancipated field-hands, led by barbers and barkeepers, fancy they knew as much about government, and were as capable of administering it, as the whites." Naturally the *Nation* approved of Hayes's withdrawal of federal troops from the South, and predicted that "the negro will disappear from the field of national politics. . . . As a 'ward of the nation' he can no longer be singled out for especial guardianship."[20]

The *Nation* was, certainly, a prime example of the desertion of the Negro by a periodical founded expressly to uphold equal rights. Of course, many of the abolitionist founders of the weekly considered themselves betrayed by Godkin, withdrew their support and capital from the *Nation*, and denounced it bitterly. But others, though they sometimes thought Godkin extreme in his statements, nevertheless continued their connection with the paper. Wendell Phillips Garrison remained as assistant editor, later as editor. J. Miller McKim retained his financial interest in the paper, and had a desk in the *Nation* office until his death in 1874. Horace White, a one-time supporter of John Brown, was a member of the editorial staff from 1877 to 1903. Henry Villard, son-in-law of William Lloyd Garrison, bought control of the *Nation* in 1881. Thus it cannot be denied that the *Nation* was, in some respects, a continuing legacy of the antislavery movement.

For thirty-five years Godkin's steady associate on the *Nation* was Wendell Phillips Garrison, who provided an interesting example of the transformation of a radical. From 1863 to 1865 young Garrison had written many articles and editorials for the *Liberator* and *Independent* advocating a "thorough" reconstruction of the South, including Negro suffrage and land reform, and had censured Lincoln for his cautious policies. Wendell was actually more radical than his father in these years. But after he joined the *Nation* in 1865, young Garrison came under the influence of Godkin's personality, and was soon parroting Godkin's mugwumpery, his elitism, and his disenchantment with Reconstruction. This led to some sharp exchanges between Wendell and his father, who had become a bitter critic of the *Nation*. In 1874 Wendell told his family that since the freedmen's "rights are now constitutionally assured, it will be no harm if they drop back . . . and refrain from taking a leading part in politics. They need more than anything else to have the gospel of education, thrift, industry, and chastity preached to them."[21] A month later, after a particularly strong anti-Reconstruction editorial in the *Nation*, William Lloyd Garrison complained to his son of the *Nation*'s "lack of sympathy with and evident contempt for the colored race. In all these respects it manifestly grows worse and worse, and utterly at variance with the hopes and expectations of those who took a special interest in its success at the outset."[22] Wendell's reply indicates how far he had departed from the faith of his father: "It is useless for you and me to exchange arguments on this matter. You see in every Southern issue a race issue, and your sympathies are naturally with the (nominally) weaker side." Wendell, on the other hand, believed that in the South and everywhere else "good government is first to be thought of and striven for, and that the incidental loss that it may seem to occasion to either race is far less mischievous than the incidental protection accorded to either by bad government."[23]

Other journalists with an antislavery background also became disillusioned with Reconstruction in the 1870s, though none went so far as the *Nation*. Another prominent civil service reformer who, like Godkin, thought the "best people" should rule, and who was eventually convinced that the best people in the South were whites of the upper and middle classes, was George William Curtis, editor of *Harper's Weekly* from 1863 until his death in 1892. Curtis had never officially joined an antislavery society, but he married the daughter of abolitionists and by the 1850s he was committed to the full range of abolitionist objectives. He was a militant racial equalitarian in the 1860s, and his editorials in the powerful *Harper's Weekly* were influential in the struggle for Negro rights.[24]

Long after many Northern intellectuals had become disenchanted with Reconstruction, Curtis still insisted that equal rights in the South must be upheld by federal power. "This is the very time to insist that the policy which has been adopted shall not be abandoned," he wrote in 1874. "No intelligent observer can doubt that [a restoration of white Democrats to power] would lead to a policy of oppression toward the colored race."[25] But by 1875 Curtis had begun to change his mind. The Fourteenth and Fifteenth Amendments, he declared, "do not change the national administration into a 'paternal government.' . . . Even when all citizens are made equal before the law . . . a great deal of injustice, disorder, and outrage will still remain. . . . [It] is not wise to expect the national power to do by force of arms what can be done only by moral processes and by time."[26]

In 1877 Curtis, after some hesitation, approved of Hayes's withdrawal of troops from the South. After all, he explained in *Harper's Weekly,* a policy of force had just not worked. All but two Southern states had been lost to the Democrats *under that policy.* Negro voters had been the targets of greater violence in states where federal troops had intervened than in states free from outside interference. Strong-arm tactics may have been necessary at first in the postwar South, said Curtis, but in the end they succeeded only in keeping a few power-hungry corruptionists in office. Efforts to enlist the friendship, loyalty, and cooperation of moderate Southern whites would in the long run provide better protection for the freedmen than the stationing of a few hundred bluecoats in Southern cities. The old policy of "hate and hostility" was bankrupt; it was time to try a new policy of conciliation and cooperation.[27]

Like *Harper's Weekly,* the *Independent* supported radical Reconstruction until about 1874, and then gradually retreated to an attitude of compromise that led to approval of Hayes's policy in 1877. The *Independent* had been founded in 1848 by Henry Bowen as a spokesman for the antislavery sentiment of the Congregational Church. Bowen was the son-in-law of Lewis Tappan and a confirmed though sometimes cautious abolitionist in his own right. As owner *and* editor of the *Independent* from 1871 until his death in 1896, Bowen proudly and repeatedly affirmed the abolitionist lineage of the paper.[28]

In 1874, amidst a growing outcry that Negro suffrage had proven a failure, the *Independent* denied that such a harsh judgment could be rendered after so short a time. "The negro, as a class, is entitled to patience and charity—or, rather, justice—at the hands of his Northern friends," declared the paper. "He is the victim still of three centuries of the white man's enforced degradation. How can he be expected to rise above it all in ten years? Give him a hundred, and then call him to account. Of the complete success finally of the experiment of negro suffrage, even in South Carolina, we do not entertain a doubt."[29] The *Independent* also insisted that the federal government must protect Negro rights with utmost vigor. Referring to the White Leagues in Louisiana, the paper demanded: "Crush them, utterly, remorselessly. They are Ku-klux under another name. . . . They are banded outlaws, sworn by intimidation, violence, or death to drive the negro from the polls and to restore white rule. . . . Crush them!"[30]

But 1874 was something of a turning point in the *Independent*'s attitude toward Reconstruction. While calling for charity—or justice—in judging the performance of Negroes, the paper itself sometimes betrayed a lack of charity. The stories of misgovernment, corruption, and outrageous conduct by Negro politicians in South Carolina caused the *Independent* to lament that "our colored fellow-citizens of South Carolina must do much better than they have done since [1867], or they will stagger the faith and disappoint the hopes of their true friends."[31] And not long after it had called for unremitting force to "crush" Southern oppressors of freedmen, the *Independent* abruptly proclaimed that "Congress should discontinue the system of special legislation in respect to the Southern States. The difficulties of the social problem in Southern society must mainly be disposed of by Southern society itself, and not by any outside power coming from Washington."[32]

Like several other abolitionists, Bowen had concluded that the race problem was more complex and difficult than it had appeared in the exciting, optimistic days of the 1860s. Constitutional amendments and legislation now seemed of limited avail in the face of Southern reality, and federal efforts at enforcement under President Grant seemed to worsen rather than help the situation. When Hayes inaugurated his policy of conciliation and good will toward the white South in 1877 the *Independent,* after a good deal of soul-searching, finally came out in favor of the policy. There seemed to be no viable alternative; the policy of the Grant administration had broken down, and the Hayes program at least gave some hope of a gradual, evolutionary improvement in race relations. Wade Hampton, L. Q. C. Lamar, and other leaders of the "better class" of Southern whites seemed well disposed toward the Negro and had promised that his rights would be protected. Negro statemanship had been less than a striking success, and the freedmen needed more education, experience, and religious uplift before they could take their rightful place as equals beside the white race. In the matter of Reconstruction, said the *Independent* in 1877, "we are passing from the era of force to the era of slow education." Force had failed, and "the question we ask, with no little anxiety is: Will religion and education solve the problem? Can they give us, at last, allowing them time enough, equality of political and social rights at the South? They *must*, for it is our only hope."[33]

III

This emphasis on time and education was a keynote in the thinking of many former abolitionists in the 1870s and 1880s. The impact of Darwinism on social thought was one cause of a transformation from immediatism to gradualism in theories of racial progress. The abolitionist movement had grown out of a complex interplay of intellectual, moral, and religious forces, including the Enlightenment's concept of natural rights, Transcendentalism's notion that human beings were basically good and capable of boundless betterment, and evangelical Christianity's belief in the immediate expiation of individual and social sins by conversion to God's truth. The reform and utopian movements of the 1830s and 1840s, with their emphasis on immediate social change produced by the purposeful action of men working in harmony with God's will, had formed the ideological substructure of abolitionism. The elements of immediatism in racial change envisaged by radical Reconstruction were, in part, products of this ideology. But by the 1870s many thinkers were beginning to apply the Darwinian concepts of biological evolution to social problems. Social change, they argued, could not be effected overnight by the conscious agency of man, but could develop only gradually, over a period of many generations, through the operation of natural forces beyond the control of man.

The effect of Darwinism on the social thought of some former abolitionists was exemplified by Abram W. Stevens, who had been converted to abolitionism as a young man in the 1850s. For twenty years Stevens was a radical reformer, hoping that his efforts would help cleanse America of sin and evil. The Thirteenth, Fourteenth, and Fifteenth Amendments had seemed to herald the dawn of racial equality. But by 1875 the impact of Darwinism plus the failure of Reconstruction to achieve the millennium had caused Stevens to change his mind. Emotionally he still shared the hope that "a messiah and a millennium are sure to come, whereby and wherein every evil will be changed to good." But intellectually he now rejected this hope. "It seems to me," Stevens wrote, "the the great gospel of the nineteenth century is the discovery of Evolution," and one of the main lessons of Darwin's (and Herbert Spencer's) revelation was that "all our efforts at reform, all our struggle and striving, are for naught. . . . We see that everything does not depend upon us alone, to make society what it should be,—that Nature works even while we are asleep." Once we learn the lesson of evolution "we become, not content with evil, but patient with it." Social change "that is hastened or brought about by violent means is, so far as true progress is concerned, a *stumble,* not a step. It may be questioned if even the antislavery reform were not at last consummated too precipitately; if a more gradual emancipation, including a preparatory education for freedom, might not have been better." Darwinism did not teach, said Stevens, that man should sit back and let Nature do all the work. But man's efforts should be those that work *with* evolution, not those that try to hurry it up, transcend it, bypass it. Education and the gradual amelioration of mitigable wrongs were the best means of working with Nature. "In *formation* rather than re-formation is my faith," concluded Stevens. "And for this work the 'eternal years of God' are needed; and all 'evils' incident to its gradual accomplishment we must be patient and brave to endure."[34]

Few other former abolitionists articulated Darwinist ideas so clearly as Stevens, but several of them were influenced directly or indirectly by the new Darwinian intellectual climate. James Russell Lowell, erstwhile poet and essayist of the antislavery movement, said in 1876 that radical Reconstruction had been based on the mistaken assumption, which he had once shared, that "human nature is as clay in the hands of a potter instead of being, as it is, the result of a long past & only to be reshaped by the slow influences of an equally long future."[35] One of the first and most faithful of the Garrisonian abolitionists, Oliver Johnson, declared in an 1877 editorial approving Hayes's Southern policy that "neither laws nor bayonets can remove the prejudices of race and social condition. For this time and patience are indispensable."[36] Referring to the condition of the Negro in 1884, George William Curtis admitted that it was far from perfect. But "little more can be done by means of law, and . . . the harmonizing and healing influence of time, with the steady pressure of sound sentiment and of the obvious interest of both races, [will] gradually complete the good work which, at least, is begun."[37]

For some erstwhile abolitionists, facile references to education and "the healing influence of time" no doubt served as rationalizations for a growing indifference to Negro rights. But for others, these concepts had genuine meaning and applicability. The abolitionists active in educational and religious missions to the freedmen did not believe that approval of Hayes's Southern policy necessarily constituted an abandonment of the Negro. "Our work," wrote one of them, "is more fundamental and important than that of either Congresses or courts." The "only safeguard" of the freedman's rights was "in his fitness to exercise and his ability to maintain them." Only through education and the development of Christian character could this fitness be attained: "Intelligence and virtue are the . . . two great pillars of the porch of American citizenship and liberty. While it rests on anything else, it is uncertain and unsafe."[38]

Several prominent Negroes concurred in this shift of emphasis from agitation and protest to education and uplift in the 1870s. John Mercer Langston, a Negro abolitionist, lawyer, and one-time dean of Howard University Law Schools, praised the motives of "earnest and tried friends of the colored people" such as Garrison and Phillips who had denounced Hayes's withdrawal of troops from the South as a sellout of the freedmen. But Langston warmly approved

Hayes's policy, and stated that the best way for the Negro to "become self-reliant and self-supporting" was through education plus economic and political "reconciliation" with Southern whites.[39] George T. Downing, a Negro businessman and formerly a militant equalitarian, sanctioned Hayes's policy and declared that the Negro race "will have to bide its time, get means, apply itself, struggle hard, become educated and skilled more in the science of government than fourteen years of freedom admits of."[40]

There has always been a tension in American Negro thought between protest and accommodation. In the two decades after Reconstruction the accommodationist viewpoint, with its accompanying emphasis on self-help, education, and uplift, gained considerable strength in the Negro community, paving the way for Booker T. Washington's enunciation of the Atlanta Compromise in 1895.[41] The tension and interaction between protest and accommodation among Negro leaders was paralleled by a similar tension between the old agitation-immediatist tradition and the new emphasis on time and education among former white abolitionists. Most of the Negroes and whites who stressed education, uplift, and gradualism did not believe they were "abandoning" the cause of equal rights; rather they looked upon their efforts as the only avenue by which the Negro could in the long run attain the character and ability to render these rights real and meaningful.

IV

Throughout American history, education has been considered an important remedy for social ills, and the faith in the schoolhouse as an instrument of racial progress after the Civil War fits comfortably into this tradition. Former abolitionists did more than talk about education for the Negro. During and after the Civil War dozens of freedmen's aid societies, most of them organized by abolitionists, set up hundreds of schools for emancipated slaves. Thousands of abolitionists and their sons and daughters went into the South to teach the freedmen. Many of the education societies had dissolved by the early 1870s but several of the larger associations, sustained by Northern churches, continued their work for many decades: the American Missionary Association, the Freedmen's Aid Society of the Methodist Episcopal Church, the Baptist Home Mission Society, the Friends' Freedmen's Relief Association, and others. These organizations had been founded largely by abolitionists within the various denominations, and their work was carried on after the war in substantial measure by men and women of antislavery background. The American Missionary Association and the Methodist and Baptist societies supported scores of academies and normal schools for Negro teachers and founded or lent support to several institutions that became the leading Negro colleges of the South: Atlanta, Fisk, and Howard Universities, Berea, Tougaloo, Talladega, Morehouse, and Spelman Colleges, Meharry Medical School, Hampton Institute, and others. Many abolitionists were on the faculties of these schools, and former abolitionists or their descendants served as presidents of Howard University from 1877 to 1889, of Atlanta University from 1867 to 1922, of Berea College from 1869 to 1920, of Fisk University from 1875 to 1900, and of several other institutions during this period.[42]

Living and working among the freedmen and witnessing at first hand their foibles as well as their virtues, some of these educators were among the earliest abolitionists to shift emphasis from equalitarian agitation and legislation to education and uplift. The American Missionary Association declared in 1875 that constitutional amendments and statute laws had destroyed the "superstructure" of slavery but had left the "foundation" untouched. The foundation was the "antagonism of races, the ignorance of the blacks, and the prejudices of the whites" which were "embedded in the *minds and hearts* of men" and "can only be overcome by education."[43] In 1877 Richard Rust, an abolitionist of long standing who was executive secretary of the Freedmen's Aid Society of the Methodist Episcopal Church, wrote that emancipation and Reconstruction had not freed the Negro from the bondage of "ignorance and degradation" imposed by slavery. It was impossible to expect a people worn down by "centuries of heathenism and oppression" to "come forth clothed with all the qualifications of citizenship. Christian

education, the development of heart and intellect . . . the
education which our schools impart, is the only hope of this
unfortunate people. Nothing else can free it from the dis-
abilities of the past, protect it from the perils of the present,
and prepare it for the mission of the future."[44]

This emphasis on "preparation" of the freedmen for the
rights and responsibilities of citizenship led some of the abolitionist educators to anticipate the gradualism of Booker T.
Washington. And the necessity of avoiding direct or provoca-
tive confrontation with the prejudices and power structure
of the white South if their institutions were to survive caused
others to anticipate Washington's reluctance to speak out
boldly against discrimination. But most of them never lost
sight of their ultimate goal of first-class citizenship for the
Negro, and some were surprisingly outspoken in their criticism of Southern mores. Though the teachers of the freedmen were often narrowly moralistic, excessively pious, or
offensive in their racial paternalism, they were nevertheless
in some respects the real heroes of their age. The unquench-
able religious faith and deep-rooted abolitionist convictions
of many gave them the strength to persist in the face of Southern white hostility, Northern indifference, personal hard-
ship, and countless disappointments in their work. Their belief in education as the chief remedy for the race problem
may have been misplaced, but their contributions to racial
progress were considerable and constituted perhaps the most
enduring legacy of the antislavery movement.

V

A major objective of Hayes's (and of his Republican successors') Southern policy was to encourage the development of
a two-party system in the South by taking the race issue out
of sectional politics and thereby removing the outside pressure that had forced nearly all Southern whites into the
Democratic party. Hayes hoped that once the color line was
removed from politics both parties would appeal to the Negro vote, thus creating the circumstances in which Southern
promises to respect freedmen's rights could be fulfilled. Several former abolitionists were optimistic that Hayes's program would serve the best interests of the Negro in the long

run, and in the late 1870s and 1880s they discerned signs that the "let-alone" policy toward the South was really working.

In 1878 Thomas Wentworth Higginson took a trip through the South Atlantic states to observe conditions and visit some of the veterans of the Negro regiment he had commanded in the Civil War. Higginson, who professed to view the South with "the eyes of a tolerably suspicious abolitionist," claimed that he found plenty of evidence of Negro prosperity and advancement under the Hayes policy. Wade Hampton's promises in South Carolina were being carried out, Negroes continued to vote and hold office in the state, and there were few signs of a reaction in the direction of wholesale disfranchisement. Most of the soldiers from his old regiment, said Higginson, "agreed that wherever the Democratic party itself began to divide on internal or local questions, each wing was ready to conciliate and consequently defend the colored vote, for its own interest, just as Northern politicians conciliate the Irish vote, even while they denounce it."[45]

In the late 1870s and early 1880s the Democratic party in several Southern states split into factions, with one faction sometimes forming a coalition with the Republicans or with the Negro vote. In Virginia the "Readjusters" under the leadership of William Mahone controlled the state government for several years with Republican support. The *Boston Transcript,* edited by William Hovey from 1875 to 1881 and Edward Clement from 1881 to 1906, both of them sons of Massachusetts abolitionists, declared in 1880 that the independent movements in Virginia and elsewhere "are pretty good evidence of the continuing and increasing disintegration of the solid South." Mahone's party was accomplishing "the wiping out of class and race distinctions, and placing Virginia alongside of Massachusetts in a national sense."[46] In 1885 the *Nation* stated that "the lively bidding for negro votes by the rival white parties in the recent contest over prohibition in Atlanta is only one of a number of signs that the color line in politics is vanishing throughout the South."[47]

The "New South" ideology of social and political regeneration through industrial progress captured the imagination of some Northern liberals, who believed that economic modernization of the South would improve the condition of both races and soften the racial animosities associated with an agrarian past and slavery. William D. Kelley, the famous high-tariff congressman from Pennsylvania who had been an outspoken champion of Negro rights during Reconstruction and whose wife was a Quaker abolitionist, toured the South in 1886 and praised the contribution of industrialization to racial melioration.[48] Edward Atkinson, a spokesman for the New England textile industry who had been involved with some phases of the abolitionist movement in the 1850s and 1860s, was a prominent advocate in the 1880s of Southern betterment through economic partnership with the North.[49] The *Boston Transcript* rejoiced that the South was becoming a "peaceful, law-respecting, industrious" section "devoted to business first and politics afterwards. . . . The freedman will . . . share in this general improvement." Southern ideals in the 1880s, said the *Transcript,* were different from those of slavery times. "Work and money have brought into vogue new ideals, new tests and new ambitions in Southern society. Capital is, after all, the greatest agent of civilization. . . . Money is the great emollient for social abrasions, and the two races . . . will move kindly together when wealth is more evenly divided between them."[50]

To bolster these optimistic conclusions the editors of the *Transcript* and others of similar outlook publicized every shred of evidence that seemed to illustrate progress in race relations. The *Transcript* noted that the Republicans polled 41½ percent of the major party vote in the former Slave States in the presidential election of 1884, a gain of nearly 1½ percent over 1880. In 1888 the Republican vote slipped back to 40 percent, but Benjamin Harrison nearly carried Virginia and West Virginia; the Republicans did well in other border states, and elected several Southern congressmen. The Republican party, declared the *Transcript* in 1888, was becoming "a power in the South by enlisting intelligent leadership there and so dividing the colored vote, thus doing away with its suppression in a natural manner without force from the outside."[51] Wendell Phillips Garrison conceded in 1888 that Negroes were often deprived of political power by various subterfuges, but they still had the legal rights granted during Reconstruction "and the nominal preservation of the suffrage is rapidly turning to real, and will in time enable them to take a hand in redressing the wrongs of legislation which yet remain. . . . The colored people have Hayes to thank for the happiest years of their lives since emancipation."[52]

Much of this talk about the promising state of affairs in the South was probably wishful thinking subconsciously calculated to assuage consciences that may have felt guilty about the Compromise of 1877. But there was some truth in a portrait of the South in the 1880s where the Negro's condition, though not ideal, at least gave promise of a gradual broadening of rights and opportunities. C. Vann Woodward and others have shown that Negroes continued to vote and hold office in substantial numbers in the 1880s, that rigid codification of Jim Crow practices had not yet taken place, and that not all the doors to better race relations in the South had yet been closed.[53] Certainly the optimism with which some Northern liberals viewed the South in the 1880s was not entirely rooted in fantasy. As they saw it, the situation during the decade after Reconstruction was better in some respects than the decade *of* Reconstruction with its turmoil, violence, hatred, and race conflicts of which the Negro was the chief victim.

VI

But events after 1890 eroded whatever basis for confidence had existed earlier. The decade of the 1890s produced a severe economic depression and a greater degree of social tension than ever before in American history. Political upheaval, the Populist movement, labor violence, jingoism, nativism, and a deterioration in race relations were some of the manifestations of this tension. The early 1890s saw an increase in the lynching rate; after 1892 the annual number of lynchings gradually declined, but the *percentage* of lynch-mob victims who were Negro rose sharply. Moreover, the lynching of Negroes was increasingly accompanied by sadism and torture and accomplished by burning at the stake. Lynching bees frequently became the occasion for a holiday, with thousands watching the saturnalia of mutilation, torture, and burning flesh. So while the total number of lynchings declined after 1892, the practice became more visible and its manifestations more ugly, stark, and alarming. In the two decades after 1890 the Southern states disfranchised all but a handful of Negro voters by means of poll taxes, white primaries, and literacy or property qualifications that were enforced against Negroes but not against whites. During the same years the Southern states also enacted a host of Jim Crow laws that segregated the Negro in virtually every aspect of public life. The conservative leaders of the South, the "Redeemers" who had ruled their states since the 1870s and who retained some of the paternalistic attitudes of slavery toward the Negro, were replaced after 1890 by a new breed of Southern politicians, the Ben Tillmans and James Vardamans and Jeff Davises who represented the "redneck" voters and whose chief stock in trade was often a virulent racism. At the same time the growth of scientific racism and the cult of Anglo-Saxon supremacy, the advent of imperialism, and the beginnings of the northward migration of Negroes produced a broadening anti-Negro sentiment in the North as well as the South. In the decade from 1898 to 1908 there were race riots at Wilmington, North Carolina, New York, New Orleans, Atlanta, and Springfield, Illinois.

These developments undermined much of the optimism of the 1880s. For a time many Northerners of antislavery descent placed their hopes in Booker T. Washington's formula for racial progress. But in the 1890s and 1900s some of these people began to feel a growing sense of desperation, anger, and militancy. The faith in gradualism, the trust in the good will of Southern whites, and the hope that evolution and education would solve the race problem broke down amidst the retrogressive events from 1890 to 1910. The "new slavery" in the South, as some former abolitionists termed it, produced a new abolitionism in the North. This new abolitionism was not so strident, radical, or well publicized as the old abolitionism of the 1830s, but it nevertheless represented a conscious revival of the antislavery impulse. The founding of the NAACP in 1909–1910 was, in part, the fruition of this new abolitionist movement.

The *Boston Transcript,* edited by Edward Clement, had been in the 1880s one of the foremost advocates of gradualism and good will toward the South. But events in the next decade caused Clement to despair of this approach to the race problem. As early as 1889 the *Transcript* declared that "race rancor" was "increasing in inverse ratio to the distance from slavery, instead of dying out. At this rate a worse civil war than that of 1861–65 will come in a few generations."[54] In the 1890s Clement became an outspoken critic of lynching and disfranchisement. He termed South Carolina's disfranchisement of Negroes in 1895 "The New Nullification," and declared that the Supreme Court's decision in Williams *v.* Mississippi (1898) upholding the disfranchisement clauses of Mississippi's 1890 constitution "wiped out as with a sponge" the "entire work of the Republican party, so far as the political rights of the southern negro are concerned."[55] In 1899 the *Transcript* lamented that "the old slavery prejudice" was "almost as strong today as it was forty years ago." There was a "new crusade against the negro" to "deprive the black race of citizenship" which must be met by a revived crusade to protect that citizenship.[56]

Wendell Phillips Garrison was also shaken out of his earlier complacency toward the race problem by events in the 1890s. In 1895 he wrote that lynching and disfranchisement were signs of "the unchanged spirit of slavery."[57] In 1903 Garrison told one of his brothers that "the great debate of the last century will be renewed in our latter years as it seemed settled in Father's." The "wave of reaction on the negro question," said Wendell, must "raise a counter wave of conscience" as it had done in the days of abolitionism.[58]

Other members of the Garrison clan expressed similar sentiments. William Lloyd Garrison, Jr., a successful wool merchant, became in the 1890s a prominent advocate of many reform causes, including woman suffrage, anti-imperialism, the single tax, and racial justice.[59] In many ways he seemed to be a reincarnation of his father. He told an audience of Negroes in 1901 that if it were possible "to resurrect the old anti-slavery guard today" they would view the racial situation with "sadness and astonishment." In the South "they would behold a race contempt unabated by emancipation, and lynching cruelties that exceed in savagery the deeds of Simon Legree." In the North, "instead of indignation and protest, they would see the old pro-slavery prejudice against color revived."[60] In 1906 Garrison proclaimed that "it is time for the colored people to organize for lawful self-defense and for white lovers of liberty to stand up for equal rights." The increasing oppression of the Negro "is the very recrudescence of slavery. It must be met with the undaunted purpose that the abolitionists displayed, for the conflict is the same irrepressible one. This Union can no more exist on the basis of the enfranchised whites and disfranchised blacks than could a Union half slave and half free."[61]

Fanny Garrison Villard said in 1911 that "father would have to begin his work all over again, if he were alive, for color-prejudice runs as high as in ante-bellum times."[62] Fanny's husband, Henry Villard, had purchased the *New York Evening Post* and the *Nation* in 1881, and had consolidated the two papers, making the *Nation,* in effect, a weekly edition of the *Evening Post.* Godkin remained as editor of the *Evening Post* until ill-health forced him to retire in 1899. When Villard died in 1900 the ownership of the *Post* and *Nation* passed into the hands of Fanny Garrison Villard and her son, Oswald Garrison Villard. Oswald, who soon became one of the leading journalists of the era, was very much aware that he was the grandson of William Lloyd Garrison. In 1898, soon after he had joined the *Evening Post*'s editorial staff, he wrote that it was his ambition to make the *Post* "a worthy follower of the 'Liberator.' "[63] After he took control of the *Post* in 1900 he began, with the help of Rollo Ogden and Wendell Phillips Garrison, editors respectively of the *Post* and *Nation,* to make these papers vigorous champions of racial justice. It had taken a long time, but the *Nation,* which William Lloyd Garrison in 1865 had hoped would become a worthy successor of the *Liberator,* finally fulfilled his hopes.

In the early 1900s Villard and his Garrison uncles were friends and supporters of Booker T. Washington. But after 1905 they became increasingly impatient with Washington's attitude. Villard wrote in 1909: "I grow very weary of hearing it said that Hampton and Tuskegee provide the absolute solution to this problem." With Washington "it is always the same thing, platitudes, stories, high praise for the Southern white man who is helping the negro up, insistence that the way to favor lies through owning lands and farms, etc., etc."[64] In 1905 a group of Negro militants under the leadership of W. E. B. Du Bois founded the Niagara Movement as a protest organization to agitate for Negro rights. Villard was in touch with Du Bois and his followers, and in 1906 Villard began to discuss with Mary White Ovington, a white social worker who was the daughter and granddaughter of abolitionists, the idea of organizing a national society of whites and Negroes to work for equal rights by challenging discriminatory legislation in the courts, forming political pressure groups, and holding protest meetings to arouse public opinion. Miss Ovington supported the project: she told Villard that "you and I were brought up on stories of heroism for a cause, and dreamed dreams of doing something ourselves some time."[65]

In the summer of 1908 a race riot at Springfield, Illinois, startled the country. Writing about the riot in the *Independent,* the Kentucky-born socialist William English Walling concluded that "either the spirit of the abolitionists, of Lincoln and of Lovejoy must be revived and we must come to treat the negro on a plane of absolute political and social equality, or Vardaman and Tillman will soon have transferred the race war to the North."[66] After reading this article, Miss Ovington arranged a meeting with Walling and Dr. Henry Moskowitz, and the three of them enlisted Villard to draft a call for a national conference to discuss the race problem. Villard's call, issued on the centenary of Lincoln's birth, proclaimed that " 'A house divided against itself cannot stand'; this government cannot exist half-slave and half-free any better today than it could in 1861. . . . [There must be] a renewal of the struggle for civil and political liberty." Among the fifty-two white signers of this call were at least fifteen former abolitionists or their children, including William Lloyd Garrison, Jr., Fanny Garrison Villard, Edward Clement, William Hayes Ward (editor of the *Independent*),

Horace White, and others whose memories and careers went back to the Civil War generation.[67]

The first meeting of the National Negro Conference was held in 1909, and out of the second meeting in 1910 grew the formal organization of the NAACP, which absorbed the Niagara Movement. The NAACP was literally as well as symbolically a revival of the abolitionist crusade. The two leading spirits of the NAACP in its early years were Villard and Ovington. Villard was treasurer of the Association and chairman of its executive committee; his organizational talent and ability to raise money kept the NAACP alive during these years.[68] The national president was Moorfield Storey, who came from an antislavery Boston family and had once been Charles Sumner's secretary. Francis Jackson Garrison was the first president of the Boston branch of the NAACP, and the executive committee of this branch contained several well-known antislavery names. Albert Pillsbury (a nephew of Parker Pillsbury) and Wendell Phillips Stafford were two of the most prominent white orators of the NAACP in its infancy. In 1911 the Association held a meeting to commemorate the centenary of Wendell Phillips' birth. The main speaker was Wendell Phillips Stafford, whose abolitionist parents had named him after the great orator. Stafford proclaimed that "we who have united to demand of the American people the rights guaranteed by the Constitution . . . have reason to believe that the master spirits of the earlier crusade are with us now. . . . In every charge we make against the forces of oppression we have a right to feel that Garrison and Phillips . . . are riding at our side."[69]

The NAACP revived some of the immediatism and fervor of the abolitionist movement. The race problem, said Villard in a 1911 speech on behalf of the Association, "will not work itself out by the mere lapse of time or by the operation of education. . . . There is only one remedy—that the colored people shall have every one of the privileges and rights of American citizens."[70] Francis Jackson Garrison said of an enthusiastic NAACP conference in Boston that "it seemed like an old-fashioned anti-slavery meeting."[71] During the NAACP's campaign in 1913 to arouse public opinion against the segregation of Negro civil servants in the Post Office and

Treasury departments, Villard responded to criticism that he was an extremist with the words: "No one who has ever made an impress in a reform movement has ever done so without being called a fanatic, a lunatic, a firebrand, etc. If in this cause of human rights I do not win at least a portion of the epithets hurled at my grandfather in his battle, I shall not feel that I am doing effective work."[72]

VII

A study of the antislavery legacy from Reconstruction to the NAACP reveals a greater complexity of attitudes and activities among former abolitionists than might appear at first glance. Many of them did not desert the cause of Negro rights in the 1870s, but persisted in the old faith until they died. Others modified their attitudes, and the nature of their modifications can tell us something about the Northern retreat from Reconstruction, the disenchantement with immediatism, the impact of Darwinism, the confidence in education, and the revival of militancy after 1890 in the face of the Negro's deteriorating status. Many of the Northern liberals who became disillusioned with Reconstruction in the 1870s did not abandon their concern for Negro rights, but were genuinely convinced that reconciliation between North and South and the cooperation of the "best people" of both sections in behalf of education and economic progress offered the best hope for ultimate racial equality. Of course, some men and women of antislavery background grew indifferent to the Negro's plight, turned to other concerns, or disappeared from public view. But in the first decade of the twentieth century several white people of antislavery descent came together with a number of other liberal whites and Negroes to found the NAACP. The NAACP was, in some respects, a self-conscious revival of the antislavery impulse. Thus one can discern a thread of continuity between the old abolitionism of the antebellum era and the new abolitionism of 1910; the thread is frayed and almost broken in places, but a close examination of its strands can tell us much about the course of race relations between the end of Reconstruction and the beginning of the NAACP.

NOTES

1. Lerone Bennett, Jr., *Confrontation: Black and White* (Chicago, 1965), p. 91.
2. C. Vann Woodward, *The Strange Career of Jim Crow* (New York, 1966), p. 70.
3. August Meier, "Negroes in the First and Second Reconstructions," *Civil War History,* XII (June 1967), 126, 128-29.
4. James M. McPherson, *The Struggle for Equality: Abolitionists and the Negro in the Civil War and Reconstruction* (Princeton, 1964); McPherson, "Grant or Greeley? The Abolitionist Dilemma in the Election of 1872," *American Historical Review,* LXXI (October 1965), 43–61; McPherson, "Abolitionists and the Civil Rights Act of 1875," *Journal of American History,* LII (December 1965), 493–510; McPherson, "Coercion or Conciliation? Abolitionists Debate President Hayes's Southern Policy," *New England Quarterly,* XXXIX (December 1966), 474–97.
5. I am working on a book-length study of this subject, which will be based on a larger sampling. The present essay is a summary of ideas and conclusions that have emerged from my research thus far.
6. Wilson to Garrison, December 17, 1874, William Lloyd Garrison Papers, Boston Public Library.
7. *Chicago Tribune,* June 10, 1874.
8. *Boston Journal,* January 16, 1875.
9. *Boston Globe,* March 28, 1877.
10. *New York Times,* January 24, 1878.
11. Garrison to Wendell Phillips, October 30, 1878, W. L. Garrison Papers, Boston Public Library.
12. *New York Times,* June 1, 1876.
13. It is difficult to determine precisely the percentage of abolitionist approval or disapproval of Hayes's Southern policy. The attitudes of some have not yet been discovered. A few of those who expressed an opinion were equivocal; others qualified their position with certain conditions; still others changed their minds at least once in the years after 1877 as circumstances changed or seemed to change. The figure of 55–60 percent is based on a sampling of only sixty former abolitionists and their descendants. Further research will enlarge the sample, but will probably not alter the percentage decisively. A breakdown of the figures into categories of Garrisonian versus non-Garrisonian abolitionists and first-generation abolitionists versus their second-generation descendants revealed some differences, but because of the smallness of the sample these differences are probably inconclusive. Approximately 65 percent of the Garrisonians opposed the withdrawal of troops, while only half or slightly less of the non-Garrisonians did so. The second-generation abolitionists whose opinions have been discovered thus far split

in proportions similar to their elders: six opposed and four approved Hayes's Southern policy.

14. *Worcester Spy,* May 29, 1886.

15. Richard P. Hallowell to William Lloyd Garrison, Jr., November 2, 1888, William Lloyd Garrison, Jr., Papers, Smith College Library.

16. Four books that contain valuable accounts of the attitudes of the federal government, the Republican party, and Northern opinion toward the race issue in the decades after Reconstruction are: Paul H. Buck, *The Road to Reunion 1865–1900* (Boston, 1937); Rayford W. Logan, *The Betrayal of the Negro: From Rutherford B. Hayes to Woodrow Wilson* (New York, 1965); Vincent P. De Santis, *Republicans Face the Southern Question: The New Departure Years, 1877–1897* (Baltimore, 1959); and Stanley P. Hirshson, *Farewell to the Bloody Shirt: Northern Republicans and the Southern Negro, 1877–93* (Bloomington, Ind., 1962). These studies contain occasional references to a few former abolitionists, but no systematic or thorough analysis of their attitudes.

17. McPherson, *Struggle for Equality,* pp. 323–25. The standard studies of Godkin and the *Nation* (Rollo Ogden, *Life and Letters of Edwin L. Godkin* [2 vols.; New York, 1907]; Gustav Pollak, ed., *Fifty Years of American Idealism: The New York Nation, 1865–1915* [Boston, 1915]; and Alan P. Grimes, *The Political Liberalism of the New York Nation, 1865–1932* [Chapel Hill, N. C., 1953]) give only incomplete accounts of the founding of the paper. Frank P. Stearns, *The Life and Public Service of George Luther Stearns* (Philadelphia, 1907), pp. 332–38; William M. Armstrong, "The Freedmen's Movement and the Founding of the *Nation*," *Journal of American History,* LIII (March 1967), 708–26; and many letters, circulars, clippings, etc., in the Edwin L. Godkin Papers and the Wendell Phillips Garrison Papers, Houghton Library, Harvard University, provide the fullest background on the establishment and early history of the *Nation.*

18. *Nation,* XII (March 30, 1871), 212, and XIV (February 22, 1872), 114.

19. *Ibid.,* XVI (January 23, 1873), 50, and XIX (October 29, 1874), 278.

20. *Ibid.,* XXIII (August 24, 1876), 114, and XXIV (April 5, 1877), 202.

21. Wendell Phillips Garrison to Francis Jackson Garrison, December 31, 1874, W. P. Garrison Papers, Houghton Library, Harvard University.

22. W. L. Garrison to W. P. Garrison, January 25, 1875, W. L. Garrison Papers, Boston Public Library.

23. W. P. Garrison to W. L. Garrison, February 7, 1875, W. P. Garrison Papers, Houghton Library, Harvard University.

24. There are two biographies of Curtis: Edward Cary, *George William Curtis* (Boston, 1894); and Gordon Milne, *George William Curtis and the Genteel Tradition* (Bloomington, Ind., 1956). The circula-

tion of *Harper's Weekly* averaged nearly 150,000 during the Civil War and Reconstruction.

25. *Harper's Weekly*, XVIII (August 29, 1874), 710.

26. *Ibid.*, XIX (February 27, 1875), 171.

27. *Ibid.*, XXI (April 14, 1877), 282, and (April 21, 1877), 302.

28. For the early history of the *Independent*, see Louis Filler, "Liberalism, Anti-Slavery, and the Founders of the *Independent*," *New England Quarterly*, XXVII (September 1954), 291–306. For biographical information on Bowen, see his obituary in the *Independent*, XLVIII (February 28, 1896), 280.

29. *Independent*, XXVI (August 27, 1874), 16.

30. *Ibid.*, XXVI (September 24, 1874), 17.

31. *Ibid.*, XXVI (March 12, 1874), 16.

32. *Ibid.*, XXVI (December 24, 1874), 14.

33. *Ibid.*, XXIX (July 5, 1877), 16.

34. *Index*, VI (March 18, 1875), 127–28, and (April 15, 1875), 175.

35. Martin Duberman, *James Russell Lowell* (Boston, 1966), 276.

36. *Orange* (N. J.) *Journal*, March 17, 1877.

37. *Harper's Weekly*, XXVIII (December 6, 1884), 796. Abolitionists from religious backgrounds also spoke about the "ameliorating influence of time," though they ascribed its benefits to God rather than Nature. The *Independent* declared in 1877 that the Lord was on the side of racial progress: "His forces are slow forces. . . . To us the way may seem a slow one; but it is the sure one." (*Independent*, XXIX [July 5, 1877], 16.) Two years later Luther Lee, a Methodist clergyman who had been one of the earliest of the militant abolitionists in his denomination, wrote that the eradication of white prejudice and Negro ignorance caused by slavery "must be the work of time. . . . Deep constitutional and long cherished wrongs are not righted in a day." The race problem would eventually be solved "under a benign Providence . . . the color line [will] be blotted out, and the white man and the colored man shall sit together under the shadow of the same palmetto tree." *Northwestern Christian Advocate*, XXVII (October 22, 1879), 1.

38. *American Missionary*, XXXIII (January 1879), p. 1.

39. John Mercer Langston, *The Other Phase of Reconstruction, a Speech Delivered at Congregational Tabernacle, Jersey City, April 17, 1877* (Washington, 1877), pp. 8–9.

40. Downing to Frederick Douglass, March 19, 1877, Frederick Douglass Papers, Douglass Memorial Home, Washington, D.C.

41. August Meier, *Negro Thought in America, 1880–1915* (Ann Arbor, Mich., 1963), pp. 3–82.

42. The statements in this paragraph are based on a reading of many educational, religious, and secular periodicals for the 1865–1915 period, plus several studies of Negro education after the Civil War.

43. *American Missionary,* XIX (April 1875), 73–74.

44. *Northwestern Christian Advocate,* XXVI (January 2, 1878), 6.

45. Thomas Wentworth Higginson, "Some War Scenes Revisited," *Atlantic Monthly,* XLII (July 1878), 1–9; Higginson, "The Southern Outlook," *Woman's Journal,* IX (March 16, 1878), 81.

46. *Boston Transcript,* February 12, 1880, June 6, 1881.

47. *Nation,* XLI (December 10, 1885), 477.

48. Ira V. Brown, "William D. Kelley and Radical Reconstruction," *Pennsylvania Magazine of History and Biography,* LXXXV (July 1961), 316–29; William D. Kelley, *The Old South and the New* (New York, 1888).

49. Harold F. Williamson, *Edward Atkinson: The Biography of an American Liberal* (Boston, 1934), pp. 3–27, 166–76.

50. *Boston Transcript,* July 16, 1877, August 11, October 21, 1885.

51. *Ibid.,* November 22, 1884, October 20, 1885, November 9, 10, 1888; the quotation is from November 9, 1888.

52. W. P. Garrison to Francis Jackson Garrison, December 19, 1888, W. P. Garrison Papers, Houghton Library, Harvard University.

53. Woodward, *The Strange Career of Jim Crow.* See also Frenise A. Logan, *The Negro in North Carolina, 1876–1894* (Chapel Hill, N.C., 1964); George B. Tindall, *South Carolina Negroes, 1877–1900* (Columbia, S.C., 1952); Vernon Lane Wharton, *The Negro in Mississippi, 1865–1890* (Chapel Hill, N.C., 1947); Charles E. Wynes, *Race Relations in Virginia, 1870–1902* (Charlottesville, Va., 1961). In Ch. 10 of *After Slavery: The Negro in South Carolina During Reconstruction, 1861–1877* (Chapel Hill, N.C., 1965), Joel Williamson argues that the basic structure of segregation in South Carolina (and by implication in other Southern states as well) was fixed during Reconstruction, and that there was no essential difference between the Jim Crow of the 1890s and that of the 1870s. The thesis is not entirely convincing: as Woodward states in the 1966 edition of *The Strange Career of Jim Crow,* there were many "cross currents and contradictions" in race relations during the 1870s and 1880s that were extinguished by the more aggressive and virulent patterns of segregation and disfranchisement of the 1890s and 1900s. (Woodward, *Strange Career,* p. 25 and *passim.*)

54. *Boston Transcript,* December 12, 1889.

55. *Ibid.,* September 13, 1895, July 20, 1898. The Court's decision in Plessy *v.* Ferguson (1896) and the general issue of Jim Crow in public accommodations elicited less concern than did Court decisions and other developments regarding lynching, disfranchisement, and peonage. The Plessy decision has come to have greater significance in retrospect than it had for contemporaries, who were more concerned with lynching, education, political rights, and economic opportunities than with segregation.

56. *Ibid.,* August 10, 1899.

57. *Nation,* LXI (November 21, 1895), 370.

58. W. P. Garrison to Francis Jackson Garrison, February 28, May 3, 1903, W. P. Garrison Papers, Houghton Library, Harvard University.

59. As in the days of the abolitionist movement, individuals participating in one reform cause often became active in others as well. Most of the former abolitionists supported woman suffrage, and many of them were active in temperance reform, the social gospel and social justice movements, or anti-imperialism. Indeed, there was a close connection between anti-imperialism and concern for Negro rights. All three of the living sons of Garrison, Albert E. Pillsbury, Moorfield Storey, Thomas Wentworth Higginson, and other former abolitionists were active in the Anti-Imperialist League. They saw the conquest and subordination of colored Filipinos as another manifestation of the ideology of white supremacy. On the other hand, a few former abolitionists were proponents of imperialism; they drew a parallel between efforts to bring the benefits of American civilization to the Filipinos and the post-Civil War mission of the freedmen's aid societies. Some former abolitionists active in the women's rights movements, particularly Susan B. Anthony, Henry B. Blackwell, and his daughter Alice Stone Blackwell, compromised and almost forgot their concern for Negro rights in their attempt to win suffragist support in the South.

60. *Boston Globe*, December 3, 1901.

61. *Springfield Republican,* November 17, 1906.

62. F. G. Villard to Francis Jackson Garrison, January 29, 1911, Fanny Garrison Villard Papers, Houghton Library, Harvard University.

63. Oswald Garrison Villard to Francis Jackson Garrison, April 28, 1898, Oswald Garrison Villard Papers, Houghton Library, Harvard University.

64. O. G. Villard to W. L. Garrison, Jr., February 24, 1909, O. G. Villard Papers, Houghton Library, Harvard University.

65. Mary White Ovington to O. G. Villard, May 6, 1908, O. G. Villard Papers, Houghton Library, Harvard University. See also M. W. Ovington to Villard, October 8, 1906, and Villard to Ovington, April 29, May 8, 1908, *ibid.*

66. *Independent,* LXV (September 3, 1908), 534.

67. Mary White Ovington, *How the National Association for the Advancement of Colored People Began* (New York, 1914). One of the most prominent of the former abolitionists, Thomas Wentworth Higginson, refused to participate in the first meeting of the National Negro Conference. He believed that the granting of universal Negro suffrage, without literacy qualifications, had been a mistake (even though Higginson himself had advocated such a policy in the 1860s). The Negro should now "turn himself to his industrial and educational development," wrote Higginson, rather than "strive for the establishment of a civil and political status which, whether or not his under existing law, can never be effectually attained or if ever, only through a conflict of terrible consequence."

(Letter from Higginson published in the *New York Sun,* May 30, 1909.) Higginson was a supporter of Booker T. Washington, and he regarded the National Negro Conference as a meeting of anti-Book-erites and thus refused to have anything to do with it. But two years later, shortly before his death, Higginson expressed a desire to join the Boston branch of the NAACP. (F. J. Garrison to Ellen Wright Garrison, May 11, 1911, O. G. Villard Papers, Houghton Library, Harvard University.)

68. The Oswald Garrison Villard Papers, Houghton Library, Harvard University, and the files of the *Evening Post* and the *Nation* provide abundant evidence of Villard's prominent role in the NAACP from 1910 to 1914. See also Charles Flint Kellogg, "Villard and the NAACP," *Nation,* CLVVVCI (February 14, 1959), 137–40. For Miss Ovington, see her autobiography, *The Walls Came Tumbling Down* (New York, 1947), which modestly understates her important role in the early years of the Association. Charles Flint Kellogg's detailed study, *NAACP: A History of the National Association for the Advancement of Colored People* (Baltimore, 1967), which appeared after this essay was written, develops the theme that the NAACP was a conscious revival of the abolitionist impulse. Professor Kellogg emphasizes the important contributions made by Villard and Ovington. Villard resigned as chairman of the executive committee in 1914 after a dispute with Du Bois concerning NAACP jurisdiction over the editorial policy of the Crisis. Du Bois refused to submit to Villard's authority, and won his point when Villard resigned.

69. Wendell Phillips Stafford, *Wendell Phillips: A Centennial Oration* (Boston, 1911), p. 27.

70. Boston *Herald,* April 2, 1911.

71. F. J. Garrison to Ellen Wright Garrison, April 6, 1911, O. G. Villard Papers, Houghton Library, Harvard University.

72. O. G. Villard to J. C. Hemphill, November 6, 1913, O. G. Villard Papers, Houghton Library, Harvard University.

URBANIZATION, MIGRATION, AND SOCIAL MOBILITY IN LATE NINETEENTH-CENTURY AMERICA

∾ Stephan Thernstrom

THE UNITED STATES, it has been said, was born in the country and has moved to the city. It was during the half-century between the Civil War and World War I that the move was made. In 1860, less than a quarter of the American population lived in a city or town; by 1890, the figure had reached a third; by 1910, nearly half. By more sophisticated measures than the mere count of heads, the center of gravity of the society had obviously tilted cityward well before the last date.

If to speak of "the rise of the city" in those years is a text-book cliché, the impact of this great social transformation upon the common people of America has never been sufficiently explored. This essay is intended as a small contribution toward that task. It sketches the process by which ordinary men and women were drawn to the burgeoning cities of post-Civil War America, assesses what little we know about how they were integrated into the urban class structure, and suggests how these matters affected the viability of the political system.

I

The urbanization of late nineteenth-century America took place at a dizzying pace. Chicago, for instance, doubled its population every decade but one between 1850 and 1890, growing from 30,000 to over a million in little more than a generation. And it was not merely the conspicuous metropolitan giants but the Akrons, the Duluths, the Tacomas that were bursting at the seams; no less than 101 American communities grew by 100 percent or more in the 1880s.[1]

Why did Americans flock into these all too often unlovely places? There were some who were not pulled to the city but rather pushed out of their previous habitats and dropped there, more or less by accident. But the overriding fact is that the cities could draw on an enormous reservoir of people who were dissatisfied with their present lot and eager to seize the new opportunities offered by the metropolis.

Who were these people? It is conventional to distinguish two broad types of migrants to the American city: the immigrant from another culture, and the farm lad who moved from a rural to an urban setting within the culture. It is also conventional in historical accounts to overlook the latter type and to focus on the more exotic of the migrants, those who had to undergo the arduous process of becoming Americanized.

This is regrettable. To be sure, immigration from abroad was extremely important in the building of America's cities down to World War I. But the most important source of population for the burgeoning cities was not the fields of Ireland and Austria, but those of Vermont and Iowa. The prime cause of population growth in nineteenth-century America, and the main source of urban growth, was simply the high fertility of natives living outside the city.

We tend to neglect internal migration from country to city, partly because the immigrants from abroad seem exotic and thus conspicuous, partly because of the unfortunate legacy left by Frederick Jackson Turner's frontier theory, one element of which was the notion that the open frontier served as a safety valve for urban discontent. When there were hard times in the city, according to Turner, the American worker didn't join a union or vote Socialist; he moved West and grabbed some of that free land. This theory has been subjected to the rather devastating criticism that by 1860 it took something like $1,000 capital to purchase sufficient transportation, seed equipment, livestock, and food (to live on until the first crop) to make a go of it; that it took even more than $1,000 later in the century; and that it was precisely the unemployed workmen who were least likely to have that kind of money at their command. It is estimated that for every industrial worker who became a farmer, twenty farm boys became urban dwellers.[2] There was an urban safety valve for rural discontent, and an extremely important one. The dominant form of population movement was precisely the opposite of that described by Turner.

Since scholarly attention has been focused upon immigrants from abroad, upon Oscar Handlin's "Uprooted," it will be useful to review what is known about their movement to the American city and then to ask how much the same generalizations might hold for native Americans uprooted from the countryside and plunged into the city.

Immigration is as old as America, but a seismic shift in the character of European immigration to these shores occurred in the nineteenth century, as a consequence of the commercial transformation of traditional European agriculture and the consequent displacement of millions of peasants.[3] Compared to earlier newcomers, these were people who were closer to the land and more tradition-bound, and they generally had fewer resources to bring with them than their predecessors. One shouldn't overwork this; a substantial fraction of the German and Scandinavian immigrants had enough capital to get to the West to pick up land. But some of the Germans and Scandinavians, and most men of other nationalities, had just enough cash to make it to the New World and were stuck for a time at least where they landed— New York, Boston, or wherever. They swelled the population appreciably and the relief rolls dramatically, particularly in the pre-Civil War years, when they entered cities which were basically commercial and had little use for men whose only skill in many cases was that they knew how to dig. Eventually, however, the stimulus of this vast pool of cheap labor and the demands of the growing city itself opened up a good many unskilled jobs—in the construction of roads, houses, and commercial buildings, and in the manufacturing that began to spring up in the cities.

That they were driven off the land in the Old World, that they arrived without resources, immobilized by their poverty, and that they often suffered a great deal before they secured stable employment is true enough. But these harsh facts may lead us to overlook other aspects which were extremely significant.

One is that immigration was a *selective* process. However powerful the pressures to leave, in no case did everyone in a community pull up stakes. This observation may be uncomfortably reminiscent of the popular opinion on this point: that it was the best of the Old World stock that came to the New—the most intelligent, enterprising, courageous. But this should not lead us to neglect the point altogether. The traits that led some men to leave and allowed them to survive the harrowing journey to the port, the trip itself, and the perils of the New World, could be described in somewhat different terms: substitute cunning for intelligence, for example, or ruthlessness for courage. Still, whatever the emphasis, the fact remains: as weighed in the scales of the marketplace, those who came—however driven by cruel circumstance—were better adapted to American life than those who remained in the village or died on the way.

The other main point about the immigrants, and especially those who suffered the most extreme hardships—the Irish in the 1840s and 1850s, the French Canadians in the 1870s, the Italians and various East Europeans after 1880—is that they appraised their new situations with standards developed in peasant society. Lowell was terrible, with its cramped stinking tenements, and factory workers labored from dawn till dark for what seems a mere pittance. Children were forced to work at a brutally early age; the factories and dwellings were deathtraps. But Lowell was a damn sight better than County Cork, and men who knew from bitter experience what County Cork was like could not view their life in Lowell with quite the same simple revulsion as the middle-class reformers who judged Lowell by altogether different standards. It is not so much the objectively horrible character of a situation that goads men to action as it is a nagging discrepancy between what *is* and what is *expected*. And what one expects is determined by one's reference group—which can be a class, an ethnic or religious subculture, or some other entity which defines people's horizon of expectation.[4] Immigration provided an ever renewed stream of men who entered the American economy to fill its least attractive and least well rewarded positions, men who happen to have brought with them very low horizons of expectation fixed in peasant Europe.

That those Americans with greatest reason to feel outrageously exploited judged their situation against the dismally low standards of the decaying European village is an important clue to the stunted growth of the labor movement and the failure of American Socialism. Working in the same direction was what might be called the Tower of Babel factor. A firm sense of class solidarity was extremely difficult to develop in communities where people literally didn't speak each other's language. Even in cases where groups of immigrant workers had unusually high expectations and previous familiarity with advanced forms of collective action—such as the English artisans who led the Massachusetts textile strikes in the 1870s—they found it hard to keep the other troops in line; a clever Italian-speaking or Polish-speaking foreman could easily exploit national differences for his own ends, and if necessary there were always the most recent immigrants of all (and the Negroes) to serve as scabs to replace the dissenters en masse.

A somewhat similar analysis applies to the migrants who left the Kansas farms for Chicago. They were linguistically and culturally set apart from many of their fellow workers; they too had low horizons of expectation fixed in the countryside and brought to the city. The latter point is often missed because of the peculiar American reverence for an idealized agrarian way of life. As we have become a nation of city dwellers, we have come more and more to believe that it is virtuous and beautiful to slave for fourteen hours a day with manure on your boots. Recently that sturdy small farmer from Johnson City, Texas, remarked that "it does not make sense on this great continent which God has blessed to have more than 70 percent of our people crammed into one percent of the land." A national "keep them down on the farm" campaign is therefore in the offing.[5] But it is damnably hard to keep them down on the farm after they've seen New York (or even Indianapolis), and it was just as hard a century ago, for the very good reason that the work is brutal, the profits are often miserably low, and the isolation is psychologically murderous. Virtuous this life may be, especially to people who don't have to live it, but enjoyable it is not—not, at least, to a very substantial fraction of our ever shrinking farm population.

This applies particularly to young men and women growing up on a farm. Their parents had a certain stake in staying where they were, even if it was a rut. And the eldest son, who would inherit the place eventually, was sometimes tempted by that. But the others left in droves, to tend machines, to dig and haul and hammer—or in the case of the girls, to sell underwear in Marshall Field's, to mind someone else's kitchen, or in some instances to follow in the footsteps of Sister Carrie.

There were some large differences between native-born migrants to the cities and immigrants from another land, to be sure. But the familiar argument that native workmen "stood on the shoulders" of the immigrant and was subjected to less severe exploitation is somewhat misleading. The advantages enjoyed by many America-born laborers stemmed more from their urban experience than their birth, and they did not generally accrue to freshly arrived native migrants to the city. The latter were little better off than their immigrant counterparts, but then they too were spiritually prepared to endure a great deal of privation and discomfort because even the bottom of the urban heap was a step up from the farms they had left behind. The two groups were one in this respect, and perceptive employers recognized the fact. In 1875, the Superintendent of one of Andrew Carnegie's steel mills summed up his experience this way: "We must steer clear as far as we can of Englishmen, who are great sticklers for high wages, small production and strikes. My experience has shown that Germans and Irish, Swedes and what I denominate 'Buckwheats'—young American country boys, judiciously mixed, make the most honest and tractable force you can find."[6]

II

The move to the city, therefore, was an advance of a kind for the typical migrant. Were there further opportunities for advancement there, or did he then find himself crushed by circumstance and reduced to the ranks of the permanent proletariat? Did his children, whose expectations were presumably higher, discover correspondingly greater opportunities open to them? Remarkably little serious research has been devoted to these issues. Historians who see American history as a success story have been content to assume, without benefit of data, that the American dream of mobility was true, apparently on the principle that popular ideology is a sure guide to social reality. Dissenting scholars have been more inclined to the view that class barriers were relatively impassable, an assumption based upon generalized skepticism about American mythology rather than upon careful empirical study. Some recent work, however, provides the basis for a tentative reappraisal of the problem.

We know most about mobility into the most rarified reaches of the social order regarding such elite groups as millionaires, railroad presidents, directors of large corporations, or persons listed in the *Dictionary of American Biography*. What is most impressive about the literature on the American elite is that, in spite of many variations in the way in which the elite is defined, the results of these studies are much the same. It is clear that growing up in rags is not in the least conducive to the attainment of later riches, and that it was no more so a century ago than it is today.[7] There have been spectacular instances of mobility from low down on the social scale to the very top—Andrew Carnegie, for instance. But colorful examples cannot sustain broad generalizations about social phenomena, however often they are impressed into service toward that end. Systematic investigation reveals that even in the days of Andrew Carnegie, there was little room at the top, except for those who started very close to it.

Furthermore, this seems to have been the case throughout most of American history, despite many dramatic alterations in the character of the economy. It seems perfectly plausible to assume, as many historians have on the basis of impressionistic evidence, that the precipitous growth of heavy industry in the latter half of the nineteenth century opened the doors to men with very different talents from the educated merchants who constituted the elite of the preindustrial age, that unlettered, horny-handed types like Thomas Alva Edison and Henry Ford, crude inventors and tinkerers, then came into their own; that the connection between parental wealth and status and the son's career was loosened, so that members of the business elite typically had lower social origins and less education, and were often of immigrant stock. Plausible, yes, but true, no. It helped to go to Harvard in Thomas Jefferson's America, and it seems to have helped just about as much in William McKinley's America. There were the Edisons and Fords, who rose spectacularly from low origins, but there were always a few such. Cases like these were about as exceptional in the late nineteenth century as they were earlier. The image of the great inventor springing from common soil, unspoiled by book-larnin', is a red herring. It is doubtful, to say the least, that the less you know, the more likely you are to build a better mousetrap. And in any event it was not the great inventor who raked in the money, in most cases—Henry Ford never invented anything —but rather the organizer and manipulator, whose talents seem to have been highly valued through all periods of American history.

These conclusions are interesting, but an important caution is in order. It by no means follows that if there was very little room at the top, there was little room anywhere else. It is absurd to judge the openness or lack of openness of an entire social system solely by the extent of recruitment from below into the highest positions of all. One can imagine a society in which all members of the tiny elite are democratically recruited from below, and yet where the social structure as a whole is extremely rigid with that small exception. Conversely, one can imagine a society with a hereditary ruling group at the very top, a group completely closed to aspiring men of talent but lowly birth, and yet with an enormous amount of movement back and forth below that pinnacle. Late nineteenth-century America could have approximated this latter model, with lineage, parental wealth, and education as decisive assets in the race for the very peak, as the business elite studies suggest, and yet with great fluidity at the lower and middle levels of the class structure.

Was this in fact the case? The evidence available today is regrettably scanty, but here are the broad outlines of an answer, insofar as we can generalize from a handful of studies.[8] At the lower and middle ranges of the class structure there was impressive mobility, though often of an unexpected and rather ambiguous kind. I will distinguish three types of mobility: geographical, occupational, and property, and say a little about the extent and significance of each.

First is geographical mobility, physical movement from place to place, which is tied up in an interesting way with movement through the social scale. Americans have long been thought a restless, footloose people, and it has been assumed that the man on the move has been the man on the make; he knows that this little town doesn't provide a grand enough stage for him to display his talents, and so he goes off to the big city to win fame and fortune, or to the open frontier to do likewise. When you examine actual behavior instead of popular beliefs, however, you discover that things are more complicated than that.

It proves to be true that Americans are indeed a footloose people. In my work on Newburyport, a small industrial city, I attempted to find out what fraction of the families present in the community in the initial year of my study—1850— were still living there in the closing year, 1880, one short generation. Less than a fifth of them, it turned out—and this not in a community on the moving frontier, like Merle Curti's Trempealeau County, where you would expect a very high turnover. There the true pioneer types, who liked to clear the land, became nervous when there was another family within a half day's ride of them and sold out to the second wave of settlers (often immigrants who knew better than to try to tame the wilderness without previous experience at it). But to find roughly the same volatility in a city forty miles north of Boston suggests that the whole society was in motion.

The statistics bear out the legend that Americans are a restless people. What of the assertion that movement and success go hand in hand, that physical mobility and upward social mobility are positively correlated? Here the legend seems more questionable. It seems likely that some who pulled up stakes and went elsewhere for a new start did improve their positions; they found better land, or discovered that they possessed talents which were much more highly valued in the big city than in the place they came from. What ever would have happened to Theodore Dreiser in small-town Indiana had there been no Chicago for him to flee to?

But the point to underline, for it is less commonly understood, is that much of this remarkable population turnover was of quite a different kind. As you trace the flow of immigrants into and then out of the cities, you begin to see that a great many of those who departed did so in circumstances which make it exceedingly hard to believe that they were moving on to bigger and better things elsewhere. There is no way to be certain about this, no feasible method of tracing individuals once they disappear from the universe of the community under consideration. These questions can be explored for contemporary America by administering questionnaires to people and collecting life histories which display migration patterns, but dead men tell no tales and fill out no questionnaires, so that part of the past is irrevocably lost. But some plausible inferences can be drawn about the nature of this turnover from the fact that so many ordinary working people on the move owned no property, had no savings accounts, had acquired no special skills, and were most likely to leave when they were unemployed. They were, in short, people who had made the least successful economic adjustment to the community and who were no longer able to hang on there. At the lower reaches of the social order, getting out of town did not ordinarily mean a step up the ladder somewhere else; there is no reason to assume that in their new destinations migrant laborers found anything but more of the same. When middle-class families, who already had a niche in the world, moved on, it was often in response to greater opportunities elsewhere; for ordinary working people physical movement meant something very different.

That is a less rosy picture than the one usually painted, but I think it is more accurate. And we should notice one very important implication of this argument: namely, that the people who were least successful and who had the greatest grievances are precisely those who never stayed put very long in any one place. Students of labor economics and trade union history have long been aware of the fact that there are certain occupations which are inordinately difficult to organize simply because they have incessant job turnover. When only 5 percent or 1 percent of the men working at a particular job in a given city at the start of the year are still employed twelve months later, as is the case with some occupations in the economic underworld today (short-order cooks or menial hospital workers, for instance), how do you build a stable organization and conduct a successful strike?

An analogous consideration applies not merely to certain selected occupations but to a large fraction of the late nineteenth-century urban working class as a whole. The Marxist model of the conditions which promote proletarian consciousness presumes not only permanency of membership in this class—the absence of upward mobility—but also, I suggest, some continuity of class membership *in one setting* so that workers come to know each other and to develop bonds of solidarity and common opposition to the ruling group above them. This would seem to entail a stable labor force in a single factory; at a minimum it assumes considerable stability in a community. One reason that a permanent proletariat along the lines envisaged by Marx did not develop in the course of American industrialization is perhaps that few Americans have *stayed* in one place, one workplace, or even one city long enough to discover a sense of common identity and common grievance. This may be a vital clue to the divergent political development of America and Western Europe in the industrial age, to the striking weakness of socialism here, as compared to Europe—though we can't be sure because we don't definitely know that the European working-class population was less volatile. I suspect that it was, to some degree, and that America was distinctive in this respect, but this is a question of glaring importance which no one has yet taken the trouble to investigate.

When I first stumbled upon this phenomenon in sifting through manuscript census schedules for nineteenth-century Newburyport, I was very doubtful that the findings could be generalized to apply to the big cities of the period. It seemed reasonable to assume that the laborers who drifted out of Newburyport so quickly after their arrival must have settled down somewhere else, and to think that a great metropolis would have offered a more inviting haven than a small city, where anonymity was impossible and where middle-class institutions of social control intruded into one's daily life with some frequency, as compared to a classic big-city lower-class ghetto, where the down-and-out could perhaps huddle together for protective warmth and be left to their own devices —for instance, those Irish wards of New York where the police made no attempt to enforce law and order until late in the century. Here if anywhere one should be able to find a continuous lower-class population, a permanent proletariat, and I began my Boston research with great curiosity about this point.

If Boston is any example, in no American city was there a sizable lower class with great continuity of membership. You can identify some more or less continuously lower-class areas, but the crucial point is that *the same people do not stay in them.* If you take a sample of unskilled and semi-skilled laborers in Boston in 1880 and look for them in 1890, you are not much more likely to find them still in the city than was the case in Newburyport.[9]

The bottom layer of the social order in the nineteenth-century American city was thus a group of families who appear to have been permanent transients, buffeted about from place to place, never quite able to sink roots. We know very little about these people, and it is difficult to know how we can learn much about them. You get only occasional glimpses into the part of this iceberg that appears above the surface, in the person of the tramp, who first is perceived as a problem for America in the 1870s and reappears in hard times after that—in the 1890s and in the great depression most notably. But what has been said here at least suggests the significance of the phenomenon.

So much for geographical mobility. What can be said about the people who come to the city and remain there under our microscope so that we can discern what happened to them? I have already anticipated my general line of argument here in my discussion of migration out of the city—which amounted to the claim that the city was a kind of Darwinian jungle in which the fittest survived and the others drifted on to try another place. Those who did stay in the city and make their way there did, in general, succeed in advancing themselves economically and socially. There was very impressive mobility, though not always of the kind we might expect.

In approaching this matter, we must make a distinction which is obscured by applying labels like "open" or "fluid" to entire whole social structures. There are, after all, two sets of escalators in any community; one set goes down. To describe a society as enormously fluid implies that there are lots of people moving down while lots of others are moving up to take their place. This would obviously be a socially explosive situation, for all those men descending against their will would arrive at the bottom, not with low horizons of expectation set in some peasant village, but with expectations established when they were at one of the comfortable top floors of the structure.

Downward mobility is by no means an unknown phenomenon in American history. There have been socially displaced groups, especially if you take into account rather subtle shifts in the relative status of such groups as professionals.[10] But the chief generalization to make is that Americans who started their working life in a middle-class job strongly tended to end up in the middle class; sons reared in middle-class families also attained middle-class occupations in the great majority of cases. Relatively few men born into the middle class fell from there; a good many born into the working class either escaped from it altogether or advanced themselves significantly within the class. There is a well-established tradition of writing about the skilled workman, associated with such names as the Hammonds, the Lynds, Lloyd Warner, and Norman Ware, which holds the contrary, to be sure.[11] This tradition still has its defenders, who argue that with industrialization "class lines assumed a new and forbidding rigidity" and that "machines made obsolete many of the skilled trades of the antebellum years, drawing the once self-respecting handicraftsmen into the drudgery and monotony of factory life, where they were called upon to perform only one step in the minutely divided and automatic processes of mass production."[12] Rapid technological change doubtless did displace some skilled artisans, doubtless produced some downward mobility into semiskilled positions. But defenders of this view have built their case upon little more than scattered complaints by labor leaders, and have not conducted systematic research to verify these complaints.

Careful statistical analysis provides a very different perspective on the matter. Two points stand out. One is that as certain traditional skilled callings became obsolete, there was an enormous expansion of *other* skilled trades, and, since many of the craftsmen under pressure from technological change had rather generalized skills, they moved rapidly into these new positions and thus retained their place in the labor aristocracy.[13] Second, it is quite mistaken to assume that the sons of the threatened artisan were commonly driven down into the ranks of the factory operatives; they typically found a place either in the expanding skilled trades or in the even more rapidly expanding white-collar occupations.[14]

As for workers on the lower rungs of the occupational ladder, the unskilled and semiskilled, they had rarely drifted down from a higher beginning point. Characteristically, they were newcomers to the urban world. A substantial minority of them appear to have been able to advance themselves a notch or two occupationally, especially among the second generation; a good many of their sons became clerks, salesmen, and other petty white-collar functionaries. And the first generation, which had less success occupationally, was commonly experiencing mobility of another kind—property mobility. Despite a pathetically low (but generally rising) wage level, despite heavy unemployment rates, many were able to accumulate significant property holdings and to establish themselves as members of the stable working class, as opposed to the drifting lower class.[15]

It may seem paradoxical to suggest that so many Americans were rising in the world and so few falling; where did the room at the top come from? The paradox is readily resolved. For one thing, our attention has been fastened upon individuals who remained physically situated in one place in which their careers could be traced; an indeterminate but substantial fraction of the population was floating and presumably unsuccessful. By no means everyone at the bottom was upwardly mobile; the point is rather that those who were not were largely invisible. Furthermore, the occupational structure itself was changing in a manner that created disproportionately more positions in the middle and upper ranges, despite the common nineteenth-century belief that industrialization was homogenizing the work force and reducing all manual employees to identical robots. The homogenizing and degrading tendencies that caught the eye of Marx and others were more than offset, it appears, by developments which made for both a more differentiated and a more top-heavy occupational structure. Third, there were important sources of social mobility that could be attained without changing one's occupation, most notably the property mobility that was stimulated by the increases in real wages that occurred in this period. Finally, there was the so-called "demographic vacuum" created by the differential fertility of the social classes, best illustrated in the gloomy late nineteenth-century estimate that in two hundred years 1,000 Harvard graduates would have only 50 living descendants while 1,000 Italians would have 100,000. The calculation is dubious, but the example nicely clarifies the point that high-status groups failed to reproduce themselves, thus opening up vacancies which had necessarily to be filled by new men from below.

For all the brutality and rapacity which marked the American scene in the years in which the new urban industrial order came into being, what stands out most is the relative absence of collective working-class protest aimed at reshaping capitalist society. The foregoing, while hardly a full explanation, should help to make this more comprehensible. The American working class was drawn into the new society by a process that encouraged accommodation and rendered disciplined protest difficult. Within the urban industrial orbit, most of its members found modest but significant opportunities to feel that they and their children were edging their way upwards. Those who did not find such opportunities were tossed helplessly about from city to city, from state to state, alienated but invisible and impotent.

NOTES

1. C. N. Glaab and A. T. Brown, *A History of Urban America* (New York, 1967), pp. 107–11.
2. Fred Shannon, "A Post Mortem on the Labor-Safety-Valve Theory," *Agricultural History,* XIX (1954), 31–37.
3. For general accounts, see Marcus L. Hansen, *The Atlantic Migration, 1607–1860* (paperback ed.; New York, 1961); Oscar Handlin, *The Uprooted* (Boston, 1951).
4. For discussion of the sociological concepts of reference groups and the theory of relative deprivation, see Robert K. Merton, *Social Theory and Social Structure,* rev. ed. (Glencoe, Ill., 1957) and the literature cited there. The problem of assessing the level of expectations of any particular migratory group in the past is extremely complicated, and it is obvious that there have been important differences between and within groups. But the generalizations offered here seem to me the best starting point for thinking about this issue.
5. *Boston Globe,* February 5, 1967.
6. Quoted in Oscar Handlin, *Immigration as a Factor in American History* (Englewood Cliffs, N.J., 1959), pp. 66–67.
7. For a convenient review of this literature, see Seymour M. Lipset and Reinhard Bendix, *Social Mobility in Industrial Society* (Berkeley, Cal., 1959), Ch. 4.
8. The main sources for the generalizations which follow, unless otherwise indicated, are: Stephen Thernstrom, *Poverty and Progress: Social Mobility in a Nineteenth Century City* (Cambridge, Mass., 1964); Merle E. Curti, *The Making of an American Frontier Community* (Stanford, Cal., 1959); Donald B. Cole, *Immigrant City: Lawrence, Massachusetts, 1845–1921* (Chapel Hill, N.C., 1963)—for my reservations about this work, however, see my review in the *Journal of Economic History,* XXIV (1964), 259–61; Herbert

G. Gutman, "Social Status and Social Mobility in 19th Century America: Paterson, N.J., A Case Study," unpublished paper for the 1964 meetings of the American Historical Association; Howard Gitelman, "The Labor Force at Waltham Watch During the Civil War Era," *Journal of Economic History*, XXV (1965), 214–43; David Brody, *Steelworkers in America: The Nonunion Era* (Cambridge, Mass., 1960); Pauline Gordon, "The Chance to Rise Within Industry" (unpublished M.A. thesis, Columbia University); Robert Wheeler, "The Fifth-Ward Irish: Mobility at Mid-Century" (unpublished seminar paper, Brown University, 1967); and the author's research in progress on social mobility in Boston over the past century, in which the career patterns of some 8,000 ordinary residents of the community are traced.

9. Recent work suggesting that even the most recent U.S. Census seriously undernumerated the Negro male population may make the critical reader wonder about the accuracy of the census and city directory canvases upon which I base my analysis. Some elaborate checking has persuaded me that these nineteenth-century sources erred primarily in their coverage—their lack of coverage, rather —of the floating working-class population. For a variety of reasons it seems clear that families which had been in the community long enough to be included in one of these canvases—and hence to be included in a sample drawn from them—were rarely left out of later canvases if they were indeed still resident in the same city. A perfect census of every soul in the community on a given day would therefore yield an even higher, not a lower, estimate of population turnover for men at the bottom, which strengthens rather than weakens the argument advanced here.

10. The assumption that discontent stemming from social displacement has been the motive force behind American reform movements has exerted great influence upon American historical writing in recent years. See for instance David Donald, "Toward a Reconsideration of Abolitionists," *Lincoln Reconsidered* (New York, 1956), pp. 19–36; Richard Hofstadter, *The Age of Reform: From Bryan to F.D.R.* (New York, 1955). Donald's essay is easily demolished by anyone with the slightest acquaintance with sociological method. Hofstadter's work, while open to a very serious objection, is at least sufficiently suggestive to indicate the potential utility of the idea.

11. J. L. and Barbara Hammond, *The Town Labourer (1760–1832)* (London, 1917); Robert S. and Helen M. Lynd, *Middletown* (New York, 1929), and *Middletown in Transition* (New York, 1937); W. Lloyd Warner and J. O. Low, *The Social System of the Modern Factory* (New Haven, Conn., 1947); Norman J. Ware, *The Industrial Worker, 1840–1860* (Boston, 1924).

12. Leon Litwak, ed., *The American Labor Movement* (Englewood Cliffs, N.J., 1962), p. 3.

13. This is evident from aggregated census data and from my Boston investigation, but we badly need an American counterpart to Eric

Hobsbawm's splendid essay on "The Labour Aristocracy in Nineteenth Century Britain," in *Labouring Men: Studies in the History of Labour* (London, 1964), pp. 272–315.

14. So, at least, the evidence from Boston and Indianapolis indicates; for the latter, see Natlic Rogoff, *Recent Trends in Occupational Mobility* (Glencoe, Ill., 1953).

15. The clearest demonstration of this is in Thernstrom, *Poverty and Progress,* Ch. 5. It might be thought, however, that the remarkable property mobility disclosed there depended upon the existence of an abundant stock of cheap single-family housing available for purchase. It could be that where real estate was less readily obtainable, laborers would squander the funds that were accumulated with such sacrifice in places where home ownership was an immediate possibility. It appears from Wheeler's unpublished study of nineteenth-century Providence, however, that the working-class passion for property did not require an immediate, concrete source of satisfaction like a home and a plot of land. The Irish workmen of Providence were just as successful at accumulating property holdings as their Newburyport counterparts; the difference was only that they held personal rather than real property.

AMERICAN

EXPANSION, 1870-1900:

THE FAR EAST

∾ Marilyn Blatt Young

> Tragedy comes to the nationalist because the
> setting of *his* kingdom of fantastic ideas is un-
> fortunately the world of reality.
>
> —Albert K. Weinberg, *Manifest Destiny*

PROMPTED perhaps by America's current military involvement in such traditional areas of imperialism as the
Caribbean and Southeast Asia, the past five years have wit-
nessed a resurgence of interest in the origins of American
imperialism. The inevitable revisionism is often only se-
mantic. Annexed islands are no longer colonies but (merely)
naval or coaling stations, as if this rectification of names at
one stroke eliminates the people living on the island and
confers on the possession itself a kind of immateriality.[1]
When this is applied to a heavily populated area like the
Philippines it is particularly inappropriate. It tends to hang
a veil over what was involved in acquiring that "stepping
stone" to China. The brutal suppression of the Filipino in-
surgency, comparable in many ways to the current American
effort in Vietnam, hardly fits an interpretation which, by its
language though not its intent, diminishes the sense of impact American imperialism had on other countries.

Several other tendencies mark the new evaluations of

American foreign policy in the last three decades of the century. In 1936, Pratt remarked that his noneconomic approach to the rising expansionist philosophy of the late nineties would "controvert . . . current fashions in historical interpretation."[2] The wheel has come full circle. The attempt to explain foreign policy in terms of the demands of American businessmen and the state of the American economy is currently being pursued with greater effort, and more intelligence, than ever before. Until recently, the flurry of island-grabbing at the turn of the century was understood primarily in terms of the Spanish-American War and its unforeseen consequences. Now the interpretive process has been nearly reversed and the war is frequently explained as the logical outcome of a policy of economic expansion pursued by, but not originating with, William McKinley.[3] Convinced that America was, or would soon be, suffering from overproduction, administrations from Grant through McKinley constantly sought to protect those markets America had and expand into those she had not. Differences of method are admitted but not stressed. The overall aim was the same: not an old-fashioned territorial empire, but a "new empire," whose rationale was commercial, whose style was "anticolonial."

The theory is an attractive, even compelling one and my disagreement with it is as much philosophic as evidential. All its proponents give full weight to the economic rhetoric of the late 1880s and 1890s while ignoring, or playing down, the religious, political, national, and racist rhetoric which was equally prominent. Thus, because economic motives are felt to be more realistic, the policy makers studied are understood as pragmatic, hardheaded men out for the sensible main chance.

Yet even a cursory reading of the materials will demonstrate the outlandishness of many of the economic claims urged by Americans in these years; in tone and formulation they are economic corollaries of the assertions of Duty and Destiny. "What seems almost bizarre in retrospect," a recent study by two economists reflects, "is the extreme rhetoric characterizing early pronouncements of new markets."[4] Nor was this only true of the period under consideration here. In

1851 the current industrial upsurge was greeted with warnings that "the accumulations of industry furnish us with a constantly augmenting capital that must seek new channels of employment."[5] Indeed the importance of the Far Eastern and Latin American markets to the health, wealth, even survival of the United States was a commonplace long before the industrial revolution rationalized it. In 1803 an enthusiastic New England congressman declared, "Geography points us to China, Persia, India, Arabia Felix and Japan." In 1848 it was asserted that "Asia has suddenly become our neighbor with a placid intervening ocean inviting our steamships upon the track of a commerce greater than that of all Europe combined." Perry's treaty with Japan was acclaimed as "the entering wedge that will, ere long, open to us the interior wealth of these unknown lands."[6] How do we distinguish between these claims and those of an acknowledged new-empire, open-door, insular imperialist like Senator Albert J. Beveridge who, in 1900, declared, "Our largest trade henceforth must be with Asia. The Pacific is our ocean"?[7] If everyone is everyone else's forerunner, historical analysis is an infinite regression and there is no way we can understand why something happened in 1898 and not 1888.

It is true, as William Appleman Williams warns us, that the failure of expectations to be fulfilled (in regard to the China market, for example) is "beside the point; at issue is the nature of American thought and action at that time."[8] Yet surely we cannot simply dispense with the objective situation. Was the predominant economic analysis of the period correct? Did America suffer, acutely, from overproduction? How important were foreign markets, and in particular markets in Latin America and Asia, to the survival of the economy? Unless we know the answers, it seems to me to be very difficult to evaluate the policies of McKinley and his predecessors. When the China market remained a dream only, was this because the government did not support business interests firmly enough, or because the initial analysis was incorrect? According to one study, exporters in the period 1895–1905 concentrated not on Asia or Latin America but on Europe. It was only in the following decade that underdeveloped nations became the focus of attention.[9] What was the actual capacity of China to absorb Western manufactured goods? In a largely self-sufficient village economy, how realistic were the ambitions of all Westerners in relation to their 400 million prospective customers? Despite the urgings of consular officials, business leaders, and politicians, American manufacturers in the period under discussion were slow to meet the trade demands of the Asian market. Members of the National Association of Manufacturers and the American Asiatic Association raised tireless paeans to the possibilities of a huge Asian market, yet manufacturers made little effort to adjust their products to Asian needs and the ex-Minister to China, Charles Denby, decried the unadventurous attitude of the business community which did not seem to "feel the necessity of cultivating foreign markets."[10] Exactly how important was government support to the expansion of America's export trade? One study indicates that where marketing techniques were vigorous and imaginative, American goods were able to maintain a leading position against all political odds; a lesser effort led to an early reduction of trade as the political situation became more unfavorable.[11]

These questions, which I shall not attempt to answer here, illustrate the degree to which the context of American policy remains unclear. While granting Williams' argument as to the importance of the subjective situation, it is impossible to discuss policy without a firmer grasp of the objective realities than is now available. Just as we do not accept Dean Rusk's public analysis of the causes of the Vietnam war, though recognizing the value of understanding why he believes what he does, so it would be foolish to simply accept, without further questioning, the rationale offered for their policies by the men of the late nineteenth century.

Recent analyses have stressed the peculiarly *American* nature of the empire built between 1870 and 1900. It was commercial, not colonial; it sought markets, not peoples to rule. Yet the resurgent imperialism of the Germans and English also stressed markets, investment rights, coaling stations to protect trade routes, and the like. When the Germans seized the port of Kiaochow in China it was only after a long period of abortive negotiations for a coaling station; they did not wish to colonize China. The exploitative rights which they extracted along with the port were justified in much the same way McKinley and others justified taking all of the Philippines rather than Manila alone: the security of the port and the proper enjoyment of the surrounding area.

The parochial attitude which discusses American imperialism without reference to the new imperialism of Europe is further illustrated in the persistent over-valuation of America's role in the Far East. From 1870 up to and including 1900, America was a secondary power in that area of the world, however much its nationals boasted of having "saved" China from disintegration. American policy was not without significance, but it was, at all points, less important than that of Great Britain, Russia, Japan, and even Germany. However interesting American Far Eastern policy may be in the context of the internal history of the United States, it would be a great mistake to believe that it was so regarded by other powers in the area or by China herself. The Chinese, whose foreign policy was reduced to a constant act of balancing one power against the other, used America as and when they could. To flatter the self-esteem of an American minister they might appear to throw themselves upon his mercy; at the same time identical appeals would be made to any other country which might possibly help in their current difficulty.[12] With few exceptions the Chinese found the United States unwilling to run any risks on China's behalf. Nor did American interests in China ever become substantial enough to permit an American administration basically to challenge the policy of another power for less altruistic reasons.

There can be no denying the fact that, by the late 1870s, there was widespread acceptance of the idea that expanding foreign markets were of vital importance to the nation.[13] Yet conflicts over policy did arise and it is utterly impossible to understand them if we identify anyone who advocated foreign trade as an imperialist. Differences of method were not necessarily less significant than differences of aim. Grover Cleveland's dispatch of a warship to protect American interests during the Brazilian revolution of 1893–1894 is not identical to Benjamin Harrison's scheming to acquire naval bases in Haiti and Santo Domingo, or to McKinley's dispatch of troops to the Philippines and China. I would distinguish, then, between annexationists, mild or extreme, and those who advocated expanding foreign markets through forceful diplomatic representation, the reform of the consular service, and the construction of an isthmian canal. Henry Cabot Lodge declared that he was opposed to a "widely extended system of colonization." What he did want, however, went far beyond the wishes of those looking simply to an expansion of trade. "We should take," Lodge told the Senate in 1895, "all outlying territories necessary to our own defense, to the protection of the Isthmian Canal, and to the upbuilding of our trade and commerce and to the maintenance of our military safety elsewhere. I would take and hold the outworks as we now hold the citadels of American powers."[14]

It seems clear that from the late 1870s on, there was general agreement that the government ought to concern itself with aiding American business abroad. William Evarts, Secretary of State under Hayes, was explicitly interested in expanding foreign trade and convinced of the responsibility of the government to foster its development. Through his efforts the State Department began, in 1880, to publish monthly consular reports whose statistics and assessments of trade opportunities would, it was hoped, be of substantial aid to businessmen.[15] But his view did not extend to the annexation of outlying territories, and he was unresponsive to the far-reaching plans of more aggressive State Department officials.[16] By the 1880s there may well have been a consensus view of the nation which held that the industrial revolution had effected a permanent transformation of the economy requiring a continuously rising tide of exports to maintain itself. The depression of 1893 appeared to confirm this. But the imperialists went on from this point. Their passionate demands for economic expansion were an integral part of a larger view which saw a strong navy, trade, political power, and the territory necessary, in their view, to maintain both trade and power, as complementary factors contributing to the wealth and strength of the nation.

Recent studies of the late nineteenth century continue to accept the 1890s as a major turning point in the history of American imperialism, but the forty years preceding them are also stressed. "The years between 1850 and 1889," Walter LaFeber writes, "were a period of preparation for the 1890s. These years provided the roots of empire, not the fruit."[17] Yet the gains LaFeber's overall view offers are balanced by a certain flattening out of history which it inevitably produces. One loses sight of the unique situation that each politician faced and the impact on his actions of day-to-day problems. Moreover, distinct changes are blurred as we follow the line of continuity. The policies of the Grant administration, for example, seem to me better understood as tied to the pre-Civil War type of imperialism than as an important link "in the chain of economic expansion running from Seward . . . and beyond."[18]

It was not at Grant's instigation that Commander Meade sailed grandly into the Samoan harbor of Pago Pago and signed a treaty of friendship and protection which gave the United States exclusive use of the harbor. Meade, true to the traditions of an older form of empire, was one of many American naval men who, "freely afloat at sea in different places, on their own motion cast about for stations and naval bases to serve as points of support for trade."[19] Indeed perhaps it would be better to look at Grant's foreign policy in terms of his total administration, whose dominant characteristic was one of grab. "The new capitalism," Matthew Josephson writes, "gave an immense impetus to official and political venality—*blindly,* by its own disorderliness and fiercely competitive character rather than out of regard for its own deeper interests."[20] The system of cooperation between businessmen and politicians which began to emerge in the 1880s and reached fruition after the turn of the century[21] had yet to evolve. The very fact that the White House seemed filled with men after " '*loot* and booty . . . ready for any Mexican invasion or Caribbean annexation . . . looking to excitements and filibustering and possibly a Spanish war,' " gave imperialism, in the Grant era a bad name, tainted it with corruption.[22]

The opposition to new departures in foreign policy was extraordinary and, in the wealth of imperialist moves described in recent studies, tends to be lost sight of. Blaine's interventionist and blundering pursuit of dominance in

Latin America under Garfield was repudiated, and Frelinghuysen's much milder moves similarly met with staunch resistance.[23] While an aggressive foreign policy might, temporarily, serve to divert attention from domestic issues, as during the Harrison administration, ultimately the voters reacted to the overriding internal problems. Harrison's imperialist efforts were not seen as advancing the interests of rich and poor alike, but as tied to the advancement of the "plutocracy." His defeat was a result of "his failure or inability to respond to the new popular forces which were beginning to appear in American politics."[24] A public newly sensitive to issues of national honor might, as in the Valparaiso case of 1891, be whipped up to war pitch. But a more sustained and broadly based support of radical foreign policies awaited the demonstration that the benefits to be reaped would be distributed among all the people, that the strength and power of the nation redounded to the glory of all its citizens. This, in 1896, the Republican party was able to accomplish, presenting itself successfully to the country as the party of "energy and change," dedicated to advancing "economic growth" and enhancing "national power."[25] For a time, at least, imperialism became both respectable and popular.

What is interesting is the conjunction, in the 1890s, of an intellectual imperialist elite, strongly influenced by European trends, and a public, seared by depression, which found their ideas welcome. It is essential, therefore, to understand the changes which had taken place in American society during the last decade of the century, changes which make comprehensible the mingled note of fear and triumph that dominates the rhetoric of this period.

Perhaps the major psychological factor operating in the years before the turn of the century was the fact, and the awareness of that fact by most Americans, that the country was no longer (if indeed it ever had been) homogeneous and united. Signs of disorganization, even disintegration, were everywhere. For Americans, no strangers to disunion and fearful of revolution, the years from 1885 to 1897 were anxious ones.

The pace of urbanization had increased tremendously.

The disrupting effect of such growth was intensified by the spectacular speed with which some cities grew. As opposed to the older urban centers, Chicago, for example, did not receive a steady flow of migrants but grew to a city of one million people in what was almost one great rush.[26] And while the service problems (such as sewage disposal, sanitation, and water supply) were no longer as serious as they had been in the cities of the early nineteenth century, the problems of social organization were much greater. Significantly, it was in the late nineteenth century that cities were first loved and cursed as "jungles."

The changing nature of immigration complicated the urban problem. A flood of impoverished alien people congregating in loathsome, sickeningly visible slums threatened and challenged the "native" American city dwellers. In every social group the city produced near-intolerable strains which each tried to meet in its own way. Everywhere clearly defined neighborhoods grew up—a geographical expression of self-definition.

People in the middle class began what proved to be a steady migration toward the suburbs where, behind white picket fences and neat lawns, they strove to demonstrate their ties with an older, simpler, native and rural America. Both upper and middle classes dissociated themselves, occasionally to the point of organized opposition, from the immigrants. For now to be an immigrant was to belong to the undifferentiated mass of unskilled workers.

The severe depression of 1893 gave actual shape to the anxieties that gripped America in its New World version of a *fin de siècle* pathology.[27] On one level, the depression weakened, perhaps destroyed, an earlier blithe belief in America's infinite material expansion. There was increased talk of economic stagnation, of overproduction, of permanent unemployment of large masses of people, of decay and decline. Fear of revolution was encouraged by two developments: the organization of the Populist party with its radical economic program, and the frequency of strikes and the actual warfare between capital and labor.

On the psychological level, the depression had an equally destructive impact. The prevailing ideology of social Darwinism, which in its most simplistic and popular form saw failure as evidence of personal inadequacy, added to the economic distress of being unemployed or bankrupt.

Other economic developments contributed to the tension and confusion of life in the nineties. The unorganized middle class found itself caught between two major contending forces: the nascent labor union movement and the increasingly powerful forces of big business. Reflecting in relative tranquillity some fifteen years later, Henry Adams saw the years of the great depression as ushering in "the capitalistic system with its methods; the protective tariff; the corporations and the trusts; the trades-unions and socialistic paternalism . . . the whole mechanical consolidation of force which ruthlessly stamped out the life of the class into which Adams was born."[28] The American dream of homogeneity, of an organic, infinitely progressive nation, had never before seemed so impossible of achievement.

One expression of the uneasiness that gripped American society at this time was the growth of a new, virulent, and for the first time nation-wide, nativist movement. The nativism of the nineties is distinguished from earlier movements by its intensity and its conscious, extreme nationalism.[29] Nativist nationalism offered two easy verbal solutions to the painful dilemma of a changed and unstable America. By blaming disunity on the evil influence of the new immigrants, it absolved from blame and protected from criticism the more basic contradictions in the economic and social system. If immigrants were the root of the trouble, the solution was comparatively simple: keep them out. Viewed as unassimilable, revolutionary, and inherently inferior, the immigrant could be made a convenient catchall scapegoat. Secondly, by indulging in an orgy of fervent nationalism, the reality of American life could be denied, even for the moment forgotten. As John Higham points out, the "two antiforeign movements—one international, the other internal—complemented each other, so that the jingoist atmosphere of the decade helps explain the depth and intensity of its nativism."[30]

It is in these terms that the emotional force of the Spanish-American War becomes comprehensible. The national neurosis described above was acted out in the fantastic fervor which preceded the war and perhaps made it inevitable. The pious references to "blue and grey marching together" were not empty bombast. The war was seen as a unifying force, killing Spaniards hand in hand a proof of that unity.

However, this general framework does not always explain why some policies were adopted, others rejected. In the Far East in particular, despite the tedious reiteration of the importance of Chinese markets, despite the ultra-nationalist boasts and the frequent opportunities for action, government policy was cautious in the extreme. In contrast to Latin America, where European powers were only minimally involved in a political or military way, China was a mare's-nest of rival claims. No amount of insistence on the purely commercial goals of American policy would persuade anyone; in China politics and commerce were one.

Yet this fact was only slowly acknowledged by the government and only fitfully and reluctantly acted upon. Efforts to assert American power for the benefit of American businessmen were, in contrast to European countries, noticeable by their absence. Opportunities were ignored or rejected in every case where pressure might have brought the United States into conflict with a European nation. On the other hand, pressure against China, which was helpless to resist, in areas which might advance American prestige without exciting the jealousy of other powers (as in missionary cases) was, in the 1890s, vigorously applied. For the convinced imperialist ideologues, as well as less ambitious politicians concerned only with staying in office, were faced with a fickle and unstable American public; a public not entirely convinced that its interests lay in "adventures" abroad. Moreover the business community, though always interested in government aid, was not consistently responsive to it. Everything dictated caution.

Thomas Bayard, Secretary of State in Cleveland's first administration, has been described as a "consistent Open Door expansionist."[31] He was outspoken in his assurances to American businessmen that the government would stand behind their enterprises in China.[32] Yet when he was faced with an actual enterprise, and one of vast proportions, Bayard retreated in haste. In 1886, Wharton Barker, a prominent Philadelphia banker, secured the very first concession ever granted by the Chinese government to a foreigner: the right to build long-distance telephone lines between the treaty ports. Moreover Governor-General Li Hung-chang, then at the peak of his power, hoped to establish, with Barker's help, a joint Sino-American bank which would in time finance railroads, mines, and a host of similar internal improvements.

Rumors of the Bank circulated in the foreign community in China, and the British-dominated English language press published "ponderous leaders against the scheme," calling the concessions rash, disastrous for China, tantamount to an American protectorate over the entire country.[33] Bayard's response was strictly to forbid Minister Denby to aid Barker and his partners in the face of rising European and Chinese opposition. It is true that one of Barker's colleagues was a dubious business risk and that the State Department had not been properly approached for aid by either Barker or his friends. Yet it is doubtful if these factors would have stopped the German, French, British, or Russian governments from exploiting the gains won by their nationals—however seedy.

The Sino-Japanese War of 1894–1895 revealed China's weakness to the world in all its fullness. The major powers acted swiftly to capitalize on it and within a few years the apportionment, though not the actual partition, of the country was well under way. Between the Treaty of Shimonoseki and the Boxer uprising (the period 1895–1900), China's railroads, mines, even some of her ports, were distributed among the European powers. At first, in contrast to Europe, the United States government tended to remain in the background, ready to help the curious group of Americans who arrived in Peking seeking concessions, but at no point instigating their activity.

Bayard's instructions to Minister Denby had been very strict: he was to make no representations on behalf of private Americans without prior State Department approval. Even Richard Olney's considerably liberalized instructions did not appreciably heighten the tempo of American economic activity. Without assuming any responsibility for American enterprises in the name of the government, Denby was to use his "personal and official influence and lend all proper countenance to secure to reputable representatives . . . the same facilities . . . as are enjoyed by any other foreign commercial enterprise in the country." Nor should Denby feel himself tied down by State Department rules:

> It is not practicable to strictly define your duties in this connection, nor is it desirable that any instructions which may have been given should be too literally followed. . . . Broadly speaking you should employ all proper methods for the extension of American interests in China. . . .[34]

In practice this meant supporting the efforts of the American China Development Company, the only group which had successfully organized itself for a major effort in China.[35] Denby, pleased to have an opportunity to browbeat the Chinese in proper European fashion, argued the Company's case vociferously. The Company's failure to win the contract it initially bid for was due, in part, to the unwillingness of American capitalists to underbid their competitors. Although disappointed, Denby felt that the Americans were right to hold out for better terms. Control over enterprises invested in was essential and the "statesmen of China will understand" that in the case of America, "control does not mean territorial absorption nor governmental interference," as was true of European countries.[36]

The Chinese may well have understood this; but they also understood its corollary: that American businessmen were not ready to take a short-term loss in the hopes of great future benefits, nor was the government prepared (as was King Leopold in the case of the Belgians who successfully won the contact) to forcefully persuade the business community to do so. Denby himself recognized this.

> If the colonial ambitions of the Great Powers of Europe lead them to support syndicates in doubtful business undertakings . . . Americans will be greatly handicapped, because commercial matters for them in Asia cannot be mixed up with the schemes of political ambition. . . . As we have no political designs to serve in the Far East we have nothing to offer China in return for concessions. It thus happens that our great boon of being removed from and independent of foreign complications constitutes a correlative weakness. . . .[37]

Thus Olney's apparently forward policy still fell far short of the European style of government stimulation and support of their nationals' enterprises in China.

The concession scramble in China, reinforcing the depression-engendered fear of businessmen and politicians, turned American attention to China as never before.[38] Although the air was filled with demands that America do something, what precisely should be done was left almost entirely up to the government.

What, for example, should the government attitude be toward a man, claiming American citizenship, who had won a valuable railroad contract in China? The concession had the full support of the Chinese government; moreover it was located in an area recently seized by Germany as a "sphere of influence." Support of the claim would, at one blow, accomplish many things: it would prove to China that the American government was behind the legitimate efforts of its nationals; it would seriously hamper the European drive to stake out exclusive areas in China; it would fulfill the repeated demands of American businessmen for an active China policy which would hold that vital market for America. Yet, because the businessman involved was Chinese and his claim to citizenship therefore in question (though he had voted in all municipal, state, and federal elections since his naturalization in 1852), the State Department refused to act. Clearly, if the McKinley administration had been interested, at this time, in making a strong stand against the growing danger of spheres of influence, Yung Wing's prospective charter was an ideal occasion. Even if the State Department were unwilling to compromise the harsh consistency of the Exclusion Acts, they could have protested on Yung Wing's behalf—as an individual who had been an American, or was close to American interests. At no time, however, did the Department even weigh the issue.[39]

Charles Beresford, tireless British spokesman for the Open Door, left a tour of the United States depressed by the vagueness of the businessmen he had met. He contrasted the attitude of the "commercial classes" in Japan and America. "Both," he noted, "saw the necessity of keeping the Door open in China" but

while on the Japanese side there was every indication of a
desire to act in some practical manner . . . I could discover
no desire on the part of the commercial communities in the
United States to engage in any practical effort for preserv-
ing what to them might become in the future a trade, the
extent of which no mortal can conjecture. On many occasions I suggested that some sort of understanding should
exist between Great Britain and the United States for the
mutual benefit of the two countries . . . but while receiving
the most cordial support to this proposal, nothing of a
definite character was suggested to me. . . .[40]

Thus, while McKinley could be sure that *some* action in
regard to China would be favored by the business community, it was not clear how much action they were willing to
countenance. The business community, through groups like
the American Asiatic Association, helped to create a climate
in which a new American China policy would be favorably
received. But they did not offer prescriptions. The linea-
ments of policy would have to be worked out by the Secretary
of State himself in the full knowledge that to overstep the
limits of public tolerance for new departures was to court
disaster.

However, if both government and business circles were
vague about what should be done in the face of apparent
European moves toward exclusive spheres, in one aspect of
China policy the State Department was quite firm—the strict
prosecution of antimissionary cases. Beginning in the Cleveland administration under Secretary of State Olney and pursued with thorough consistency by Secretaries Sherman, Day,
and Hay, the new, firm missionary policy marked a real
break with the past.

Disregarding the niceties of the separation of Church and
State, which could be interpreted to preclude government
intervention on behalf of sectarians, Secretary of State Olney
was determined to demonstrate that the "United States government is an effective factor in securing due rights for
Americans resident in China."[41] When it seemed that cooperating with other foreign powers in missionary cases, as
had been done in the past, resulted in a slighting of American demands, or a delay in the proceedings, Olney was pre-

pared to establish independent inquiry commissions despite the protests of the Chinese. Moreover, for the first time a general approach to missionary riots was worked out, one which took full advantage of the Chinese legal system and Chinese administrative norms. Thus, the highest government official of the area in which such an outbreak took place would be held responsible, though his only crime was ignorance or, on the local level, helplessness in the face of concerted mob action.[42]

In a manner reminiscent of France in the 1860s, when patronage of Roman Catholic missionaries substituted for real commercial or financial interests in China, this new missionary policy offended no European power, pleased a vested domestic interest, and served notice to China that its earlier image of America—mediating, gentle, supporting China against the rapacious world—was increasingly unattractive to Americans and certainly not to be depended upon.

The point is not that the government eschewed one approach for another, but that it acted with utmost caution in pursuit of the general goal of asserting American interest in China. Responding most directly to immediate situations and pressures, the administration was chary of any open-ended involvement, which firm support of a contested railroad contract might produce, but was ready enough to bully the Chinese on missionary cases, request firm assurances on trade, and, when the moment came, produce an all-around state paper—the Open Door Note—aimed at achieving limited objectives upon which vast claims might later be based.

Concerned, even at the height of the Cuban controversy, with the growing encroachment of European powers on China, McKinley decided, on the basis of assurances received from Russia and Germany, not to join England in a joint protest against recent Russian and German acquisitions. So long as "no discriminating treatment of American citizens and their trade" developed in the spheres of influence,[43] and so long, of course, as the United States remained fully engaged with Spain, no major diplomatic *démarche* could be expected.

The "ideal policy," John Hay wrote Henry Adams in 1900, "is . . . to do nothing, and yet be around when the watermelon is cut. Not that we want any watermelon, but it is always pleasant to be seen in smart colored circles on occasions of festivity."[44] Missionaries apart, the vagueness Beresford had complained of was characteristic of both business and government. Attempting to elucidate policy toward China in March of 1899, Hay confessed that it was "not very easy to formulate with any exactness the view of the Government in regard to the present condition of things in China." Opposed to dismemberment of the Empire and convinced that "the public opinion of the United States would [not] justify the Government in taking part in the great game of spoliation now going on," Hay was also concerned to keep all alternatives open.[45] Both Hay and McKinley were careful not to commit the United States to a policy of total territorial abstention in China. Discreet inquiries into the possibilities of a naval station were in fact made, for nothing in the Open Door notes precluded such an effort.

The notes themselves answered the immediate need for a policy which would satisfactorily indicate American concern to both the American public and the European powers. The first note, circulated in September 1899, was a statement of minimum demands. What America sought was *not* equality of opportunity. That, William Rockhill, Hay's chief adviser on China policy, pointed out "we cannot hope to have . . . though we should." Rather, "absolute equality of treatment" should be insisted upon.[46] In other words, America could not expect an equal opportunity for a railroad concession in the German-dominated province of Shantung; it would, however, insist that goods carried on that road should not be subject to discriminatory taxation. The aim was to lay down ground rules for the operation of trade within the spheres of influence. No one pretended that the spheres could be abolished—indeed Rockhill stressed that their existence must be accepted as *faits accomplis*. The attempt was only to limit the range of advantages enjoyed within the spheres.[47]

If America could not herself have a sphere, it was hoped that, through the Open Door Note, she might yet gain the prestige of leading a struggle to neutralize them. Whatever the modest realism Rockhill displayed when he drew up the note, he was soon making the broadest claims for it. Amer-

ica, he wrote a friend, "holds the balance of power in China.
. . . What we have obtained will undoubtedly help to insure,
for the time being, the integrity of the Chinese Empire. . . ."[48]
In public statements, articles, instructions to the American
legation in Peking, the same inflated notion of what the note
had accomplished was pushed. The hope seemed to be that,
by referring often enough to the way in which America had
secured China's integrity and independence, the powers
would begin to feel that they had committed themselves to
it; or at least China might believe it and be suitably grateful
to America. At the very least the American people might
believe it and the administration could thus, at one blow,
satisfy those who demanded a vigorous China policy and disarm the growing anti-imperialist movement. As Rockhill's
British friend and adviser Alfred Hippisley pointed out, "the
announcement . . . that the U.S. had secured China's independence and so served the cause of peace and civilization
would be a trump card for the Admin. and crush the life out
of the anti-imperialism agitation."[49]

The greatest deterrent to the actual dismemberment of
China was that no one stood to gain from it. Profit with a
minimum of expensive colonial responsibility was the goal
of all the powers, and the spheres-of-influence mechanism
satisfied all requirements. The danger of the situation lay in
its instability. An unforeseen crisis could shake the delicate
balance of interests and lead to genuine partition. Again, it
was not in the interest of any one of the powers to precipitate
such an event. Yet each country, fearing the unknown motives of the other, might initiate a panic policy of grab that
could not be easily arrested. The Boxer uprising was just
such a crisis, and from its inception, American efforts were
bent toward avoiding the calamity of disintegration. "The
thing to do—the only thing," John Hay wrote Henry Adams,
"was to localize the storm if possible. . . ."[50] Total war and
partition might have occurred through accident or inertia.
The vigorous diplomacy of Chinese officials in the south and
central areas of the country, strongly supported by the
United States, saved China for other upheavals.

McKinley's position was very delicate indeed. With the
legations under siege and the fate of the American Min-

ister unknown, he clearly had to do something. But American participation in an international expedition was just the kind of danger the anti-imperialists had warned the country McKinley's policies would lead to. This was what happened when you went around annexing Pacific islands, they claimed. At the same time the crisis in China worked nicely to justify the annexation of the islands: without them effective American aid to its nationals would have been impossible. This was what we wanted the islands for, the imperialists argued. However, a formal statement of the terms under which America fought in China was essential. For McKinley had found even the most ardent imperialists unenthusiastic about American military action in China. Cushman K. Davis, for example, feared that America would find itself involved in a struggle for "partition, concessions . . . and other advantages." America's "commanding isolation" would be lost, and with it freedom of action in Asia.[51] Whitelaw Reid, owner of the powerful pro-administration *Tribune,* also believed that the United States could exert a major influence in China without the expense and danger of a military effort. Yet if "the Administration does not strain every nerve to save [Minister Conger] there will be a whirlwind." It was, he reflected, similar to the situation

> in which the country found itself after the explosion of the Maine. None of us wanted war with Spain, and yet war was inevitable. None of us want now to go into the business of killing Chinamen, and yet the country will probably not permit American troops to be absent from the column which ultimately enters Peking.[52]

With most of the Western world convinced that the Chinese had slaughtered all the inhabitants of the legations, a dramatic move was necessary to prevent the abandonment of the careful fiction under which foreign forces fought Chinese soldiers but not the Chinese government. The note circulated on July 3, 1900, was designed to meet that need. It would, it was hoped, make clear that the goal of American troops in China was the rescue of the legations and not plunder, that American policy sought only a solution which would bring the "permanent safety and peace of China, preserve Chinese territorial and administrative entity, protect all rights guaranteed to friendly powers . . . and safeguard . . . the principle of equal and impartial trade."[53] By formally and publicly stating that the powers would cooperate in every way with the efforts of those Chinese officials trying to stem the revolt, America sought to tie the powers down to what till then had been only a very informal modus vivendi.

American participation in the Boxer expedition was the logical culmination of a China policy which had been shaping itself along interventionist lines since 1896. From that year, when antimissionary riots were met with a vigor and harshness absent from earlier American dealings with the Chinese on this subject, to the strong diplomatic representations regarding American trade made to China and the powers in 1898 and 1899, the lines of an independent, active China policy were laid down. A policy of passive cooperation with foreign forces in 1900 was impossible; no longer would an American Secretary of State leave the protection of nationals and their interests to the British. Danger to Americans now required an American armed presence, and more than that, it was hoped that an American force would give the nation increased weight and influence in the diplomatic maneuvering that was sure to follow the suppression of the antiforeign movement.

The genius, and the weakness, of American China policy was that it satisfied immediate, realistic needs through major verbal commitments. "We do not want to rob China ourselves," Hay complained

> and our public opinion will not permit us to interfere, with an army, to prevent others from robbing her. Besides, we have no army. The talk . . . about "our pre-eminent moral position giving us authority to dictate to the world" is mere flap-doodle. [54]

Yet the July 3 note talked about bringing "permanent peace" to China, and Rockhill, architect of much of the Open Door policy, spoke of America, with the acquisition of the Philippines, becoming "an eastern power and an active participator in Asiatic politics." "We had now to endeavor," he wrote, "to prevent preponderant political control within the Empire by any one foreign state, to give aid in every legitimate way to establishing a balance of power between them. . . ."[55] In fact, the United States was hardly in a position to balance powers. It took two hard years of negotiation to wring from Russia the assurance, "if assurances are to count for anything," that "no matter what happens eventually in northern China and Manchuria, the U.S. will not be placed in any worse position than while the country was under the unquestioned domination of China."[56] But the impulse to attempt, from a limited base of either power or interest, to play a role in Asia, was difficult to resist.

In the late nineteenth century Americans came to feel that having influence in Asia was a categorical imperative for a world power. America, after the Spanish-American War, was a world power, *ergo* it must take a key part in Far Eastern affairs. And while the degree of actual activity, diplomatic or commercial, fluctuated wildly over the years, the notion of the importance of playing a role there remained. Expectations of future power and interest were often confused with present realities. In relation to no other country did the rhetoric of politicians and businessmen, diplomats and missionaries so quickly become a force, influencing behavior, coloring reality, determining policy—or at least policy statements. However specific and realistic the response to any one situation might be (as in the dealing with Russia over Manchurian trade), whatever was accomplished was stated in the broadest possible terms. Policy decisions firmly rooted in the necessities of a particular situation (as in the two Open Door Notes) became, almost at the moment of inception, sacred doctrine.

This was due in part, at least, to the success of the propaganda of specific interest groups. Arguments intended to spur the interest of the public were accepted as facts and themselves became elements of policy in a dizzying spiral increasingly remote from reality. Thus the notion of a special friendship between China and America, of the riches of the China market, of America's role as balancer of powers in Asia, were all accepted as actual descriptions of the situation and not, as they were in fact, the possibilities merely. The

American public was given to believe that its most vital national interests were involved in China, yet the commercial and financial interests which might have given substance to this claim were absent.

I have been suggesting that, for the sake of clarity, we restrict our use of the term imperialist to those who advocated the acquisition of bases and coaling stations, an aggressive foreign policy, a large navy, and the constant nurturing of American interests in the undeveloped world. Active in the period before 1893, the group reached its peak of influence and power after the disastrous effects of the depression had made their impact on the country. Influenced by Europe, the newness of their ideas consisted mainly in a recognition of what was new in European imperialism and a strong desire that America follow a similar course.

In Asia, American policy clearly went beyond the simple pressure of economic facts, though fears for the health of the economy, real or imagined, were part of the imperialist argument. Unwilled events, such as the Boxer rebellion, were dealt with primarily with an eye to the domestic situation and out of a deep-seated concern that the administration neither fall behind the impulses of the public nor stand too far in the vanguard. The firm assumption was made that whatever the given state of material interests in Asia, America had a role to play there.

American policy is usually criticized for the imbalance between the broadness of its assertions and the actual military power used to back them up. America, however, did use force during the Boxer crisis. No war to safeguard Chinese integrity (as against Russian encroachments, for example) was undertaken, but neither did Britain, whose interests in the Far East were so much greater, fight any power in defense of Chinese integrity. Indeed America's restraint of arms is unique only in regard to China. The United States, in contrast to Britain, France, Germany, Japan, and Russia, was slow to use the threat of force against the Chinese government in order to gain its ends. Looked at in this light, American pacifism is hardly so startling.

A more recent approach to American policy finds it very much in balance—commercial ends were pursued diplomatically and backed by the judicious acquisition of suitable bases to protect trade. It seems to me that, perhaps disappointingly, the truth lies in between. The economic arguments used by the imperialists were an integral part of a larger complex of nationalist ideas. In a given situation, the response of the administration might well be rational, calculated, designed to avoid ultimate conflicts. Consistently, however, such a policy was presented to the public in a form likely to fulfill the self-image of the most ardent jingo. In time a sense of the importance of power in the Far East to America's very survival grew stronger so that today, when America finds herself engaged in the virtual extinction of an Asian nation, with a military force that makes the Boxer expedition look like a friendly street-corner fight, assertions of our "endangered vital interests" are everywhere, yet there seems to be no one who can spell out precisely what those interests are.

NOTES

1. Thomas McCormick, "Insular Imperialism and the Open Door: The China Market and the Spanish-American War," *Pacific Historical Review*, XXXII, 156, talks of this " 'insular imperialism' " and its use of "island stepping-stones."
2. Julius W. Pratt, *Expansionists of 1898: The Acquisition of Hawaii and the Spanish Islands* (Quadrangle edition; Chicago, 1964), p. 22.
3. Walter LaFeber, *The New Empire, An Interpretation of American Expansion, 1860–1898* (Ithaca, N.Y., 1963), Ch. I.
4. Matthew Simon and David E. Novack, "Commercial Responses to the American Export Invasion, 1871–1914: An Essay in Attitudinal History," *Essays in Entrepreneurial History*, 2nd Ser. (Winter 1966), p. 139.
5. *Hunt's Merchant Magazine*, quoted in LaFeber, *New Empire*, p. 24.
6. Quoted in William L. Neumann, *America Encounters Japan* (Baltimore, 1963), pp. 4–5, 23, 46.
7. Quoted in Norman K. Graebner, ed. *Ideas and Diplomacy: Readings in the Intellectual Tradition of American Foreign Policy* (New York, 1964), p. 370.
8. William A. Williams, *The Tragedy of American Diplomacy*, rev. and enlarged ed. (New York, 1962), p. 35.
9. Simon and Novack, "Commercial Responses," pp. 138–39.
10. Charles Denby, *China and Her People* (Boston, 1906), II, 38.

11. Dana C. Munro, *American Commercial Interests in Manchuria,* American Academy of Political and Social Science. Publication No. 654. Reprinted from the *Annals,* January, 1912. Munro shows that Standard Oil successfully resisted Russian and Japanese discrimination for some time, in contrast to cotton interests, which made no effort to retain the American import lead in Manchuria through proper marketing techniques.

12. See for example Chinese diplomacy during the Sino-Japanese War as reflected in the dispatches of Charles Denby to the State Department, National Archives, *China: Dispatches,* Vols. 97 and 98.

13. LaFeber, *New Empire,* pp. 17–24.

14. Quoted in Merze Tate, *The United States & the Hawaiian Kingdom, A Political History* (New Haven, Conn., 1965), pp. 262–63.

15. Edward C. Kirkland notes that, in its requests for aid, "Private enterprise was asking the government to do what it had failed to accomplish." *Industry Comes of Age: Business, Labor and Public Policy, 1860–1897* (New York, 1961), p. 303.

16. John A. Kasson, Minister to Vienna, for example, urged that in the event of an Anglo-Russian war, American privateers, licensed by Russia, be used to destroy the British merchant marine, thus leaving the admittedly poor American service supreme by default. The efforts of De Lesseps in Panama threw Kasson into a panic, and in 1880 he insisted that the United States establish control over any Pacific islands "which will be of importance to our national commerce and trade." The opposition to possessing outlying territory he described as "simply imbecile." See Edward Younger, *John A. Kasson: Politics and Diplomacy from Lincoln to McKinley* (Iowa City, 1955), pp. 284–85, 293–95.

17. LaFeber, *New Empire,* p. 61.

18. *Ibid.,* p. 32.

19. Charles Beard, *The Idea of National Interest* (New York, 1934), p. 60.

20. Matthew Josephson, *The Politicos, 1865–1896* (New York, 1938), p. 103.

21. See Gabriel Kolko, *The Triumph of Conservatism, A Reinterpretation of American History, 1900–1916* (New York, 1963), p. 2.

22. Quoted in Josephson, *The Politicos,* p. 119.

23. David Pletcher, *The Awkward Years: American Foreign Relations under Garfield and Arthur* (Columbia, Mo., 1963), Chs. 7 and 14 in particular.

24. D. M. Dozer, "Benjamin Harrison and the Presidential Campaign of 1892," *American Historical Review,* LIV, 76.

25. Carl Degler, "The Nineteenth Century," in William H. Nelson, ed. *Theory and Practice in American Politics* (Chicago, 1964), pp. 38, 39.

26. Oscar Handlin, *The American People in the Twentieth Century* (Cambridge, Mass., 1954), p. 6. By 1900 almost 40 percent of the population lived in cities.

27. Henry Adams, rather dramatically, describes how, in the year of the depression, men "died like flies under the strain, and Boston grew suddenly old, haggard, and thin." *The Education of Henry Adams* (Modern Library ed.; New York, 1931), p. 338. A more prosaic description of the effects of the depression is Charles Hoffman, "The Depression of the Nineties," *Journal of Economic History*, XVI, 137–64.

28. Adams, *Education*, pp. 344–45.

29. John Higham, *Strangers in the Land* (New Brunswick, N.J., 1955), pp. 69–73.

30. *Ibid.*, p. 77.

31. LaFeber, *New Empire*, p. 54.

32. *Ibid.*, p. 56.

33. Denby to Bayard, August 13, 1887, *China: Dispatches*, Vol. 81. Wharton Barker's papers are deposited in the Library of Congress and constitute a fascinating repository of information on one man's obsession with the China market.

34. Olney to Denby, December 19, 1896, *Papers Relating to the Foreign Relations of the United States*, 1897, p. 56.

35. The most complete account is by William Braisted, "The United States and the American China Development Company," *Far Eastern Quarterly*, XI (February 1953), 147–65. The James Harrison Wilson papers, deposited in the Library of Congress, contain the story of another, even more unsuccessful American effort to secure railroad concessions in China.

36. Edward H. Zariskie, *American Russian Rivalry in the Far East, 1895–1914* (Philadelphia, 1946), pp. 34ff.

37. Denby to Sherman, May 24, 1897, *China: Dispatches*, Vol. 102.

38. Pratt, in his *Expansionists of 1898,* underlines the effect of the concessions scramble on hitherto anti-imperialist businessmen who "saw the foundations" of their faith "crumbling as a result of the threatened partition of China." Pp. 258–62.

39. See correspondence between Denby and Sherman, January–April, 1898, *China: Dispatches*, Vols. 103, 104.

40. Charles Beresford, *The Break-Up of China* (London, 1899), pp. 443–44.

41. Olney to Denby, September 19, 1895, *For. Rel.*, 1895, Part I, p. 138.

42. See correspondence in *ibid.*, concerning antimissionary riots: also Sherman to Denby, May 15, 1897, *ibid.*, 1897, pp. 66ff.; Rockhill to Denby Jr., July 28, 1896, *ibid.*, 1896, pp. 58, 59.

43. McKinley's speech is reproduced in *For. Rel.*, 1898, p. xxii.

44. Hay to Henry Adams, July 8, 1900, Hay Papers.

45. Hay to Paul Dana, March 16, 1899, Hay Papers.

46. Rockhill to Hay, August 28, 1899, Rockhill Papers.

47. In this same letter Rockhill wrote that " 'spheres of influence' *are an accomplished fact,* this cannot be too much insisted on." (Underlining in original.)

48. Rockhill to Edwin Denby, January 13, 1900, Rockhill Papers.

49. Hippisley to Rockhill, August 21, 1899, Rockhill Papers.
50. Hay to Adams, July 8, 1900, Hay Papers.
51. Davis to Reid, July 4, 1900, Reid Papers.
52. Reid to Davis, July 20, 1900, Reid Papers.
53. Circular Note of July 3, 1900, to the powers cooperating in China, *For. Rel.*, 1901, Appendix I, p. 18.
54. Hay to A. A. Adee, September 14, 1900, Hay Papers.
55. Rockhill, "The United States and the Chinese Question," Speech at Naval War College, Newport, August 5, 1904, Rockhill Papers.
56. Hay to Theodore Roosevelt, May 1, 1902, Hay Papers.

AMERICAN FOREIGN POLICY 1900-1921: A SECOND LOOK AT THE REALIST CRITIQUE OF AMERICAN DIPLOMACY

∞   Lloyd C. Gardner

FOR MORE than a decade, George F. Kennan's "realist" critique, *American Diplomacy, 1900–1950,* has dominated debate in American universities and elsewhere. Though these famous lectures were hardly solely responsible for the rise of this critique of American foreign policy to its present position, they have yet to be rivaled by any other writing on twentieth-century American foreign relations. The book is now in its twentieth printing.

Since many key points Kennan sought to establish in these lectures pertained to the earlier years (1900–1921); and since many of these contentions have served as foundation, not only for the author's discussion of later policy decisions, but for the realist school in general, it may be useful to review these events from a radical perspective with the hope that meaningful distinctions may emerge separating that view from other efforts to make sense out of the developments and personalities of these years. Hopefully, also, there will appear something of a general dialogue between what is really a conservative criticism of the American liberal "world view," and a radical explanation of the development of that outlook at the beginning of this century.

Kennan saw an overriding theme in the events leading up to John Hay's Open Door Notes on China in 1899 and 1900, in the rapid growth of the arbitration movement before the First World War, and in the aura cast by Woodrow Wilson's crusade to make the world safe for democracy. Reduced to its simplest expression, that theme was the American's "legalistic-moralistic approach to international problems." It ran "like a red skein through our foreign policy of the last fifty years."[1]

Before testing specifics against this generalization, as he set it forth during the lectures, Kennan gave his audience an atmospheric description of the State Department at the turn of the century when it was "a quaint old place, with its law-office atmosphere, its cool dark corridors, its swinging doors, its brass cuspidors, its black leather rocking chairs, and the grandfather's clock in the Secretary of State's office."[2]

After that marvelous word picture of an institution at the end of an "innocent" era, one expects an amiable, if slightly condescending, discussion of the origins of the Open Door policy. We are not disappointed. Kennan assures his audience that John Hay's Far Eastern policy "was not an American policy but one long established in British relations with China."[3] A strong Anglophile, the Secretary of State thought he was being "responsive to a request the British had made of us." Indeed, there was "no evidence that . . . [Secretary Hay] understood fully its practical significance." The policy apparently was as innocent and parochial as the institution and its inhabitants. As for commercial motives, these took a very small place, sandwiched in between the really important matters. "The formula had a high-minded and idealistic ring; it would sound well at home; it was obviously in the interests of American trade; the British had been known to advocate it—still did, so far as he knew—and it was hard to see what harm could come from trying it on the other powers."[4]

State Department officials from the time of the Open Door Notes to the Second World War were indeed constantly frustrated by the failure of the "Great China market." But the ongoing assumption behind the policy was that American Far Eastern trade, and our national interests in general, would be better served by equal access to all of China than by a preferred position in a sphere of influence. It was, in theory and in fact, the foreign policy of a confident industrial power. And as such it soon became the United States approach to its dealings with other areas of the world, particularly colonial and underdeveloped areas.

From this point of view, as another career Foreign Service officer, Stanley K. Hornbeck, wrote in 1918 (and in contrast to the emphasis in *American Diplomacy, 1900–1950*), the specific matter of how the actual notes came to be sent to the powers interested in China was of little significance, as the "Republican administration was enthusiastic over the possibilities of American commercial expansion in the Pacific." America had sent the notes instead of Great Britain because the world order was at a crucial transition point, but the "idea of defending China's integrity and of gradually securing wider opening of her doors to foreign trade on terms enjoyable mutually by all comers had long been cardinal features of the policies of both countries." And a number of recent monographs have drawn upon similar evidence to establish the strength and variety of domestic economic pressures behind the inauguration of a more forceful China policy.[5]

Similarly, Kennan also dismissed the contrary views of American expansionists, such as Brooks Adams and Charles A. Conant,[6] noting that their "thinking was distorted by the materialism of the time; by the over-estimation of economics, of trade, as factors in human events and by corresponding under-estimation of psychological and political reactions."[7] Among the most popular of American imperial theorists at the time, these thinkers developed a rationale much like that of Great Britain's John A. Hobson; but they were much less critical of capitalism than was Hobson, and much more optimistic about the chances for American economic expansion.

That they may have failed to assess properly "such things as fear, ambition, insecurity, jealousy, and perhaps even boredom—as prime movers of events," as Kennan asserts, may be true, but that probably explains only their optimism, not their assessment of the needs of industrial America. Modern psychology was certainly not absent from another career officer's attempt to convey the mood of Imperial America in 1902. "We were suffering from a sense of constraint," wrote Frederic Emory, "a vague feeling that we were not exerting ourselves to the full extent of our powers. . . ." But at the source of that feeling, Emory then went on to say, there was a general agreement: "We were not in need of more territory but commercial expansion had become a matter of pressing urgency if we were to advance along the existing lines of our accelerated industrial development."[8]

On the other hand, Kennan was also apparently suggesting that the "materialism of the time," as an attitude or habit of mind, was more important to the development of Adams's and Conant's rationalization of American expansion than the actual needs of our "accelerated industrial development." If so, then we have already established the realist position sufficiently so that the basic differences will become more apparent in the discussion below.

Turning from the China policy of the McKinley administration, Kennan explains the similar phenomena of the arbitration movement, the League of Nations, and finally the United Nations as resulting (on the American side) from an idealization of our own past political experience projected onto the world at large. His criticism of these efforts was directed at the unreal expectations stemming from such delusions in the first place, and at the American assumption that "the things for which other peoples in this world are apt to contend are for the most part neither creditable nor important and might justly be expected to take second place behind the desirability of an orderly world, untouched by international violence."[9]

The American policy maker's attempt to impose an American-organized and American-led security system on the world at the end of the First World War was premature; but his world view had developed from a much keener insight into the nature of his society (and its needs) than would appear from the realist critique. We may criticize his naive moralism or idealism along with the realists, but a full account of the development of that outlook is a much more difficult problem. The rhetoric of all great nations and empire builders is, after all, usually sounded in moralistic themes. The American policy maker in the Progressive Era was confronted with a set of conditions at home and abroad, and a collection of traditions about himself and his role in the world. As world conditions changed, so did the formulas he used to match them to, the new opportunities and challenges. World conditions changed very rapidly in these years; so rapidly, in fact, that his formulas were often outdated at once. Even so, these formulations need much more analysis than is presently available in the realist critique.

As Charles Seymour once pointed out, Wilson's closest adviser, Colonel Edward M. House, was already thinking about a union of industrial nations in 1913. He once told the German ambassador to the United States that such a league "could ensure peace and proper development of the waste places, besides maintaining an open door and equal opportunity everywhere."[10] House's suggestion stood more than halfway in time between the 1895 crisis with Great Britain over the Venezuelan boundary and the 1919 domestic crisis over the League of Nations as embodied in the Treaty of Versailles; it also stood at an intellectual and political midpoint between the arbitration movement and the League to Enforce Peace.

The modern arbitration movement received its biggest boost into the twentieth century when the "Nervous Nellies" of 1895 decided to do something about preventing recurrences of the surprising conflict with Great Britain over Venezuela. Deeply worried about the long-lasting depression which followed the Panic of 1893, they wrung their hands over the prospect of such a showdown. At the same time, a growing number of economic and political leaders had concluded that Great Britain could not be allowed to "Africanize" Latin America.[11] The depression had quickly sharpened their focus on Latin American markets.

Though temporarily absorbed in their domestic difficulties, business leaders like Andrew Carnegie thought the dispute was an opening and an opportunity "to publicize two . . . pet projects: the disposal by Great Britain of her colonial empire in the Western Hemisphere, and international arbitration."[12] Carnegie's sustained optimism was well founded; in a very few years there was much talk at home and abroad of an "American Commercial Invasion" of the world. The problems of dealing with additional conflicts in the undeveloped world where American interests were intruding brought other men to the arbitration movement; Elihu Root, William Howard Taft, and Robert Lansing were prominent among them. As Carl Schurz put it: "The institution of a regulated and permanent system of arbitration between the United States and Great Britain would not be a mere sentimental cooing between loving cousins, nor a mere stage show gotten up for the amusement of the public, but a very serious contrivance intended for very serious business."[13] That business, thought Schurz and others, was to be the transfer (ultimately) of world leadership to the United States.

By 1904 the general business community was convinced. That year the Second American Conference on International Arbitration brought Carnegie's friend, the farm implement manufacturer A. B. Farquhar, to the Washington Meeting. "I am here as the representative of the National Association of Manufacturers," he declared, "which is, perhaps, the greatest business organization in the world—to tell you that we are with the cause of arbitration—heart and soul."[14]

Farquhar's commitment to international peace and harmony had very practical backgrounds. In the depression of the 1870s his company had gone abroad in search of markets to absorb its surplus production; by the next depression he had become a strong leader in the arbitration movement.[15] There is important work yet to be done to see how many other business leaders found their way into the movement by this route. There were other routes, but the best-known peace advocate of the age, William Jennings Bryan, also tied the problem of world peace to increased international trade. Though he was the anticolonialist presidential candidate in 1900, Bryan was always for foreign economic expansion, and a defender of John Hay's Open Door to China. After completing his world tour, the Great Commoner attacked the Chinese boycott against foreign goods and ideas in a plainly worded pamphlet, *Letters to a Chinese Official.* "In proportion as nations trade with each other," he insisted, "they are slow to engage in a war, for business is a sort of hostage which each nation gives to the other."[16] Bryan's position was not fully defined, however, until his tenure as Secretary of State. By that time he was ready to proclaim the moral value of American economic expansion to the whole world. He managed to match his own specific traditional role as anti-imperialist to hemispheric conditions without even a slip of rhetoric, ending with a justification of American suppression of disorder in Haiti and Santo Domingo.

Theodore Roosevelt's dislike of the arbitration movement and his effort to manipulate power balances in Asia and Europe have won him some admiration from the "realists," though others retain a good deal of skepticism about his "romantic exercises in global foreign policy."[17] In any evaluation (including his own), T. R. was thought to be the very opposite of Bryan.

Yet Roosevelt agreed essentially with Brooks Adams that if America expected to maintain the Open Door policy and expansionism in general, it must engage more in international diplomacy. He took Adams's article "Reciprocity or the Alternative" almost literally.[18] Adams had written that other world powers would not allow the United States to dominate world trade outlets and raw-materials sources without a fight. It might be possible to avoid such a conflict through lower tariffs and reciprocity. The alternative was to build a great navy. T.R. chose the alternative—the Great White Fleet. Roosevelt distrusted the peace movement, but not key men in it. He very much appreciated, for example, the work of his Secretary of State, Elihu Root, in Latin American arbitration. Following the pacification of Cuba with the Platt Amendment and the 1903 Cuban-American Reciprocity Treaty, and the initiation of a Santo Domingo Customs Receivership shortly thereafter, Root had turned his attention to the major causes of internal disturbance and foreign (i.e., non-United States) intervention in the five

Central American countries. With Roosevelt's warm approval, the Secretary of State brought about the creation of a Central American Court of Justice to obviate the very problems which nevertheless, plagued all three presidents from 1901 to 1921.[19]

Roosevelt then assured Andrew Carnegie, whose money helped supply the brick and mortar for many Pan-American peace projects, "Gradually we are coming to a condition which will insure permanent peace in the Western Hemisphere."[20] With good reason, William Howard Taft prayed that his predecessor would prove to be right. He soon discovered that his prayer would go unanswered.

It had been hoped that the intervention in Cuba in 1906 (which Taft oversaw) would be the last, but to insure permanent peace, Taft finally intervened militarily against an obstreperous dictator in Nicaragua, thus beginning an "affair" which itself lasted more than twenty years and initiated a new tradition in Central America. Secretary of State Philander C. Knox had explained to the President that it was "impossible for the United States to sit by and see this whole region racked with turbulence and insurrection with the result that the progress and prosperity of the inhabitants is prevented and the development of the resources of the region is paralyzed."[21] Knox's phrases were startlingly like the arguments Colonel House made to the German Ambassador in 1913, especially since we have attempted to polarize "Dollar Diplomacy" and "Wilsonian Moralism."

Roosevelt had dodged the tariff issue which Taft also inherited after 1909. Instead of the reciprocity treaties negotiated by William McKinley's commissioner, John A. Kasson,[22] T.R. chose once again the alternative posed by Brooks Adams: military and naval strength. He was not insensitive to the building pressure for tariff reciprocity, but feared that if attempted too soon it would divide the Republican party. He was right, so Woodrow Wilson was made a gift of the tariff issue in 1912.

Pressures behind reciprocity were the same pressures behind the arbitration movement. Farm-implement manufacturers were prominent in both. In 1900, for example, one representative of the industry testified before the Senate

Foreign Relations Committee: "We are ready to go forth to conquer the industrial world, and we believe that the path to freedom and equality of American commerce in the markets of the world lies through reciprocity. We believe that it is the manifest destiny of this country, through one history of protection, through another history of reciprocity to reach the largest measure in value of foreign commerce that has ever been known in the history of Industry."[23]

Arbitration and reciprocity were bound to another issue in the Progressive outlook: the problem of a new national banking law to replace an outdated system was both a domestic and foreign policy issue. Again men like Farquhar reasoned that Bryan was right about the need for immediate expansion of credit facilities to still the agrarian and Western discontent in the 1890s, even if they thought he was dead wrong on free silver. But more than that they reasoned that doing business with dissatisfied farmers and overseas customers presented very similar problems: "We should open branch banks in every country where we wish trade, just as we ought to open them throughout our own country."[24]

And in 1911 an official of the National City Bank of New York told a State Department officer about the "ease, facility, and safety of financial transactions, afforded to the Englishman and his interests" in Latin America as a result of his branch banks which brought the credit and funds to the place where sales were made or lost.[25] Two years later this problem was recognized in a specific provision of the Federal Reserve Act permitting members of the new national banking system to establish branches overseas.[26] Secretary of State Bryan's role in securing passage of this legislation is incomplete without noting his statement to the National Foreign Trade Convention that the Act would "do more to promote trade in foreign lands than any other one thing that has been done in our history."[27]

When looked at in this context of industrial expansion, the quest for a stable international order does not appear quixotic at all. It is certainly true that many in the arbitration movement failed to take into account the impact of American expansion itself on an already shaky world order which, out in the fringes of European empire, was threatening to collapse at even a small shock. They also assumed, perhaps, that the inevitable transition from European to American world leadership could be accomplished smoothly without disrupting the lower echelons of the world system directed from Europe. Their faith in progress—especially American progress—was in large part a celebration of the triumph of American capitalism behind the leadership of its corporate giants.

American diplomacy therefore was not simply a quest to bring law and order into international relations, but also a desire to put American banks into underdeveloped areas of the world; not only an optimistic idealization of American political experience, but a drive to expand trade and cultural influence into world marketplaces. When these surfaces are added to the prism, the image of Progressive Era foreign policy breaks down quite differently than post-World War II critics have assumed.

Walter Lippmann put it all together neatly in 1915, when he and several other young intellectuals forged ahead to build the *New Republic*. Reviewing events leading to the First World War, Lippmann said: "Algeciras grasped the problem of diplomacy—the conflict of empires in weak territory. Algeciras gallantly tried to control it. The men at Algeciras failed. If we cannot succeed where they failed, the outlook for the future is desperate."[28]

Writing in the midst of the Great War, this young editor of the leading liberal periodical could have had but a partial vision of the impact that was yet to be made by the 1910 Mexican Revolution, the Chinese Revolution of 1911, and the yet unborn Russian Revolution of 1917. Colonel House also foresaw the dangers; he warned a leader in one of the warring countries of Europe that "Western civilization had broken down, and there was not a marketplace or a mosque in the East where the West of to-day was not derided."[29]

Cohesion of the West against alien races and civilizations was important in House's plan for a league of industrial nations; and Woodrow Wilson paused on the brink of war in 1917 to consider whether plunging his nation into the conflict would not indeed endanger the cause of Anglo-Saxon predominance. These developing revolutions, even more than the war itself, provided the ultimate challenge to American foreign policy in this era—as in later times. The response was already shaped to a large degree by a decade of experience and intervention in world affairs, and by two decades of experience with the problems of a mature industrial society dominated more and more by expansion-minded manufacturers and agricultural interests, both large and small.

Deeply concerned with rapid industrialization's threat to American political well-being, Woodrow Wilson came to the presidency from a Southern-Presbyterian heritage, modified by executive experience in the North. We should not be misled by his revulsion against the tainted morals of the men around him, as he grew up in the Gilded Age. Wilson perceived the Progressive spirit to be a repudiation of the Gospel of Wealth, but an affirmation of the Gospel of Efficiency. "I do not wish to make the analysis tedious," he lectured a group of businessmen in May 1912. "I will merely ask you, after you go home, to think over this proposition; that what we have been witnessing for the past hundred years is the transformation of a Newtonian Constitution into a Darwinian Constitution."[30] Wilson was certainly a social-political "Darwinist," particularly when it came to economic relations among nations. That he later wanted to contain that struggle within a League of Nations does not refute this view at all. By then America had, he thought, achieved world leadership and responsibility for Western civilization.

What followed from that belief? On the tariff issue, this followed: Ambassador Walter Hines Page exclaimed over the Tariff Act of 1913: "Score One! You have done a great historic deed and demonstrated and abundantly justified your leadership. . . . I have been telling . . . the editorship of the *Economist* that the passing of commercial supremacy to the United States will be dated in the economic histories from the tariff act of 1913. . . ."[31] Wilson responded, not as a naive low-tariff Southern Democrat, but as an assertive nationalist who was fully aware of what free-trade expansionism had done for Great Britain: "I do know in my mind that what we are accomplishing with regard to the tariff is going to be just as epoch-making as you indicate and in just the way you foresee."[32] When the war destroyed European commercial treaties and tariff structure, Wilson moved to put the United States in a competitive position after the war through the creation of a "scientific" tariff commission to maintain the Open Door policy in foreign empires, though he had previously rejected such a proposal on the grounds that it would lead back to excessive protectionism.[33]

Wilson's advisers made similar adjustments; most of them had never been "New Freedom" oriented except in a limited rhetorical sense for the duration of the campaign of 1912. Secretary of Commerce William C. Redfield, for example, who had much more influence in the administration than has generally been recognized, was a keen student of new methods in industry, such as "scientific" commercial education. He had written about these innovations in *The New Industrial Day* (1912), stressing a common theme—the elimination of waste and the preservation of wealth and democracy in a postfrontier society. Woodrow Wilson's references to his own indebtedness to Frederick Jackson Turner are well known;[34] Redfield's book also relied on a frontier thesis to explain American development: "For many years the great expanse of our own land and the demands of its increasing people gave our factories enough to do. As time went on our shops waxed large and their output grew larger, till one day we found, some of us, that we were making that which we could not sell at home."[35]

Then Americans went out beyond "territorial and traditional lines." "We must stay there or shut down our shops. We have gone out into the world because we must." Germany and England based their industrial prosperity on foreign trade: "Our foreign trade is also a safety valve that relieves the pressure of over-production at home."[36]

Wilson's Secretary of Commerce organized the first National Foreign Trade Convention, which met in Washington in June 1914; and he was the key Cabinet officer in the fight for the Webb-Pomerene and Edge Acts, which permitted (indeed encouraged) American manufacturers and bankers to combine to meet European cartels in postwar competition.[37]

Colonel House fictionalized his views in a utopian novel,

Philip Dru: Administrator, published under a pseudonym in 1912. Without an iota of literary merit or interest, the novel is not even good "camp" material today. Beneath its cellophane plot, however, the pages do reveal something of the author's conception of national and international problems. At the point in the novel where Dru has turned the corner of one crisis, with European powers and Japan, the next pages reveal other problems to challenge the new Administrator of the United States. The unseen narrator speaks: "In spite of repeated warnings from the United States, Mexico and the Central American Republics had obstinately continued their old-time habit of revolutions without just cause, with the result that they neither had stable governments within themselves, nor any hope of peace with each other."[38]

In a confrontation with the commander of these revolutionary forces, Dru proclaimed during a battlefield truce: "Our citizens and those of other countries have placed in your Republic vast sums for its development, trusting to your treaty guarantees, and they feel much concern over their properties, not only to the advantage of your people, but to those to whom they belong."[39]

The truce over, Dru's army smashed the opponents of law and order. He never considered the counterproposition that other nations might be entitled to define and carry out their own revolutions, just as he had overthrown a plutocracy of entrenched wealth and corrupt politicians.

What Redfield implied and House made explicit came down to this: United States leaders identified colonial and undeveloped areas as neo-frontier wastelands—wasted in the sense that their resources were not being developed and used by the industrial nations for the benefit of the whole world economy. There would continue to be international conflict among the industrial powers until that situation was corrected. America's mission, or new manifest destiny, was to bring to "waste areas" political democracy (as much as such peoples could absorb) and stability. In this view, selfish exploitation (such as colonial monopoly systems), which did not contribute to the overall system, was almost as bad as not making use of the area at all. Though very often covered with the thick rhetoric of morality (especially in the Wilson years), this was the foreign policy reflection of the Gospel of Efficiency, or of a Darwinian Constitution.

Wilson and House, therefore, sought the "Road Away from Revolution." The latter proposed early in the administration a Dru-like plan for promoting Western Hemisphere stability by encouraging the most politically advanced countries, and ABC Powers—Argentina, Brazil, and Chile—to guarantee each other's territorial integrity, and to settle boundary disputes, "by means of international arbitration."[40]

He revealed the plan to European leaders in July 1914 in this way: "We all thought the best way to do this was to appeal to the A.B.C. powers, ostensibly for the good of both Americas. I suggested that the President should say to them that we were all borrowing countries . . . and that we should have some better understanding in order that interest rates might be lessened. To do this capital would have to have better assurances of safety than now."[41]

Bryan had his own proposals for Latin America. To begin with, he heartily approved the President's own statement at the outset of his administration that the United States would prefer as friends "those who act in the interest of peace and honor, who protect private rights, and respect the institutions of constitutional power."[42] Though Wilson had soundly denounced "Dollar Diplomacy," this statement was issued because the administration feared a resurgence of revolutionary activity as a result of the changes in Washington. If there was a significant difference in Central and South American revolutions between genuine social upheavals and more simple *coups d'état,* the new administration's policy pronouncement did not take cognizance of it.

Besides his pacifism, and his Protestant temperance ideals, the Secretary of State brought to the State Department an equally strong belief in what he termed the "economic value of righteousness." "When the people of other countries understand that the United States will investigate claims before it puts its moral force behind them," he informed a newspaper reporter, "and that when it does approve a claim it will support that claim only by methods consistent with the nation's honor and the tradition of fair dealing—when the people of all other nations understand this, they will welcome American capital and American capitalists." Lest he miss the point, Bryan also said: "The preceding administration attempted to till the fields of foreign investment with a penknife; President Wilson intends to cultivate it with a spade."[43]

Making good use of his experiences in Nebraska during the Populist revolt, Bryan converted them into positive plans for Central American financing that would benefit both the northern and southern halves of the hemisphere. In July 1913, he suggested to the President a program for lending countries in the Americas the "credit" standing of the United States government. Most injustices in inter-American relations, he insisted, came from situations where the borrowers had to pay usurious interest rates; sometimes these countries were forced to grant concessions to bankers and investors in the United States and Europe (especially Europe) to secure the loans they needed.[44]

The President replied that the idea was too radical, so Bryan's first suggestion for a means of preventing revolutions and encouraging "stable and just government" was shelved. Later Secretaries of State picked up similar ideas when post-World War II foreign aid plans were designed.[45]

Anything but stymied, the Secretary of State turned to the alternative of securing "Platt Amendment" treaties to secure financial control and the right of intervention in Nicaragua, Haiti, and other Central American countries. Haitian leaders resisted the proposal, countering with offers of unlimited economic concessions. These, they hoped, would preserve their own ambitions and forestall American political control. Bryan's reply to this gambit has been misinterpreted; true enough, he rejected the offer as beneath Washington's dignity, but he noted pointedly: "While we desire to encourage in every proper way American investments in Haiti, we believe that this can be better done by contributing to stability and order than by favoring special concessions to Americans."[46]

In 1914 Haiti verged on anarchy—a prime example of a "waste place." Along with that, without American control, the island might become a strategic danger point. R. L. Farnham, an American banker concerned about financial interests in Haiti, soon became one of Bryan's closest advisers on the situation there. He expressed the problem this way: "With a population of something over 2,000,000 of people; with exceptional natural agricultural conditions and particularly good climatic conditions, Haiti would be one of the richest and most prosperous of all the Caribbean countries, were it not for the almost continuous revolutionary disturbances which are imposed on the country by a relatively small number of political aspirants."[47]

When all else failed, Bryan and Wilson, like Taft and Knox, reluctantly accepted the final option of military intervention. If anything, the Wilson administration actually displayed the big stick more often in dealing with revolutionaries in Latin America than that of either Roosevelt or Taft. Of course, the strategic problem was heightened by the World War, as in the Haitian situation, but the basic trend seems clear in any event.

Military intervention in a small island country was one thing; the Mexican Revolution, however, was not so easily contained and turned into peaceful democratic channels. The long-time stability of the Porfirio Díaz regime came to an end in 1910; a man and his era were over. He had been a personage "to be held up to the hero worship of mankind," Elihu Root said.[48] Mexico's apparent progress toward constitutional government was interrupted, unfortunately, when Francisco Madero's short-lived government was overthrown by one of its own generals, Victoriano Huerta. Mexicans then divided into several warring camps, each led by a claimant to the leadership of the original revolution. Huerta held Mexico City, fully expecting diplomatic recognition from Europe and the United States. Taft demurred, leaving it all up to Wilson.

Upon satisfying himself that Huerta had acted illegally and violently against Madero (and progress), and that the usurper did not hold, and probably could not establish, effective control throughout his country within a short time, the President decided to force Huerta into honoring democratic procedures and institutions. He went about this by sending a representative to Mexico to offer the dictator badly needed financial aid if the General would pledge himself to hold free elections, at which he would not stand as a candidate, and abide by the results.[49]

When Huerta scornfully rejected the "bribe" and looked defiantly to Europe for support, Wilson was temporarily thwarted in what had become a personal issue as well as a public policy. Finally Wilson found an excuse to intervene militarily at Vera Cruz in April 1914. War was averted in part because the ABC Powers displayed their political maturity by making it possible to ease Huerta out of power. Accommodation with the revolution, however, was still a long way off.[50]

The administration's Mexican policy had brought on a storm of criticism at home and abroad. Reacting to this questioning, Wilson assured foreign leaders that the United States "will seek, here as elsewhere, to show itself the consistent champion of the open door." And:

> Each conspicuous instance in which usurpations of this kind are prevented will render their recurrence less likely, and in the end a state of affairs will be secured in Mexico and elsewhere upon this continent which will assure the peace of America and the untrammeled development of its economic and social relations with the rest of the world.[51]

In 1917 the Mexican government proclaimed a new constitution, but Washington, despite its passion for constitutional government, was dismayed by Article 27 of that document, which placed ownership of subsoil oil and mineral rights in the hands of the central government. To meet this threat the administration supported the creation of an American-controlled International Bankers Committee. Its goal was to employ financial aid to divert Mexico City from expropriation of foreign investments. These plans were still pending when Warren Harding came into the White House.[52]

By that time there was yet another aspect to Washington's relations with the Mexican Revolution—its influence on other Latin American countries. In 1919 a special committee in the government had reached the conclusion that "the confiscation or destruction of petroleum properties controlled by United States interests or the existence of conditions which make impossible their operation, is an injury to the national interests and an injury which cannot be remedied by apologies or pecuniary compensation after the damage has occurred."[53] Such a declaration pretty well froze Washington's attitude toward Mexican revolutions—even constitutional ones! It has not completely thawed out yet.

Wilson's early recognition of the Chinese "Republic" and his dramatic break with the Taft-sponsored International Banking Consortium have often been cited as evidences of the purely moralistic foreign policy of the first Wilson administration. Like the Mexican situation, however, the Chinese upheaval was simply not well enough defined in 1913 to enable American policy makers to see that efforts to influence its outcome were even less likely to succeed. Moreover, Wilson urged American business to participate in the modernization of China.

In the Far East, Washington devoted most of its energy to blocking a Japanese forward movement, which became virulent after the outbreak of the war, culminating in the Twenty-One Demands. The break with the old Consortium had been well received by those who had urged a stronger anti-Japanese, go-it-alone, "original" Open Door policy. They had applauded the President's call for support of the new regime in China, and for increased traffic through the Open Door: ". . . one thing has now become clear, namely, that from now on, American business and financial interests will have a clear field in China, and . . . they can look for all the diplomatic support from this Government that they need or that is proper for them to have."[54]

Critics once again equated Wilsonian idealism with anti-business sermonizing, but the President's new ambassador to China, Paul S. Reinsch, turned out to be the very model of a modern Dollar Diplomat. The most ambitious project he undertook was the financing of the proposed Huai River Valley Conservancy.[55] Reinsch caught the vision from American Red Cross engineers who portrayed for him a scene filled with Americans hard at work reclaiming millions of acres of land for cultivation in the flood-plagued Huai River valley. American efficiency would triumph over yet another backward waste area. Altruist though he said he was (and may have been), Ambassador Reinsch was strongly anti-Japanese as well; he saw the project from that vantage point and as a step toward securing a foothold in China's modernization programs.

Washington caught the vision, too. The Counselor of the State Department, John Bassett Moore, urged it on the President. "In talking with certain bankers today I had further assurances that under proper conditions and with the moral support of the Department of State, we could get the assistance we need in this country, *without going abroad for it.* This, as you can imagine, is a most satisfying statement. We wish it to be known of this project, first, that it is one of the activities of the Red Cross, and, second, that it is supported morally and financially by the American people alone, so that the Chinese will understand that it is, in truth and in fact, an American enterprise."[56]

But it never was. The first shots fired in the Great War chased venturesome capital into hiding. And although a representative of the former Consortium bankers thought such a loan to China might "be the bridge over which we can enter once again upon Chinese business," the idea emerged later in a radically different form—as part of a new plan for cooperation with Japan in China.[57]

A decision to pursue the possibility of at least a limited *modus operandi* with Tokyo in the Far East led to the 1917 Lansing-Ishii Agreement and then, ultimately, to the formation of a Second International Consortium.[58] Tokyo expected concessions to its position on former German island bases and control of the Shantung Peninsula as part of the bargain; moreover, before joining the Consortium it wanted recognition of several unfinished projects in Manchuria and Mongolia.[59]

These demands put the United States in an even more difficult position, where it seemed that Washington would have to choose between cooperation with Japan and a full commitment to Chinese national aims. Of course this dilemma was exactly the type of problem that those who desired a league of industrial powers hoped could be avoided in the postwar world. Traditional national sympathy with Chinese reform weighted one side of the balance against the proven quality of relations with Japan on the other. The United States wanted the Open Door policy to equalize the situation. To seek a delicate equilibrium, J. P. Morgan & Co.'s Thomas Lamont went to Japan and China to convince each to accept the international cooperation of the Consortium plan. He reached a modicum of agreement in Tokyo; in China, the Shantung decision at the Versailles Conference had further speeded up an awakening nationalism. Revolutionary groups now blamed the United States as well as their old enemies, even as they cursed their own impotence and inability to defend Chinese national interests. Realizing the futility of dependence upon any foreign nation, no matter how well-intentioned it might be, they looked inward to shaping their own revolution.[60]

Japan's frank claims to German rights in Shantung were heard all over the world, especially in the United States. Along with the revelations of Allied "secret treaties" pertaining to the Middle East, Japan's demands soured the great crusade for many who had followed Woodrow Wilson to Versailles. His Fourteen Points, even the League of Nations itself, said the disillusioned, had been stolen by the reactionaries.[61] Wilson's supporters countered that the League was the only way to rectify any of the wrongs done at Paris; it was the only way for civilized nations to live together.[62]

So the great crusade to make the world safe for democracy ended in bitter disagreements among Americans of all political views. From the very first day of the Great War, advisers had urged President Wilson to attempt mediation among the warring nations, premising their arguments most often upon the opportunity that had suddenly been presented to the United States to construct a true society of nations.[63] Some in the arbitration movement faltered in their belief in the essential harmony of world interests; but others, like Colonel House (of course), were more than ever convinced that America's time had come to complete the assigned task. First, said House, German "militarism" had to be eliminated, for it was a greater danger to American interests and to the world than British "navalism." The latter could be dealt with at leisure after the war.[64]

With the President's full support, House made two trips to Europe to convince its disturbed statesmen that they should accept American political intervention to end the war. The second time he sought—almost out of desperation, one feels—to exchange a promise of American military intervention in favor of the Allies for a guarantee that President Wilson would be recognized at the peace conference as the principal spokesman for world opinion.[65] Not wanting to make such a commitment to the United States, the Allies simply hoped all along that America's position of neutrality would become untenable, that Washington would be forced to enter the war in anger against the outrages of German submarine warfare—a simple unbinding reaction against brutality.

In part they were prevented from asking for American political intervention by the promises they had made to one another, and the resolutions of the Allied Economic Conference which met in Paris during June 1916. Fear that the war might end inconclusively and then be transferred back into economic conflict, as well as a good deal of concern about America's swelling commercial and financial power, had brought them together. Their meeting produced a long series of narrow resolutions which had immediate repercussions in the United States.[66]

With a flurry of activity in New York and Washington, economic and political leaders charged that the Allies had opened an economic campaign against neutrals as well as the Central Powers.[67] Secretary of State Lansing called the meeting to Wilson's attention: "We neutrals, as well as the Central Powers, will have to face a commercial combination which has as its avowed purpose preferential treatment for its members. . . . The consequent restrictions upon profitable trade with these commercial allies will cause a serious, if not critical, situation for nations outside the Union by creating unusual and artificial conditions."[68]

An American "Commercial Preparedness" campaign to overcome Sherman Act restrictions against cooperation among foreign traders was led in the private sector by the National Foreign Trade Council, and in the government by Commerce Secretary Redfield. "American firms must be given definite authorization to cooperate for foreign selling operations," Wilson told a magazine writer, "in plain words to organize for foreign trade just as the 'rings' of England and cartels of Germany are organized."[69]

But the resolutions of the Paris Economic Conference seemed to Washington only a part of the pattern—a pattern the administration believed was being woven to deny the United States a major role in the peace to come, economic or political. So when America finally did enter the war because of Germany's resumption of submarine warfare, it did so not as the Allies had hoped, but with a whole series of self-declared conditions which served the purpose Colonel House had been trying to achieve earlier. President Wilson had laid out a wholly independent position he expected to advance at the final peace conference.

Upon his return from Paris, the President explained his achievement:

> Mr. Taft was speaking of Washington's utterance about entangling alliances, and if he will permit me to say so, he put the exactly right interpretation that is inevitable if you read what he said. . . . And the thing that he longed for was just what we are about to supply; an arrangement which will disentangle all the alliances in the world.[70]

Wilson's attempt to take the final giant step to complete what had been started by the arbitration movement after 1895 divided his own backers: some preferred to have an ordinary military alliance with Great Britain and France, rather than take on the ambiguous burdens lurking behind Article Ten of the League Covenant; even the President seemed unclear about the exact nature of America's commitment under that clause. His opponents made good use of his vagueness.

Such questions were also linked to the problem of how to deal with the Russian Revolution, which had already split American and European liberals. Those who opposed the policy charged that the League and all its sanctions were being employed by reactionaries in the same way the Holy Alliance had been used to defeat nineteenth-century revolutions against tyranny. And there were a good many people who reacted against the intervention in Russia in the same way that they disagreed with the notion of fighting for other dubious propositions such as the Versailles settlements of the Shantung question—or Fiume—or German reparations.[71]

The April 1917 revolution had raised false hopes that the fall of czardom would eliminate yet one more carryover from the Dark Ages. It was a triumph over cultural inertia, the removal of the last block to the rise of a league of democracies. The American response, the railroad mission to set the Trans-Siberian Railway back running in apple-pie order, was comparable, it is suggested, to Paul Reinsch's vision for the modernization of China.

"E. H. Harriman," reported the engineer sent to carry out this mission, "described the Chinese Eastern as one of the greatest possibilities of any railroad property in the world. It is true. It taps a wonderful region. It is, say, thirteen or fourteen hundred miles long. It ought to have in branch lines, or feeders, like teeth in a rake as J. J. Hill used to call them, a thousand miles more." And former Secretary of Commerce Redfield explained to Wilson's last Secretary of State, Bainbridge Colby, what American exporters wanted to see done with the teeth in the rake: "That road is the direct route between our Pacific ports and Siberia and Russia. Were it to fall into hands whose interests were adverse to our own, the results would be disastrous, for no alternative route of equal directness and efficiency exists. . . . It is of vital importance therefore, to the future of Russia's trade and of our own commerce, that the direct route be maintained as an open passage."[72]

This reaction to the Bolshevik triumph a few months after the April revolution was typical. The Bolsheviks had opened the way, as these men feared, to a Japanese forward movement in Manchuria. In European Russia, the second revolution raised the likely probability that German efficiency methods would triumph there, not American techniques. And given the war-ravaged state of Europe, worst of all, it conjured up fears of a red wave pouring out across the continent—perhaps even across the channel—or the ocean!

Refusing to accept Anglo-French proposals for large-scale military intervention in European Russia, Wilson did use American economic power against the Bolsheviks—calling it, as Herbert Hoover remarked much later, the "Second American Expeditionary Force to Save Europe."[73] In Manchuria and Siberia, the United States also tried to rally anti-Bolshevik forces around various white leaders, making use of American troops in the endeavor. Finally, Wilson placed a moral embargo on Lenin's government that lasted down to 1933.

When Wilson began his climactic tour for the League of Nations he made it plain to critics and the citizenry in general that he saw in it the only alternative to the most dangerous kind of international anarchy. Without it, he warned repeatedly, the country would have to spend its resources (wastefully) in creating a gigantic military and naval establishment. Once again, the alternatives T.R. saw were posed for the nation by a new leader.

The country was nearly paralyzed, he told the Senate Foreign Relations Committee, while the nations that ratify the treaty "will be in a position to lay their plans for controlling the markets of central Europe without competition from us if we do not presently act. . . . There are large areas of Europe whose future will lie uncertain and questionable until their people know the final settlements of peace and the forces which are to administer and sustain it. Without determinate markets our production cannot proceed with intelligence or confidence."[74]

It was difficult for many to believe, however, that the League of Nations as Wilson had outlined it could meet the challenge presented by the three revolutions. Nor was it by any means sure that Wilson's supporters were right in saying that the only chance to rectify the mistakes in the Treaty of Versailles was through the League organization.

Had the arbitration movement, then, come to a dead end? There was no question but that Progressives were disillusioned by the peace-making experience; it had turned out to be a piece-taking orgy. However naive the Wilsonian crusade seemed then, at the end of 1919, or now, it does not follow that the realist critique applies as a wholly satisfactory generalization about foreign policy from the Open Door Notes to 1921. Far greater challenges faced American leaders in the first two decades of this century than had faced the first leader in the industrial era, Great Britain. Both had attempted to find the way to increase their chances to expand in a stable and orderly world. Starting afresh, the Harding administration tried to apply some of the lessons of those two decades in dealing with social revolution; it succeeded most with Mexico, not very much with Russia, and not at all in Asia.

Instead of pursuing the League question further, the new administration adopted a more limited approach at the Washington Naval Conference, a regional "arbitration" policy not unlike Colonel House's ABC plan for the Western Hemisphere. But when these arrangements broke down, followed by another great war, the American people were ready to follow leaders who took them into a new League of Nations.

The realist critique questioned certain manifestations of American foreign policy. Its contributions may be appreciated for what they are without admitting that its criticisms go to the center of the problem. On the other hand, one fears that this critique has been distorted too often in order to deny the relevance of all save the most "tough-minded" alternative in a given situation. Its major use seems to be to justify "elitism" as opposed to "popular" diplomacy. If it falls short as an explanation, it may well prove disastrous as a justification for basically unsound policies. And if Kennan set out to question America's extended commitments, his followers (as he now seems aware) have ironically increased those dubious undertakings in the name of realism. In the end, the realist critique leads one to believe that the rhetoric surrounding the foreign policy of a John Hay, or a Woodrow Wilson, was in fact the core substance of the policy: the radical perspective, on the other hand, sees the development of America's world view as a logical result of national expansion.

NOTES

1. George F. Kennan, *American Diplomacy, 1900–1950* (Mentor MP360; New York, 1952), p. 93. No attempt will be made to survey the literature of this interpretation, with all its variations. It has influenced writing about all periods of American diplomatic history. The bibliography of any standard textbook will provide the reader with a list of samples to test.

2. *Ibid.,* p. 90.

3. *Ibid.,* p. 39

4. *Ibid.,* pp. 39, 36.

5. Stanley K. Hornbeck, "The Enunciation of the Open Door Policy in Reference to China," August 14, 1918, *The Papers of the Inquiry,* File 232, National Archives. Secondary works which substantiate and develop Hornbeck's thesis are: Charles S. Campbell, Jr., *Special Business Interest and the Open Door Policy* (New Haven, Conn., 1951); William Appleman Williams, *The Tragedy of American Diplomacy* (Cleveland and New York, 1959); and Walter LaFeber, *The New Empire* (Ithaca, N.Y., 1963). Soon to be published by Quadrangle Books, Chicago, is Thomas McCormick's study of the origins of the Open Door policy, a revision of his "Fair Field and No Favor; American China Policy during the McKinley Administrations" (unpublished Ph.D. dissertation, University of Wisconsin, 1960).

6. See Brooks Adams, *The New Empire* (New York, 1901) and Charles A. Conant, *The United States in the Orient* (New York, 1900), not only to see what Kennan is refuting, but to examine their arguments first-hand in the light also of the studies cited above.

7. Kennan, *American Diplomacy,* p. 12.

8. As cited in the author's *A Different Frontier: Selected Readings in the Foundations of American Economic Expansion* (Chicago, 1966), pp. 134–35.

9. Kennan, *American Diplomacy,* p. 94.

10. Diary Entry, May 9, 1913, reprinted in Charles Seymour, ed., *The Intimate Papers of Colonel House* (4 vols.; Boston, 1926–28), I, 239, 273–75.

11. Literature on the peace movement is particularly unsatisfactory. A beginning toward understanding that was never taken up is Merle Curti's *Peace or War: The American Struggle, 1636–1936* (New York, 1938); Joseph Schumpeter also made some valuable suggestions even earlier that have never been examined. In his *Imperialism and Social Classes* (New York, 1955), he noted that the United States was "the first advocate of disarmament and arbitration . . . doing so most zealously, by the way, when economic interest in expansion was at its greatest" (see pp. 72–73). On the Venezuelan crisis, see Walter LaFeber, "The American Business

Community and Cleveland's Venezuelan Message," *Business History Review*, XXXIV (Winter 1960), 393–402.

12. LaFeber, "American Business Community."

13. Schurz is quoted in John Morley, "Arbitration with America," *Nineteenth Century*, XL (August 1896), 320–27.

14. National Arbitration Committee, *The Second American Conference on International Arbitration* (Washington, 1904), pp. 47–52.

15. Background on Farquhar's views on low tariffs and other international economic problems can be found in his *Economic and Industrial Delusions* (New York, 1891). He outlines his start in the peace movement in a letter to William Howard Taft, November 18, 1911, William Howard Taft Papers, Library of Congress. (hereafter, Taft Mss.).

16. William Jennings Bryan, *Letters to a Chinese Official* (New York, 1906), pp. 31–32.

17. Howard K. Beale's *Theodore Roosevelt and the Rise of America to World Power* (Baltimore, 1956) is the most recent study of T.R.'s acts in foreign policy. It is critical of Roosevelt, by the way, for being too much of a realist. Beale so thoroughly accepts the realist thesis that his study is framed to its dimensions. The quotation, however, is taken from Walt W. Rostow, *The United States in the World Arena* (New York, 1960), to point up varieties of interpretation within the general hypothesis (see p. 23).

18. See the article in the *Atlantic Monthly*, LXXXVIII (August 1901), 145–55. Background can be found in Gardner, *A Different Frontier*, pp. 159–83.

19. See, for example, Samuel Flagg Bemis, *The United States as a World Power*, rev. ed. (New York, 1955), pp. 61–62.

20. Roosevelt to Carnegie, August 6, 1906, Theodore Roosevelt Papers, Library of Congress.

21. Knox to Taft, June 23, 1911, Taft Mss. A realist interpretation of these events is Dana G. Munro, *Intervention and Dollar Diplomacy in the Caribbean, 1900–1921* (Princeton, 1964), Ch. 5.

22. Materials on Kasson's efforts can be found in the *Kasson Reciprocity Papers*, National Archives. See also Gardner, *A Different Frontier*, Introduction.

23. U.S. Senate, Committee on Foreign Relations, 56th Cong., 1st Sess., *Senate Document 225, Hearings and Exhibits on Reciprocity*, pp. 98–99.

24. Speech to the Philadelphia Commercial Museum, undated [December] 1897, enclosed in Farquhar to Kasson, December 9, 1897, Kasson Reciprocity Papers.

25. Charles L. Chandler to Knox, May 18, 1911, Department of State, Decimal File 811.516/6, National Archives. (hereafter, NA plus file number).

26. See Clyde William Phelps, *The Foreign Extension of American Banks* (New York, 1927), and Paul M. Warburg, *The Federal Re-*

serve *System, Its Origins and Growth* (2 vols.; New York, 1930), II, 187–88.

27. Bryan's speech is in, *Official Report of the National Foreign Trade Convention, 1914* (New York, 1914), pp. 207–11.
28. *The Stakes of Diplomacy* (New York, 1915), p. 149.
29. Seymour, *Intimate Papers of Colonel House*, II, 142.
30. Economic Club Address, May 23, 1912, reprinted in Ray Stannard Baker and William E. Dodd, eds., *The Public Papers of Woodrow Wilson* (8 vols.; New York, 1927), II, 430–51.
31. Quoted in Ray Stannard Baker, *Woodrow Wilson: Life and Letters* (8 vols.; New York, 1927–1939), IV, 128–29.
32. *Ibid.*
33. See Arthur S. Link, *Wilson: Confusions and Crises, 1915–1916* (Princeton, 1964), p. 343.
34. See, for example, "The Ideals of America," *Public Papers*, I, 419–41.
35. *New Industrial Day*, pp. 46–47.
36. *Ibid.*, and see pp. 1–17.
37. See Redfield to Wilson, April 11, 1914 and May 5, 1914, Woodrow Wilson Papers, Library of Congress (hereafter, Wilson Mss.).
38. *Philip Dru: Administrator*, p. 280.
39. *Ibid.*
40. Bemis, *U.S. as a World Power*, pp. 288–89.
41. Diary entry, July 8, 1914, Edward M. House Papers, Yale University Library (hereafter, House Mss.).
42. Circular Telegram to all American Diplomatic Officers in Latin America, March 12, 1913, Department of State, *Papers Relating to the Foreign Relations of the United States, 1913*, p. 7 (hereafter, *For. Rel.* followed by year).
43. *St. Louis Post-Dispatch*, April 20, 1913.
44. Bryan to Wilson, July 17, 1913, and August 6, 1913, William Jennings Bryan Papers, Library of Congress. Bryan may have had in mind the problem discussed in the context of his own experience in the West by Henry George in *Protection or Free Trade* (New York, 1886), p. 121: "Our internal commerce also involves the flow from country to city, and from West to East, of commodities for which there is no return. Our large mine-owners, ranch-owners, land-speculators, and many of our large farmers, live in the great cities. Our small farmers have had in large part to buy their farms on mortgage of men who live in cities to the east of them; the bonds of national, State, county, and municipal governments are largely so held, as are the stocks and bonds of railway companies. . . ." If we replace a few of the terms, we have Bryan's proposal for Latin America, and open up new possibilities for investigation of both situations.
45. *Ibid.*
46. Bryan to Thomas Bailly-Blanchard, December 19, 1914, *For. Rel.*, 1914, pp. 370–71.
47. Farnham to Bryan, January 22, 1914, NA 838.00/901.

48. Edward I. Bell, *The Political Shame of Mexico* (New York, 1914), p. 2.

49. This episode is well known, but see the discussion in Arthur S. Link, *Wilson: The New Freedom* (Princeton, 1956), pp. 347–78.

50. The most recent detailed retelling of this story is Robert Quirk's *An Affair of Honor: Woodrow Wilson and the Occupation of Vera Cruz* (Lexington, Ky., 1962).

51. November 24, 1913: Link, *New Freedom*, pp. 386–87.

52. For the background of the effort to use economic coercion on Mexico, see House to Lansing, August 4, 1915, *The Papers of Robert Lansing*, Library of Congress, Washington, D.C. For what this letter finally evolved into, see Robert F. Smith, "The Formation and Development of the International Banker's Committee on Mexico," *Journal of Economic History*, XXIII (December 1963), 574–86.

53. Economic Liaison Committee, "Petroleum Policy of the United States," n.d., 1919, Frank L. Polk Papers, Yale University Library.

54. Jacob W. Binder to Joseph Tumulty, March 26, 1913, NA 893.51/1356. There are a whole pile of similar letters in this file in the National Archives.

55. Reinsch's involvement in the plan can be followed in his *An American Diplomat in China* (New York, 1922), Ch. 1.

56. Moore to Wilson, February 11, 1914, NA 893.811/119b.

57. Willard Straight to Reinsch, February 25, 1914, Paul S. Reinsch Papers, State Historical Society of Wisconsin, Madison, Wis.

58. The most recent discussion of this effort is Burton F. Beers, *Vain Endeavor: Robert Lansing's Attempts to End the American-Japanese Rivalry* (Durham, N.C., 1962).

59. Japanese Embassy to the Department of State, March 2, 1920, and Memorandum by the Third Assistant Secretary of State, April 30, 1920, *For. Rel.*, 1920, I, pp. 500–503, 538–39.

60. Lamont's mission and its problems are discussed briefly in his *Across World Frontiers* (New York, 1948).

61. This point is made plain in Wolfgang J. Helbich's, "American Liberals in the League of Nations Controversy," soon to be published in *Public Opinion Quarterly*.

62. *Ibid.*

63. Ernest R. May, *The World War and American Isolation, 1914–1917* (Chicago, 1966), Ch. 4.

64. The Wilson-House correspondence is replete with examples of these ideas, but see two good examples: House to Wilson, June 16, 1915, and November 19, 1915, House Mss. The whole story may be followed in either May, *World War and American Isolation* or Arthur S. Link, *Wilson: The Struggle for Neutrality* (Princeton, 1960).

65. *Ibid.*

66. See Carl Parrini, "American Empire and Creating a Community

of Interest, 1916–1922" (unpublished Ph.D. thesis, University of Wisconsin, 1960).

67. *Ibid.*

68. Lansing to Wilson, June 23, 1916, *For. Rel., The Lansing Papers,* I, 311–12. And Lansing, "The Blunder of the Allied Economic Conference in Paris in June, 1916," August 25, 1917, Lansing Mss.

69. George Creel, "The Next Four Years: An Interview with the President," *Everybody's Magazine,* XXXVI (February 1917), 129–39; and Wilson's remarks in his Annual Message, December 5, 1916, *For. Rel.* 1916, p. xii.

70. March 4, 1919: copy in *Wilson MSS.*

71. For example, see Elihu Root to Henry Cabot Lodge, June 19, 1919, Elihu Root Papers, Library of Congress.

72. Thomas W. Lamont, "Memorandum," given by Ambassador Roland Morris to the Secretary of State, June 8, 1920, NA 861.77/1574; Redfield to Colby, November 5, 1920, NA 861.77/1811.

73. Herbert Hoover, *The Ordeal of Woodrow Wilson* (New York, 1958), p. 87 *et passim.*

74. Quoted by David F. Houston, *Eight Years with Wilson's Cabinet* (2 vols.; New York, 1926), II, 7–8.

AMERICAN FOREIGN

RELATIONS, 1920–1942

∽ Robert Freeman Smith

MANY HISTORIANS of United States foreign relations view the period from 1920 to 1942 through the smoke-filled air of the Pearl Harbor attack. In combination with the "Adolf Hitler syndrome" this has produced a basic plot and a series of acceptable phrases which characterize a considerable amount of writing in the field. A. J. P. Taylor pointedly discussed this conformity of historical interpretation, and also the possibility that the so-called "lessons of history" derived from this interpretation provided useful arguments for the Cold War policies of Great Britain and the United States.[1]

After the Second World War a nationalistic school of historical interpretation became predominant in the field of United States foreign relations. An older group of anti-Beardian historians provided the nucleus (with some assistance from geopoliticians) for a "patriotic" history which articulated the emotions of the Second World War and the Cold War.[2] The resulting interpretative consensus stressed the primacy of political factors, external pressures upon the United States, and the universal validity of the "American way of life."

Within this context the period from 1920 to 1940 has been generally described in terms of a retreat into isolationism which was only reversed when totalitarian aggressors forced a passive United States to fight for its survival. The elements in the plot vary, but most historians within this consensus begin with the argument that the United States' refusal to join the League of Nations represented a retreat from Wilsonian idealism and its promise of world peace through American enforcement of those ideals. The activities of the policy makers of the 1920s (especially in regard to the Kellogg-Briand Pact and the disarmament conferences) are pictured as naive, unrealistic attempts to shield the country from power politics. The fact of United States involvement in World War II is given as automatic evidence that the policies of this period were isolationist and wrong. For the 1930s, these historians portray a generally "internationalist" Franklin D. Roosevelt whose hands are tied by the depression and the political power of the isolationists. Thus, for most of the 1930s the United States is described as an "innocent bystander" (with emphasis on innocent) whose foreign policy is made in Berlin and Tokyo. In the late 1930s Roosevelt begins to try to lead the nation toward its "proper involvement" in world affairs, but it is only with the attack on Pearl Harbor that the President gains the final triumph over the isolationists. Then the United States again takes up the Wilsonian torch of "world leadership" and returns to its destiny of restoring peace to the world.

The ultimate logic of this interpretation provides "patriotic" justification for United States involvement in World War II, and links this to the policies of the Cold War. The isolationists, we are told, vainly attempt to regain power after the war, but the United States had "learned the lessons of history" and did not repeat the "mistakes" of the post-World War I period.

Another aspect of this plot is the portrayal of Japan, Germany, and Italy (and in some cases Soviet Russia) as "evil" aggressor nations which refused to accept their legitimate place in the world. Conversely the United States is described as an unambitious nation which only wanted peace in the world. Implicit in all of this is the assumption that the ideals and goals of the United States are right and that other nations have legitimate interests only when these coincide with the views of the United States and when these nations accept the role assigned to them by the United States formula for world order.

This emphasis on destiny, inevitability, and "good guys *vs*. bad guys" moralism is a characteristic of much writing about this period. We are informed *ad infinitum* that the United States "abdicated its responsibilities," "refused to accept the burden of world leadership," and "believed it could escape the contagion of war." This litany of power determinism is also characterized by a "devil theory" of noninvolvement. The isolationists were the naive, backward-looking people who fought to try to keep the United States from assuming its proper (and inevitable) role in the world. The heroes of the story are those who advocated the active military involvement of the United States in every corner of the world; the champions of "assuming international responsibilities," restoring the "balance of power" and accepting the "challenge of aggression." These recurrent phrases provide little real explanation for the foreign policy of the United States, but they do provide an insight into the beliefs of some historians and policy makers. Except for analyzing the isolationist deviates, this interpretation gives little attention to internal, socio-economic elements.

Much of the historical rhetoric and interpretation of this period reflects the debates and labels of the 1930s. The bad guys are anti-Roosevelt on both foreign and domestic issues, and isolationists and conservatives are both portrayed as unified groups. The good guys are the New Dealers-internationalists. In part, this interpretation may stem from the political views of some historians who consider themselves to be "vital center" (or New Deal) liberals. As defenders of the Wilson-Roosevelt-Truman reform tradition, these historians usually defend the foreign policies of these administrations. A related factor here may be the postwar attacks of some Republicans on New Deal legislation, which were often phrased in terms of "twenty years of treason" or the "Red Decade." One defense against such charges was to link the militant anti-communist policies of the Truman period to the policy of saving the world from fascist aggression, so as to demonstrate the "patriotism" of New Deal liberals. Thus, the emotions engendered by the Cold War may well have delayed a realistic evaluation of the causes of United States participation in World War II because orthodox interpretation of this was necessary for the historical arguments supporting containment and the Truman Doctrine.

The influence of geopolitical theorists is more in evidence among those consensus historians who are less sympathetic to the Wilson-Roosevelt tradition. On the surface the vocabulary of power (usually referred to as "balance of power") seems more objective and realistic since it avoids moralizing. But in many cases these historians have used the concept of power in a deterministic fashion, and United States world objectives become the inevitable products of geopolitical factors. In most cases the conclusions of historians who stress the logic of power are indistinguishable from those who stress manifest destiny. Whatever the intellectual or political genesis, consensus historians tend to accept with few questions the basic assumption that war with Japan and Germany was inevitable, realistic, and right.

The major scholarly efforts of this school are devoted to studying the tactics of foreign policy. Questions are raised in this area and some controversy takes place, but the basic goals and underlying motives of policy are rarely questioned or subjected to critical analysis. In fact, this deeper analysis has been called unobjective by some historians, who maintain that the only role of the historian is to describe what happened. One historian has designated this latter approach as neo-Rankean.[3] This is an apt term, since Ranke once wrote that he was only "following the footsteps of God in history." As with Ranke, the works of the neo-Rankeans in the United States are far more than mere descriptions of events. In the last analysis, many are also briefs in support of an imperial role for the United States, whether this is euphemistically called world leadership or international responsibility.

Perhaps the basic element in the approach of the neo-nationalists is the fact that they believe (and implicitly promulgate) the myth of the unique nation; a nation which is unselfish, unambitious, and whose world goals are good for all people. Those nations and groups which challenge this assumption are therefore labeled aggressors or appeasers. In reality, this world view is the ideological baggage of Manifest Destiny presented in modern terminology and in more sophisticated rhetoric. The relationship between this view of the righteousness and wisdom of the American concept of world order, the idea of inevitability, and the imperial stance of a *Pax Britannica-Pax Americana* are well illustrated in Samuel Eliot Morison's *Strategy and Compromise*. According to Morison, *all* of the United States and British military involvements since the 1860s have been part of a common effort to achieve a stable world, "in which they can 'do business' in other ways than at the point of a gun."[4]

Such a proposition as this, and the beliefs behind it, should certainly be subjected to critical analysis. Historians, however, have been reluctant to challenge the consensus position —perhaps through fear of being labeled Beardians, Marxists, or neo-Actonians. Some develop their analysis to the point where it seems that some basic questions are about to be raised. In too many instances, however, the writer suddenly shifts his analysis to the cloudy area of philosophical determinism, and the reader is informed that the events (and their consequences) were really "tragically inevitable."

Other historians have criticized the results of United States policy, but have shifted the focus of their criticism to public opinion. This vague entity has been called uninformed, and a moralistic obstruction to policy makers who were trying to carry out "international responsibilities."[5] But the use of inevitability or misdirected public opinion allows the historian to criticize tactics without challenging the assumptions of the unique-nation mythology.

Historical writing is not stagnant, however, and signs of a deeper degree of analysis and a greater flexibility are much in evidence. The concept of "retreat to isolationism" in the 1920s has been seriously challenged and the goals of the so-called isolationists of the 1930s have also received more serious treatment.[6]

A minority group of foreign relations historians have been particularly active in reinvigorating the internal analysis of the goals of United States policy. While emphases vary, these men tend to reject the nationalistic view of the unique nation, and to focus upon the ideas, beliefs, and interests which constituted the framework in which policy makers interpreted the world. Their works reject the view of a somewhat befuddled, defensive United States facing a world of predatory aggressors, and instead present the United States as a rather imperial-minded power with ambitions and goals which on the whole are rather similar to those of most other modern powers. This group generally rejects the position of inevitability in history, and emphasizes the role of policy makers as representatives of groups in a society.

The works of these historians present various aspects of the theme that United States policy makers have adhered to a relatively consistent world view since at least the late nineteenth century. In the process, rhetorical terms such as "collective security" and "international responsibilities" are revealed as modern terminology for older ambitions and goals.[7] Some of these historians have also broadened the scope of the foreign relations field by analyzing the impact of United States policy on other countries and the reactions which in turn created new problems for the policy makers.[8]

New insights and much basic research have placed the foreign relations of the United States in the 1920s and 1930s in a fresh context. Perhaps we are even on the verge of a major synthesis concerning the road to World War II. The signs of such a development are clearer in the field of United States-Japanese relations than in the field of United States-German relations, since very few historians have any empathy for Nazism. Yet, as A. J. P. Taylor has indicated, the "Adolf Hitler syndrome" is too simplistic an explanation for such a major catastrophe. In the last analysis, the study of the historical development of the underlying motives and internal pressures involved in the foreign relations of all the major powers must be integrated to achieve the needed perspective.

One of the basic concerns of United States policy makers from 1920 to 1941 was the establishment and maintenance of a world order which would be conducive to the prosperity and power of the United States. Since the latter part of the nineteenth century government officials, intellectuals, and businessmen had been actively promoting various means for the extension and protection of the new frontiers created by the economic expansion of the country. By 1920 one of these tactics had been modified (colonialism), and another had been rejected (international organization directed by the major powers). Officials had developed a combination of other tactics, however, which they hoped would ensure an "Open Door World"; a stable world order in which the United States could enjoy the fruits of an imperial position without the military, financial, and administrative burdens of a colonial empire. "Dollar Diplomacy," protectorates, intervention, and the extension of the political and value systems of the industrial United States were all involved in the drive to establish this broad system of influence and control. The belief that the nation's prosperity depended upon free access to markets, raw materials, and investment opportunities was a basic element in all of these formulations.

In a similar manner, definitions of security and strategic necessities generally followed these interpretations of economic frontiers. This entanglement of security and prosperity was noted by Representative Carl Vinson of Georgia in 1932 when he said:

> Not alone are free seas necessary to enable us to import our necessities, but they are vital to our prosperity, for without the ability to export our surplus farm products, our surplus manufactured articles . . . an economic situation would quickly be brought about which would make our present depression seem an era of prosperity.[9]

Beliefs concerning the mission and destiny of the United States added an emotional ingredient to this world view. These beliefs were linked to a faith in the humanitarian nature of United States goals, and this was an important part of the self-image which the government tried to project in its international affairs. Relief missions for the victims of famine, flood, and earthquake were expressions of a desire to do good. Such manifestations of peace and good will were not hypocritical. But they did obscure for Americans the impact which the United States had on other countries and the reasons why some people in the world opposed American formulas for political and economic relations (even when mixed with charitable acts). This in turn produced frustration and anger in the United States, as in 1919 when Fiorello H. La-Guardia told the House of Representatives that he would go to Mexico with beans in one hand and hand grenades in the other and, "God help them in case they do not accept our well-intended and sincere friendship."[10]

United States officials wanted peace, stability, and good will in the world, but they also wanted a variety of other things. The latter often collided with other people's interpretations of their own national interests and ideals. The contradictory elements in United States policy could not be resolved simply by charitable acts or professions of good will.

The First World War was a bloody contest between the major Western nations for positions of dominant influence in Europe and in the underdeveloped world. The struggle for predominance in the underdeveloped areas—especially in Africa and the area from the Balkans to the islands of the Pacific—had been a major factor behind the creation of the prewar alliance systems, but neither the alliances nor the war resolved the basic problems. The United States was deeply involved in this struggle, and Warren Harding expressed a prevalent belief when he told the National Association of Manufacturers:

> When Europe . . . turns to the rehabilitation and reconstruction of peace, there will be a struggle for commercial and industrial supremacy such as the world has never witnessed. And if this land of ours desires to maintain its eminence, it must be prepared for that struggle. (Applause.)[11]

Yet many government officials realized that such a continued struggle could produce another major war between the industrial nations which might have disastrous consequences for all concerned. Norman H. Davis wrote to William Gibbs McAdoo about the "disastrous experiences" of World War I and noted:

> The paramount interest of the United States beyond its frontiers is the maintenance of peace, because experience has proven that the repercussions from armed disturbances of the peace do not stop at our frontiers, but may choke up

our channels of trade and commerce, and threaten our political rights and freedom of action.[12]

Davis believed that international organization, such as the League of Nations, provided the "only practical means in this industrial era" of advancing the interests of the United States. But the opposition to this method from the advocates of various other kinds of world order (not isolationists) meant that the policy makers of the 1920s would have to extend the "Open Door" concept by methods which did not involve organizational commitments. Thus, between 1921 and 1931, Secretaries of State Charles Evans Hughes, Frank B. Kellogg, and Henry L. Stimson tried to build a world order through treaties and other arrangements. The goal was a "law-bound" world in which the industrial powers would agree to maintain the status quo, respect the Open Door concept, and generally cooperate in policing the underdeveloped areas. Such a goal was based on the assumption that these industrial-creditor nations were basically satisfied with the division of the world's resources and territory, that their interests were basically the same, and that recognizing these conditions they would settle their disputes peacefully and "legally."[13]

The first major step toward establishing this world order was the Washington Conference of 1921. The treaties produced by this conference established an up-to-date set of ground rules for East Asia—with the Open Door as a key element—limited naval armaments, and enunciated a thinly veiled American-British predominance on the oceans of the world. The latter aspect was a reflection of the important role which the British Empire—and memories of the *Pax Britannica*—played in the "Open Door World" concept of United States officials. In a confidential memorandum prepared during the conference, J. V. A. McMurray stated that Japan had no choice but to cooperate with the United States and Britain, since this "strongest political and naval grouping" could isolate Japan and destroy its economy.[14] The abrogation of the Anglo-Japanese Alliance and the 5:5:3 capital ship ratio were symbols of this cooperative supremacy. For several years the Japanese accepted this system, which an official later described as "Rolls Royce: Rolls Royce: Ford."

The Kellogg-Briand Pact and the disarmament conferences of 1927 and 1930 were other steps in the development of a treaty system to stabilize the Open Door World. The United States government also took an active part in negotiating settlements with the various European powers to guarantee the Open Door in Asia and Africa. The British and French did resist the entry of American oil companies into the Middle East, but the State Department—in conjunction with these companies—forced an accommodation which gave the American companies an important stake in these oil regions.[15] Similarly, the government used its influence at the Lausanne Conference (1922–1923) to protect United States access to the Black Sea and to the natural resources of Turkey.[16]

The State Department policy concerning stabilization of the Open Door in underdeveloped regions was succinctly stated by Secretary Hughes in 1924 when Representative Theodore Burton complained that the mandates were not being used to benefit the "backward people." Hughes wrote, "We have proceeded upon the policy of negotiating treaties to protect American interest in the mandated regions." Burton was further informed that the United States had negotiated—or was negotiating—treaties with France, Belgium, Japan, and Britain to ensure an "equal position" for the United States. Hughes also suggested that Burton refrain from mentioning the problem of commercial exploitation of the mandated regions in his proposed speech.[17]

The United States version of world order was also promoted by Dollar Diplomacy. The Dawes and Young plans for the economic rehabilitation of Germany were examples of this. In addition, the State Department refused to give approval for American bankers' loans to France and Belgium until these two countries gave "written assurances" that they would purchase their share of the Dawes Plan annuities.[18] The Department used the same tactic to curtail what were called "unproductive or militaristic purposes" in Rumania, Greece, and Austria, and to protect American economic interests which were supposedly threatened by Brazil (coffee valorization), Germany (Potash Syndicate), and Japan (Japanese business interests in China).[19]

All of these activities to promote an industrial-creditor version of stability, in a world open to the economic and ideological penetration of the United States, were not intended simply to "secure peace as an end in itself, but to make available the opportunities of peace."[20] The latter phrase was written by Secretary Hughes, who also told the United States Chamber of Commerce:

> The Department of State is carrying the flag of the twentieth century. It aims to be responsive in its own essential sphere to what it recognizes as the imperative demands of American business. It aims at the coordination of the work of all departments bearing upon the same great object of American prosperity.[21]

This was a common theme among government officials. The prosperity of the nation was inextricably connected to a multidimensional foreign policy which in general was supposed to ensure a stable and protective world order for trade and investments, and specifically promote and protect these interests by direct action.

Secretary Stimson in 1932 summarized the European and Asiatic policies of the United States as these had developed since 1921. The Secretary stated that the United States enjoyed "a unique position of national security," but the prosperity of the nation was at stake, since "An armed camp is not a favorable breeding place for either trade or investment." Stimson cited the various treaties and conferences of the period and noted:

> These striking steps toward peace and good-will in Europe directly conduce to the cause of ultimate stability in that Continent. They directly strengthen the normal foundations of the greatest foreign pillar upon which rests American trade and industrial development.[22]

The Secretaries pointed out that the policies of the Open Door ("so vital to our commercial interests") and the interrelated treaty structure were the East Asian versions of the same world strategy.

United States officials believed that one of the major

threats to this world status quo came from nationalistic revolutions. Such upheavals not only destroyed property and disrupted trade, but also threatened the basic economic and legal framework which had been developed by the industrial-creditor nations. Reform-minded nationalists in the underdeveloped nations wanted to assert control over natural resources, institute land reform, promote industrial development, and generally modify—or break completely—the international order of the developed, capitalistic nations.

In 1922 former Secretary of the Interior Franklin K. Lane expressed a common attitude toward such developments when he wrote:

> When I say that Russia may go her own way, and Mexico hers, I say so with a sense that I have a right in Russia and in Mexico, and also a right to see that they do not go their own way to the extent of blocking my way to what of good they hold.[23]

Secretary Hughes elaborated on this theme in a speech concerning Mexico, and said:

> Intercourse, from the standpoint of business, consists in the making of contracts and the acquisition of property rights. . . . and the most important principle to be maintained at this time with respect to international relations is that no State is entitled to a place within the family of nations if it destroys the foundations of honorable intercourse by resort to confiscation and repudiation.[24]

Calvin Coolidge also referred to the extension and protection of these principles as giving "support to the side of freedom."[25]

The Soviet Union made the most complete break with this world order, and not only asserted absolute control over the internal economy of the country but also encouraged other nations to follow this example. United States policy makers believed that no regime could follow such "heretical" and "unsound" economic policies and survive for long. Thus, the United States government refused to recognize the Soviet government. Instead the United States concentrated on discouraging revolutions in other areas, and on trying to stabilize capitalist economies in countries such as Germany, Cuba, and Peru.

Latin America was regarded as one of the most sensitive areas in the world because of the belief that United States predominance was a *sine qua non* for the prosperity and power of the nation. The reforms emanating from the Mexican Revolution seemed especially to threaten the United States position, and officials feared that the Mexican "contagion" would spread. As James R. Sheffield—Ambassador to Mexico from 1924 to 1927—told President Coolidge, the future of the United States as a creditor nation depended on a firm stand in Mexico, since "Any weakness in our attitude here is certain to be reflected almost immediately in other foreign countries."[26] But the earlier use of military force to maintain order and protect foreign property had created a major dilemma in Latin American relations. Anti-United States sentiment was increasing during the early 1920s, and officials believed that this also threatened the nation's predominant position in the hemisphere.

The Latin American policy of the second Woodrow Wilson administration was marked by a revival of Dollar Diplomacy. Wilson, however, was still prepared to use military tactics in 1920. An Army division was secretly prepared for use in Cuba, and a Marine Emergency Expeditionary Force of 1,200 men was on standby alert for a Mexican intervention during the upheaval of May 1920.[27] The Republican administrations of the 1920s de-emphasized military intervention, and instead concentrated on a variety of economic, diplomatic, and cultural tactics to reinforce the status quo in Latin America. A treaty system, United States mediation of disputes, and the manipulation of private loans were important tools of policy. In addition, policy makers and businessmen believed that the expansion of educational facilities would help to convert Latin Americans to North American "ideals," thus smoothing the way for the extension of United States influence.[28]

Whatever the tactics used, the basic goals of United States policy had not changed. The instructions to the United States delegates to the 1928 Pan-American Conference stated:

> It may be observed that the United States is uninfluenced
> even by the willingness or desire of any American State to
> . . . submit to any form of political control or influence
> of a non-American State. In maintaining its position, the
> United States has been governed primarily by its own in-
> terests, involving its conception of what was essential to its
> security and its distinctive position in this hemisphere.[29]

In actual practice, United States officials even objected to
the possibility of another American state exerting influence
beyond its borders. The decision to send the Marines back to
Nicaragua in 1927 was based partly on the fear that Mexico
was trying to exert some pressure in Central America.

By 1929 the United States seemed largely to have achieved
the goal of an Open Door world order. Outside of the Soviet
Union the international legal-economic-ideological system
of the industrial-creditor nations was predominant, and the
United States had been generally successful in molding this
along the lines of a *Pax Americana*.[30] Military garrisons were
still being utilized in China, Nicaragua, Haiti, and the Dominican Republic, but Herbert Hoover's administration was
planning gradually to terminate the Western Hemisphere
"interpositions." In addition, Mexico had returned to the
fold of "well-behaved" underdeveloped nations, and the oil-
fields of the Middle East had been opened to American companies. This predominant position had been achieved without a large military establishment or the acquisition of a
major colonial empire.

The great depression, however, created a basic foreign
policy dilemma for the United States: how to maintain an
imperial position in the world without fighting those nations
which tried to challenge the status quo by threatening the
Open Door world order. The tactics and treaty systems devised by United States policy makers in the 1920s began to
break down after 1930 as the struggle for economic survival
intensified economic and political nationalism in all of the
industrial nations. In the process latent ambitions, old
wounds, and lingering frustration over Anglo-American predominance in the world unleashed rivalries which produced
a decade of foreign-policy debate in the United States.

At the same time the New Deal recovery program was based partly upon the recovery and expansion of foreign markets. To further this aim the Roosevelt administration expanded the activities of the Reconstruction Finance Corporation to include foreign operations, and created the Export-Import Bank. Both of these were designed to subsidize exports (as private lending had done prior to 1930), as well as stimulate other foreign activities of American business. The Trade Agreements program proved to be particularly useful in promoting trade with underdeveloped nations, since the United States could grant reciprocity to raw-material imports which were largely noncompetitive.[31]

United States officials believed that Latin America was of prime importance for the recovery of the export trade. The highly publicized "Good Neighbor" Policy was basically a continuation of previous policies. New tactics (trade agreements, Export-Import Bank loans) were introduced, the Latin Americans were courted with more fervor, and the United States government became the principal financial element in the revised Dollar Diplomacy. But, the economic and political hegemony of the United States was still the basic objective.[32]

The success of these measures, however, depended upon the maintenance of the Open Door World, and the general agreement of the other industrial nations concerning international economic rules. The crisis of the early 1930s prompted these nations to adopt varying degrees of governmental control, and even the British with their Imperial Preference System seemed to be moving away from the Open Door concept. Cordell Hull and Roosevelt believed that this trend away from "liberal" trade practices presented a threat to the United States, and the diplomatic notes of the period were filled with charges of "economic aggression"—especially against Japan and Germany. While attacking the policies of other nations, the United States government did some of the same things. The first trade agreement (Cuba, 1934) was clearly intended to drive Japan out of the Cuban market and establish what Sumner Welles called the "practical control" of that market by the United States. The Jones-Costigan Act (1934) created a closed sugar-marketing system

in the United States based upon subsidies and rigid government controls. In addition, Export-Import Bank loans were
generally tied to requirements that the funds be used to
purchase United States goods. In some instances these loans
were used as subsidies to pro-United States regimes or as
rewards for legislation favorable to United States interests.[33]

In 1935, United States officials began to call Germany and
Japan "aggressors" because of their economic activities. A
War Department memorandum in 1935 defined the ultimate
"threat" in Asia largely in economic terms and stated that
Japan's desire to be the dominant power in East Asia would
have "a direct influence on those people of Europe and
America who depend on trade and commerce with this area
for their livelihood."[34] The same year Cordell Hull decided
that Germany was "straining every tendon to undermine
United States trade relations with Latin America."[35] This
anxiety over economic "aggression" grew more intense, and
in May 1940, Assistant Secretary of State Breckinridge Long
commented that the subordination of Europe to German
control would mean that "every commercial order will be
routed to Berlin and filled under its orders somewhere in
Europe rather than in the United States." The result would
be "falling prices and declining profits here and a lowering
of our standard of living with the consequent social and
political disturbances."[36] These arguments were repeated
ad infinitum, and clearly indicate that the concept of security
was thoroughly entangled with the belief that the preservation of private enterprise capitalism in the United States
depended upon a world order in which this system was free
to operate with few restrictions.

A subordinate element in this world view was the identification of capitalism with such concepts as democracy and
constitutional government. This was not stressed with any
consistency (and could be ignored as in the case of Spain
after the Civil War), but it did become another element in
defining the "German threat" after 1936. Some began to
argue that Nazism was genuine socialism, and one writer
stated the moral of this connection in these words:

> Capitalism is lost where it is not built on liberalism and
> democracy. And liberalism and democracy are lost where

they fail to convince the people of the necessity of capitalism as the only available economic safeguard of political, intellectual and spiritual freedom.[37]

This argument was useful for defending capitalism at home, and also for attempting to heal a foreign policy split in the business community. Some in the business sector, with investment ties to the German economy, believed that the policies of National Socialism provided economic rationalization and stability in Central Europe, while others viewed these as a broad threat to the economic and political interests of the United States.[38]

The basic element in the foreign policy debate of the 1930s was not a division between isolationists and internationalists, but rather a disagreement between various groups over the most expeditious tactics for maintaining the world position of the United States. Various kinds of internationalists advocated tactics involving cooperation with the other status quo powers, while a multifarious assortment of unilateralists—usually called isolationists—generally stressed a political nonentanglement policy. There were few genuine isolationists in any positions of power, and Felix Morley (editor of the *Washington Post*) pointed out this fact in an attack on the supporters of the Neutrality Acts. Morley indicated his respect for the "man who talks real isolation," and stated: "But for the political isolationists, who believe that at one and the same time we can be *economically dominant throughout the world* and politically isolated, I cannot say that I have any intellectual respect."[39]

These groups were basically divided over the kinds of foreign policy tactics best suited to promote the prosperity of private-enterprise capitalism in the United States. This was complicated by disagreements over the use of military force, the relative importance to the United States of different regions of the world (some of the unilateralists advocated aggressive tactics in East Asia), and the question of which nations really threatened capitalism. A significant number of so-called isolationists really feared Soviet Russia and radicalism in general. Representative Hamilton Fish, Jr., provided a good illustration of this in a 1931 speech:

> So far as we are concerned, the economic phase of it [communism] is the most serious at the present time to the American people because free American labor cannot compete with labor in Russia. . . . Furthermore, we have more to fear from Russia than from any other country, because it is a great country like our own, with enormous natural resources in wheat, oil, lumber, and cotton. It is not Russian imports in this country, but Russian competition in the world markets, that we have to fear.[40]

This fear of Soviet Russia was also present in administration circles, and was a part of the world view of such men as Ambassadors Joseph P. Kennedy and William C. Bullitt, and Breckinridge Long. The latter noted in his diary (October 11, 1939) that the "eventual enemy" of the United States was Russia, and that if the "responsible" Nazis would replace Adolf Hitler with Hermann Goering then the Western powers might be able to obtain a rapid settlement with Germany.[41] In East Asia, United States officials were still suspicious of the radicalism of some leaders of the Kuomintang and feared the possibility of attacks on foreign property.[42]

For an administration dedicated to restoring domestic prosperity these conflicting interests and views helped to produce some ambiguities and heated controversies in the formulations of tactics. But the basic agreement of most political figures (in both the executive and the legislative branches) in regard to the relationship between the Open Door World and United States prosperity is clearly revealed by the history of the Neutrality Acts. Those who were closest to true isolationism lost all of the major contests. Some aspects of trade and financing were regulated, but these had only a limited effect on the world economic position of the country. Senator Key Pittman voiced a common opinion in 1939 when he argued for repeal of the arms embargo on the grounds "that further obstructions to our exports would bankrupt large sections of our country."[43] United States commercial interests were quite active also in attacking restrictions on trade, and in 1939 they were instrumental in limiting the cash-and-carry restrictions solely to the North Atlantic area.[44]

Military preparations provide another insight into this

fundamental agreement over goals. In June 1933 Franklin D. Roosevelt allotted $238 million of NRA funds to a naval building program—the largest single construction undertaken by any nation since the end of Word War I.[45] This trend continued, and as Wayne Cole has described it, "Congress never failed to appropriate the funds requested by the Roosevelt Administration for the army and navy." In fact, Congress usually appropriated more than Roosevelt requested.[46]

This does not mean that the leaders of the United States wanted war. But most of them wanted to preserve an international order in which the country could have the fruits of an imperial position. The British and French empires were important elements in the maintenance of this system (although United States officials wanted to eliminate some aspects of empire which were not conducive to United States interests). Thus, when the French collapsed and the British began to falter in mid-1940, United States officials were faced with the dilemma of when and how militarily to engage the disruptors of the status quo.

After September 1939 the German policy of military conquest became the paramount issue for United States policy makers—especially as this affected Britain and France (the traditional guarantors of an open Europe). The military problem was in part based upon the economic ambitions of Germany, and the belief that Germany could only gain economic (and military) security by breaking the world order dominated by Britain, the United States, and France. Early in 1937 Hjalmar Schacht, the German Finance Minister, wrote that Germany must have some control over markets, sources of raw materials, and investment outlets. He concluded with the blunt warning that the German "colonial problem" was "simply and solely a problem of economic existence. Precisely for that reason the future of European Peace depends upon it."[47]

Cordell Hull repeatedly told the Germans that they should follow "our program of peace, orderly progress, and normal international relations," since the only alternative was the "course of force, militarism, and territorial aggression." In a similar vein, he suggested to the Italian ambassador in No-

vember 1935 that massive investments be used in Ethiopia
instead of military conquest.[48] On the eve of conflict both
Britain and the United States offered the Germans an improved position in the existing world order. The United
States proposed a vague program of armament reduction,
and the establishment of a "liberal, unconditional most-
favored-nation international trade relationship."[49] The un-
official British proposals were more specific. These involved armament reduction, nonaggression pacts, and the
recognition of a German "sphere of activity" in eastern and
southern Europe. Some British officials also proposed "far
reaching plans for a joint Anglo-German working arrangement for opening up new markets or expanding existing
ones." China and Russia were cited as areas for this cooperation, and competition in other markets was to be eliminated.[50]

Perhaps the Germans would not have accepted these offers
at any time. Whatever the case, by August 1939 Adolf Hitler
had decided to make Europe a bastion of German power.
The Nazi racist policy was indeed repugnant to many leaders
in Western Europe and the United States, but if Hitler had
concentrated on Eastern Europe and Soviet Russia he probably could have avoided a war with these nations.[51] The general reluctance of the American public toward participation
in another European war did delay the actual involvement of
the United States. But, given the attack on Britain and
France, and an official United States concept of world order
substantially the same as that of the policy makers of 1914–
1917, this involvement may well have come even if the Germans had employed less barbaric practices.

The actual defense of the United States was one factor involved in the move to an "all-out aid short of war" policy,
but the restoration of the Open Door world order was of at
least equal importance to the Roosevelt administration. The
United States also used this opportunity to try to force the
British to accept completely the Open Door ground rules.
The British were in desperate straits in March 1941, but
many United States officials seemed more concerned with
squeezing concessions from them—as *quid pro quos* for Lend-
Lease aid—than with the war effort. J. P. Moffat noted in his

diary that the most important of these was the modification
of the Ottawa Agreements.[52] Roosevelt did moderate these
demands, but at the Atlantic Conference he informed Win-
ston Churchill that the economic policies of the Empire must
be changed. In his conversations with the Prime Minister,
Roosevelt based this demand on the United States' concern
for colonial peoples. In private, he was more explicit. As he
told his son:

> It's something that's not generally known, but British bank-
> ers and German bankers have had world trade pretty well
> sewn up in their pockets for a long time. . . . Well, now,
> that's not so good for American trade, is it? . . . If in the past
> German and British economic interests have operated to
> exclude us from world trade, kept our merchant shipping
> down, closed us out of this or that market, and now Ger-
> many and Britain are at war, what should we do?

The President's answer was that the United States should
help the British, but insist on changes in imperial policy
which hampered the economic interests of the United States.
The formula for postwar reorganization of the world was
presented to Churchill in the traditional rhetoric of the Open
Door: "Equality of peoples involves the utmost freedom of
competitive trade."[53] This is not to argue that Roosevelt was
not sincerely convinced that what was good for the interests
of the United States was also good for the peoples of the
world. But Churchill sincerely believed the same thing about
the Empire, and the Japanese believed in the goodness of the
Greater East Asia Co-Prosperity Sphere.

Roosevelt and Hull were able proponents of the twentieth-
century version of American "Manifest Destiny." Both
wanted peace, but they also wanted a particular kind of
world order and conceived of an American mission to establish this. In a speech given in 1932 Hull criticized the
Republicans for not following the policies of Woodrow
Wilson, and declared:

> America, thus exceptionally equipped to lead the world to
> heights of wealth and civilization undreamed of, had but to
> gird herself, yield to the law of manifest destiny, and go
> forward as the supreme world factor economically and mor-
> ally.[54]

Thus, Roosevelt, Hull, and other officials moved, with varying degrees of speed, to an acceptance of a kind of military involvement which would lead to a world policed by the United States and other developed nations with the same view of the world order.[55]

The ideological basis of this development obscured the real differences between Japan and Germany and paved the way for a double war. Paul Schroeder has documented the Japanese efforts for a peaceful settlement, the relative unimportance of the German-Japanese Alliance, and the desire of some United States military leaders for a compromise in East Asia.[56] Japan did not want to rule the world (German intentions are less clear), but in 1941 the United States rigidly asserted that any order in Asia would have to be in terms of "the basic objectives of American Far Eastern policy"[57] Hull's last note to the Japanese made this abundantly clear.

Why did the United States take a position which the policy makers knew would probably lead to war? Some undoubtedly wanted a "back door" to war in Europe (Henry L. Stimson, Harold Ickes), and others had been advocating a militant Asian policy for several years (Stanley Hornbeck, Admiral Leahy). Mixed up with these views was the belief that Germany and Japan were absolutely united in a worldwide conspiracy, and that the two (with Italy, the very junior partner) were identical in terms of ideologies and objectives. This was reinforced in 1941 by British pressure for United States military action in Asia, which added a note of emotional urgency and—to some—seemed to confirm the worldwide threat to the British Empire and the Open Door World.[58]

Until 1941 the United States followed two fairly separate roads to war. The one would probably not have been taken had Germany attacked Russia in 1940 instead of Western Europe. Certainly during the winter of 1939-1940 the British and French seemed more willing to fight Russia than Germany, and there were similar reactions in the United States.[59]

The war with Japan might have taken place anyway. Roosevelt described the causes of United States involvement in a traditional idiom of "Manifest Destiny," the frontier. He compared the United States to the "peaceful" frontiersmen who were attacked by the aggressive Indians, and who restored peace by shooting some of these aggressors and by driving the remainder into reservations.[60] The "omnipotent sophistry of interest and passion" which was used to define aggression in the Indian Wars was still useful in the twentieth century.[61] By asserting an American frontier in Asia, however, the United States confronted a Japan with national ambitions, and the stage was set for a double war when Germany moved west.

In 1901 the philosopher of empire, Brooks Adams, wrote:

> Destruction has awaited the gambler who backs his luck, the braggart who would be at once rich, aggressive, and unarmed. . . . America enjoys no immunity from natural laws. She can pay for what she takes, or she can fight for it, but she cannot have the earth for nothing. . . .

The attack on Pearl Harbor vividly revealed the full implications of this imperial logic.[62]

III

Historians play an important role in shaping beliefs about the past, and these in turn have a significant effect on decisions about present and future policy. Thus historians help to provide the intellectual justification for current foreign policy activities. The "lessons" of the 1920s and 1930s are constantly cited in defense of United States foreign policy around the world. We have been warned of the dangers of another "Munich" so often that the word has become a descriptive noun. The word "appeasement" (which at one time was a good diplomatic term for bargaining) has become linked to a historical interpretation that a series of "surrenders" in the 1930s produced World War II. In this same context we are informed that history teaches us that the opposition, or aggressors, will always accept our solutions if threatened with enough military power. Thus, United States policy from the Dominican Republic to Vietnam is explained in the light of historical lessons which in turn are derived from a nationalistic interpretation of the past.[63]

By linking the Cold War policies of the United States to this interpretation of American involvement in World War

II (or applying the lessons of history) historians have portrayed Russia and China as identical twins (or triplets) of Nazi Germany. Since there is no difference between these "aggressive" powers, the problems of the postwar era are treated as repetitions of the 1930s. Secretary of State Dean Rusk has relied heavily on this use of historical analogy. In discussing the United States stake in Vietnam in 1965 he said:

> Can those of us in this room forget the lesson that we had in this issue of war and peace when it was only 10 years from the seizure of Manchuria to Pearl Harbor; about 2 years from the seizure of Czechoslovakia to the outbreak of World War II in Western Europe?

The term Communist is now used as the unifying word to link to China and Russia all those groups in the world which oppose the United States concept of world order, and from Vietnam to the Dominican Republic guerrillas and revolutionaries can be compared to the Nazi legions (and handled in the same way). This distorted use of historical analogy vastly oversimplifies not only the policies of Russia and China, but also the nationalistic reform movements around the world.

An ironic aspect of this is that consensus scholars are quite critical of the revisionist historians of the 1920s and 1930s (who challenged the "patriotic" interpretation of United States entry into World War I), and accuse them of using the so-called lessons of the period 1914–1917 to support measures such as the Neutrality Acts. Yet these same consensus scholars adhere to the idea that "history repeats itself" when they apply the lessons of the pre-World War II period to the postwar era.

A critical re-evaluation of the period 1920–1941 produces no simple formula for United States foreign policy. It does reveal the inherent problems involved in trying to maintain a particular concept of world order based upon what United States leaders believed about the national necessities of the United States.

A variety of tactics have been developed in the struggle to achieve a relatively status quo world. But these have not been uniformly successful, and by the mid-1960s the United States had reverted to such older tactics as armed intervention (Dominican Republic) and military colonialism (Vietnam). This is not due to history repeating itself, but to the essential dilemma involved in a national attempt to maintain a world imperium with its double standard of international conduct. When other nations or groups reject the United States definition of their place in the world and their vital interests, then conflict develops. The maintenance of an imperial position (whatever the form) in effect becomes a declaration of perpetual war, and this could be suicidal in the nuclear age.

The world is no more stable or peaceful in 1967 than it was in 1920. Perhaps it is time to reconsider the basic ideas, interests, and beliefs undergirding a utopian concept of world order which interprets the world in terms of an American frontier. The "Garden of Eden" of a stable world run by the Western industrial-capitalistic nations was a half-truth even in the nineteenth century.[64] To pursue this will-o-the-wisp with fire and sword in the mid-twentieth century can only be rationalized by scholars and officials who see the world through star-spangled glasses.

NOTES

1. A. J. P. Taylor, *The Origins of the Second World War* (Greenwich, Conn., 1963), pp. 16–20.
2. For a discussion of some of these see Wayne Cole, "American Entry into World War II: A Historiographical Appraisal," *Mississippi Valley Historical Review,* XLIII (March 1957), 603–6.
3. Earnest R. May, "Emergence to World Power," in John Higham, ed., *The Reconstruction of American History* (London, 1963), pp. 180–81, 195–96. Contrary to this view, many of the historians designated as "Actonians" do utilize the multinational approach; and in fact handle it more objectively since they do not use the goals of the United States as the major criteria for evaluating the policies of other nations.
4. Samuel Eliot Morison, *Strategy and Compromise* (Boston and Toronto, 1958), p. 6. See also Samuel Flagg Bemis, "American Foreign Policy and the Blessings of Liberty," *American Historical Review,* LXVII (January 1962).

5. George F. Kennan, *American Diplomacy, 1900–1950* (New York, 1952); Robert Divine, *The Reluctant Belligerent: American Entry into World War II* (New York, 1965); Robert Osgood, *Ideals and Self-Interest in America's Foreign Policy* (Chicago, 1953).

6. L. Ethan Ellis, *Frank B. Kellogg and American Foreign Policy* (New Brunswick, N.J., 1961); John A. De Novo, *American Interests and Policies in the Middle East, 1900–1939* (Minneapolis, 1963); Joseph Brandes, *Herbert Hoover and Economic Diplomacy: Department of Commerce Policy, 1921–1928* (Pittsburgh, 1962). For a discussion of these historiographical trends see Burl Noggle, "The Twenties: A New Historiographical Frontier," *Journal of American History*, LII (September 1966), 312–14; Robert Divine, *The Illusion of Neutrality* (Chicago, 1962); John E. Wiltz, *In Search of Peace: The Senate Munitions Inquiry, 1934–1936* (Baton Rouge, La., 1963); Manfred Jonas, *Isolationism in America, 1935–1941* (Ithaca, N.Y., 1966); James J. Martin, *American Liberalism and World Politics, 1931–1941* (2 vols.; New York, 1965); Warren I. Cohen, *The American Revisionists: the Lessons of Intervention in World War I* (Chicago, 1967).

7. Richard Current, *Secretary Stimson: A Study in Statecraft* (New Brunswick, N.J., 1954); William Appleman Williams, *The Tragedy of American Diplomacy*, rev. ed. (New York, 1962); William L. Neumann, *America Encounters Japan: From Perry to MacArthur* (Baltimore, 1963); Arthur A. Ekirch, Jr., *Ideas, Ideals, and American Diplomacy: A History of Their Growth and Interaction* (New York, 1966); Lloyd C. Gardner, *Economic Aspects of New Deal Diplomacy* (Madison, Wis., 1964); Willard Range, *Franklin D. Roosevelt's World Order* (Athens, Ga., 1959); Wayne Cole, *Senator Gerald P. Nye and American Foreign Relations* (Minneapolis, 1962). The author of this chapter owes a substantial intellectual debt to these historians. Their research and ideas (as well as those of other historians cited in these notes) have played an important part in the writing of this chapter.

8. D. F. Fleming, *The Cold War and Its Origins, 1917–1960* (2 vols.; Garden City, N.Y., 1961); Robert F. Smith, *The United States and Cuba: Business and Diplomacy, 1917–1960* (New York, 1960); Theodore P. Wright, *American Support of Free Elections Abroad* (Washington, 1964); O. Edmund Smith, *Yankee Diplomacy: U.S. Intervention in Argentina* (Dallas, Tex., 1953); Fredrick Pike, *Chile and the United States, 1800–1962* (South Bend, Ind., 1963); Donald Dozer, *Are We Good Neighbors?* (Gainesville, Fla., 1959).

9. *Congressional Record,* 72nd Cong., 1st Sess. (1932), Vol. LXXV, Part 3, p. 2426. Similar views in Henry L. Stimson, *The United States and the Other American Republics,* U.S. Department of State, Latin American Series No. 4 (Washington, 1931), pp. 5–6.

10. *Congressional Record,* 66th Cong., 1st Sess. (1919), Vol. LVIII, Part 3, p. 2421.

11. National Association of Manufacturers, *Twentieth Annual Con-*

vention—1915 (New York, 1915), p. 298. For the relationship between revolutionary nationalism in Asia and the European alliance structure, see Ivar Spector, *The First Russian Revolution: Its Impact on Asia* (Englewood Cliffs, N.J., 1962).

12. Davis to McAdoo November 20, 1923, Norman H. Davis Papers, Library of Congress, Washington, D.C. Davis had served in the State Department during the Wilson administration, and had been Under Secretary in 1920–1921. After this he returned to private banking.

13. Some prominent Americans viewed the World Court as the legal forum for such arrangements and advocated U.S. membership.

14. Confidential Memorandum on the Shantung Question, Charles Evans Hughes Papers, Library of Congress, Washington, D.C. McMurray was Chief of the Division of Far Eastern Affairs. In 1932 Secretary Stimson told the U.S. delegation to the Naval Conference that the guiding principle must be, "the superiority on the seas of the Anglo-Saxon nations." Nancy H. Hooker, ed., *The Moffat Papers: Selections from the Diplomatic Journals of Jay Pierrepont Moffat, 1919–1943* (Cambridge, Mass., 1956), p. 51.

15. De Novo, *American Interests in the Middle East,* pp. 179–80, 198–206.

16. Joseph C. Grew, *Turbulent Era: A Diplomatic Record of Forty Years, 1904–1945* (2 vols.; Boston, 1952), I, 480–585.

17. Hughes to Burton, June 3, 1924, C. E. Hughes Papers, Library of Congress, Washington, D.C.

18. Memorandum, "The Department of State and the Flotation of Foreign Loans," April 2, 1925, Leland Harrison Papers, Library of Congress, Washington, D.C. This was a discussion of the implementation of the Department's loan statement of March 3, 1922.

19. *Ibid.* See also Herbert Feis, "The Export of American Capital," *Foreign Affairs,* III (July 1925), 668–86.

20. Charles Evans Hughes, *Foreign Relations* (NP: Republican National Committee, 1924), p. 53.

21. Charles Evans Hughes, *Some Aspects of the Work of the Department of State,* 67th Cong., 2nd Sess. (1922), Senate Document No. 206, p. 10. Similar views in, J. Butler Wright, "The Department of State and American Enterprise Abroad," *Official Report of the Twelfth National Foreign Trade Convention* (New York, 1925), pp. 163–71.

22. This speech to the Union League Club of Philadelphia was printed in *The Commercial and Financial Chronicle,* CXXXV (November 26, 1932), 3624–25.

23. Lecture prepared for delivery at Princeton University, March, 1922; Franklin K. Lane Papers, Bancroft Library, Berkeley, Cal.

24. Speech by Secretary Hughes, May 18, 1922, Records of the Department of State, National Archives, Record Group, 59; File No. 711.1211/223 (hereafter cited as SD). For similar views see the

speech by Henry Cabot Lodge, *Congressional Record,* 67th Cong., 1st Sess. (1921), Vol. 61, Part 1, pp. 160–68.

25. "Address Delivered by President Coolidge at the Dinner of the United Press Association at New York, April 25, 1927," *Papers Relating to the Foreign Relations of the United States, 1927* (3 vols.; Washington, 1942), III, 209–21.

26. Sheffield to Coolidge, April 5, 1926, SD 711.12/744.

27. Newton D. Baker (Secretary of War) to President Wilson, October 16, 1920; Wilson to Bainbridge Colby, October 18, 1920, Bainbridge Colby Papers, Library of Congress, Washington, D.C. Josephus Daniels (Secretary of the Navy) to Colby, June 14, 1920, SD 812.00/24210.

28. Examples: Central American Treaty of Peace and Amity (1922), Central American Court of Arbitration (1922), Inter-American Court of Arbitration (1928), and the Gondra Convention (1923); mediation of the Tacna-Arica dispute, and numerous boundary controversies. Memorandum, "The Pros and Cons Regarding the Establishment of a School in Central America," (no date, probably 1924, or 1925), Leland Harrison Mss.; Memorandum by U. Grant Smith (Ambassador to Uruguay), "Latin America and the United States of America," March 30, 1927, Henry P. Fletcher Papers, Library of Congress, Washington, D.C.; Diary of Henry L. Stimson, entry of April 4, 1931, Henry L. Stimson Papers, Yale University Library.

29. U.S. Department of State, *Papers Relating to the Foreign Relations of the United States, 1928* (3 vols.; Washington, 1942), I, 578.

30. Secretary Hughes used this term in a speech in 1924; cited in Williams, *Tragedy of American Diplomacy,* p. 123.

31. U.S. Tariff Commission, *The Foreign Trade of Latin America* (Washington, 1941), Part 1, p. 97. Cordell Hull, *The Memoirs of Cordell Hull* (2 vols.; New York, 1948), I, 375–76. For the economic value of the "Good Neighbor" Policy see Sumner Welles, *"Good Neighbor" Policy in the Caribbean: Address before the Institute of Public Affairs, University of Virginia, July, 1935,* U.S. Department of State, Latin American Series No. 12 (Washington, 1935).

32. Charles C. Griffin, ed., "Welles to Roosevelt: A Memorandum on Inter-American Relations, 1933," *Hispanic American Historical Review,* XXXIV (May 1954), 190–92; Arthur P. Whitaker, "From Dollar Diplomacy to the Good Neighbor Policy," *Inter-American Economic Affairs,* IV (Spring 1951); Smith, *United States and Cuba,* pp. 141–64. Dollar Diplomacy was also used to abort the revolutionary movement in Cuba (1933–1934) and to provide a settlement with Mexico *in re* compensating the oil companies after the expropriation of 1938.

33. *Ibid.,* pp. 146, 159–64, 172–74.

34. Memorandum on the Pacific Campaign, June, 1935; found in William Gibbs McAdoo Papers, Library of Congress, Washington,

D.C.; this memorandum also recommended turning Japanese expansion toward Siberia and northern China.

35. Hull, *Memoirs,* I, 496.

36. Fred L. Israel, ed., *The War Diary of Breckinridge Long: Selections from the Years 1939–1944* (Lincoln, Neb., 1966), p. 98. For similar views see Thomas W. Lamont, *The Defense of the Republic,* Remarks before a luncheon meeting of the Merchants' Association of New York, January 28, 1941 (pamphlet published by the Association, 1941); Walter Lippmann, "The Economic Consequences of a German Victory," *Life,* IX (July 22, 1940); Francis P. Miller, ed., *Some Regional Views of Our Foreign Policy, 1940,* (New York, 1940; this book was printed by the Council on Foreign Relations for private distribution only, and the introductory chapter by Alvin H. Hansen, as well as the reports of the various city committees of the Council, stressed the economic aspects of national interest); Gardner, *Economic Aspects of New Deal Diplomacy,* Ch. 8; Hull, *Memoirs,* I, 523, 577; Allen W. Dulles and Hamilton Fish Armstrong, *Can We Be Neutral?* (New York, 1936), pp. 118–20.

37. V, "The Destruction of Capitalism in Germany," *Foreign Affairs,* XV (July 1937), 607 (V was Gustav Stolper, founder and editor of *Der Deutsche Volkswirt,* and at one time a member of the Reichstag: Hamilton Fish Armstrong to author, February 28, 1967); Lippmann, "Economic Consequences of a German Victory," *Life;* Lamont, *Defense of the Republic,* pp. 2, 6; Gabriel Kolko, "American Business and Germany, 1930–1941," *Western Political Quarterly,* XV (December 1962), 715.

38. For the involvement of American business in the German economy see Kolko, *ibid.,* pp. 716–28; Mira Wilkins and Frank E. Hill, *American Business Abroad: Ford on Six Continents* (Detroit, 1964), pp. 282–85.

39. Felix Morley, "Political Implications of American Neutrality Policy," *Annals of the American Academy of Political and Social Science,* CLXXXVI (July 1936), 52 (italics mine).

40. Hamilton Fish, Jr., "The Menace of Communism," *ibid.,* CLVI (July 1931), 59.

41. Israel, *War Diary of Breckinridge Long,* pp. 27–28. For related views and/or discussions of this fear see *ibid.,* pp. 24–26, 123, 236, 296, 320; Hooker, *The Moffat Papers,* p. 236; William F. Kaufmann, "Two American Ambassadors: Bullitt and Kennedy," Gordon A. Craig and Felix Gilbert, eds., *The Diplomats: 1919–1939* (2 vols.; New York, 1963), II, 652–68; Jonas, *Isolationism in America,* p. 113; Robert E. Sherwood, *Roosevelt and Hopkins: An Intimate History,* rev. ed. (New York, 1950), pp. 160–61, 322, 485; Gerhard L. Weinberg, "Hitler's Image of the United States," *American Historical Review,* LXIX (July 1964), 1012 (pro-German elements in the U.S. Army).

42. Gardner, *Economic Aspects of New Deal Diplomacy,* pp. 72–73.

This concern in 1934 was rooted in the fears of the late 1920s—
J. MacMurray (American Minister to China) to Secretary Stimson,
July 22, 1929, U.S. Department of State, *Papers Relating to the
Foreign Relations of the United States, 1929* (3 vols.; Washington,
1944), II, 227; other letters on pp. 466–70, 579. See also *ibid., For-
eign Relations, 1934* (5 vols.; Washington, 1950), III, 467–68.

43. Cole, *Senator Gerald P. Nye*, pp. 165–66.

44. Divine, *Illusion of Neutrality;* pp. 319–25.

45. Neumann, *America Encounters Japan*, p. 203. Japanese naval
spending had been declining, and totaled $26.9 million for 1932–
1933.

46. Cole, *Senator Gerald P. Nye*, pp. 131, 154.

47. Hjalmar Schacht, "Germany's Colonial Demands," *Foreign Affairs*,
XV (January 1937), 226–34.

48. Hull, *Memoirs,* I, 585, 594, 439.

49. Sumner Welles, *The Time for Decision* (New York and London,
1944), pp. 104–05.

50. Herbert von Dirksen, *Moscow, Tokyo, London: Twenty Years of
German Foreign Policy* (Norman, Okla., 1952), pp. 224–27.

51. Taylor, *Origins of the Second World War,* pp. 254–56, 267; A. L.
Rowse, *Appeasement: A Study in Political Decline*, 1933–39 (New
York, 1961), pp. 98–100.

52. Hooker, *The Moffat Papers,* pp. 352–53.

53. Elliott Roosevelt, *As He Saw It* (New York, 1946), pp. 24–25, 35–37.

54. *Congressional Record,* 72nd Cong., 1st Sess., LXXV, Part 4 (1932),
3505.

55. Range, *Roosevelt's World Order,* pp. 2–3, 15–16, 175–76.

56. Paul Schroeder, *The Axis Alliance and Japanese-American Relations, 1941* (Ithaca, N.Y., 1958), pp. 175–82.

57. William C. Johnstone, *The United States and Japan's New Order*
(Toronto, 1941), p. 362. Johnstone's recommendations for an ulti-
matum to Japan were very similar to the Hull proposals.

58. Neumann, *America Encounters Japan,* pp. 264–67. Raymond A.
Esthus, "President Roosevelt's Commitment to Britain to Intervene
in a Pacific War," *Mississippi Valley Historical Review,* L (June
1963), 28–38.

59. D. F. Fleming, *The Cold War,* I, 101–3. In February 1940, the Allied Supreme War Council decided to send troops to Finland (six
divisions from Britain and 50,000 men from France). See also Divine, *Reluctant Belligerent,* pp. 78–79.

60. Range, *Roosevelt's World Order,* p. 84.

61. An expression used by William Wirt in opposing the removal of
the Cherokee Indians from the Eastern states, Albert K. Weinberg,
*Manifest Destiny: A Study of Nationalist Expansionism in Ameri-
can History* (Chicago, 1963), p. 87.

62. Brooks Adams, "Reciprocity or the Alternative," *Atlantic Monthly*,
LXXXVIII (August 1901), 155.

63. For an excellent analysis of this misuse of historical analogy see

"Munich, Dominos, and Containment," in Howard Zinn, *Vietnam: The Logic of Withdrawal* (Boston, 1967).

64. For nostalgic references to the pre-1914 world, which also link the *Pax Britannica* of the nineteenth century to the *Pax Americana* of the 1950s and 1960s, see remarks by George V. Allen, Director of the Foreign Service Institute of the U. S. State Department, at the seventeenth annual meeting of the American Academy of Political and Social Science, April 1966 (*Philadelphia Inquirer,* April 16, 1966); editorial, "The American 'Empire,'" *Fortune,* August 1965, pp. 119–20; Raymond Moley, "Mahan's Long Shadow," *Newsweek,* July 18, 1966, p. 100. An excellent analysis of this myth is Walter Lippmann, "LBJ's Manila Madness: The Old 'White Man's Burden,'" *Capital Times* (Madison, Wis.), November 19, 1966, p. 20.

THE NEW DEAL:

THE CONSERVATIVE

ACHIEVEMENTS OF LIBERAL

REFORM

∽ Barton J. Bernstein

WRITING from a liberal democratic consensus, many American historians in the past two decades have praised the Roosevelt administration for its nonideological flexibility and for its far-ranging reforms. To many historians, particularly those who reached intellectual maturity during the depression,[1] the government's accomplishments, as well as the drama and passion, marked the decade as a watershed, as a dividing line in the American past.

Enamored of Franklin D. Roosevelt and recalling the bitter opposition to welfare measures and restraints upon business, many liberal historians have emphasized the New Deal's discontinuity with the immediate past. For them there was a "Roosevelt Revolution," or at the very least a dramatic achievement of a beneficent liberalism which had developed in fits and spurts during the preceding three decades.[2] Rejecting earlier interpretations which viewed the New Deal as socialism[3] or state capitalism,[4] they have also disregarded theories of syndicalism[5] or of corporate liberalism.[6] The New Deal has generally commanded their approval for such laws or institutions as minimum wages, public housing, farm assistance, the Tennessee Valley Authority, the Wagner Act, more progressive taxation, and social security. For most liberal historians the New Deal meant the replenishment of democracy, the rescuing of the federal government from the clutches of big business, the significant redistribution of political power. Breaking with laissez faire, the new administration, according to these interpretations, marked the end of the passive or impartial state and the beginning of positive government, of the interventionist state acting to offset concentrations of private power, and affirming the rights and responding to the needs of the unprivileged.

From the perspective of the late 1960s these themes no longer seem adequate to characterize the New Deal. The liberal reforms of the New Deal did not transform the American system; they conserved and protected American corporate capitalism, occasionally by absorbing parts of threatening programs. There was no significant redistribution of power in American society, only limited recognition of other organized groups, seldom of unorganized peoples. Neither the bolder programs advanced by New Dealers nor the final legislation greatly extended the beneficence of government beyond the middle classses or drew upon the wealth of the few for the needs of the many. Designed to maintain the American system, liberal activity was directed toward essentially conservative goals. Experimentalism was most frequently limited to means; seldom did it extend to ends. Never questioning private enterprise, it operated within safe channels, far short of Marxism or even of native American radicalisms that offered structural critiques and structural solutions.

All of this is not to deny the changes wrought by the New Deal—the extension of welfare programs, the growth of federal power, the strengthening of the executive, even the narrowing of property rights. But it is to assert that the elements of continuity are stronger, that the magnitude of change has been exaggerated. The New Deal failed to solve the problem of depression, it failed to raise the impoverished, it failed to redistribute income, it failed to extend equality and generally countenanced racial discrimination and segregation. It failed generally to make business more responsible to the social welfare or to threaten business's pre-eminent political power. In this sense, the New Deal, despite the shifts in tone and spirit from the earlier decade, was profoundly conservative and continuous with the 1920s.

I

Rather than understanding the 1920s as a "return to normalcy," the period is more properly interpreted by focusing on the continuation of progressive impulses, demands often frustrated by the rivalry of interest groups, sometimes blocked by the resistance of Harding and Coolidge, and occasionally by Hoover.[7] Through these years while agriculture and labor struggled to secure advantages from the federal government, big business flourished. Praised for creating American prosperity, business leaders easily convinced the nation that they were socially responsible, that they were fulfilling the needs of the public.[8] Benefitting from earlier legislation that had promoted economic rationalization and stability, they were opponents of federal benefits to other groups but seldom proponents of laissez faire.[9]

In no way did the election of Herbert Hoover in 1928 seem to challenge the New Era. An heir of Wilson, Hoover promised an even closer relationship with big business and moved beyond Harding and Coolidge by affirming federal responsibility for prosperity. As Secretary of Commerce, Hoover had opposed unbridled competition and had transformed his department into a vigorous friend of business. Sponsoring trade associations, he promoted industrial self-regulation and the increased rationalization of business. He had also expanded foreign trade, endorsed the regulation of new forms of communications, encouraged relief in disasters, and recommended public works to offset economic declines.[10]

By training and experience, few men in American political life seemed better prepared than Hoover to cope with the depression. Responding promptly to the crisis, he acted to stabilize the economy and secured the agreement of businessmen to maintain production and wage rates. Unwilling to let the economy "go through the wringer," the President requested easier money, self-liquidating public works, lower personal and corporate income taxes, and stronger commodity stabilization corporations.[11] In reviewing these unprecedented actions, Walter Lippmann wrote, "The national government undertook to make the whole economic order operate prosperously."[12]

But these efforts proved inadequate. The tax cut benefitted the wealthy and failed to raise effective demand. The public works were insufficient. The commodity stabilization corporations soon ran out of funds, and agricultural prices kept plummeting. Businessmen cut back production, dismissed employees, and finally cut wages. As unemployment grew, Hoover struggled to inspire confidence, but his words seemed hollow and his understanding of the depression limited. Blaming the collapse on European failures, he could not admit that American capitalism had failed. When prodded by Congress to increase public works, to provide direct relief, and to further unbalance the budget, he doggedly resisted. Additional deficits would destroy business confidence, he feared, and relief would erode the principles of individual and local responsibility.[13] Clinging to faith in voluntarism, Hoover also briefly rebuffed the efforts by financiers to secure the Reconstruction Finance Corporation (RFC). Finally endorsing the RFC,[14] he also supported expanded lending by Federal Land Banks, recommended home-loan banks, and even approved small federal loans (usually inadequate) to states needing funds for relief. In this burst of activity, the President had moved to the very limits of his ideology.

Restricted by his progressive background and insensitive to politics and public opinion, he stopped far short of the state corporatism urged by some businessmen and politicians. With capitalism crumbling he had acted vigorously to save it, but he would not yield to the representatives of business or disadvantaged groups who wished to alter the government.[15] He was reluctant to use the federal power to achieve through compulsion what could not be realized through voluntary means. Proclaiming a false independence, he did not understand that his government already represented business interests; hence, he rejected policies that would openly place the power of the state in the hands of business or that would permit the formation of a syndicalist state in which power might be exercised (in the words of William Appleman Williams) "by a relatively few leaders of each functional bloc formed and operating as an oligarchy."[16]

Even though constitutional scruples restricted his efforts, Hoover did more than any previous American president to combat depression. He "abandoned the principles of laissez faire in relation to the business cycle, established the conviction that prosperity and depression can be publicly controlled by political action, and drove out of the public consciousness the old idea that depressions must be overcome by private adjustment," wrote Walter Lippmann.[17] Rather than the last of the old presidents, Herbert Hoover was the first of the new.

II

A charismatic leader and a brilliant politician, his successor expanded federal activities on the basis of Hoover's efforts. Using the federal government to stabilize the economy and advance the interests of the groups, Franklin D. Roosevelt directed the campaign to save large-scale corporate capitalism. Though recognizing new political interests and extending benefits to them, his New Deal never effectively challenged big business or the organization of the economy. In providing assistance to the needy and by rescuing them from starvation, Roosevelt's humane efforts also protected the established system: he sapped organized radicalism of its waning strength and of its potential constituency among the unorganized and discontented. Sensitive to public opinion and fearful of radicalism, Roosevelt acted from a mixture of motives that rendered his liberalism cautious and limited, his experimentalism narrow. Despite the flurry of activity, his government was more vigorous and flexible about means than goals, and the goals were more conservative than historians usually acknowledge.[18]

Roosevelt's response to the banking crisis emphasizes the conservatism of his administration and its self-conscious avoidance of more radical means that might have transformed American capitalism. Entering the White House when banks were failing and Americans had lost faith in the financial system, the President could have nationalized it—

"without a word of protest," judged Senator Bronson Cutting.[19] "If ever there was a moment when things hung in the balance," later wrote Raymond Moley, a member of the original "brain trust," "it was on March 5, 1933—when unorthodoxy would have drained the last remaining strength of the capitalistic system."[20] To save the system, Roosevelt relied upon collaboration between bankers and Hoover's Treasury officials to prepare legislation extending federal assistance to banking. So great was the demand for action that House members, voting even without copies, passed it unanimously, and the Senate, despite objections by a few Progressives, approved it the same evening. "The President," remarked a cynical congressman, "drove the money-changers out of the Capitol on March 4th—and they were all back on the 9th."[21]

Undoubtedly the most dramatic example of Roosevelt's early conservative approach to recovery was the National Recovery Administration (NRA). It was based on the War Industries Board (WIB) which had provided the model for the campaign of Bernard Baruch, General Hugh Johnson, and other former WIB officials during the twenties to limit competition through industrial self-regulation under federal sanction. As trade associations flourished during the decade, the FTC encouraged "codes of fair competition" and some industries even tried to set prices and restrict production. Operating without the force of law, these agreements broke down. When the depression struck, industrial pleas for regulation increased.[22] After the Great Crash, important business leaders including Henry I. Harriman of the Chamber of Commerce and Gerard Swope of General Electric called for suspension of antitrust laws and federal organization of business collaboration.[23] Joining them were labor leaders, particularly those in "sick" industries—John L. Lewis of the United Mine Workers and Sidney Hillman of Amalgamated Clothing Workers.[24]

Designed largely for industrial recovery, the NRA legislation provided for minimum wages and maximum hours. It also made concessions to pro-labor congressmen and labor leaders who demanded some specific benefits for unions—recognition of the worker's right to organization and to collective bargaining. In practice, though, the much-heralded Section 7a was a disappointment to most friends of labor.[25] (For the shrewd Lewis, however, it became a mandate to organize: "The President wants you to join a union.") To many frustrated workers and their disgusted leaders, NRA became "National Run Around." The clause, unionists found (in the words of Brookings economists), "had the practical effect of placing NRA on the side of anti-union employers in their struggle against trade unions. . . . [It] thus threw its weight against labor in the balance of bargaining power."[26] And while some far-sighted industrialists feared radicalism and hoped to forestall it by incorporating unions into the economic system, most preferred to leave their workers unorganized or in company unions. To many businessmen, large and independent unions as such seemed a radical threat to the system of business control.[27]

Not only did the NRA provide fewer advantages than unionists had anticipated, but it also failed as a recovery measure. It probably even retarded recovery by supporting restrictionism and price increases, concluded a Brookings study.[28] Placing effective power for code-writing in big business, NRA injured small businesses and contributed to the concentration of American industry. It was not the government-business partnership as envisaged by Adolf A. Berle, Jr., nor government managed as Rexford Tugwell had hoped, but rather, business managed, as Raymond Moley had desired.[29] Calling NRA "industrial self-government," its director, General Hugh Johnson, had explained that "NRA is exactly what industry organized in trade associations makes it." Despite the annoyance of some big businessmen with Section 7a, the NRA reaffirmed and consolidated their power at a time when the public was critical of industrialists and financiers.

III

Viewing the economy as a "concert of organized interests,"[30] the New Deal also provided benefits for farmers—the Agricultural Adjustment Act. Reflecting the political power of larger commercial farmers and accepting restrictionist economics, the measure assumed that the agricultural problem was overproduction, not underconsumption. Financed by a processing tax designed to raise prices to parity, payments encouraged restricted production and cutbacks in farm labor. With benefits accruing chiefly to the larger owners, they frequently removed from production the lands of share-croppers and tenant farmers, and "tractored" them and hired hands off the land. In assisting agriculture, the AAA, like the NRA, sacrificed the interests of the marginal and the un-recognized to the welfare of those with greater political and economic power.[31]

In large measure, the early New Deal of the NRA and AAA was a "broker state." Though the government served as a mediator of interests and sometimes imposed its will in divisive situations, it was generally the servant of powerful groups. "Like the mercantilists, the New Dealers protected vested interests with the authority of the state," acknowl-edges William Leuchtenburg. But it was some improvement over the 1920s when business was the only interest capable of imposing its will on the government.[32] While extending to other groups the benefits of the state, the New Deal, however, continued to recognize the pre-eminence of business inter-ests.

The politics of the broker state also heralded the way of the future—of continued corporate dominance in a politi-cal structure where other groups agreed generally on corpo-rate capitalism and squabbled only about the size of the shares. Delighted by this increased participation and the ab-sorption of dissident groups, many liberals did not under-stand the dangers in the emerging organization of politics. They had too much faith in representative institutions and in associations to foresee the perils—of leaders not represent-ing their constituents, of bureaucracy diffusing responsi-bility, of officials serving their own interests. Failing to per-ceive the dangers in the emerging structure, most liberals agreed with Senator Robert Wagner of New York: "In order that the strong may not take advantage of the weak, every group must be equally strong."[33] His advice then seemed appropriate for organizing labor, but it neglected the prob-lems of unrepresentative leadership and of the many millions to be left beyond organization.[34]

In dealing with the organized interests, the President acted frequently as a broker, but his government did not simply express the vectors of external forces.[35] The New Deal state was too complex, too loose, and some of Roosevelt's subordinates were following their own inclinations and pushing the government in directions of their own design.[36] The President would also depart from his role as a broker and act to secure programs he desired. As a skilled politician, he could split coalitions, divert the interests of groups, or place the prestige of his office on the side of desired legislation.

In seeking to protect the stock market, for example, Roosevelt endorsed the Securities and Exchange measure (of 1934), despite the opposition of many in the New York financial community. His advisers split the opposition. Rallying to support the administration were the out-of-town exchanges, representatives of the large commission houses, including James Forrestal of Dillon, Read, and Robert Lovett of Brown Brothers, Harriman, and such commission brokers as E. A. Pierce and Paul Shields. Opposed to the Wall Street "old guard" and their companies, this group included those who wished to avoid more radical legislation, as well as others who had wanted earlier to place trading practices under federal legislation which they could influence.[37]

Though the law restored confidence in the securities market and protected capitalism, it alarmed some businessmen and contributed to the false belief that the New Deal was threatening business. But it was not the disaffection of a portion of the business community, nor the creation of the Liberty League, that menaced the broker state.[38] Rather it was the threat of the Left—expressed, for example, in such overwrought statements as Minnesota Governor Floyd Olson's: "I am not a liberal . . . I am a radical. . . . I am not satisfied with hanging a laurel wreath on burglars and thieves . . . and calling them code authorities or something else."[39] While Olson, along with some others who succumbed to the rhetoric of militancy, would back down and soften their meaning, their words dramatized real grievances: the failure of the early New Deal to end misery, to re-create prosperity. The New Deal excluded too many. Its programs were inadequate.

While Roosevelt reluctantly endorsed relief and went beyond Hoover in support of public works, he too preferred self-liquidating projects, desired a balanced budget, and resisted spending the huge sums required to lift the nation out of depression.

IV

For millions suffering in a nation wracked by poverty, the promises of the Left seemed attractive. Capitalizing on the misery, Huey Long offered Americans a "Share Our Wealth" program—a welfare state with prosperity, not subsistence, for the disadvantaged, those neglected by most politicians. "Every Man a King": pensions for the elderly, college for the deserving, homes and cars for families—that was the promise of American life. Also proposing minimum wages, increased public works, shorter work weeks, and a generous farm program, he demanded a "soak-the-rich" tax program. Despite the economic defects of his plan, Long was no hayseed, and his forays into the East revealed support far beyond the bayous and hamlets of his native South.[40] In California discontent was so great that Upton Sinclair, food faddist and former socialist, captured the Democratic nomination for governor on a platform of "production-for-use"—factories and farms for the unemployed. "In a cooperative society," promised Sinclair, "every man, woman, and child would have the equivalent of $5,000 a year income from labor of the able-bodied young men for three or four hours per day."[41] More challenging to Roosevelt was Francis Townsend's plan —monthly payments of $200 to those past sixty who retired and promised to spend the stipend within thirty days.[42] Another enemy of the New Deal was Father Coughlin, the popular radio priest, who had broken with Roosevelt and formed a National Union for Social Justice to lead the way to a corporate society beyond capitalism.

To a troubled nation offered "redemption" by the Left, there was also painful evidence that the social fabric was tearing—law was breaking down. When the truckers in Minneapolis struck, the police provoked an incident and shot sixty-seven people, some in the back. Covering the tragedy, Eric Sevareid, then a young reporter, wrote, "I understood deep in my bones and blood what fascism was."[43] In San Francisco union leaders embittered by police brutality led a general strike and aroused national fears of class warfare. Elsewhere, in textile mills from Rhode Island to Georgia, in cities like Des Moines and Toledo, New York and Philadelphia, there were brutality and violence, sometimes bayonets and tear gas.[44]

Challenged by the Left, and with the new Congress more liberal and more willing to spend, Roosevelt turned to disarm the discontent. "Boys—this is our hour," confided Harry Hopkins. "We've got to get everything we want—a works program, social security, wages and hours, everything —now or never. Get your minds to work on developing a complete ticket to provide security for all the folks of this country up and down and across the board."[45] Hopkins and the associates he addressed were not radicals: they did not seek to transform the system, only to make it more humane. They, too, wished to preserve large-scale corporate capitalism, but unlike Roosevelt or Moley, they were prepared for more vigorous action. Their commitment to reform was greater, their tolerance for injustice far less. Joining them in pushing the New Deal left were the leaders of industrial unions, who, while also not wishing to transform the system, sought for workingmen higher wages, better conditions, stronger and larger unions, and for themselves a place closer to the fulcrum of power.

The problems of organized labor, however, neither aroused Roosevelt's humanitarianism nor suggested possibilities of reshaping the political coalition. When asked during the NRA about employee representation, he had replied that workers could select anyone they wished—the Ahkoond of Swat, a union, even the Royal Geographical Society.[46] As a paternalist, viewing himself (in the words of James Mac-Gregor Burns) as a "partisan and benefactor" of workers, he would not understand the objections to company unions or to multiple unionism under NRA. Nor did he foresee the political dividends that support of independent unions could yield to his party.[47] Though presiding over the reshaping of politics (which would extend the channels of power to some of the discontented and redirect their efforts to competition within a limited framework), he was not its architect, and he was unable clearly to see or understand the unfolding design.

When Senator Wagner submitted his labor relations bill, he received no assistance from the President and even struggled to prevent Roosevelt from joining the opposition. The President "never lifted a finger," recalls Miss Perkins. ("I, myself, had very little sympathy with the bill," she wrote.[48]) But after the measure easily passed the Senate and seemed likely to win the House's endorsement, Roosevelt reversed himself. Three days before the Supreme Court invalidated the NRA, including the legal support for unionization, Roosevelt came out for the bill. Placing it on his "must" list, he may have hoped to influence the final provisions and turn an administration defeat into victory.[49]

Responding to the threat from the left, Roosevelt also moved during the Second Hundred Days to secure laws regulating banking, raising taxes, dissolving utility-holding companies, and creating social security. Building on the efforts of states during the Progressive Era, the Social Security Act marked the movement toward the welfare state, but the core of the measure, the old-age provision, was more important as a landmark than for its substance. While establishing a federal-state system of unemployment compensation, the government, by making workers contribute to their old-age insurance, denied its financial responsibility for the elderly. The act excluded more than a fifth of the labor force leaving, among others, more than five million farm laborers and domestics without coverage.[50]

Though Roosevelt criticized the tax laws for not preventing "an unjust concentration of wealth and economic power,"[51] his own tax measure would not have significantly redistributed wealth. Yet his message provoked an "amen" from Huey Long and protests from businessmen.[52] Retreating from his promises, Roosevelt failed to support the bill, and it succumbed to conservative forces. They removed the inheritance tax and greatly reduced the proposed corporate and individual levies. The final law did not "soak the rich."[53] But it did engender deep resentment among the wealthy for increasing taxes on gifts and estates, imposing an excess-profits tax (which Roosevelt had not requested), and raising surtaxes. When combined with such regressive levies as social security and local taxes, however, the Wealth Tax of 1935 did not drain wealth from higher-income groups, and the top one percent even increased their shares during the New Deal years.[54]

V

Those historians who have characterized the events of 1935 as the beginning of a second New Deal have imposed a pattern on those years which most participants did not then discern.[55] In moving to social security, guarantees of collective bargaining, utility regulation, and progressive taxation, the government did advance the nation toward greater liberalism, but the shift was exaggerated and most of the measures accomplished far less than either friends or foes suggested. Certainly, despite a mild bill authorizing destruction of utilities-holding companies, there was no effort to atomize business, no real threat to concentration.

Nor were so many powerful businessmen disaffected by the New Deal. Though the smaller businessmen who filled the ranks of the Chamber of Commerce resented the federal bureaucracy and the benefits to labor and thus criticized NRA,[56] representatives of big business found the agency useful and opposed a return to unrestricted competition. In 1935, members of the Business Advisory Council—including Henry Harriman, outgoing president of the Chamber, Thomas Watson of International Business Machines, Walter Gifford of American Telephone and Telegraph, Gerard Swope of General Electric, Winthrop Aldrich of the Chase National Bank, and W. Averell Harriman of Union Pacific —vigorously endorsed a two-year renewal of NRA.[57]

When the Supreme Court in 1935 declared the "hot" oil clause and then NRA unconstitutional, the administration moved to measures known as the "little NRA." Re-establishing regulations in bituminous coal and oil, the New Deal also checked wholesale price discrimination and legalized "fair trade" practices. Though Roosevelt never acted to revive the NRA, he periodically contemplated its restoration. In the so-called second New Deal, as in the "first," government remained largely the benefactor of big business, and some more advanced businessmen realized this.[58]

Roosevelt could attack the "economic royalists" and endorse the TNEC investigation of economic concentration, but he was unprepared to resist the basic demands of big business. While there was ambiguity in his treatment of oligopoly, it was more the confusion of means than of ends, for his tactics were never likely to impair concentration. Even the antitrust program under Thurman Arnold, concludes Frank Freidel, was "intended less to bust the trusts than to forestall too drastic legislation." Operating through consent degrees and designed to reduce prices to the consumer, the program frequently "allowed industries to function much as they had in NRA days." In effect, then, throughout its variations, the New Deal had sought to cooperate with business.[59]

Though vigorous in rhetoric and experimental in tone, the New Deal was narrow in its goals and wary of bold economic reform. Roosevelt's sense of what was politically desirable was frequently more restricted than others' views of what was possible and necessary. Roosevelt's limits were those of ideology; they were not inherent in experimentalism. For while the President explored the narrow center, and some New Dealers considered bolder possibilities, John Dewey, the philosopher of experimentalism, moved far beyond the New Deal and sought to reshape the system. Liberalism, he warned, "must now become radical. . . . For the gulf between what the actual situation makes possible and the actual state itself is so great that it cannot be bridged by piecemeal policies undertaken *ad hoc*."[60] The boundaries of New Deal experimentalism, as Howard Zinn has emphasized, could extend far beyond Roosevelt's cautious ventures. Operating within very safe channels, Roosevelt not only avoided Marxism and the socialization of property, but he also stopped far short of other possibilities—communal direction of production or the organized distribution of surplus. The President and many of his associates were doctrinaires of the center, and their maneuvers in social reform were limited to cautious excursions.[61]

VI

Usually opportunistic and frequently shifting, the New Deal was restricted by its ideology. It ran out of fuel not because of the conservative opposition,[62] but because it ran out of ideas.[63] Acknowledging the end in 1939, Roosevelt proclaimed, "We have now passed the period of internal conflict in the launching of our program of social reform. Our full energies may now be released to invigorate the processes of recovery in order to preserve our reforms. . . ."[64]

The sad truth was that the heralded reforms were severely limited, that inequality continued, that efforts at recovery had failed. Millions had come to accept the depression as a way of life. A decade after the Great Crash, when millions were still unemployed, Fiorello LaGuardia recommended that "we accept the inevitable, that we are now in a new normal."[65] "It was reasonable to expect a probable minimum of 4,000,000 to 5,000,000 unemployed," Harry Hopkins had concluded.[66] Even that level was never reached, for business would not spend and Roosevelt refused to countenance the necessary expenditures. "It was in economics that our troubles lay," Tugwell wrote. "For their solution his [Roosevelt's] progressivism, his new deal was pathetically insufficient. . . ."[67]

Clinging to faith in fiscal orthodoxy even when engaged in deficit spending, Roosevelt had been unwilling to greatly unbalance the budget. Having pledged in his first campaign to cut expenditures and to restore the balanced budget, the President had at first adopted recovery programs that would not drain government finances. Despite a burst of activity under the Civil Works Administration during the first winter, public works expenditures were frequently slow and cautious. Shifting from direct relief, which Roosevelt (like Hoover) considered "a narcotic, a subtle destroyer of the human spirit," the government moved to work relief.[68] ("It saves his skill. It gives him a chance to do something socially useful," said Hopkins.[69]) By 1937 the government had poured enough money into the economy to spur production to within 10 percent of 1929 levels, but unemployment still hovered over seven million. Yet so eager was the President to balance the budget that he cut expenditures for public works and relief, and plunged the economy into a greater depression. While renewing expenditures, Roosevelt remained cautious in his fiscal policy, and the nation still had almost nine million unemployed in 1939. After nearly six years of struggling with the depression, the Roosevelt administration could not lead the nation to recovery, but it had relieved suffering.[70] In most of America, starvation was no longer possible. Perhaps that was the most humane achievement of the New Deal.

Its efforts on behalf of humane *reform* were generally faltering and shallow, of more value to the middle classes, of less value to organized workers, of even less to the marginal men. In conception and in practice, seemingly humane efforts revealed the shortcomings of American liberalism. For example, public housing, praised as evidence of the federal government's concern for the poor, was limited in scope (to 180,000 units) and unfortunate in results.[71] It usually meant the consolidation of ghettos, the robbing of men of their dignity, the treatment of men as wards with few rights. And slum clearance came to mean "Negro clearance" and removal of the other poor. Of much of this liberal reformers were unaware, and some of the problems can be traced to the structure of bureaucracy and to the selection of government personnel and social workers who disliked the poor.[72] But the liberal conceptions, it can be argued, were also flawed for there was no willingness to consult the poor, nor to encourage their participation. Liberalism was elitist. Seeking to build America in their own image, liberals wanted to create an environment which they thought would restructure character and personality more appropriate to white, middle-class America.

While slum dwellers received little besides relief from the New Deal, and their needs were frequently misunderstood, Negroes as a group received even less assistance—less than they needed and sometimes even less than their proportion in the population would have justified. Under the NRA they were frequently dismissed and their wages were sometimes below the legal minimum. The Civilian Conservation Corps left them "forgotten" men—excluded, discriminated against, segregated. In general, what the Negroes gained—relief, WPA jobs, equal pay on some federal projects—was granted them as poor people, not as Negroes.[73] To many black men the distinction was unimportant, for no government had ever given them so much. "My friends, go home and turn Lincoln's picture to the wall," a Negro publisher told his race. "That debt has been payed in full."[74]

Bestowing recognition on some Negro leaders, the New Deal appointed them to agencies as advisers—the "black cabinet." Probably more dramatic was the advocacy of Negro rights by Eleanor Roosevelt. Some whites like Harold Ickes and Aubrey Williams even struggled cautiously to break down segregation. But segregation did not yield, and Washington itself remained a segregated city. The white South was never challenged, the Fourteenth Amendment never used to assist Negroes. Never would Roosevelt expend political capital in an assault upon the American caste system.[75] Despite the efforts of the NAACP to dramatize the Negroes' plight as second-class citizens, subject to brutality and often without legal protection, Roosevelt would not endorse the anti-lynching bill. ("No government pretending to be civilized can go on condoning such atrocities," H. L. Mencken testified. "Either it must make every possible effort to put them down or it must suffer the scorn and contempt of Christendom.")[76] Unwilling to risk schism with Southerners ruling committees, Roosevelt capitulated to the forces of racism.[77]

Even less bold than in economic reform, the New Deal left intact the race relations of America. Yet its belated and cautious recognition of the black man was great enough to woo Negro leaders and even to court the masses. One of the bitter ironies of these years is that a New Dealer could tell the NAACP in 1936: "Under our new conception of democracy, the Negro will be given the chance to which he is entitled. . . ." But it was true, Ickes emphasized, that "The greatest advance [since Reconstruction] toward assuring the Negro that degree of justice to which he is entitled and that equality of opportunity under the law which is implicit in his American citizenship, has been made since Franklin D. Roosevelt was sworn in as President. . . ."[78]

It was not in the cities and not among the Negroes but in rural America that Roosevelt administration made its (philosophically) boldest efforts: creation of the Tennessee Valley Authority and the later attempt to construct seven little valley authorities. Though conservation was not a new federal policy and government-owned utilities were sanctioned by municipal experience, federal activity in this area constituted a challenge to corporate enterprise and an expression of concern about the poor. A valuable example of regional planning and a contribution to regional prosperity, TVA still fell far short of expectations. The agency soon retreated from social planning. ("From 1936 on," wrote Tugwell, "the TVA should have been called the Tennessee Valley Power Production and Flood Control Corporation.") Fearful of antagonizing the powerful interests, its agricultural program neglected the tenants and the sharecroppers.[79]

To urban workingmen the New Deal offered some, but limited, material benefits. Though the government had instituted contributory social security and unemployment insurance, its much-heralded Fair Labor Standards Act, while prohibiting child labor, was a greater disappointment. It exempted millions from its wages-and-hours provisions. So unsatisfactory was the measure that one congressman cynically suggested, "Within 90 days after appointment of the administrator, she should report to Congress whether anyone is subject to this bill."[80] Requiring a minimum of twenty-five cents an hour ($11 a week for 44 hours), it raised the wages of only about a half-million at a time when nearly twelve million workers in interstate commerce were earning less than forty cents an hour.[81]

More important than these limited measures was the administration's support, albeit belated, of the organization of labor and the right of collective bargaining. Slightly increasing organized workers' share of the national income,[82] the new industrial unions extended job security to millions who were previously subject to the whim of management. Unionization freed them from the perils of a free market.

By assisting labor, as well as agriculture, the New Deal started the institutionalization of larger interest groups into a new political economy. Joining business as tentative junior partners, they shared the consensus on the value of large-scale corporate capitalism, and were permitted to participate in the competition for the division of shares. While failing to redistribute income, the New Deal modified the political structure at the price of excluding many from the process of decision making. To many what was offered in fact was symbolic representation, formal representation. It was not the industrial workers necessarily who were recognized, but their unions and leaders; it was not even the farmers, but their organizations and leaders. While this was not a conscious design, it was the predictable result of conscious policies. It could not have been easily avoided, for it was part of the price paid by a large society unwilling to consider radical new designs for the distribution of power and wealth.

VII

In the deepest sense, this new form of representation was rooted in the liberal's failure to endorse a meaningful egalitarianism which would provide actual equality of opportunity. It was also the limited concern with equality and justice that accounted for the shallow efforts of the New Deal and left so many Americans behind. The New Deal was neither a "third American Revolution," as Carl Degler suggests, nor even a "half-way revolution," as William Leuchtenburg concludes. Not only was the extension of representation to new groups less than full-fledged partnership, but the New Deal neglected many Americans—sharecroppers, tenant farmers, migratory workers and farm laborers, slum dwellers, unskilled workers, and the unemployed Negroes. They were left outside the new order.[83] As Roosevelt asserted in 1937 (in a classic understatement), one third of the nation was "ill-nourished, ill-clad, ill-housed."[84]

Yet, by the power of rhetoric and through the appeals of political organization, the Roosevelt government managed to win or retain the allegiance of these peoples. Perhaps this is one of the crueller ironies of liberal politics, that the marginal men trapped in hopelessness were seduced by rhetoric, by the style and movement, by the symbolism of efforts seldom reaching beyond words. In acting to protect the institution of private property and in advancing the interests of corporate capitalism, the New Deal assisted the middle and upper sectors of society. It protected them, sometimes, even at the cost of injuring the lower sectors. Seldom did it bestow much of substance upon the lower classes. Never did the New Deal seek to organize these groups into independent political forces. Seldom did it risk antagonizing established interests. For some this would constitute a puzzling defect of liberalism; for some, the failure to achieve true liberalism. To others it would emphasize the inherent shortcomings of American liberal democracy. As the nation prepared for war, liberalism, by accepting private property and federal assistance to corporate capitalism, was not prepared effectively to reduce inequities, to redistribute political power, or to extend equality from promise to reality.

NOTES

1. The outstanding examples are Arthur Schlesinger, Jr., Frank Freidel, Carl Degler, and William Leuchtenburg. Schlesinger, in *The Crisis of the Old Order* (Boston, 1957), emphasized the presence of reform in the twenties but criticized the federal government for its retreat from liberalism and condemned Hoover for his responses to the depression. The next two volumes of his *The Age of Roosevelt, The Coming of the New Deal* (Boston, 1958) and *The Politics of Upheaval* (Boston, 1960), praise the New Deal, but also contain information for a more critical appraisal. His research is quite wide and has often guided my own investigations. For his theory that the New Deal was likely even without the depression, see "Sources of the New Deal: Reflections on the Temper of a Time," *Columbia University Forum*, II (Fall 1959), 4–11. Freidel affirmed that the New Deal was a watershed (*American Historical Review*, October 1965, p. 329), but in *The New Deal in Historical Perspective* (Washington, 1959), he has suggested the conservatism of the New Deal as a reform movement. Degler, in *Out of Our Past* (New York, 1959), pp. 379–416, extolled the New Deal as a "Third American Revolution." But also see his "The Ordeal of Herbert Hoover," *Yale Review*, LII (Sumner 1963), 565–83. Leuchtenburg, *Franklin D. Roosevelt and the New Deal, 1932–1940* (New York, 1963), offers considerable criticism of the New Deal, but finds far more to praise in this "half-way revolution." He cites Degler approvingly but moderates Degler's judgment (pp. 336–47). The book represents years of research and has often guided my own investigations.

2. Eric Goldman, *Rendezvous with Destiny* (New York, 1952); Henry Steele Commager, "Twelve Years of Roosevelt," *American Mercury*, LX (April 1945), 391–401; Arthur Link, *American Epoch* (New York, 1955), pp. 377–440. In his essay on "Franklin D. Roosevelt: the Patrician as Opportunist" in *The American Political Tradition* (New York, 1948), pp. 315–52, Richard Hofstadter was critical of the New Deal's lack of ideology but treated it as a part of the larger reform tradition. In *The Age of Reform* (New York, 1955), however, while chiding the New Deal for opportunism, he emphasized the discontinuity of the New Deal with the reform tradition of Populism and Progressivism.

3. Edgar E. Robinson, *The Roosevelt Leadership, 1933–1945* (Philadelphia, 1955), the work of a conservative constitutionalist, does accuse the administration of having objectives approaching the leveling aims of communism (p. 376).

4. Louis Hacker, *American Problems of Today* (New York, 1938).

5. William Appleman Williams, *The Contours of American History* (Chicago, 1966), pp. 372–488; and his review, "Schlesinger: Right Crisis—Wrong Order," *Nation*, CLXXXIV (March 23, 1957), 257–60. Williams' volume has influenced my own thought.

6. Ronald Radosh, "The Corporate Ideology of American Labor Leaders from Gompers to Hillman," *Studies on the Left*, VI (November–December 1966), 66–88.

7. Arthur Link, "What Happened to the Progressive Movement?" *American Historical Review*, LXIV (July 1959), 833–51.

8. James Prothro, *The Dollar Decade* (Baton Rouge, La., 1954).

9. Louis Galambos, *Competition and Cooperation* (Baltimore, 1966), pp. 55–139; Link, "What Happened to the Progressive Movement?"

10. Joseph Brandes, *Herbert Hoover and Economic Diplomacy* (Pittsburgh, 1962); Hofstadter, *American Political Tradition*, pp. 283–99.

11. William S. Myers, ed., *The State Papers and Other Writings of Herbert Hoover* (New York, 1934), I, 84–88 (easier money), 137, 411, 431–33; II, 202 (public works); I, 142–43, 178–79 (lower taxes). The Commodity Stabilization Corporation was created before the crash.

12. Lippmann, "The Permanent New Deal," *Yale Review*, XXIV (June 1935), 651.

13. Myers, ed., *State Papers*, II, 195–201, 214–15, 224–26, 228–33 (on the budget); II, 405, 496–99, 503–5 (on relief).

14. Gerald Nash, "Herbert Hoover and the Origins of the Reconstruction Finance Corporation," *Mississippi Valley Historical Review*, XLVI (December 1959), 455–68.

15. W. S. Myers and W. H. Newton, eds., *The Hoover Administration: A Documentary History* (New York, 1936), p. 119; "Proceedings of a Conference of Progressives," March 11–12, 1931, Hillman Papers, Amalgamated Clothing Workers (New York).

16. *Contours of American History,* p. 428.

17. Lippmann, "The Permanent New Deal," p. 651.

18. For an excellent statement of this thesis, see Howard Zinn's introduction to his *New Deal Thought* (New York, 1966), pp. xv–xxxvi. So far historians have not adequately explored the thesis that F.D.R. frequently acted as a restraining force on his own government, and that bolder reforms were often thwarted by him and his intimates.

19. Bronson Cutting, "Is Private Banking Doomed?" *Liberty,* XI (March 31, 1934), 10; cf. Raymond Moley, *The First New Deal* (New York, 1966), pp. 177–80.

20. Moley, *After Seven Years* (New York, 1939), p. 155; Arthur Ballantine, "When All the Banks Closed," *Harvard Business Review,* XXVI (March 1948), 129–43.

21. William Lemke, later quoted in Lorena Hickok to Harry Hopkins, November 23, 1933, Hopkins Papers, Franklin D. Roosevelt Library (hereafter called FDRL).

22. Baruch to Samuel Gompers, April 19, 1924, Baruch Papers, Princeton University; Schlesinger, *Coming of the New Deal,* pp. 88–89; Gerald Nash, "Experiments in Industrial Mobilization: WIB and NRA," *Mid-America,* XLV (July 1963), 156–75.

23. Gerard Swope, *The Swope Plan* (New York, 1931); Julius H. Barnes, "Government and Business," *Harvard Business Review,* X (July 1932), 411–19; Harriman, "The Stabilization of Business and Employment," *American Economic Review,* XXII (March 1932), 63–75; House Committee on Education and Labor, 73rd Cong., 1st Sess., *Thirty-Hour Week Bill, Hearings,* pp. 198–99.

24. *Ibid.,* pp. 884–97; Hillman, "Labor Leads Toward Planning," *Survey Graphic,* LXVI (March 1932), 586–88.

25. Irving Bernstein, *The New Deal Collective Bargaining Policy* (Berkeley, Cal., 1950), pp. 57–63.

26. Quotes from Hofstadter, *American Political Tradition,* p. 336. "It is not the function of NRA to organize . . . labor," asserted General Hugh Johnson. "Automobile Code Provides for Thirty-Five Hour Week," *Iron Age,* CXXXII (August 3, 1933), 380.

27. Richard C. Wilcock, "Industrial Management's Policy Toward Unionism," in Milton Derber and Edwin Young, eds., *Labor and the New Deal* (Madison, Wis., 1957), pp. 278–95.

28. Leverett Lyon, *et al., The National Recovery Administration* (Washington, 1935).

29. The characterization of Berle, Tugwell, and Moley is from Schlesinger, *Coming of the New Deal,* pp. 181–84, and Johnson's address at the NAM is from NRA press release 2126, December 7, 1933, NRA Records, RG 9, National Archives.

30. "Concert of interests" was used by F.D.R. in a speech of April 18, 1932, in Samuel Rosenman, ed., *The Public Papers and Addresses of Franklin D. Roosevelt* (13 vols.; New York, 1938–52), I, 627–39. (Hereafter referred to as *FDR Papers.*)

31. M. S. Venkataramani, "Norman Thomas, Arkansas Sharecroppers, and the Roosevelt Agricultural Policies," *Mississippi Valley Historical Review*, XLVII (September 1960), 225–46; John Hutson, Columbia Oral History Memoir, pp. 114ff.; Mordecai Ezekiel, Columbia Oral History Memoir, pp. 74ff.

32. Quoted from Leuchtenburg, *F.D.R.*, p. 87, and this discussion draws upon pp. 87–90; John Chamberlain, *The American Stakes* (Philadelphia, 1940): James MacGregor Burns, *Roosevelt: The Lion and the Fox* (New York, 1956), pp. 183–202.

33. Quoted from House Committee on Education and Labor, 74th Cong., 1st Sess., *National Labor Relations Board Hearings*, p. 35.

34. For a warning, see Paul Douglas, "Rooseveltian Liberalism," *Nation*, CXXXVI (June 21, 1933), 702–3.

35. Leuchtenburg, *F.D.R.*, p. 88, uses the image of "a parallelogram of pressures."

36. For example see the Columbia Oral Histories of Louis Bean, Hutson, and Ezekiel.

37. *New York Times*, January 30, 1934; House Interstate and Foreign Commerce Committee, 73rd Cong., 2nd Sess., House Report No. 1383, *Securities Exchange Bill of 1934*, p. 3; "SEC," *Fortune*, XXI (June 1940), 91–92, 120ff.; Ralph DeBedts, *The New Deal's SEC* (New York, 1964), pp. 56–85.

38. Frederick Rudolph, "The American Liberty League, 1934–1940," *American Historical Review*, LVI (October 1950), 19–33; George Wolfskill, *The Revolt of the Conservatives* (Boston, 1962). Emphasizing the Liberty League and focusing upon the rhetoric of business disaffection, historians have often exaggerated the opposition of the business communities. See the correspondence of James Forrestal, PPF 6367, FDRL, and at Princeton; of Russell Leffingwell, PPF 886, FDRL; of Donald Nelson, PPF 8615, FDRL, and at the Huntington Library; and of Thomas Watson, PPF 2489, FDRL. On the steel industry, see *Iron Age*, CXXXV (June 13, 1935), 44. For very early evidence of estrangement, however, see Edgar Mowrer to Frank Knox, November 8, 1933, Knox Papers, Library of Congress.

39. Quoted from Donald McCoy, *Angry Voices: Left of Center Politics in the New Deal Era* (Lawrence, Kan., 1958), p. 55, from *Farmer-Labor Leader*, March 30, 1934.

40. Long, *My First Days in the White House* (Harrisburg, Pa., 1935).

41. Quoted from Sinclair, *The Way Out* (New York, 1933), p. 57. See Sinclair to Roosevelt, October 5 and 18, 1934, OF 1165, FDRL.

42. Nicholas Roosevelt, *The Townsend Plan* (Garden City, N.Y., 1935). Not understanding that the expenditures would increase consumption and probably spur production, critics emphasized that the top 9 percent would have received 50 percent of the income, but they neglected that the top income-tenth had received (before taxes) nearly 40 percent of the national income in 1929. National Indus-

trial Conference Board, *Studies in Enterprise and Social Progress* (New York, 1939), p. 125.

43. Sevareid, *Not So Wild a Dream* (New York, 1946), p. 58.

44. Sidney Lens, *Left, Right and Center* (Hinsdale, Ill., 1949), pp. 280–89.

45. Quoted in Robert Sherwood, *Roosevelt and Hopkins,* rev. ed. (New York, 1950), p. 65.

46. Roosevelt's press conference of June 15, 1934, *FDR Papers,* III, 301; cf., Roosevelt to John L. Lewis, February 25, 1939, Philip Murray Papers, Catholic University.

47. Burns, *The Lion and the Fox,* pp. 217–19; quotation from p. 218.

48. Perkins, Columbia Oral History Memoir, VII, 138, 147, quoted by Leuchtenburg, *F.D.R.,* p. 151.

49. Irving Bernstein, *The New Deal Collective Bargaining Policy,* pp. 100–8; Burns, *The Lion and the Fox,* p. 219.

50. Margaret Grant, *Old Age Security* (Washington, 1939), p. 217. Under social security, payments at sixty-five ranged from $10 a month to $85 a month, depending on earlier earnings.

51. Roosevelt's message to Congress on June 19, 1935, *FDR Papers,* IV, 271.

52. *New York Times,* June 20 and 21, 1935; *Business Week,* June 22, 1935, p. 5.

53. John Morton Blum, *From the Morgenthau Diaries: Years of Crisis, 1928–1938* (Boston, 1959), pp. 302–4.

54. Simon Kuznets, *Shares of Upper Income Groups in Income and Savings,* National Bureau of Economic Research, Occasional Paper 35 (New York, 1950), pp. 32–40.

55. Otis L. Graham, Jr., "Historians and the New Deals: 1944–1960," *Social Studies,* LIV (April 1963), 133–40.

56. *New York Times,* November 19, 1933; May 1, September 30, November 17, December 23, 1934; May 1, 3, 5, 28, 1935; "Chamber to Vote on NIRA," *Nation's Business,* XXII (December 1934), 51; "Business Wants a New NRA," *ibid.,* XXIII (February 1935), 60; "Listening in as Business Speaks," *ibid.,* XXIII (June 1935), 18, 20; William Wilson, "How the Chamber of Commerce Viewed the NRA," *Mid-America,* XLIII (January, 1962), 95–108.

57. *New York Times,* May 3, 4, 12, 1935. On the steel industry see L. W. Moffet, "This Week in Washington," *Iron Age,* CXXXV (March 21, 1935), 41; *ibid.* (April 18, 1935), 49; "NRA Future Not Settled by Senate Committee's Action for Extension," *ibid.* (May 9, 1935), 58.

58. Ellis W. Hawley, *The New Deal and the Problem of Monopoly* (Princeton, 1966), pp. 205–86.

59. Freidel, *The New Deal,* pp. 18–19. On Arnold's efforts, see Wendell Berge Diary, 1938–1939, Berge Papers, Library of Congress; and Gene Gressley, "Thurman Arnold, Antitrust, and the New Deal," *Business History Review,* XXXVIII (Summer, 1964), 214–31. For

characteristic Roosevelt rhetoric emphasizing the effort of his government to subdue "the forces of selfishness and of lust for power,"
see his campaign address of October 31, 1936, his press conference
of January 4, 1938, and his message of April 29, 1938, in *FDR
Papers,* V, 568–69 and VII, 11, 305–32.

60. Dewey, *Liberalism and Social Action* (New York, 1935), p. 62.
61. Howard Zinn, in *New Deal Thought,* pp. xxvi–xxxi, discusses this
    subject and has influenced my thought. Also consider those whom
    Zinn cites: Edmund Wilson, "The Myth of Marxist Dialectic,"
    Partisan Review, VI (Fall, 1938), 66–81; William Ernest Hocking,
    "The Future of Liberalism," *The Journal of Philosophy,* XXXII
    (April 25, 1935), 230–47; Stuart Chase, "Eating Without Working:
    A Moral Disquisition," *Nation,* CXXXVII (July 22, 1933), 93–94.
62. See James T. Patterson, "A Conservative Coalition Forms in Con-
    gress, 1933–1939," *Journal of American History,* LII (March 1966),
    757–72.
63. Hofstadter, *American Political Tradition,* p. 342; cf., Freidel, *The
    New Deal,* p. 20.
64. Roosevelt's annual message to the Congress on January 4, 1939,
    FDR Papers, VIII, 7.
65. Fiorello LaGuardia to James Byrnes, April 5, 1939, Box 2584, La-
    Guardia Papers, Municipal Archives, New York City.
66. Hopkins, "The Future of Relief," *New Republic,* XC (February
    10, 1937), 8.
67. Tugwell, *The Stricken Land* (Garden City, N.Y., 1947), p. 681.
68. Roosevelt's speech of January 4, 1935, *FDR Papers,* IV, 19.
69. Hopkins, "Federal Emergency Relief," *Vital Speeches,* I (December
    31, 1934), 211.
70. Broadus Mitchell, *Depression Decade: From New Era Through
    New Deal* (New York, 1947), pp. 37–54.
71. Housing and Home Finance Agency, *First Annual Report* (Wash-
    ington, 1947), pp. 24–25. Timothy McDonnell, *The Wagner Hous-
    ing Act* (Chicago, 1957), pp. 53, 186–88, concludes that the Wagner
    bill would have passed earlier if Roosevelt had supported it.
72. Jane Jacobs, *The Life and Death of Great American Cities* (New
    York, 1963). Racial policy was locally determined. U.S. Housing
    Authority, *Bulletin No. 18 on Policy and Procedure* (1938), pp. 7–8;
    Robert C. Weaver, "The Negro in a Program of Public Housing,"
    Opportunity, XVI (July 1938), 1–6. Three fifths of all families, re-
    ported Weaver, were earning incomes "below the figure necessary
    to afford respectable living quarters without undue skimping on
    other necessities." (p. 4)
73. Allen Kifer, "The Negro Under the New Deal, 1933–1941," (un-
    published Ph.D. dissertation, University of Wisconsin, 1961), *pas-
    sim.* The National Youth Agency was an exception, concludes Kifer,
    p. 139. For Negro protests about New Deal discrimination, John P.
    Davis, "What Price National Recovery?," *Crisis,* XL (December

1933), 272; Charles Houston and Davis, "TVA: Lily-White Construction," *Crisis*, XLI (October 1934), 291.

74. Robert Vann of the *Pittsburgh Courier*, quoted in Joseph Alsop and William Kintner, "The Guffey," *Saturday Evening Post*, CCX (March 26, 1938), 6. Vann had offered this advice in 1932.

75. See Eleanor Roosevelt to Walter White, May 2, 29, 1934, April 21, 1938, White Papers, Yale University; Frank Freidel, *F.D.R. and the South* (Baton Rouge, La., 1965), pp. 71–102.

76. Quoted from Senate Judiciary Committee, 74th Cong., 1st Sess., *Punishment for the Crime of Lynching, Hearings,* p. 23. Cf. Harold Ickes, "The Negro as a Citizen," June 29, 1936, Oswald Garrison Villard Papers, Harvard University.

77. Roy Wilkins, Columbia Oral History Memoir, p. 98; Lester Granger, Columbia Oral History Memoir, p. 105, complains that Wagner had refused to include in his labor bill a prohibition against unions excluding workers because of race. When Wagner counseled a delay, Negroes felt, according to Granger, that the New Deal "was concerned with covering up, putting a fine cover over what there was, not bothering with the inequities."

78. Ickes, "The Negro as a Citizen." Ickes had said, "since the Civil War."

79. Schlesinger, *Politics of Upheaval*, pp. 362–80; quotation from Tugwell p. 371.

80. Martin Dies, quoted by Burns, *Congress on Trial* (New York, 1949), p. 77.

81. The law raised standards to thirty cents and forty-two hours in 1939 and forty cents and forty hours in 1945. U.S. Department of Labor, BLS, *Labor Information Bulletin* (April 1939), pp. 1–3.

82. Arthur M. Ross, *Trade Union Wage Policy* (Berkeley, Cal., 1948), pp. 113–28.

83. Leuchtenburg, *F.D.R.*, pp. 346–47. The Bankhead-Jones Farm Tenancy Act of 1937 provided some funds for loans to selected tenants who wished to purchase farms. In 1935, there were 2,865,155 tenants (about 42 percent of all farmers), and by 1941, 20,748 had received loans. *Farm Tenancy: Report of the President's Committee* (Washington, February 1937), Table I, p. 89; *Report of the Administrator of the Farm Security Administration*, 1941 (Washington, 1941), p. 17.

84. Roosevelt's Inaugural Address of January 20, 1937, *FDR Papers*, VI, 5.

AMERICA IN
WAR AND PEACE: THE TEST
OF LIBERALISM

∞ Barton J. Bernstein

THE DOMESTIC EVENTS of the war and postwar years have failed to attract as much scholarly effort as have the few years of the New Deal. The reforms of the thirties and the struggle against depression have captured the enthusiasm of many liberal historians and have constituted the major themes shaping their interpretations. Compared with the excitement of the New Deal years, the events at home during the next decade seem less interesting, certainly less dramatic.

The issues of these years also seem less clear, perhaps because the period lacks the restrictive unity imposed upon the New Deal. Despite the fragmentary scholarship, however, the major issues are definable: economic policies,[1] civil rights, civil liberties,[2] and social welfare policies.[3] The continued dominance by big business, the consolidation of other groups within the economy, the challenge of racial inequality—these are the themes of the wartime Roosevelt administration. Toward the end of Roosevelt's years, they are joined by another concern, the quest for social reform, and in Truman's years by such themes as economic readjustment, the

renewed struggle against inflation, and the fear of disloyalty
and communism. These problems are largely the legacy of
the New Deal: the extension of its limited achievements, the
response to its shortcomings, the criticism of its liberalism.

It was during the war years that the nation climbed out of
depression, that big busines regained admiration and increased its power, and that other interests became effective
partners in the political economy of large-scale corporate
capitalism. While the major interests focused on foreign
policy and on domestic economic problems—on mobilization and stabilization, later on reconversion and inflation—
liberal democracy was revealing serious weaknesses. Opposing fascism abroad as a threat to democratic values, the nation
remained generally insensitive to the plight of its citizens who
suffered indignity or injury because of their color. Violating
liberal values in the process of saving American democracy,
Roosevelt's government, swept along by a wave of racism,
victimized Japanese-Americans. Uncommitted to advancing
the Negroes' cause, the war government resisted their demands for full participation in democracy and prosperity,
and grudgingly extended to them only limited rights.

Though the New Deal had gone intellectually bankrupt
long before Pearl Harbor and reform energies were submerged during most of the war, they reappeared in the last
years of the conflict. Reviving the reform spirit in 1944,
Roosevelt called for an "Economic Bill of Rights" for postwar America. In his last year, however, he was unable to
achieve his goals, and Truman's efforts were usually too
weak to overcome the conservative coalition blocking his
expanded reform program. Mobilized by apprehension, liberals wrongly believed that the conservative bloc wished to
destroy unions, to reorganize the corporate economy, and to
leave the nation without protection from depression. But as
unions endured and the economy grew, the fears and energies of liberals waned. Exaggerating the accomplishments of
past reforms and believing that widespread prosperity had
been achieved, they lost much of their social vision: they
came to praise big business, to celebrate pluralism, to ignore
poverty. Yet to their surprise they fell under vigorous attack
from the right, in a new assault on civil liberties. In viewing

McCarthyism as an attack upon the reform tradition, however, liberals failed to understand that they and the Democratic administration, as zealous anticommunists, also shared responsibility for the "red scare."

I

During the war and postwar years, big business regained national admiration and received lavish praise for contributing to victory over fascism. Yet few realized that business had not initially been an enthusiastic participant in the "arsenal of democracy." Such firms as Standard Oil of New Jersey, Dow Chemical, United States Steel, Dupont, General Motors, and the Aluminum Company of America had assisted the growth of Nazi industry and delayed America's preparation for war. Even after most Americans had come to condemn fascism, these corporations had collaborated with German business, sharing patents and often blocking production of defense materials in America.[4] The general ideology of these firms was probably best expressed by Alfred Sloan, Jr., the chairman of the General Motors board, when he replied to a stockholder: ". . . an international business operating throughout the world should conduct its operations in strictly business terms without regard to the political beliefs in its management, or the political beliefs of the country in which it is operating."[5]

In the two years before Pearl Harbor, major industries were also reluctant to prepare for defense. Though the aircraft industry ended its "sit-down" strike after the government had relaxed profit restrictions and improved terms for amortization,[6] other industries continued to resist expansion and production for defense. Sharing the common opinion that American intervention was unlikely, and painfully recalling the glutted markets of the depression decade, the steel industry and the aluminum monopoly (Alcoa) opposed growth, which might endanger profits. Nor were the automobile makers and larger producers of consumer durables willing to take defense contracts which would convert assembly lines from profitable, peacetime goods to preparation for a war that many believed, and President Roosevelt seemed to promise, America would never enter.[7]

Fearful of bad publicity, the leaders of these industries never challenged the administration nor demanded a clear statement of their responsibility. They avoided a dialogue on the basic issues. Still suffering from the opprobrium of the depression, industrialists would not deny corporate responsibility to the nation. Though privately concerned about the welfare of their companies, industrialists never argued that they owed primary responsibility to their stockholders. Fearful of jeopardizing their firms' well-being, company officials did not publicly express their doubts. Yet they could have objected publicly to executive suasion and contended that the issues were so grave that a Congressional mandate was necessary. Instead, they publicly accepted their obligation to risk profits for American defense, but in practice they continued to avoid such risks. Often they made promises they did not fulfill, and when they resisted administration policy, they took refuge in evasion. They restricted the dialogue to matters of feasibility and tactics—that expansion in steel and aluminum was unnecessary, that partial conversion was impossible, and that available tools could not produce defense goods.

The government also avoided opening the dialogue. The prewar mobilization agencies, administered largely by dollar-a-year men, did not seek to embarrass or coerce recalcitrant industries. Protecting business from public censure, the directors of mobilization—such men as William Knudsen of General Motors and Edward Stettinius of United States Steel —resisted the efforts of other government officials to force prompt expansion and conversion. In effect, Knudsen, Stettinius, and their cohorts acted as protectors of "business as usual." Despite the protests of the service secretaries, Roosevelt permitted the businessmen in government to move slowly. Though he encouraged some assistants to prod business, and occasionally spurred the dollar-a-year men, he avoided exerting direct pressure on big business.

The President was following the strategy of caution. Reluctant to encourage public criticism of, or even debate on, his foreign policy, he maneuvered to avoid conflict or challenge. Because the nation respected big businessmen, he chose them to direct mobilization. He too had faith in their ability, and he hoped to win cooperation from the suspicious business community by selecting its leaders as his agents.

While many liberals criticized Roosevelt's reliance upon big business, the most direct, public challenge to business power came from Walter Reuther, vice-president of the recently formed United Automobile Workers, and from Philip Murray, president of the CIO and the United Steel Workers.[8] Criticizing "business as usual" policies, they proposed a labor-management council to guide industry during war. The plan shocked industrialists. It was radicalism, an invasion of management's prerogatives, a threat to private enterprise, asserted business leaders.[9] They would not share power or sanction a redefinition of private property. Having grudgingly recognized industrial unions shortly before the war, they remained suspicious of organized labor and were unwilling to invite its leaders into the industrial councils of decision making.[10]

Despite these suspicions, the administration called upon labor leaders and their organizations for cooperation in the war effort. Needing their support, Roosevelt appointed union chiefs to positions in the stabilization and mobilization agencies, and thus bestowed prestige upon organized labor. Calling for a labor-management partnership, he secured a wartime no-strike pledge.[11] As junior partners in the controlled economy, labor leaders generally kept the pledge.[12] Cooperating with business leaders in the defense effort, union representatives, by their actions, convinced many businessmen that organized labor did not threaten large-scale corporate capitalism.[13] By encouraging labor-management cooperation, the war years, then, provided a necessary respite between the industrial violence of the thirties and sustained collective bargaining, and speeded the consolidation of the new organization of the American economy.

It was within a government-controlled economy (dominated by business) that the major interests struggled for economic advantages. Farmers, rescued from the depression by enlarged demand, initially battled price controls but soon acceded to them and tried simply to use political power to increase their benefits. Also reaping the gains of war, workers received higher incomes but bitterly criticized the tight restraints on hourly wage increases. Business, also recovering from the depression, complained about price controls, which indirectly limited profits. Though all interests chafed under the restraints, none disputed in principle the need for government-imposed restraints on wages and prices: all agreed that a free price system during war, when civilian demand greatly outstripped consumer goods, would have created inequity and chaos.[14]

Despite price restrictions and the excess-profits tax, the major corporations prospered, benefitting from cost-plus contracts and the five-year amortization plan (which made the new plants partial gifts from the government).[15] As dollar-a-year men poured into Washington, big firms gained influence and contracts. Smaller businessmen, unable to match the influence and mistrusted by procurement officers, declined in importance. In a nation that prized the large corporation, few had confidence in small business. Even the creation of a government agency to protect small business failed to increase significantly its share in the war economy.[16]

The interests of big business were defended and advanced by the dollar-a-year men, and particularly by those on the War Production Board (WPB), the agency controlling resources. In many wartime Washington agencies, and especially on the WPB, the leaders of big business and the military served together and learned to cooperate. Burying earlier differences about preparation for war, they developed similar views of the national interest and identified it with the goals of their own groups. The reconversion controversy of 1944, which C. Wright Mills views as the beginning of the military-industrial alliance,[17] is the outstanding example of this coalition of interests.

In early 1944, big business was experiencing large military cutbacks and withdrawing subcontracts from smaller firms, often leaving them idle. Temporarily proponents of strong controls, most of the WPB executives from industry and finance would not allow these smaller firms to return to consumer goods. They collaborated with representatives of the military to block the reconversion program. Desiring control of the wartime economy, such military leaders as Robert P. Patterson, Under Secretary of War, James Forrestal, Under

Secretary of the Navy, and Major General Lucius Clay, Assistant Chief of Staff for Matériel, feared that reconversion would siphon off scarce labor and disrupt vital production. Joining them were such WPB executives as Charles E. Wilson, president of General Electric, Lemuel Boulware, a Celotex executive and later a General Electric vice-president, and financiers Arthur H. Bunker of Lehman Brothers and Sidney Weinberg of Goldman, Sachs. Sympathetic to military demands, they were also afraid that the earlier return of small producers to consumer markets would injure big business. While some may have acted to protect their own companies, most were simply operating in a value system that could not accept a policy which seemed to threaten big business. Through cunning maneuvering, these military and industrial leaders acted to protect the prewar oligopolistic structure of the American economy.[18]

The war, while creating the limited prosperity that the New Deal had failed to create, did not disrupt the economic distribution of power. Nor did the extension of the wartime income tax significantly reallocate income and wealth, for the Congress even rebuffed Roosevelt's effort to limit the war incomes of the wealthy. Though the wartime measures and not the New Deal increased the tax burden on the upper-income groups, "the major weight," emphasizes Gabriel Kolko, "fell on income groups that had never before been subjected to the income tax."[19]

II

Failing to limit business power or to reallocate wealth, the wartime government was more active in other areas. Yielding to pressures, Roosevelt slightly advanced the welfare of the Negro, but the President also bowed to illiberal pressures and dealt a terrible blow to civil liberties when he authorized the forced evacuation of 110,000 loyal Americans of Japanese descent.

It was the "worst single wholesale violation of civil rights" in American history, judged the American Civil Liberties Union.[20] Succumbing to the anti-Japanese hysteria of Westerners (including the pleas of California Attorney-General Earl Warren and the Pacific coast congressional delegation under Senator Hiram Johnson) and the demands of the military commander on the coast, the President empowered the Army to remove the Japanese-Americans.[21] ("He was never theoretical about things. What must be done to defend the country must be done," Roosevelt believed, later wrote Francis Biddle, his Attorney-General.[22]) "Japanese raids on the west coast seemed not only possible but probable in the first months of war, and it was quite impossible to be sure that the raiders would not receive important help from individuals of Japanese origin," was the explanation later endorsed by Secretary of War Henry Stimson.[23]

Privately Stimson called the episode a "tragedy," but he supported it as War Department policy.[24] Opposing the decision, Biddle could not weaken the resolve of Roosevelt. Though liberals protested the action, the Supreme Court later upheld Roosevelt and the War Department.[25] "The meaning of the decision," concludes Arthur Link, "was clear and foreboding: in future emergencies no American citizen would have any rights that the President and the army were bound to respect when, *in their judgment,* the emergency justified drastic denial of civil rights."[26]

Though anti-Japanese feeling was most virulent on the Pacific coast, racism was not restricted to any part of America. In most of America, Negroes had long been the victims of hatred. Frequently lacking effective legal protection in the South, Negroes also encountered prejudice, fear, and hatred in the North. During the war there were racial clashes in Northern cities. New York narrowly averted a major riot. In Los Angeles whites attacked Negroes and Mexicans, and in Detroit whites invaded the Negro sector and pillaged and killed.[27]

Despite the evidence of deep racism, liberal historians have usually avoided focusing upon the hatred in white America and the resort to violence.[28] Curiously, though emphasizing the disorganization of the Negro community, they have also neglected the scattered protests by organized Negroes—boycotts of white-owned stores in Negro areas of Memphis and Houston when they would not hire Negroes, a sit-in in a public library in Alexandria, Virginia, a Harlem boycott of a bus line to compel the hiring of Negro drivers.[29]

Condemned to inferiority in nearly all sectors of American life, Negroes did not share in the benefits of the early defense economy.[30] Denied jobs in many industries, they also met discrimination by the military. The Air Corps barred them, the Navy segregated them to the mess corps, and the Army held them to a small quota, generally restricting them to menial tasks.[31] During the 1940 campaign, Negro leaders attacked the administration for permitting segregation and discrimination, and demanded the broadening of opportunity in the military. It is not "a fight merely to wear a uniform," explained *Crisis* (the NAACP publication). "This is a struggle for status, a struggle to take democracy off a parchment and give it life."[32]

Negroes gained admission to the Air Corps when it yielded under White House pressure, but they failed to gain congressional support for wider participation in the military. At Roosevelt's direction the War Department did raise its quota of Negroes—to their proportion in the population. But the Army remained segregated. Though unwilling to challenge segregation, the administration still courted Negro leaders and the black vote. Rather than bestowing benefits upon the masses, Roosevelt maintained their allegiance by offering symbolic recognition: Colonel Benjamin O. Davis, the Army's highest ranking Negro, was promoted to Brigadier General, and some prominent Negroes were appointed as advisers to the Secretary of War and the Director of Selective Service.[33] ("We asked Mr. Roosevelt to change the rules of the game and he countered by giving us some new uniforms," complained the editors of the *Baltimore Afro-American*. "That is what it amounts to and we have called it appeasement."[34])

As the nation headed toward war, Negroes struggled to wring other concessions from a president who never enlisted in their cause and would not risk antagonizing powerful Southerners. Discriminated against by federal agencies during the depression and denied an equal share of defense prosperity, Negroes were unwilling to acquiesce before continued injustice. In some industrial areas the NAACP and *ad hoc* groups organized local protests. After numerous unsuccessful appeals to the President, Negro leaders planned more dramatic action—a march on Washington.[35]

Demanding "the right to work and fight for our country," the leaders of the March on Washington Movement—A. Philip Randolph, head of the Brotherhood of Sleeping Car Porters, Walter White, executive secretary of the NAACP, and Lester Granger, executive secretary of the Urban League—publicly requested executive orders ending racial discrimination in federal agencies, the military and defense employment.[36] In private correspondence with the President they sought more: the end of segregation in these areas. So bold were their goals that some still have not been enforced by the government, and it is unlikely that Negro leaders expected to secure them.[37]

Refusing to give up the march for the promise of negotiations, Negro leaders escaped the politics of accommodation. Though white liberals urged Randolph and his cohorts to call off the march, they would not yield.[38] Applying pressure on an uncomfortable administration, they ultimately settled for less than they had requested (and perhaps less than they had anticipated[39])—an executive order barring discrimination in defense work and creating a Federal Employment Practices Committee (FEPC). Meager as the order was, it was the greatest achievement in American history for organized Negro action.[40]

FEPC did not contribute significantly to the wartime advancement of the Negro. His gains were less the results of federal efforts than of the labor shortage. Undoubtedly, the committee would have been more effective if Roosevelt had provided it with a larger budget, but the Negro's cause never commanded the President's enthusiasm. Yet he did protect FEPC from its enemies, and by maintaining the agency, stressed its symbolic importance.[41]

It affirmed the rights of Negroes to jobs and focused attention on the power of the federal government to advance the interests of its black citizens. It did not smash the walls of prejudices; it only removed a few bricks. FEPC, concludes Louis Ruchames, "brought hope and a new confidence into their [Negro] lives. It gave them cause to believe in democracy and in America. It made them feel that in answering the call to their country's colors, they were defending, not the oppression and degradation, to which they were accustomed, but democracy, equality of opportunity, and a better world for themselves and their children."[42]

Still relegated to second-class citizenship, Negroes had found new dignity and new opportunity during the war. Loyal followers of Roosevelt, loving him for the few benefits his government had extended, black Americans had become important members of the shifting Democratic coalition. By their presence in Northern cities, they would also become a new political force.[43] For the Democratic party and the nation, their expectations and needs would constitute a moral and political challenge. By its response, white America would test the promise of liberal democracy.

III

When the nation joined the Allies, Roosevelt had explained that "Dr. Win-the-War" was taking over from "Dr. New Deal," and there were few liberal legislative achievements during the war years. Those benefits that disadvantaged groups did receive were usually a direct result of the labor shortage and the flourishing economy, not of liberal politics. By 1944, however, Roosevelt was prepared to revive the reform spirit, and he revealed his liberal vision for the post-war years. Announcing an "Economic Bill of Rights," he outlined "a new basis for security and prosperity": the right to a job, adequate food, clothing, and recreation, a decent home, a good education, adequate medical care, and protection against sickness and unemployment.[44]

Noble as was his vision of the future society, Roosevelt was still unprepared to move far beyond rhetoric, and the Congress was unsympathetic to his program.[45] While approving the GI Bill of Rights,[46] including educational benefits and extended unemployment pay, Congress resisted most liberal programs during the war. Asserting its independence of the executive, the war Congress also thwarted Roosevelt in other ways—by rejecting a large tax bill designed to spread the cost of war and to reduce inflationary pressures.[47] and by liquidating the National Resources Planning Board, which had originated the "second bill of rights" and also studied post-war economic planning.[48]

By its opposition to planning and social reform, Congress increased the anxieties of labor and liberals about the post-war years and left the new Truman administration poorly prepared for the difficult transition to a peacetime economy when the war suddenly ended.[49] Fearing the depression that most economists forecast, the administration did, however, propose a tax cut of $5 billion. While removing many low-income recipients from the tax rolls, the law was also of great benefit to large corporations. Charging inequity, organized labor found little support in Congress or the executive, for the government was relying upon business activity, rather than on consumer purchasing power, to soften the economic decline. Significantly, despite the anticipated $30 billion deficit (plus the $5 billion tax), no congressman expressed any fear of an unbalanced budget. Clearly fiscal orthodoxy did not occupy a very high place in the scale of values of congressional conservatives, and they accepted in practice the necessity of an unbalanced budget.[50]

Before the tax bill passed, the wartime harmony of the major interest groups had crumbled: each struggled to consolidate its gains and advance its welfare before the anticipated economic collapse. Chafing under the no-strike pledge and restrictions on wage raises, organized labor compelled the administration to relax its policy and free unions to bargain collectively.[51] Farmers, fearful of depression, demanded the withdrawal of subsidies which artificially depressed prices.[52] Big business, despite anticipated shortages, secured the removal of most controls on the allocation of resources.[53]

As the economic forecasts shifted in late autumn, the administration discovered belatedly that inflation, not depression, was the immediate economic danger. The President acted sporadically to restrain inflationary pressures, but his efforts were too occasional, often misguided, and too weak to resist the demands of interest groups and the actions of his own subordinates.[54]

Beset by factionalism and staffed often by men of limited ability, Truman's early government floundered. By adopting the practice of cabinet responsibility and delegating excessive authority to department chiefs, Truman created a structure that left him uninformed: problems frequently developed unnoticed until they had swelled to crises, and the choice then was often between undesirable alternatives. Operating in a new politics, in the politics of inflation, he confronted problems requiring greater tactical skill than those Roosevelt had confronted. Seeking to maintain economic controls, and compelled to deny the rising expectations of major interest groups, his administration found it difficult to avoid antagonizing the rival groups. In the politics of depression, the Roosevelt administration could frequently maintain political support by bestowing specific advantages on groups, but in the politics of inflation the major interest groups came to seek freedom from restrictive federal controls.[55]

So difficult were the problems facing Truman that even a more experienced and skilled president would have encountered great difficulty. Inheriting the hostile Congress that had resisted occasional wartime attempts at social reform, Truman lacked the skill or leverage to guide a legislature seeking to assert its independence of the executive. Unable to halt fragmentation of the Democratic coalition, and incapable of ending dissension in his government, he also found that conservative subordinates undercut his occasional liberalism. Though he had gone on record early in endorsing a reform program[56] ("a declaration of independence" from congressional conservatives, he called it),[57] he had been unsuccessful in securing most of the legislation—a higher minimum wage, public housing, expanded unemployment benefits, and FEPC. Even the employment act was little more, as one congressman said, than a license to look for a job.[58] The President, through ineptitude or lack of commitment, often chose not to struggle for his program. Unable to dramatize the issues or to command enthusiasm, he was an ineffectual leader.[59]

So unsuccessful was his government that voters began jibing, "To err is Truman." Despairing of a resurgence of liberalism under Truman, New Dealers left the government in droves. By the fall of 1946, none of Roosevelt's associates was left in a prominent position. So disgruntled were many liberals about Truman and his advisers, about his unwillingness to fight for price controls, housing, benefits for labor, and civil rights, that some turned briefly to serious consideration of a new party.[60]

IV

Achieving few reforms during his White House years, Truman, with the notable exception of civil rights, never moved significantly beyond Roosevelt. The Fair Deal was largely an extension of earlier Democratic liberalism,[61] but Truman's new vigor and fierce partisanship ultimately made him more attractive to liberals who despairingly watched the GOP-dominated Eightieth Congress and feared a repeal of the New Deal.

Their fears were unwarranted, as was their enthusiasm for the Fair Deal program. In practice it proved very limited— the housing program only provided for 810,000 units in six years of which only 60,000 were constructed;[62] social security benefits were extended to ten million[63] and increased by about 75 percent, and the minimum wage was increased to 75 cents, but coverage was reduced by nearly a million.[64] But even had all of the Fair Deal been enacted, liberal reform would have left many millions beyond the benefits of government. The very poor, the marginal men, those neglected but acknowledged by the New Deal, went ultimately unnoticed by the Fair Deal.[65]

While liberals frequently chafed under Truman's leadership and questioned his commitment, they failed generally to recognize how shallow were his reforms. As the nation escaped a postwar depression, American liberals gained new faith in the American economy. Expressing their enthusiasm, they came to extoll big business for its contributions. Believing firmly in the success of progressive taxation, they exaggerated its effects, and congratulated themselves on the redistribution of income and the virtual abolition of poverty. Praising the economic system, they accepted big agriculture and big labor as evidence of healthy pluralism that protected freedom and guaranteed an equitable distribution of resources.[66]

Despite the haggling over details and the liberals' occasional dismay at Truman's style, he expressed many of their values. Like Roosevelt, Truman never challenged big business, never endangered large-scale capitalism. Indeed, his efforts as well as theirs were directed largely to maintaining and adjusting the powers of the major economic groups.

Fearing that organized labor was threatened with destruction, Truman, along with the liberals, had been sincerely frightened by the postwar rancor toward labor.[67] What they failed to understand was that most Americans had accepted unions as part of the political economy. Certainly most major industrialists had accepted organized labor, though smaller businessmen were often hostile.[68] Despite the overwrought rhetoric of debates, Congress did not actually menace labor. It was not seeking to destroy labor, only to restrict its power.

Many Americans did believe that the Wagner Act had unduly favored labor and was creating unions indifferent to the public welfare and hostile to corporate power. Capitalizing on this exaggerated fear of excessive union power, and the resentment from the postwar strikes, businessmen secured the Taft-Hartley Act.[69] Designed to weaken organized labor, it tried but failed to protect the membership from leaders; it did not effectively challenge the power of established unions. However, labor chiefs, recalling the bitter industrial warfare of the thirties, were still uneasy in their new positions. Condemning the legislation as a "slave-labor" act, they responded with fear, assailed the Congress, and declared that Taft-Hartley was the major political issue.[70]

Within a few years, when unions discovered that they were safe, Taft-Hartley faded as an issue. But in 1948 it served Truman well by establishing the GOP's hostility to labor and casting it back into the Democratic ranks. Both the President and union chiefs conveniently neglected his own kindling of antilabor passions (as when he had tried to draft strikers).[71] Exploiting Taft-Hartley as part of his strategy of patching the tattered Democratic coalition, Truman tied repeal of the "slave-labor" law to price controls, farm benefits, anticommunism, and civil rights in the campaign which won his election in his own right.

V

In courting the Negro the Truman administration in 1948 made greater promises to black citizens than had any previous federal government in American history. Yet, like many Americans, Truman as a senator had regarded the Negro's plight as peripheral to his interests, and with many of his generation he believed that equality was compatible with segregation.[72] As President, however, he found himself slowly prodded by conscience and pushed by politics. He moved cautiously at first and endorsed only measures affirming legal equality and protecting Negroes from violence.

Reluctant to fragment the crumbling Democratic coalition, Truman, in his first year, had seemed to avoid taking positions on civil rights which might upset the delicate balance between Northern and Southern Democrats. While he endorsed legislation for a statutory FEPC that the Congress would not grant, his efforts on behalf of the temporary FEPC (created by Roosevelt's executive order) were weaker. Having already weakened the power of the temporary agency, he also acquiesced in the legislative decision to kill it.[73] Despite the fears of Negro leaders that the death of FEPC would leave Negroes virtually unprotected from discrimination in the postwar job market, Truman would not even issue an order requiring nondiscrimination in the federal service and by government contractors.[74]

Though Truman was unwilling to use the prestige or power of his great office significantly on behalf of Negroes, he did assist their cause. While sidestepping political conflict, he occasionally supported FEPC and abolition of the poll tax. When Negroes were attacked, he did condemn the racial violence.[75] Though generally reluctant to move beyond rhetoric during his early years, Truman, shortly before the 1946 election, found conscience and politics demanding more. So distressed was he by racial violence that when Walter White of the NAACP and a group of white liberals urged him to assist the Negro, he promised to create a committee to study civil rights.[76]

The promise of a committee could have been a device to

resist pressures, to delay the matter until after the election. And Truman could have appointed a group of politically safe men of limited reputation—men he could control. But instead, after the election, perhaps in an effort to mobilize the liberals for 1948, he appointed a committee of prominent men sympathetic to civil rights. They were men he could not control and did not seek to control.[77]

The committee's report, undoubtedly far bolder than Truman's expectations,[78] confirmed charges that America treated its Negroes as second-class citizens. It called for FEPC, an antilynching law, an anti-poll tax measure, abolition of segregation in interstate transportation, and the end of discrimination and segregation in federal agencies and the military. By attacking Jim Crow, the committee had moved to a redefinition of equality and interpreted segregation as incompatible with equality.[79]

Forced by the report to take a position, he no longer could easily remain an ally of Southern Democrats and maintain the wary allegiance of Negro leaders and urban liberals. Compelled earlier to yield to demands for advancement of the Negro, pressures which he did not wish fully to resist, Truman had encouraged these forces and they were moving beyond his control. On his decision, his political future might precariously rest. Threatened by Henry Wallace's candidacy on a third-party ticket, Truman had to take a bold position on civil rights or risk losing the important votes of urban Negroes. Though he might antagonize Southern voters, he foresaw no risk of losing Southern Democrats, no possibility of a bolt by dissidents, and the mild Southern response to the Civil Rights Report seemed to confirm this judgment.[80]

On February 2, 1948, Truman asked the Congress to enact most of the recommendations of his Civil Rights Committee (except most of those attacking segregation). Rather than using his executive powers, as the committee had urged, to end segregation in federal employment or to abolish segregation and discrimination in the military, he *promised* only to issue orders ending discrimination (but not specifying segregation) in the military and in federal agencies.[81] Retreating to moderation, the administration did not submit any of the legislation, nor did Truman issue the promised executive orders. "The strategy," an assistant later explained, "was to start with a bold measure and then temporize to pick up the right-wing forces. Simply stated, backtrack after the bang."[82]

Truman sought to ease Southern doubts by inserting in the 1948 platform the party's moderate 1944 plank on civil rights. Most Negro leaders, fearing the taint of Wallace and unwilling to return to the GOP, appeared stuck with Truman and they praised him. Though they desired a stronger plank, they would not abandon him at the convention, for his advocacy of rights for Negroes was unmatched by any twentieth-century president. To turn their backs on him in this time of need, most Negroes feared, would be injuring their own cause. But others were prepared to struggle for a stronger plank. Urban bosses, persuaded that Truman would lose, hoped to save their local tickets, and prominent white liberals sought power and principle. Triumphing at the convention, they secured a stronger plank, but it did not promise social equality. By promising equality when it was still regarded as compatible with segregation, they were offering far less than the "walk forthrightly into the bright sunshine of human rights," which Hubert Humphrey, then mayor of Minneapolis, had pledged in leading the liberal effort.[83]

When some of the Southerners bolted and formed the States Rights party, Truman was freed of any need for tender courtship of the South. He had to capture the Northern vote. Quickly he issued the long-delayed executive orders, which established a federal antidiscrimination board, declared a policy of equal opportunity in the armed forces, and established a committee to end military discrimination and segregation. (In doing so, Truman courted Negro voters and halted the efforts of A. Philip Randolph to lead a Negro revolt against the draft unless the military was integrated.[84]) Playing politics carefully during the campaign, Truman generally stayed away from civil rights and concentrated on inflation, public housing, and Taft-Hartley.

In the new Democratic Congress Truman could not secure the civil rights program, and a coalition of Southern Democrats and Northern Republicans blocked his efforts. Though liberals were unhappy with his leadership, they did not question his proposed legislation. All agreed on the emphasis on social change through legislation and judicial decisions. The liberal way was the legal way, and it seldom acknowledged the depth of American racism or even considered the possibility of bold new tactics. Only occasionally—in the threatened March on Washington in 1941, in some ride-ins in 1947,[85] and in the campaign of civil disobedience against the draft in 1948—had there been bolder means. In each case Negroes had devised and carried out these tactics. But generally they relied upon more traditional means: they expected white America to yield to political pressure and subscribe to the dictates of American democracy. By relying upon legal change, however, and by emphasizing measures to restore a *modicum* of human dignity, Negroes and whites did not confront the deeper problems of race relations which they failed to understand.[86]

Struggling for moderate institutional changes, liberals were disappointed by Truman's frequent unwillingness to use his executive powers in behalf of the cause he claimed to espouse. Only after considerable pressure did he create a FEPC-type agency during the Korean War.[87] His loyalty-and-security program, in its operation, discriminated against Negroes, and federal investigators, despite protests to Truman, apparently continued to inquire into attitudes of interracial sympathy as evidence relevant to a determination of disloyalty.[88] He was also slow to require the Federal Housing Administration to stop issuing mortgages on property with restrictive covenants, and it continued, by its policies, to protect residential segregation.[89]

Yet his government was not without significant achievements in civil rights. His special committee had quietly acted to integrate the armed forces,[90] and even the recalcitrant Army had abolished racial quotas when the President secretly promised their restoration if the racial imbalance became severe.[91] And the Department of Justice, despite Truman's apparent indifference,[92] had been an active warrior in the battle against Jim Crow. Entering cases as an *amicus curiae,* Justice had submitted briefs arguing the unconstitutionality of enforcing restrictive covenants and of requiring separate-but-equal facilities in interstate transportation and in higher education.[93] During the summer of 1952, the Solicitor-General's Office even won the administration's approval for a brief directly challenging segregated primary education.[94]

The accomplishments of the Truman years were moderate, and the shortcomings left the nation with a great burden of unresolved problems. Viewed from the perspective of today, Truman's own views seem unduly mild and his government excessively cautious; viewed even by his own time he was a reluctant liberal, troubled by terror and eager to establish limited equality. He was ahead of public opinion in his legislative requests, but not usually in his actions. By his occasional advocacy, he educated the nation and held high the promise of equality. By kindling hope, he also may have prevented rebellion and restrained or delayed impulses to work outside of the system. But he also unleashed expectations he could not foresee, and forces which future governments would not be able to restrain.

VI

Never as committed to civil rights as he was opposed to communism at home and abroad, Truman ultimately became a victim of his own loyalty-and-security policies. Mildly criticized in 1945 and 1946 for being "soft on communism," the administration belatedly responded after the disastrous election of 1946.[95] Truman appointed a committee to investigate loyalty and security, promptly accepted its standard of judgment ("reasonable grounds of belief in disloyalty"), and created a system of loyalty boards.[96]

Outraging many liberals, his loyalty program provoked vigorous criticisms—for its secret investigations, for the failure to guarantee the accused the right to know the identity of and cross-examine the accuser, for its loose standards of proof, for its attempt to anticipate disloyal behavior by inquiring into attitudes.[97] In seeking to protect the nation, the government seemed to be searching for all who *might* be disloyal—"potential subversives," Truman called them.[98]

Dangerously confusing the problems of loyalty and security, the administration, in what might seem a burst of democratic enthusiasm, decided to apply the same standards to diplomats and gardeners. Disloyalty at any level of government would endanger the nation. "The presence within the government of any disloyal or subversive persons constitutes a threat to democratic processes," asserted Truman in launching the program.[99] Anxious to remove communism in government as a possible issue, Truman had exaggerated the dangers to the nation. And by assuming that disloyalty could be determined and subversives discovered, Truman seemed also to be promising *absolute* internal security.[100]

Shocked by earlier lax security procedures and unwilling to rely exclusively upon counterintelligence to uncover spies, the administration had responded without proper concern for civil liberties. So extreme was the program that it should have removed loyalty and security as a political issue. But by failing to distinguish between radical political activity and disloyalty, the administration endangered dissent and liberal politics: it made present or past membership in organizations on the Attorney-General's list evidence of possible disloyalty. Thus, in justifying investigations of political activity, it also legitimized occasional right-wing attacks on the liberal past and encouraged emphasis on the radicalism of a few New Dealers as evidence of earlier subversion.[101]

In their own activities, many liberals were busy combatting domestic communism. Taking up the cudgels, the liberal Americans for Democratic Action (ADA) came often to define its purpose by its anticommunism. As an enemy of those liberals who would not renounce association with Communists, and, hence, as vigorous foes of the Progressive party, the ADA was prepared to do battle. Following Truman's strategy, ADA members assailed Wallace and his supporters as Communists, dupes of the Communists, and fellow travelers. To publicize its case the ADA even relied upon the tactic of guilt by association and paid for advertisements listing the Progressive party's major donors and the organizations on the Attorney-General's list with which they were or had been affiliated.[102] (Truman himself also red-baited. "I do not want and will not accept the political support of Henry Wallace and his Communists. . . . These are days of high prices for everything, but any price for Wallace and his Communists is too much for me to pay.")[103] In the labor movement liberals like the Reuther brothers led anticommunist crusades, and the CIO ultimately expelled its Communist-led unions. ("Granting the desirability of eliminating Communist influence from the trade union movement," later wrote Irving Howe and Louis Coser, "one might still have argued that mass expulsions were not only a poor way of achieving this end but constituted a threat to democratic values and procedures.")[104]

Expressing the administration's position, Attorney-General J. Howard McGrath proclaimed a "struggle against pagan communist philosophies that seek to enslave the world." "There are today many Communists in America," he warned. "They are everywhere—in factories, offices, butcher stores, on street corners, in private business. And each carries in himself the death of our society."[105] ("I don't think anybody ought to be employed as instructors [sic] for the young people of this country who believes in the destruction of our form of government," declared Truman.)[106]

Calling for a crusade against evil, viewing communism as a virulent poison, the administration continued to emphasize the need for *absolute* protection, for *absolute* security. By creating such high standards and considering their fulfillment easy, by making success evidence of will and resolution, the administration risked assaults if its loyalty-and-security program was proved imperfect. To discredit the administration, all that was needed was the discovery of some red "spies," and after 1948 the evidence seemed abundant— Alger Hiss, William Remington, Judith Coplon, Julius and Ethel Rosenberg.[107]

In foreign policy, too, Truman, though emphasizing the danger of communism, had promised success. Containment could stop the spread of communism: military expansion could be restrained and revolutions prevented. Since revolutions, by liberal definition, were imposed on innocent people by a small minority, a vigilant American government could block them. By his rhetoric, he encouraged American innocence and left many citizens little choice but to believe in their own government's failure when America could not thwart revolution—when the Chinese Communists triumphed. If only resolute will was necessary, as the administration suggested, then what could citizens believe about America's failure? Was it simply bungling? Or treason and betrayal?[108]

By his rhetoric and action, Truman had contributed to the loss of public confidence and set the scene in which Joseph McCarthy could flourish. Rather than resisting the early movement of anticommunism, he had acted energetically to become a leader, and ultimately contributed to its transformation into a crusade which threatened his administration. But the President could never understand his own responsibility, and his failure handicapped him. Because he had a record of vigorous anticommunism, Truman was ill-prepared to respond to McCarthy's charges. At first the President could not foresee any danger and tried to dispense with McCarthy as "the greatest asset the Kremlin has."[109] And later, as the Senator terrorized the government, Truman was so puzzled and pained that he retreated from the conflict and sought to starve McCarthy without publicity. Rather than responding directly to charges, the President tried instead to tighten his program. But he could not understand that such efforts (for example, revising the loyalty standard to "reasonable doubt as to the loyalty of the individual")[110] could not protect the administration from charges of being soft on communism. He only encouraged these charges by seeming to yield to criticism, admitting that the earlier program was unnecessarily lax.

The President was a victim of his own policies and tactics. But bristling anticommunism was not simply Truman's way, but often the liberal way.[111] And the use of guilt by association, the discrediting of dissent, the intemperate rhetoric —these, too, were not simply the tactics of the Truman administration. The rancor and wrath of these years were not new to American politics, nor to liberals.[112] Indeed, the style of passionate charges and impugning opponents' motives may be endemic to American democratic politics. Submerging the issues in passion, using labels as substitutes for thought, questioning motives, these tactics characterized much of the foreign policy debate of the prewar and postwar years as well—a debate in which the liberals frequently triumphed. Developing a more extreme form of this rancorous style, relying upon even wilder charges and more flagrant use of guilt by association, McCarthy and his cohorts flailed the liberals and the Democratic administration.

VII

In looking at the war and postwar years, liberal scholars have emphasized the achievements of democratic reform, the extension of prosperity, the movements to greater economic and social equality. Confident that big business had become socially responsible and that economic security was widespread, they have celebrated the triumph of democratic liberalism. In charting the course of national progress, they frequently neglected or minimized major problems, or they interpreted them as temporary aberrations, or blamed them on conservative forces.[113]

Yet the developments of the sixties—the rediscovery of poverty and racism—suggest that the emphasis has been misplaced in interpreting these earlier years. In the forties and fifties white racism did not greatly yield to the dictates of American democracy, and the failure was not only the South's. The achievements of democratic liberalism were more limited than its advocates believed, and its reforms left many Americans still without adequate assistance. Though many liberal programs were blocked or diluted by conservative opposition, the liberal vision itself was dim. Liberalism in practice was defective, and its defects contributed to the temporary success of McCarthyism. Curiously, though liberalism was scrutinized by some sympathizers[114] who attacked its faith in progress and by others who sought to trace McCarthyism to the reform impulses of earlier generations,[115] most liberals failed to understand their own responsibility for the assault upon civil liberties or to respond to the needs of an "other America" which they but dimly perceived.

NOTES

1. See Bernstein, "The Economic Policies of the Truman Administration: A Bibliographic Essay," in Richard Kirkendall, ed., *The Truman Period as a Research Field* (Columbia, Mo., 1967).
2. Also see William Berman, "Civil Rights and Civil Liberties in the Truman Administration," in *ibid.*
3. Also see Richard O. Davies, "Harry S. Truman and the Social Service State," in *ibid.*
4. Gabriel Kolko, "American Business and Germany, 1930–1941," *Western Political Quarterly,* XV (December 1962), 713–28; cf. Roland Stromberg, "American Business and the Approach of War, 1935–1941," *Journal of Economic History,* XIII (Winter 1953), 58–78.
5. Quoted in Corwin Edwards, *Economic and Political Aspects of International Cartels,* A Study for the Subcommittee on War Mobilization of the Senate Committee on Military Affairs, 78th Cong., 2nd Sess., pp. 43–44.
6. House Committee on Ways and Means and Senate Committee on Finance, 76th Cong., 3rd Sess., *Joint Hearings on Excess Profits Taxation,* p. 22; *New York Times,* July 26, August 9, 1940; *Wall Street Journal,* July 15, 1940.
7. The next four paragraphs draw upon Bernstein, "The Automobile Industry and the Coming of the Second World War," *Southwestern Social Science Quarterly,* XLVII (June 1966), 24–33.
8. Walter Reuther, *500 Planes a Day* (1940); *CIO News,* December, 1940.
9. Bruce Catton to Robert Horton, Policy Documentation File 631.-0423, War Production Board Records, RG 179, National Archives.
10. Richard Wilcock, "Industrial Management's Policies Towards Unionism," in Milton Derber and Edwin Young, *Labor and the New Deal* (Madison, Wis., 1957), pp. 305–8.
11. Joel Seidman, *American Labor from Defense to Reconversion* (Chicago, 1953), pp. 41–87.
12. *Ibid.,* pp. 131–51. It was in response to the coal strikes led by John Lewis that Congress passed the Smith-Connally Act.
13. "With few exceptions, throughout the war years labor, not management, made the sacrifices when sacrifices were necessary," concludes Paul A. C. Koistinen, "The Hammer and the Sword: Labor, the Military, and Industrial Mobilization" (unpublished Ph.D. dissertation, University of California at Berkeley, 1965), p. 143.
14. Bernstein, "The Truman Administration and the Politics of Inflation" (unpublished Ph.D. dissertation, Harvard University, 1963), Ch. 2.
15. Senate Special Committee to Study Problems of American Small Business, 79th Cong., 2nd Sess., Senate Document 208, *Economic*

Concentration and World War II, pp. 42–64. On concentration, see *ibid., passim;* cf. M. A. Adelman, "The Measurement of Industrial Concentration," *Review of Economics and Statistics,* XXXIII (November 1951), 269–96.

16. *Economic Concentration and World War II,* pp. 22–39.

17. C. Wright Mills, *The Power Elite* (New York, 1956), p. 273.

18. This paragraph is based on Bernstein, "Industrial Reconversion: The Protection of Oligopoly and Military Control of the War Economy," *American Journal of Economics and Sociology,* XXVI (April 1967), 159–72. Cf. Jack Peltason, *The Reconversion Controversy* (Washington, 1950).

19. Gabriel Kolko, *Wealth and Power in America* (New York, 1962), pp. 9–45; quotation from p. 31. Also see U.S. Bureau of the Census, *Income Distribution of the United States* (Washington, 1966), pp. 2–27; and Simon Kuznets, *Shares of Upper Income Groups in Income and Savings* (New York, 1953).

20. Quoted from Francis Biddle, *In Brief Authority* (Garden City, N.Y., 1962), p. 213.

21. Stetson Conn *et al., Guarding the United States and Its Outposts,* in *United States Army in World War II: The Western Hemisphere* (Washington, 1964), pp. 115–49. The Canadian government also moved Japanese away from the coast.

22. Biddle, *In Brief Authority,* p. 219.

23. Quoted from Henry L. Stimson and McGeorge Bundy, *On Active Service* (New York, 1948), p. 406. The prose is presumably Bundy's, but Stimson apparently endorsed the thought (p. xi). Also see War Department, *Final Report: Japanese Evacuation from the West Coast* (Washington, 1943), pp. 9–10.

24. Quoted from Biddle, *In Brief Authority,* p. 219.

25. *Korematsu* v. *U.S.,* 323 US 214, at 219. The Court split and Justice Black wrote the opinion. Justices Roberts, Murphy and Jackson dissented. Also see *Hirabayshi* v. *U.S.,* 320 US 81.

26. *American Epoch* (New York, 1955), p. 528 (italics in original).

27. Apparently Roosevelt refused to condemn the riots. Vito Marcantonio to Roosevelt, June 16, 1943, and reply, July 14, 1943, Vito Marcantonio Papers, New York Public Library. Also see Roosevelt's Proclamation No. 2588, in Samuel Rosenman, ed., *The Public Papers of Franklin D. Roosevelt,* (13 vols.; New York, 1938–50), XII, 258–59.

28. "This was the dark side of an otherwise bright picture," concludes Link, *American Epoch,* p. 529. Also see Frank Freidel, *America in the Twentieth Century* (New York, 1960), p. 405. Oscar Handlin, *The American People in the Twentieth Century* (Cambridge, Mass., 1954), p. 215; Everett C. Hughes, "Race Relations and the Sociological Imagination," *American Sociological Review,* XXVIII (December 1963), 879–90.

29. *Pittsburgh Courier,* July 15, September 2, 9, November 11, 1939; March 2, 9, 1940; April 26, 1941; cited in Richard Dalfiume, "De-

segregation of the United States Armed Forces, 1939–1953" (unpublished Ph.D. dissertation, University of Missouri, 1966), pp. ix–x. For other protests, see *Pittsburgh Courier,* September 16, 30, 1939, November 23, and December 7, 1940.

30. *Amsterdam News,* May 10, 1940; Louis Ruchames, *Race, Jobs, and Politics* (New York, 1953), pp. 11–17.

31. Ulysses Lee, *The Employment of Negro Troops,* in *United States Army in World War II: Special Studies* (Washington, 1966), pp. 35–52.

32. Quoted from "For Manhood in National Defense," *Crisis,* XLVII (December 1940), 375. Also see Lee, *Employment of Negro Troops,* pp. 62–65.

33. Lee, *ibid.,* pp. 69–84.

34. Dalfiume, "Desegregation of the Armed Forces," p. 57, is the source of this quotation from the *Baltimore Afro-American,* November 2, 1940. Cf. *Pittsburg Courier,* November 2, 1940.

35. Herbert Garfinkel, *When Negroes March* (Glencoe, Ill., 1959), pp. 37–38.

36. Quoted from the *Pittsburgh Courier,* January 25, 1941, and from the *Black Worker,* May 1941.

37. "Proposals of the Negro March-on-Washington Committee" (undated), OF 391, Roosevelt Library. This was called to my attention by Dalfiume, "Desegregation of the Armed Forces," pp. 172–73.

38. Edwin Watson to Roosevelt, June 14, 1941; A. Philip Randolph to Roosevelt, June 16, 1941; both in OF 391, Roosevelt Library; Garfinkel, *When Negroes March,* pp. 60–61.

39. Dalfiume, "Desegregation of the Armed Forces," pp. 173–76, concludes that the Negro leaders may have met defeat. Cf. "The Negro's War," *Fortune,* XXV (April 1942), 76–80ff.; *Amsterdam News,* July 5, 1941; *Chicago Defender,* July 5, 1941; Randolph, "Why and How the March Was Postponed" (mimeo, n.d.), Schomburg Collection, New York Public Library.

40. For the notion that the events of the war years constitute the beginnings of the civil rights revolution, see Dalfiume, "Desegregation of the Armed Forces," pp. 177–89.

41. Ruchames, *Race, Jobs & Politics,* pp. 162–64.

42. *Ibid.,* p. 164.

43. Samuel Lubell, *The Future of American Politics* (New York, 1952), *passim.*

44. Message on the State of the Union, January 11, 1944, in Rosenman, ed., *Public Papers of Roosevelt,* XIII, p. 41. For some evidence that Roosevelt was at least talking about a new alignment of politics, see Samuel Rosenman, *Working with Roosevelt* (London, 1952), pp. 423–29. Probably this was a tactical maneuver.

45. Mary Hinchey, "The Frustration of the New Deal Revival, 1944–1946" (Unpublished Ph.D. dissertation, University of Missouri, 1965), Chs. 1–2.

46. President's statement on signing the GI Bill of Rights, June 22, 1944, in Rosenman, ed., *Public Papers of Roosevelt*, XIII, 180–82, and Rosenman's notes, pp. 183–84. The GI Bill has generally been neglected as an antidepression measure.

47. President's veto of the tax bill, February 22, 1944, in Rosenman, ed., *Public Papers of Roosevelt*, XIII, 80–84.

48. Charles Merriam, "The National Resources Planning Board: A Chapter in American Planning Experience," *American Political Science Review*, XXXVIII (December 1944), 1075–88.

49. Bernstein, "The Truman Administration and the Politics of Inflation," Chs. 3–4.

50. Bernstein, "Charting a Course Between Inflation and Deflation: Secretary Fred Vinson and the Truman Administration's Tax Bill," scheduled for *Register of the Kentucky Historical Society*.

51. Bernstein, "The Truman Administration and Its Reconversion Wage Policy," *Labor History*, VI (Fall 1965), 214–31.

52. Bernstein, "Clash of Interests: The Postwar Battle Between the Office of Price Administration and the Department of Agriculture," *Agricultural History*, XL (January 1967), 45–57; Allen J. Matusow, "Food and Farm Policies During the First Truman Administration, 1945–1948" (unpublished Ph.D. dissertation, Harvard University, 1963), Chs. 1–3.

53. Bernstein, "The Removal of War Production Board Controls on Business, 1944–1946," *Business History Review*, XXXIX (Summer 1965), 243–60.

54. Bernstein, "The Truman Administration and the Steel Strike of 1946," *Journal of American History*, LII (March 1966), 791–803; "Walter Reuther and the General Motors Strike of 1945–1946," *Michigan History*, IL (September 1965), 260–77; "The Postwar Famine and Price Control, 1946," *Agricultural History*, XXXIX (October 1964), 235–40; and Matusow, "Food and Farm Policies," Chs. 1–3.

55. Bernstein, "The Presidency Under Truman," IV (Fall 1964), 8ff.

56. Truman's message to Congress, September 6, 1945, in *Public Papers of the Presidents of the United States* (8 vols.; Washington, 1961–66), pp. 263–309 (1948).

57. Quoted in Jonathan Daniels, *The Man of Independence* (Philadelphia, 1950), p. 288. For evidence that Truman was trying to head off a bolt by liberals, see *New York Times*, August 12, 1945; Harold Smith Daily Record, August 13, 1945, Bureau of the Budget Library, Washington, D.C.

58. Harold Stein, "Twenty Years of the Employment Act" (unpublished ms., 1965, copy in my possession), p. 2. Also see Stephen K. Bailey, *Congress Makes a Law: The Story Behind the Employment Act of 1946* (New York, 1950).

59. Lubell, *The Future of American Politics*, pp. 8–27, while emphasizing the continuation of the prewar executive-legislative stalemate

and the strength of conservative forces in the postwar years, has also been critical of Truman. "All his skills and energies ., . . were directed to standing still. . . . When he took vigorous action in one direction it was axiomatic that he would contrive soon afterward to move in the conflicting direction" (p. 10). Cf. Richard Neustadt, "Congress and the Fair Deal: A Legislative Balance Sheet," in Carl Friedrich and John Galbraith, eds., *Public Policy*, V, 351–81.

60. Curtis MacDougall, *Gideon's Army* (3 vols.; New York, 1965–66), I, 102–27. The National Educational Committee for a New Party, which would be explicitly anticommunist, included John Dewey, A. Philip Randolph, Daniel Bell, and Lewis Corey.

61. On the continuity, see Mario Einaudi, *The Roosevelt Revolution* (New York, 1959), pp. 125, 334; Neustadt, "Congress and the Fair Deal"; Eric Goldman, *Rendezvous with Destiny* (New York, 1952), pp. 314–15; and Goldman, *The Crucial Decade and After, America 1945–1960* (New York, 1960).

62. Richard O. Davis, *Housing Reform during the Truman Administration* (Columbia, Mo.) p. 136. The original measure aimed for 1,050,000 units in seven years, at a time when the nation needed more than 12,000,000 units to replace inadequate housing. During the Truman years, the government constructed 60,000 units of public housing (pp. 105–38). Rather than creating programs to keep pace with urban needs, the government in these years fell further behind. In contrast, private industry was more active, and it was assisted by noncontroversial federal aid. Under Truman's government, then, the greatest achievement in housing was that private capital, protected by the government, built houses for the higher-income market.

63. Under the old law, the maximum benefit for families was $85 a month and the minimum was $15, depending on prior earnings. The new minimum was $25 and the maximum $150. (*Social Security Bulletin,* September 1950, p. 3). Unless couples also had other sources of income, even maximum benefits ($1,800 a year) placed them $616 under the BLS "maintenance" standard of living and $109 above the WPA-based "emergency" standard of living—the poverty level. (Calculations based on Kolko, *Wealth and Power,* pp. 96–98.) Since the payments were based on earnings, lower-income groups would receive even fewer benefits. They were the people generally without substantial savings or significant supplementary sources of income, and therefore they needed even more, not less, assistance.

64. *Congressional Quarterly Almanac,* V (1949), 434–35.

65. Bernstein, "Economic Policies of the Truman Administration." Truman had achieved very little: improved unemployment benefits, some public power and conservation projects, agricultural assistance, and a National Science Foundation. He failed to secure the ill-conceived Brannan Plan and two programs suggested by

Roosevelt: federal aid to education and health insurance. For his health insurance programs, see his messages of November 19, 1945, in *Public Papers of Truman* (1945), pp. 485–90, and of May 19, 1947, in *ibid.*, (1947), pp. 250–52. In 1951, when the BLS calculated that a family of four needed $4,166 to reach the "maintenance" level, 55.6 percent of the nation's families had incomes beneath that level (Bureau of the Census, *Income Distribution in the United States,* p. 16.).

66. Bernstein, "Economic Policies of the Truman Administration."

67. Truman to William Green, September 13, 1952, PPF 85, Truman Papers, Truman Library.

68. Wilcock, "Industrial Management's Policies Toward Unionism," pp. 305–11; "Public Opinion on the Case Bill," OF 407B, Truman Papers, Truman Library; Robert Brady, *Business as a System of Power* (New York, 1943), pp. 210–15; Harry Millis and Emily Clark Brown, *From the Wagner Act to Taft-Hartley* (Chicago, 1950), pp. 286–98.

69. R. Alton Lee, *Truman and Taft-Hartley: A Question of Mandate* (Lexington, Ky. 1966), pp. 22–71.

70. Lee, *Truman and Taft-Hartley,* pp. 79–130.

71. Truman's message to Congress, May 25, 1946, in *Public Papers of Truman* (1946), pp. 277–80.

72. Truman's address of July 14, 1940, reprinted in *Congressional Record,* 76th Cong., 3rd Sess., 5367–69.

73. Ruchames, *Race, Jobs & Politics,* pp. 130–36. This section relies upon Bernstein, "The Ambiguous Legacy: The Truman Administration and Civil Rights" (paper given at the AHA, December 1966; copy at the Truman Library).

74. Truman to David Niles, July 22, 1946, and drafts (undated) of an order on nondiscrimination; and Philleo Nash to Niles (undated), Nash Files, Truman Library.

75. Truman to Walter White, June 11, 1946, PPF 393, Truman Papers, Truman Library.

76. Walter White, *A Man Called White* (New York, 1948), pp. 331–32.

77. Robert Carr to Bernstein, August 11, 1966.

78. Interview with Philleo Nash, September 19, 1966.

79. President's Committee on Civil Rights, *To Secure These Rights* (Washington, 1947), pp. 1–95.

80. Clark Clifford, "Memorandum for the President," November 17, 1947, Clifford Papers (his possession), Washington, D.C.

81. Truman's message to Congress, February 2, 1948, in *Public Papers of Truman* (1948), pp. 117–26.

82. Interview with Nash.

83. On the struggle, see Clifton Brock, *Americans for Democratic Action: Its Role in National Politics* (Washington, 1962), pp. 94–99; quotation at p. 98.

84. Grant Reynolds, "A Triumph for Civil Disobedience," *Nation,* CLXVI (August 28, 1948), pp. 228–29.

85. George Houser and Bayard Rustin, "Journey of Reconciliation" (mimeo, n.d., probably 1947), Core Files, Schomburg Collection New York Public Library.

86. There was no urging of special programs to assist Negroes left unemployed (at roughly double the white rate) in the mild recession of 1949–1950, nor was there open acknowledgement of race hatred.

87. National Council of Negro Women to Truman, November 18, 1950, Nash Files, Truman Library; Senator William Benton to Truman, October 21, 1951, OF 526B, Truman Library.

88. Carl Murphy to Truman, April 10, 1950, OF 93 misc.; Walter White to Truman, November 26, 1948, OF 252K; both in Truman Library.

89. NAACP press release, February 4, 1949, Schomburg Collection, New York Public Library; Hortense Gabel to Raymond Foley, February 26, 1953, Foley Papers, Truman Library; Housing and Home Finance Agency, *Fifth Annual Report* (Washington, 1952), p. 413.

90. President's Committee on Equality of Treatment and Opportunity in the Armed Forces, *Freedom to Serve* (Washington 1950); Dalfiume, "Desegregation of the Armed Forces."

91. Gordon Gray to Truman, March 1, 1950, OF 1285B, Truman Library.

92. Interview with Philip Elman, December 21, 1966.

93. *Shelley* v. *Kraemer,* 334 US 1; *Henderson* v. *United States* 339 US 816; *McLaurin* v. *Board of Regents,* 339 US 641.

94. Interview with Elman; *Brown* v. *Board of Education,* 347 US 483.

95. "The Report of the President's Temporary Commission on Employee Loyalty," Appendix III, Charles Murphy Papers, Truman Library; Rep. Jennings Bryan to Truman, July 25, 1946, OF 2521, and Stephen Spingarn, "Notes on Meeting of Subcommittee of February 5, 1947," Spingarn Papers, Truman Library.

96. E.O. 9806, 11 Fed. Reg. 13863; "The Report of the President's Temporary Commission on Employee Loyalty," quotation at 3; E.O. 9835, 12 F.R. 1935. On earlier programs, see Eleanor Bontecou, *The Federal Loyalty-Security Program* (Ithaca, N.Y., 1953), pp. 1–19.

97. Letter by Zechariah Chafee, Jr., Erwin Griswold, Milton Katz, and Austin Scott, in *New York Times,* April 13, 1947; L. A. Nikoloric, "The Government Loyalty Program," *American Scholar,* XIX (Summer 1950), 285–98; Bontecou, *Federal Loyalty-Security Program,* pp. 30–34.

98. Quoted from Bontecou, *Federal Loyalty-Security Program,* p. 32, who suggests that Truman may have really meant Communists who might be subject to future orders by the party. Also see Truman's statement of November 14, 1947, in *Public Papers of Truman* (1947), pp. 489–91.

99. Quoted from E.O. 9835, 12 Fed. Reg. 1935.

100. Much of the analysis of this program and its contribution to the rise of McCarthyism is indebted to Athan Theoharis, "The Rhetoric of Politics: Foreign Policy, Internal Security and Domestic Politics in the Truman Era, 1945–1950" (paper delivered at the Southern Historical Association, November 1966). Cf. Daniel Bell, ed., *The New American Right* (New York, 1955). On the need for absolute security, see Tom Clark to A. Devitt Vanech, February 14, 1947, OF 2521, Truman Library; "Report of the President's Temporary Commission on Employee Loyalty"; Theoharis, "Rhetoric of Politics," pp. 26–32.

101. Theoharis, "Rhetoric of Politics," pp. 29–31.

102. Karl M. Schmidt, *Henry A. Wallace: Quixotic Crusade, 1948* (Syracuse, N.Y., 1960), pp. 159–60, 252–53, 261–62. On the strategy of letting the liberal intellectuals attack Wallace, see Clifford, "Memorandum for the President," November 17, 1947. On the split in liberal ranks on cooperation with Communists, see Curtis MacDougall, *Gideon's Army*, I, 122–25.

103. Truman's address of March 17, 1948, in *Public Papers of Truman* (1948), p. 189.

104. Howe and Coser, *The American Communist Party*, 2nd. ed. (New York, 1962), p. 468; see pp. 457–68 for the activity of labor.

105. McGrath's address of April 8, 1949, McGrath Papers, Truman Library, which was called to my attention by Theoharis. Also see Theoharis, "Rhetoric of Politics," n. 37.

106. Quoted from transcript of President's News Conference of June 9, 1949, Truman Library. Also see Sidney Hook, "Academic Integrity and Academic Freedom." *Commentary*, VIII (October 1949), cf., Alexander Meiklejohn, *New York Times Magazine*, March 27, 1949, pp. 10ff. In his veto of the McCarran Act, Truman failed to defend civil liberties effectively and instead emphasized that the act would impair the government's anticommunist efforts. Veto message of September 22, 1950, *Public Papers of Truman* (1950), pp. 645–53.

107. Theoharis, "Rhetoric of Politics," pp. 32–38.

108. See Truman's addresses of March 17, 1948, in *Public Papers of Truman* (1948), pp. 182–86; and of June 7, 1949, in *ibid.* (1949), pp. 277–80. See Theoharis, "Rhetoric of Politics," pp. 17–27.

109. Quoted from transcript of President's News Conference, March 30, 1950, Truman Library.

110. E.O. 10241, 16 Fed. Reg. 9795.

111. On liberal confusion about this period, see Joseph Rauh, "The Way to Fight Communism," *Future*, January 1962. For the argument that liberal naiveté about Stalinism had led to McCarthyism, see Irving Kristol, "Civil Liberties, 1952—A Study in Confusion," *Commentary*, XIII (March 1952), 228–36.

112. For earlier antitotalitarianism, see Freda Kirchway, "Curb the Fascist Press," *Nation*, CLIV (March 28, 1942), 357–58.

113. Although there are no thorough, scholarly histories of these years, there are many texts that embody these characteristics. In addition, much of the monographic literature by other social scientists conforms to the pattern described in this paragraph. For a discussion, see Bernstein, "Economic Policies of the Truman Administration."

114. In particular see the works of Reinhold Niebuhr and the new realism that he has influenced: Niebuhr, *Moral Man and Immoral Society* (New York, 1932); *The Children of Light and the Children of Darkness* (New York, 1944); Arthur Schlesinger, Jr., *The Vital Center* (Cambridge, Mass., 1947). What is needed is a critical study of wartime and postwar liberalism, an explanation for many on "Where We Came Out" (to use the title of Granville Hicks's volume). See Jason Epstein, "The CIA and the Intellectuals," *New York Review of Books*, VII (April 20, 1967), 16–21.

115. See Bell, ed., *The New American Right,* and the tendency to trace McCarthyism back to earlier reform movements and often to Populism. The volume, interestingly, is dedicated to the managing editor of the *New Leader*. For a former radical's attempt to reappraise the liberal past, see Richard Hofstadter, *The Age of Reform* (New York, 1956).

THE CULTURAL
COLD WAR: A SHORT
HISTORY OF THE
CONGRESS FOR
CULTURAL FREEDOM

∞ Christopher Lasch

HISTORIANS, like other scholars, need to become more conscious of the social conditions under which they work—the general influences shaping intellectual life in a bureaucratized industrial society organized for war, and more particularly, the conditions created by the Cold War of the 1950s. The essays in this volume in one way or another attack the prevailing historiographical orthodoxy in the United States. The following essay examines some of the social and political circumstances that have helped to create it. The established premises of historical interpretation, from which scholars are beginning to dissent, are the product, in part, of the intellectual's identification of himself with the interests of the modern state—interests he serves even while maintaining the illusion of detachment. Especially in the fifties,

American intellectuals, on a scale that is only beginning to be understood, lent themselves to purposes having nothing to do with the values they professed—purposes, indeed, that were diametrically opposed to them.

The defection of intellectuals from their true calling—critical thought—goes a long way toward explaining not only the poverty of political discussion but the intellectual bankruptcy of so much recent historical scholarship. The infatuation with consensus; the vogue of a disembodied "history of ideas" divorced from considerations of class or other determinants of social organization; the obsession with "American studies" which perpetuates a nationalistic myth of American uniqueness—these things reflect the degree to which historians have become apologists, in effect, for American national power in the holy war against communism. But the propagandistic import of this scholarship, because it seldom takes crude or obvious forms, is not always easy to detect. The nature of intellectual freedom itself, moreover, is a difficult and complicated subject that cannot be understood as simply the absence of political censorship. In the following pages I have tried to explore the complexities of cultural freedom by examining the activities of its self-designated defenders—the Congress for Cultural Freedom and its American affiliate, the American Committee for Cultural Freedom. The record of these organizations, both of them devoted to the proposition that a respect for cultural freedom continues to be one of the distinguishing features of Western society, furnishes compelling evidence of how precarious it has in fact become.

I

From the beginning the Congress for Cultural Freedom had a quasi-official character, even to outward appearances. It was organized in 1950 by Michael Josselson, formerly an officer in the Office of Strategic Services, and Melvin J. Lasky, who had earlier served in the American Information Services and as editor of *Der Monat,* a magazine sponsored by the United States High Commission in Germany. The decision to hold the first meeting of the Congress in West Berlin, an outpost of Western power in communist east Europe and one of the principal foci and symbols of the Cold War, fitted very well the official American policy of making Berlin a showcase of "freedom." The United Press reported in advance that "the five-day meeting will challenge the alleged freedoms of Soviet-dominated Eastern Europe and attempt to unmask the Soviet Union's and Soviet-sponsored 'peace' demonstrations as purely political maneuvers." H. R. Trevor-Roper, one of the British delegates, noted that "a political tone was set and maintained throughout the congress." Nobody would have objected to a political demonstration, he observed, if it had been avowed as such. The question was whether "it would have obtained all its sponsors or all its delegates if it had been correctly advertised."

The sponsors of the meeting included such eminent figures as Eleanor Roosevelt, Upton Sinclair, the philosophers G. A. Borgese and A. J. Ayer, Walter Reuther, the French writer Suzanne Labin, and Dr. Hans Thirring, a Viennese atomic scientist. Delegates attended from twenty-one countries, but the most conspicuous among them were militant anticommunists (some of them also ex-Communists) from the European continent and from the United States: Arthur Koestler, Franz Borkenau of Austria, Lasky, Sidney Hook, James Burnham, James T. Farrell, Arthur Schlesinger, Jr. A number of themes quickly emerged from their speeches which would become polemical staples in the following decade. One was the end of ideology, the assertion that conventional political distinctions had become irrelevant in the face of the need for a united front against Bolshevism. Arthur Koestler announced that "the words 'socialism' and 'capitalism,' 'Left' and 'Right' have today become virtually empty of meaning." Sidney Hook looked forward "to the era when references to 'right' 'left,' and 'center' will vanish from common usage as meaningless." Franz Borkenau made the same point and went on to explain the deeper sense in which ideology could be said to have died.* For more than

---

* References to Borkenau in the following discussion are based on a translation of his prepared address by G. D. Arnold which appeared in *The Nineteenth Century* for November 1960. Borkenau also delivered an extemporaneous speech which was described by Trevor-Roper in the *Manchester Guardian Weekly* (July 20, 1950) as fol-

a century utopian "extremes"—visions of total freedom competing with visions of total security—had "increasingly turned the history of the occident into a tragic bedlam." But having observed at first hand the devastating effects of utopianism, particularly in Russia, reasonable men had at last learned the importance of a more modest and pragmatic view of politics.

At the same time, the pragmatists who met at Berlin announced that in the present crisis, a moral man could not remain neutral from the struggle of competing ideologies. Robert Montgomery, the American film actor, declared that "no artist who has the right to bear that title can be neutral in the battles of our time. . . . Today we must stand up and be counted." "In varying phraseology and in different languages but concentrating on one basic point, delegates . . . admonished listeners," according to the correspondent of the *New York Times,* ". . . that the time is at hand for a decision as between the East and West." "Man stands at a crossroads," Koestler said, "which only leaves the choice of this way or that." At such moments "the difference between the very clever and the simple in mind narrows almost to the vanishing point"; and only the "professional disease" of the intellectual, his fascination with logical subtleties and his "estrangement from reality," kept him from seeing the need to choose between slavery and freedom.

The attack on liberal intellectualism, and on liberalism

lows: "Pouring out his German sentences with hysterical speed and gestures, he screamed that he was a convert from Communism and proud of it; that past guilt must be atoned for; that the ex-Communists alone understood Communism and the means of resisting it; that Communism could only mean perpetual war and civil war; and that it must be destroyed at once by uncompromising frontal attack. And yet, terrible though it was, this fanatical speech was less frightening than the hysterical German applause which greeted it. It was different from any other applause at that congress. It was an echo of Hitler's Nuremberg."

Arnold charged that Trevor-Roper's account created "misleading impressions." "No one would have guessed from Mr. Trevor-Roper's report . . . that one of the calmest and weightiest contributions was made by Dr. Borkenau—in writing." In dealing with this latter speech, therefore, we are dealing with what passed for calm and weighty political analysis in 1950.

in general, ran through a number of speeches. Borkenau argued that totalitarianism grew dialectically out of liberalism. "The liberal utopia of absolute individual freedom found its counterpart in the socialist utopia of complete individual security." With liberalism in decline, intellectuals looking for "a ready-made doctrine of salvation and a prefabricated paradise" turned in the twenties and thirties to communism and "permitted themselves to be led by the nose through Russia without noticing anything of the reality." During the Second World War—which Borkenau called "a second edition of the Popular Front"—even experienced politicians allowed themselves to be deceived by Stalin's professions of good faith. "Thus in the course of a quarter century Communism ran a course which brought it in contact with every stratum of society, from extreme revolutionaries to ultra-conservatives." But the very pervasiveness of communism, by another turn of Borkenau's dialectic, meant that "the entire body of occidental society has received an increasingly strong protective inoculation against Communism. Every new wave of Communist expansion led to a deepening of the anti-Communist current: from the ineffective opposition of small groups to the rise of an intellectual countercurrent, and finally to the struggle in the arena of world politics."

The attack on liberalism, together with the curious argument that exposure to communism was the only effective form of "inoculation" against it, points to another feature of the anticommunist mentality as revealed at Berlin: a strong undercurrent of ex-Communism, which led Trevor-Roper to describe the whole conference as "an alliance between . . . the ex-communists among the delegates . . . and the German nationalists in the audience." Borkenau, Koestler, Burnham, Hook, Lasky, and Farrell had all been Communists during the thirties, and it requires no special powers of discernment to see that their attack on communism in the fifties expressed itself in formulations that were themselves derived from the cruder sort of Marxist cant. Borkenau's defense of "freedom," for instance, rested not on a concern for institutional safeguards of free thought, let alone for the independence of critical thought from national power, but rather on an assertion of man's capacity to transcend the "narrow materialism" posited, according to Borkenau, by liberalism and socialism alike. The defense of freedom merged imperceptibly with the dogmatic attack on historical materialism which, in another context, had done so much to impede historical and sociological scholarship in the period of the Cold War. It is significant that Borkenau still regarded Leninism as a "great achievement," not, however, because Lenin had contributed to the materialist interpretation of society but because Lenin rejected Marx's "fatalism" and converted socialism "into the free act of a determined, ruthless and opportunist elite." Elitism was one of the things that attracted intellectuals to Leninism in the first place (more than to orthodox Marxism); and even after they had dissociated themselves from its materialist content, they clung to the congenial view of intellectuals as the vanguard of history and to the crude and simplified dialectic (of which Borkenau's speech is an excellent example, and James Burnham's *The Managerial Revolution* another) which passed for Marxism in left-wing circles of the thirties.

These things not only demonstrate the amazing persistence and tenacity of the Bolshevik habit of mind even among those who now rejected whatever was radical and liberating in Bolshevism, they also suggest the way in which a certain type of anticommunist intellectual continued to speak from a point of view "alienated" from bourgeois liberalism. Anticommunism, for such men as Koestler and Borkenau, represented a new stage in their running polemic against bourgeois sentimentality and weakness, bourgeois "utopianism," and bourgeois materialism. That explains their eagerness to connect Bolshevism with liberalism—to show that the two ideologies sprang from a common root and that it was the softness and sentimentality of bourgeois liberals which had paradoxically allowed communism—liberalism's deadly enemy, one might have supposed—to pervade Western society in the thirties and early forties. In attributing "twenty years of treason" to an alliance between liberals and Communists, the anticommunist intellectuals put forth their own version of the right-wing ideology that was gaining adherents, in a popular and still cruder form, in all the countries of the West, particularly in Germany and the United States. In the fifties, this high-level McCarthyism sometimes served as a defense of McCarthyism proper. More often it was associated with official efforts to pre-empt a modified McCarthyism while denouncing McCarthy as a demagogue. In both capacities it contributed measurably to the Cold War.

At still another point on its multifaceted surface, the ideology of the anticommunist Left tended to merge with fascism, which has served as yet another vehicle for the intellectual's attack on bourgeois materialism. Borkenau, for instance—in so many ways the embodiment of a Central European, quasi-totalitarian sensibility—denounced totalitarianism at length without referring, except in passing and in the most general terms, to its most horrifying manifestation, the Nazi regime in Germany. In the United States, anticommunism found a more congenial basis in "pragmatism," which, however, shared with European neo-fascism the capacity to furnish a perspective—a quite different perspective —from which to belabor "utopianism." And whereas the elitism of European intellectuals expressed itself in a cult of charismatic leadership, the American variety based its distrust of the masses precisely on their susceptibility to extreme political solutions; that is, to the same utopianism which the Europeans attacked as a vice of deluded intellectuals. Thus a neat twist of logic permitted those who opposed McCarthyism to argue that McCarthyism was itself a form of Populism. This condemned it sufficiently in the eyes of a generation that tended to confuse intellectual values with the interests of the intellectuals as a class, just as they confused freedom with the national interests of the United States.

II

The Berlin meetings, meanwhile, broke up in a spirit of rancor which must have alarmed those who had hoped for a "united front" against Bolshevism. A resolution excluding totalitarian sympathizers "from the Republic of the Spirit" was withdrawn, "Professor Hook and Mr. Burnham," according to Trevor-Roper, "protesting to the end." The opposition came largely from the English and Scandinavian delegates—a revealing fact for two reasons. In the first place it showed how closely the division of opinion among intellectuals (who supposedly take a more detached view of things than governments do) coincided with the distribution of power in the world. In 1950, the United States had already emerged as the leader of an anticommunist coalition on the European continent, and Great Britain had fallen into her role of a reluctant and not very influential member of a partnership which increasingly tended to revolve around the West Germans. The discussions at Berlin—even the choice of the meeting place—accurately reflected these political facts.

In the second place, the reluctance of the British delegates to join a rhetorical crusade against communism, in this first of the postwar struggles for cultural freedom, seems to have suggested to the officers of the Congress for Cultural Freedom that British intellectuals needed to be approached more energetically than before, if they were not to lapse completely into the heresy of neutralism. The founding of *Encounter* magazine in 1953, with Irving Kristol, Stephen Spender and later Lasky at its head, was the official answer to the "anti-Americanism," as it was now called, which disfigured the English cultural scene. The editors of *Encounter* addressed themselves with zeal to its destruction.

The new magazine lost no time in establishing its point of view and its characteristic tone of ultra-sophistication. The very first issue contained a spirited polemic on the Rosenberg case by Leslie Fiedler, whose uncanny instinct for cultural fashions, combined with a gift for racy language ("Come Back to the Raft Ag'in, Huck Honey"), made him a suitable spokesman for cultural freedom in the fifties. Fiedler had already, in "Hiss, Chambers, and the Age of Innocence," exhorted intellectuals to accept their common guilt in the crimes of Alger Hiss. With an equal disregard for the disputed facts of the case, he now went on to berate sentimentalists who still believed the Rosenbergs to be innocent. "As far as I am concerned the legal guilt of the Rosenbergs was clearly established at their trial." From the fact of their guilt, Fiedler spun an intricate web of theory intended to show, once again, what a pervasive and deplorable influence Stalinism had exercised, for twenty years, over the life of the mind in America.

"To believe that two innocents had been falsely condemned," Fiedler argued, ". . . one would have to believe the judges and public officials of the United States to be not merely the Fascists the Rosenbergs called them, but monsters, insensate beasts." Whereas in fact, the implication seemed to be, they were dedicated humanitarians. Just so; and in order to believe that the CIA had infiltrated (for instance) the National Student Association, one would have to believe—heaven forbid!—that the CIA was a corrupter of youth. The absurdity of such a thing is self-evident; the case collapses of its own weight.

For a group of intellectuals who prided themselves on their realism, skepticism, and detachment (qualities they regularly displayed in cogent analyses of the deplorable state of affairs in Russia), the editors of *Encounter* and their contributors showed an unshakable faith in the good intentions of the American government. It was inconceivable to them that American officials were not somehow immune to the temptations of great power. The defense of "cultural freedom" was wholly entwined, in their minds, with the defense of the "free world" against communism. Criticism of the men who presided over the free world—even mild criticism— tended automatically to exclude itself from their minds as a subject of serious discussion. These men might make occasional mistakes; but there could be no question of their devotion to freedom.

Encounter, wrote Denis Brogan (a frequent contributor) in 1963, "has been the organ of protest against the *trahison des clercs.*" Julian Benda's point, in the book from which Brogan took this phrase, was that intellectuals should serve truth, not power. *Encounter*'s claim to be the defender of intellectual values in a world dominated by ideology rested, therefore, on its vigorous criticism of all influences tending to undermine critical thought, whether they emanated from the Soviet Union or from the United States. This is indeed the claim that the editors and friends of *Encounter* have made. As we shall see, the Cold War liberals have not hesitated to criticize American popular culture or popular politics, but the question is whether they have criticized the American government or any other aspect of the officially sanctioned order. And the fact is that *Encounter,* like other journals sponsored by the Congress for Cultural Freedom (except perhaps for *Censorship,* which recently expired), consistently approved the broad lines and even the details of American policy, until the war in Vietnam shattered the Cold War coalition and introduced a new phase of American politics. Writers in *Encounter* denounced the Soviet intervention in Hungary without drawing the same conclusions about the Bay of Pigs. The magazine published Theodore Draper's diatribes against Castro, which laid a theoretical basis for American intervention by depicting Castro as a Soviet puppet and a menace to the Western Hemisphere. Writers in *Encounter* had little if anything to say about the American coup in Guatemala, the CIA's intervention in Iran, its role in the creation of Diem, or the American support of Trujillo; but these same writers regarded communist "colonialism" with horror. The plight of the communist satellites wrung their hearts; that of South Korea and South Vietnam left them unmoved. They denounced racism in the Soviet Union while ignoring it in South Africa and the United States until it was no longer possible to ignore it, at which time (1962) *Encounter* published an overly optimistic issue on the "Negro Crisis," the general tone of which was quite consistent with the optimism then being purveyed by the Kennedy administration.

In 1958, Dwight Macdonald submitted an article to *Encounter*—"America! America!"—in which he wondered whether the intellectuals' rush to rediscover their native land (one of the obsessive concerns of the fifties, at almost every level of cultural life) had not produced a somewhat uncritical acquiescence in the American *imperium.* The editors told Macdonald to publish his article elsewhere; in the correspondence that followed, according to Macdonald, "the note sounded more than once . . . that publication of my article might embarrass the Congress in its relations with the American foundations which support it." When the incident became public, Nicholas Nabokov, secretary-general of the Congress, pointed in triumph to the fact that Macdonald's article had eventually appeared in *Tempo Presente,* an Italian periodical sponsored by the Congress. That proved, he said, that the Paris headquarters of the Congress did not dictate editorial policy to the magazines it supported. But the question was not whether the Paris office dictated to the editors what they could publish and what they could not; the question was whether the editors did not take it upon themselves to avoid displeasing the sponsors, whoever they were, standing behind the Congress for Cultural Freedom. To point to their independence from overt official control did not necessarily prove their independence from the official point of view. It was possible that they had so completely assimilated and internalized that point of view that they were no longer aware of the way in which their writings had come to serve as rationalizations of American world power. Even when subsequent disclosures had made their complicity, in the larger sense, quite clear, they continued to protest their innocence, as if innocence, in the narrow and technical sense, were the real issue in the matter.

III

In 1951 the Congress sponsored a large conference in India, attended by such luminaries as Denis de Rougemont, W. H. Auden, Stephen Spender, Ignazio Silone, Louis Fischer, Norman Thomas, and James Burnham. The *Times* correspondent understated the case when he wrote that "many of the delegates are said to be former Communists, who have become critics." He noted further: "The meeting has been described as an answer to the 'World Peace Conference' supported by the Soviet Union." (The Berlin conference of the year before, it will be recalled, was also conceived as a response to Soviet "peace propaganda." Its immediate stimulus was a series of peace congresses in East Germany.)

The delegates meeting in India hoped to bring home to the nonaligned nations the immorality of neutralism. As usual, they could count on the American press to echo the party line. Anne O'Hare McCormick wrote in one of her dispatches: "There is no middle ground in the world conflict"; that was the message which the Congress hoped to impress on the Indians. When transferred to a non-Western setting, however, the reiteration of this theme, which had gone down so well with the Berliners, led to an "unexpected undertone of dissatisfaction," according to the *Times*. When Denis de Rougemont "compared the present Indian neutrality with that of the lamb that is neutral between the wolf and the shepherd," one of the Indian delegates drew from the fable a moral quite different from the one intended. He pointed out that the shepherd, having saved the lamb from the wolf, "shears the lamb and possibly eats it." Many Indians boycotted the Congress because it had been "branded widely as a U.S. propaganda device"—an unwarranted assumption of course, but one that many Indians seemed to share. The Indian government took pains to withhold its official sanction from the meeting, insisting that it be moved from New Delhi, the capital and original site of the conference, to Bombay.

It seemed at times that the Indians did not want to be free. Robert Trumbull, a correspondent of the *Times,* tried to reassure his readers about their "peculiar" point of view. The Indian speakers weren't really neutralists, they were only "manifesting the common Indian oratorical tendency to stray from the real point of the issue in hand." A dispassionate observer might have concluded that they understood the point all too well. The Congress, having suffered a rebuff, made no more direct attacks on neutralism in the Third World. In 1958 it held a conference on the problems of developing nations on the isle of Rhodes, which produced no notable results. Probably it was not expected to have any. A new official style was emerging, faithfully reflected in the Congress for Cultural Freedom—urbane, cool, and bureaucratic. The old slogans had become passé (even as the old policies continued). The union of intellect and power deceptively presented itself as an apparent liberalization of official attitudes, an apparent relaxation of American anticommunism. The day was rapidly approaching when officials in Washington would value ideas for their own sake (as long as they had no consequences). McCarthyism was dead and civilized conversation in great demand. The Congress flew people to Rhodes and encouraged them to participate in a highly civilized, nonideological discussion of economic development—a gratifying experience for everybody concerned, all the more so since it made so few demands on the participants. Expansive and tolerant, the Congress asked only that intellectuals avail themselves of the increasing opportunities for travel and enlightenment that the defense of freedom made possible.

IV

Shortly after the founding of the Congress for Cultural Freedom, its more active members set up subsidiaries in various countries. The American Committee for Cultural Freedom was founded in 1951 by Burnham, Farrell, Schlesinger, Hook, and others, to hold annual forums on topics like "The Ex-Communist: His Role in a Democracy" or "Anti-Americanism in Europe"; to "counteract the influence of mendacious Communist propaganda"; to defend academic freedom; and in general "to resist the lengthening shadow of thought-control." The Committee had a limited though illustrious membership, never exceeding six hundred, and it claimed to subsist on grants from the Congress and on public contributions. It repeatedly made public appeals for money, even announcing, in 1957, that it was going out of business for lack of funds. It survived; but ever since that time, it has been semimoribund, for reasons that will become clear in a moment.

Sidney Hook was the first chairman of the ACCF. He was succeeded in 1952 by George S. Counts of Teachers College, Columbia, who was followed in 1954 by Robert Gorham Davis of Smith. James T. Farrell took Davis' place in the same year, but resigned in 1956 after a quarrel with other members of the Committee.

Farrell, in resigning, said that "his travels had convinced him that he and other members had been 'wrong' in earlier struggles against Paris office policies." His statement, incidentally, suggests that the Paris office sometimes tried to enforce its own views on subsidiary organizations, in spite of its disclaimers. It also shows—what should already be apparent—that the Congress in its early period took an exceptionally hard line on neutralism.

Farrell's resignation, along with other events, signaled the breakdown of the coalition on which the American Committee was based, a coalition of moderate liberals and reactionaries (both groups including a large number of ex-Communists) held together by their mutual obsession with the Communist conspiracy. James Burnham had already resigned in 1954. Earlier Burnham had resigned as a member of the advisory board of *Partisan Review* (which was then and still is sponsored by the Committee) in a dispute with the editors over McCarthyism. Burnham approved of McCarthy's actions and held that McCarthyism was a "diversionary" issue created by Communists. William Phillips and Philip Rahv, adopting a favorite slogan of the Cold War to their own purposes, announced, however, that there was no room on *Partisan Review* for "neutralism" about McCarthy.

Originally, the ACCF took quite literally the assertion, advanced by Koestler and others at Berlin, that the Communist issue overrode conventional distinctions between Left and Right. Right-wingers like Burnham, Farrell, Ralph De Toledano, John Chamberlain, John Dos Passos, and even Whittaker Chambers consorted with Schlesinger, Hook, Irving Kristol, Daniel Bell, and other liberals. In the early fifties, this uneasy alliance worked because the liberals generally took positions that conceded a good deal of ground to the Right, if they were not indistinguishable from those of the Right. But the end of the Korean War and the censure of McCarthy in 1954 created a slightly less oppressive air in which the right-wing rhetoric of the early fifties seemed increasingly inappropriate to political realities. Now that McCarthy was dead as a political force, the liberals courageously attacked him, thereby driving the Right out of the Committee for Cultural Freedom. The collapse of the anticommunist coalition coincided with the Committee's financial crisis of 1957 and with the beginning of its long period of inactivity. These three developments are obviously related. The ACCF and its parent, the Congress for Cultural Freedom, took shape in a period of the cold war when official anticommunism had not clearly distinguished itself, rhetorically, from the anticommunism of the Right. In a later period official liberalism, having taken over essential features of the rightist world view, belatedly dissociated itself from the cruder and blatantly reactionary type of anticommunism, and pursued the same anticommunist policies in the name of anti-imperialism and progressive change. Once again, the Kennedy administration contributed decisively to the change of style, placing more emphasis on "counterinsurgency" than on military alliances, advocating an "Alliance for Progress," de-emphasizing military aid in favor of "development," refraining from attacks on neutralism, and presenting itself as the champion of democratic revolution in the undeveloped world. The practical result of the change was a partial détente with communism in Europe and a decidedly more aggressive policy in the rest of the world (made possible by that détente), of which the most notable products were the Bay of Pigs, the Dominican intervention, and the war in Vietnam. The European détente made the anticommunist rhetoric of the fifties obsolete, although it of course did not make anticommunism obsolete. The particular brand of anticommunism that flourished in the fifties grew out of the postwar power struggles in Europe and out of traumas of twentieth-century history—fascism, Stalinism, the crisis of liberal democracy—all of which had concerned Europe, not Asia. The prototype of the anticommunist intellectual in the fifties was the disillusioned ex-Communist, obsessed by the corruption of Western politics and culture by the pervasive influence of Stalinism and driven by a need to exorcise the evil and expatiate his own past. The anticommunism of the sixties, on the other hand, focused on the Third World and demanded another kind of rhetoric.

The ACCF, then, represented a coalition of liberals and reactionaries who shared a conspiratorial view of communism and who agreed, moreover, that the Communist conspiracy had spread through practically every level of American society. (It is the adherence of liberals to these dogmas that shows how much they had conceded to the right-wing view of history.) Sidney Hook's "Heresy, Yes—Conspiracy, No!"—published in the *New York Times Magazine* in 1950–1951 and distributed as a pamphlet by the ACCF—set forth the orthodox position and tried to distinguish it (not very successfully) from that of the Right, as well as from "ritualistic liberalism." Heresy—the open expression of dissenting opinions—had to be distinguished, according to Hook, from secret movements seeking to attain their ends "not by normal political or educational processes but by playing outside the rules of the game." This distinction did not lead Hook to conclude that communism, insofar as it was a heresy as opposed to a conspiracy, was entitled to Constitutional protection. On the contrary, he argued that communism was a conspiracy by its very nature; since they were members of an international conspiracy—servants of a foreign power—Communists could not expect to enjoy the same liberties enjoyed by other Americans. Academic freedom did not extend to a Communist teacher; nor was it necessary to "catch him in the act" of conspiring against the country before dismissing him from his job—mere membership in the Communist party was sufficient evidence of conspiracy.

The American Committee's official position on academic freedom started from the same premise. "A member of the Communist party has transgressed the canons of academic responsibility, has engaged his intellect to servility, and is therefore professionally disqualified from performing his functions as scholar and teacher." The Committee on Academic Freedom (Counts, Hook, Arthur O. Lovejoy, and Paul R. Hays) characteristically went on to argue that the matter of Communists should be left "in the hands of the colleges, and their faculties." "There is no justification for a Congressional committee to concern itself with the question." Academic freedom meant self-determination for the academic community. The full implications of this position will be explored in due time.

"Liberalism in the twentieth century," Sidney Hook declared in the spirit of the Berlin manifesto, "must toughen its fibre, for it is engaged in a fight on many different fronts." A sentimental and unrealistic tradition of uncritical tolerance might prove to be a fatal handicap in the struggle with totalitarianism. "Ritualistic liberals," according to Hook, not only failed to distinguish between heresy and conspiracy, they helped to "weaken the moral case of Western democracy against Communist totalitarianism" by deploring witchhunts, giving the unfortunate impression that America was "on the verge of Fascism." He conceded that some demagogues—he tactfully refrained from mentioning them by name—sought to discredit unpopular reforms by unfairly labeling them communist. But the important point was that these activities were not the official policy of "our government," they were the actions of "cultural vigilantes." Ignorant people saw progressive education, for example, or the federal withholding tax, as evidence of Communist subversion—an absurdity which suggested to Hook, not the inherent absurdity of the anticommunist ideology, but the absurdity of untutored individuals concerning themselves with matters best left to experts. The student of these events is struck by the way in which ex-Communists seem always to have retained the worst of Marx and Lenin and to have discarded the best. The elitism which once glorified intellectuals as a revolutionary avant-garde now glorifies them as experts and social technicians. On the other hand, Marx's insistence that political issues be seen in their social context —his insistence, for example, that questions of taxation are not "technical" but political questions, the solutions to which reflect the type of social organization in which they arise—this social determinism, which makes Marx's ideas potentially so useful as a method of social analysis, has been sloughed off by Sidney Hook without a qualm. These reflections lead one to the conclusion, once more, that intellectuals were more attracted to Marxism in the first place as an elitist and antidemocratic ideology than as a means of analysis which provided, not answers, but the beginnings of a critical theory of society.

Hook's whole line of argument reflected one of the dominant values of the modern intellectual—his acute sense of himself as a professional with a vested interest in technical solutions to political problems. The attack on "cultural vigilantism" paralleled the academic interpretation of McCarthyism as a form of populism and a form of anti-intellectualism, except that it did not even go so far as to condemn McCarthyism itself.

Some liberals, in fact, specifically defended McCarthy. Irving Kristol, in his notorious article in the March 1952 issue of *Commentary,* admitted that McCarthy was a "vulgar demagogue" but added: "There is one thing that the American people know about Senator McCarthy: he, like them, is unequivocally anticommunist. About the spokesmen for American liberalism, they feel they know no such thing." This article has been cited many times to show how scandalously the anticommunist Left allied itself with the Right. Kristol's article was a scandal, but it was no more a scandal than the apparently more moderate position which condemned unauthorized anticommunism while endorsing the official variety. By defining the issue as "cultural vigilantism," the anticommunist intellectuals lent themselves to the dominant drive of the modern state—not only to eliminate the private use of violence (vigilantism) but, finally, to discredit all criticism which does not come from officially recognized experts. The government had a positive interest in suppressing McCarthy, as the events of the Eisenhower administration showed—not because of any tender solicitude for civil liberties, but because McCarthy's unauthorized anticommunism competed with and disrupted official anticommunist activities like the Voice of America. This point was made again and again during the Army-McCarthy hearings. (Indeed, the fact that it was the Army that emerged as McCarthy's most powerful antagonist is itself suggestive.) The same point dominated the propaganda of the ACCF. "Government agencies," said Hook, "find their work hampered by the private fevers of cultural vigilantism which have arisen like a rash from the anti-Communist mood." "Constant vigilance," he added, "does not require private citizens to usurp the functions of agencies entrusted with the task of detection and exposure."

In effect—though they would have denied it—the intellectuals of the ACCF defined cultural freedom as whatever best served the interests of the United States government. When James Wechsler was dropped from a television program, the *New Leader* (a magazine which consistently took the same positions as the ACCF) wrote: "This lends substance to the Communist charge that America is hysteria-ridden." Diana Trilling agreed that "the idea that America is a terror-stricken country in the grip of hysteria is a Communist-inspired idea." After McCarthy's attack on the Voice of America, even Sidney Hook criticized McCarthy because of "the incalculable harm he is doing to the reputation of the United States abroad." The ACCF officially condemned McCarthy's investigation of the Voice of America. "The net effect, at this crucial moment, has been to frustrate the very possibility of the United States embarking on a program of psychological warfare against world communism." A few months later, the ACCF announced the appointment of Sol Stein as its executive director. Stein had been a writer and political affairs analyst for the Voice of America. He was succeeded in 1956 by Norman Jacobs, chief political commentator of the Voice of America and head of its Central Radio Features Branch from 1948 to 1955.

V

While avoiding a principled attack on McCarthyism, the ACCF kept up a running fire on "anti-anticommunism." (It was characteristic of the period that issues so often presented themselves in this sterile form and that positions were formulated not with regard to the substance of a question, but with regard to an attitude or "posture" which it was deemed desirable to hold.) In January 1953 the ACCF handed down a directive setting out the grounds on which it was permissible to involve oneself in the Rosenberg case. "[The] preeminent fact of the Rosenbergs' guilt must be openly acknowledged before any appeal for clemency can be regarded as having been made in good faith. Those who allow the Communists to make use of their name in such a way as to permit any doubt to arise about the Rosenbergs' guilt are doing a grave disservice to the cause of justice—and of mercy, too."

In 1954 a group calling itself the Emergency Civil Liberties Committee sponsored a conference at Princeton, at which Albert Einstein, along with Corliss Lamont, I. F. Stone, Dirk Struik, and others, urged intellectuals not to cooperate with "witch-hunting" congressional committees. Sol Stein immediately announced that the ACCF opposed any "exploitation" of academic freedom and civil liberties "by persons who are at this late date still sympathetic to the cause of the Soviet Union." Following its usual practice, the ACCF proceeded to lay down a standard to which any "sincere" criticism of American life, even of McCarthyism, had to conform. "The test of any group's sincerity is whether it is opposed to threats of freedom anywhere in the world and whether it is concerned about the gross suppression of civil liberties and academic freedom behind the Iron Curtain. The Emergency Civil Liberties Committee has not met that test."* The validity of criticism, in other words, depended not so much on its substance as on its adherence to a prescribed ritual of dissent.

The ACCF did not stop with this rebuke and also accused the Emergency Civil Liberties Committee of being "a Communist front with no sincere interest in liberty in the United States or elsewhere." No evidence was adduced to support this statement. The conclusion followed logically, perhaps, from the ACCF's test of "sincerity." The Civil Liberties Committee, in reply, pointed out that even the Attorney-General had not thought to list it as a subversive organization. In this case, the standards of the ACCF were even more rigorous than those of the government itself.

On another occasion, the ACCF tried to plant with the *New York World Telegram and Sun* a story, already circulated by the *New Leader,* that a certain liberal journalist was a "Soviet espionage agent." Sol Stein called the city desk with what he described as a "Junior Alger Hiss" story. The reporter who took the call asked whether the proper place to determine the truth of these charges was not a court of law.

---

* As late as 1966, one finds Arthur Schlesinger, Jr., still resorting to the same tired old formula, as well as to the catchword, "anti-anticommunism." When Conor Cruise O'Brien accused intellectuals in the West of serving the "power structure" at the same time that they praised Russian writers for resisting the power structure of the Soviet Union (he added that "sympathy with the hard lot of writers in communist countries is sometimes so copiously expressed as to make the lot of these writers actually harder" by alerting bureaucrats to antiparty tendencies they might otherwise have overlooked), Schlesinger, completely avoiding these issues, made the stock response: "How in the year 1966 can anyone, even Mr. O'Brien, write a piece about 'Politics and the Writer' and not mention Sinyavsky and Daniel or their Chinese counterparts?" (*Book Week,* September 11, 1966).

Stein replied, in this reporter's words, that "libel suits were a Communist trick to destroy opposition by forcing it to bear the expense of trial." The reporter then asked whether the ACCF was "upholding the right of people to call anyone a Communist without being subject to libel suits." Stein said: "You misunderstand the context of the times. Many reckless charges are being made today. But when the charges are documented, the Committee believes you have the right to say someone is following the Communist line without being brought into court." The reporter asked if Stein had any proof that the journalist in question was a Soviet spy. Stein said no, "but we have mountains of material that show he consistently follows the Soviet line."

When they took positions of which the ACCF disapproved, the "ritualistic liberals" were Communist tools. When they took positions critical of the Soviet Union, the ACCF denied their right to take them. Arthur Miller in 1956 wrote a statement condemning political interference with art in the Soviet Union. The ACCF did not congratulate him; it asked why he had not taken the same position in 1949. The Committee also noted that Miller, in any case, had made an unforgivable mistake: he had criticized political interference with art not only in the Soviet Union but in the United States, thereby implying that the two cases were comparable. American incidents, the Committee declared, were "episodic violations of the tradition of political and cultural freedom in the United States," whereas "the official government policy" of the USSR was to "impose a 'party line' in all fields of art, culture, and science, and enforcing such a line with sanctions ranging from imprisonment to exile to loss of job." Having dutifully rapped Miller's knuckles, the ACCF then went on to use his statement by challenging the Soviet government to circulate it in Russia.

VI

In 1955 a *New York Times* editorial praised the ACCF for playing a vital role in "the struggle for the loyalty of the world's intellectuals"—in itself a curious way of describing the defense of cultural freedom. The *Times* went on to make the same claim that was so frequently made by the Committee itself: "The group's authority to speak for freedom against Communist slavery has been enhanced by its courageous fight against those threatening our own civil liberties from the Right." But even when it found itself confronted with cultural vigilantism in its most obvious forms, the Committee stopped short of an unambiguous defense of intellectual freedom. In 1955, for instance, Muhlenberg College canceled a Charlie Chaplin film festival under pressure from a local post of the American Legion. The ACCF protested that "while it is perfectly clear that Chaplin tends to be pro-Soviet and anti-American in his political attitudes, there is no reason why we should not enjoy his excellent movies, which have nothing to do with Communist totalitarianism." This statement left the disturbing implication that if Chaplin's films could be regarded as political, the ban would have been justified. The assertion that art has nothing to do with politics was the poorest possible ground on which to defend cultural freedom.

But whatever the nature of the ACCF's critique of vigilantism, a better test of its "authority to speak for freedom" would have been its willingness to criticize *official* activities in the United States—the real parallel to Soviet repression. (In the Soviet Union, attacks on vigilantism are doubtless not only not proscribed but encouraged. It is attacks on Soviet officials that are not permitted.)

In March 1955 the Committee did criticize a Post Office ban on *Pravda* and *Izvestia* as "unreasonable and ineffective in dealing with the Communist conspiracy." A year later the Committee deplored the Treasury Department's raid on the office of the *Daily Worker*. "However much we abominate the *Daily Worker*, . . . we must protest even this much interference with the democratic right to publish freely." The ACCF criticized the Agriculture Department's dismissal of Wolf Ladejinsky and the Atomic Energy Commission's persecution of Oppenheimer, in both cases arguing that the victims had established themselves in recent years as impeccably anticommunist. On one occasion the ACCF attacked the United States Information Agency because it had canceled an art show in response to charges that four of the artists represented were subversive. Diana Trilling, chairman of the Committee's board of directors, insisted that "actions of this kind hold us up to derision abroad." She went on to question the judgment of government officials "who mix politics and art to the detriment of both."

On the other hand, when 360 citizens petitioned the Supreme Court to invalidate or to declare unconstitutional the 1950 Internal Security Act (which created the Subversive Activities Control Board), James T. Farrell issued a statement for the ACCF calling them "naive," accusing them of a "whitewash" of the Communist party, and declaring that "if freedom were left in the hands of the petitioners it would have no future."

The infrequency of complaints against American officials, together with the triviality of the issues that called them forth—as contrasted with the issues against which others protested out of their "naiveté"—show that the anticommunist liberals cannot claim to have defended cultural freedom in the United States with the same consistency and vigor with which they defended it in Russia. Claiming to be the vanguard of the struggle for cultural freedom, the anticommunist intellectuals in reality brought up the rear.

The Cold War intellectuals revealed themselves as the servants of bureaucratic power; and it was not altogether surprising, years later, to find that the relation of intellectuals to power was even closer than it had seemed at the time. They had achieved both autonomy and affluence, as the social value of their services became apparent to the government, to corporations, and to the foundations. Professional intellectuals had become indispensable to society and to the state (in ways which neither the intellectuals nor even the state always perceived), partly because of the increasing importance of education—especially the need for trained experts—and partly because the Cold War seemed to demand that the United States compete with communism in the cultural sphere as well as in every other. The modern state, among other things, is an engine of propaganda, alternately manufacturing crises and claiming to be the only instrument which can effectively deal with them. This propaganda, in order to be successful, demands the cooperation of writers, teachers, and artists not as paid propagandists or state-censored time-servers but as "free" intellectuals capable of policing their own jurisdictions and of enforcing acceptable standards of responsibility within the various intellectual professions.

A system like this presupposes two things: a high degree of professional consciousness among intellectuals, and general economic affluence which frees the patrons of intellectual life from the need to account for the money they spend on culture. Once these conditions exist, as they have existed in the United States for some time, intellectuals can be trusted to censor themselves, and crude "political" influence over intellectual life comes to seem passé. In the Soviet Union, on the other hand, intellectuals are insufficiently professionalized to be able effectively to resist political control. As one would expect in a developing society, a strong commitment to applied knowledge mitigates against the development of "pure" standards, which is one of the chief prerequisites of professionalization. It can be demonstrated that in the nineteenth-century United States professionalization of intellectual activities went hand in hand with the acceptance of pure research as a legitimate enterprise, first among intellectuals themselves and then among their patrons. Only when they win acceptance for pure research do intellectuals establish themselves as masters in their own house, free from the nagging public scrutiny that naively expects to see the value of intellectual activity measured in immediate practical applications. This battle having been won, the achievement of "academic freedom" is comparatively easy, since academic freedom presents itself (as we have seen) not as a defense of the necessarily subversive character of good intellectual work, but as a prerequisite for pure research. Moreover, the more intellectual purity identifies itself with "value-free" investigations, the more it empties itself of political content and the easier it is for public officials to tolerate it. The "scientific" spirit, spreading from the natural sciences to social studies, tends to drain the latter of their critical potential while at the same time making them ideal instruments of bureaucratic control.

Pure science, once it comes to dominate the organized life of the intellect, paradoxically establishes itself as even more useful to the prevailing social order than the practical knowledge it displaces—useful, if not in the immediate present, in the not-too-distant future. The high status enjoyed by American intellectuals depends on their having convinced their backers in government and industry that "basic research" produces better results in the long run than mindless empiricism. But for intellectuals to win this battle it was necessary not only to convince themselves of these things, but to overcome the narrowly utilitarian approach to knowledge that usually prevails (particularly in bourgeois society) among the patrons of learning. The patrons' willingness to be convinced depended, in turn, on their having at their disposal almost unlimited funds; and more than that, on a positive predilection for useless expenditure. The advancement of pure learning on a large scale demands that the sponsors of learning be willing to spend large sums of money without hope of immediate return. In advanced capitalism, this requirement happily coincides with the capitalists' need to engage in conspicuous expenditure; hence the dominant role played by "captains of industry" in the professionalization of higher education (with the results described by Veblen in *Higher Learning in America*). At a still later stage of development, the same role is played by the foundations and directly by government, both of which need to engage in a form of expenditure (not necessarily conspicuous in all its details) that shares with the conspicuous expenditure of the capitalist a marked indifference to results. Modern bureaucracies are money-spending agencies. The more money a bureaucracy can spend, the larger the budget it can claim. Since the bureaucracy is more interested in its own aggrandizement than in doing a job, the bureaucrat is restrained in his expenditure only by the need to account to some superior and ultimately, perhaps, to the public; but in complicated bureaucracies it is hard for anyone to account for the money, particularly since a state of continual emergency can be invoked to justify secrecy in all the important operations of government. This state of perfect nonaccountability, which is the goal toward which bureaucracies ceaselessly strive, obviously works to the indirect advantage of pure research and of the professionalized intellectuals.

In Soviet Russia, a comparatively undeveloped economy cannot sustain the luxury of unaccounted expenditure, and the bureaucracy is still infected, therefore, by a penny-pinching mentality that begrudges expenditures unless they can be justified in utilitarian terms. This attitude, together with the lack of professional consciousness among intellectuals themselves (many of whom share the belief that knowledge is valuable not for itself but for the social and political uses to which it can be put), is the source of the political interference with knowledge that is so widely deplored in the West. It is obvious that the critical spirit cannot thrive under these conditions. Even art is judged in narrowly utilitarian terms and subjected to autocratic regulation by ignorant bureaucrats.

What needs to be emphasized, however, is that the triumph of academic freedom in the United States, under the special conditions which have brought it about, does not necessarily lead to intellectual independence and critical thinking. It is a serious mistake to confuse academic freedom with cultural freedom. American intellectuals are not subject to political control, but the very conditions which have brought about this result have at the same time undermined their capacity for independent thought. The American press is free, but it censors itself. The university is free, but it has purged itself of ideas. The literary intellectuals are free, but they use their freedom to propagandize for the state. What has led to this curious state of affairs? The very freedom of American intellectuals blinds them to their unfreedom. It leads them to confuse the political interests of intellectuals as an official minority with the progress of intellect. Their freedom from overt political control (particularly from "vigilantes") blinds them to the way in which the "knowledge industry" has been incorporated into the state and the military-industrial complex. Since the state exerts so little censorship over the cultural enterprises it subsidizes—since, on the contrary, it supports basic research, congresses for cultural freedom, and various liberal organizations—intellectuals do not see that these activities serve the interests of the state, not the interests of intellect. All they can see is the absence of censorship; that and that alone proves to their satisfaction that Soviet intellectuals are slaves and American intellectuals free men. Meanwhile their own self-censorship makes them eligible for the official recognition and support that sustain the illusion that the American government, unlike the Soviet government, greatly values the life of the mind. The circle of illusion is thus complete; and even the revelation that the campaign for "cultural freedom" was itself the creation and tool of the state has not yet torn away the veil. It has only led to the further illusion that the state is even more enlightened than the intellectuals had supposed.

It is possible to hope, nevertheless, that when the matter is more completely understood, it will force people to quite different conclusions.

VII

That there is no necessary contradiction between the interests of organized intellectuals and the interests of American world power, that the intellectual community can be trusted to police itself and should be left free from annoying pressures from outside, that dissenting opinion within the framework of agreements on Cold War fundamentals not only should be tolerated but can be turned to effective propaganda use abroad—all these things were apparent, in the early fifties, to the more enlightened members of the governmental bureaucracy; but they were far from being universally acknowledged even in the bureaucracy, much less in Congress or in the country as a whole. "Back in the early 1950's," says Thomas W. Braden, the man who supervised the cultural activities of the CIA, ". . . the idea that Congress would have approved many of our projects was about as likely as the John Birch Society's approving Medicare." There was resistance to these projects in the CIA itself. To a man of Braden's background and inclinations, the idea of supporting liberal and socialist "fronts" grew naturally out of the logic of the Cold War. During the Second World War Braden served with the OSS—next to the communist movement itself the most fruitful source, it would appear, of postwar anticommunism (the same people often having served in both). Before joining the CIA in 1950, Braden served as president of the California Board of Education. He represented a new type of bureaucrat, equally at home in government and in academic circles; but when in 1950 he proposed that "the CIA ought to take on the Russians by penetrating a battery of international fronts," his more conventional colleagues made the quaint objection that "this is just another one of those goddamned proposals for getting into everybody's hair." Allen Dulles intervened to save the project after it had been voted down by the division chiefs. "Thus began the first centralized effort to combat Communist fronts."

Before they had finished, the directors of the CIA had infiltrated the National Student Association, the Institute of International Labor Research, the American Newspaper Guild, the American Friends of the Middle East, the National Council of Churches, and many other worthy organizations. "We . . . placed one agent in a Europe-based organization of intellectuals called the Congress for Cultural Freedom," Braden notes. This "agent" was Michael Josselson, who was born in Russia in 1908, educated in Germany, represented American department stores in Paris in the mid-thirties, came to the United States just before the war, and was naturalized in 1941. During the war Josselson, like Braden, served in the OSS. Afterwards he was sent to Berlin as an officer for cultural affairs in Patton's army. There he met Melvin J. Lasky. In 1947 he and Lasky led a walkout of anticommunists from a cultural meeting in the Russian sector of Berlin. When they organized the Congress for Cultural Freedom in 1950, Josselson became its executive director—a position he still holds, in spite of the exposure of his connection with the CIA.

"Another Agent became an editor of *Encounter*." The usefulness of these agents, Braden says, was that they "could not only propose anti-Communist programs to the official leaders of the organizations but they could also suggest ways and means to solve the inevitable budgetary problems. Why not see if the needed money could be obtained from 'American foundations'?" Note that he does not describe the role of the CIA as having been restricted to financing these fronts; its agents were also to promote "anti-Communist programs." When it became public that the Congress for Cultural Freedom had been financed for sixteen years by the CIA, the editors of *Encounter* made a great point of the fact that the Congress had never dictated policy to the magazine; but the whole question takes on a different color in light of Braden's disclosure that one of the editors worked for the CIA. Under these circumstances, it was unnecessary for the Congress to dictate policy to *Encounter;* nor would the other editors, ignorant of these connections, have been aware of any direct intervention by the CIA.

On April 27, 1966, the *New York Times,* in a long article on the CIA, reported that the CIA had supported the Congress for Cultural Freedom and other organizations through a system of dummy foundations, and that "*Encounter* magazine . . . was for a long time—though it is not now—one of the indirect beneficiaries of C.I.A. funds." (Rumors to this effect had circulated for years.) The editors of *Encounter*— Stephen Spender, Lasky, and Irving Kristol—wrote an extremely disingenuous letter to the *Times* in which they tried to refute the assertion without denying it outright. They asserted—what was a half-truth at best—that the Congress's funds "were derived from various recognized foundations— all of them (from such institutions as the Ford and Rockefeller Foundations to the smaller ones) publicly listed in the official directories." What was not publicly listed, of course, was the fact that some of these "smaller ones" received money from the CIA for the express purpose of supporting the Congress for Cultural Freedom. Thus between 1961 and 1966, the CIA through some of its phony foundations gave $430,700 to the Hoblitzelle Foundation, a philanthropical enterprise established by the Dallas millionaire Karl Hoblitzelle, and the Hoblitzelle Foundation obligingly passed along these funds to the Congress for Cultural Freedom. Needless to say, no hint of these transactions appeared in the Lasky-Spender-Kristol letter to the *Times.*

Privately, Lasky went much further and declared categorically that *Encounter* had never received funds from the CIA. (Later he admitted that he had been "insufficiently frank" with his colleagues and friends.) In public, however, the magazine's defense was conducted in language of deliberate ambiguity. Another letter to the *Times,* signed by John

Kenneth Galbraith, George Kennan, Robert Oppenheimer, and Arthur Schlesinger, Jr., completely avoided the question of *Encounter*'s financing and argued merely that the magazine's editorial independence proved that it had never been "used" by the CIA—a statement, however, which carried with it the implication that the CIA had had nothing to do with the organization at all. One must ask why these men felt it necessary to make such a guarded statement, and why, since they had to state their position so cautiously, they felt it necessary to make any statement at all. The matter is even more puzzling in view of Galbraith's statement in the New York *World Journal Tribune* (March 13, 1967) that "some years ago," while attending a meeting of the Congress in Berlin (he probably refers to a conference held there in 1960), he had been told by a "knowledgeable friend" that the Congress for Cultural Freedom might be receiving support from the CIA. Galbraith says that he "subjected its treasurer to interrogation and found that the poor fellow had been trained in ambiguity but not dissemblance." "I was disturbed," he says, "and I don't think I would have attended any more meetings" if his entrance into government service had not ended his participation. In another interview Galbraith told Ivan Yates of the London *Observer* (May 14, 1967), that he "made a mental note to attend no more meetings of the Congress." Yates asked "how in that case he could possibly have signed the letter to the *New York Times*. He replied that at the time, he had 'very strong suspicions' that the CIA had been financing the Congress. 'I was writing really with reference to *Encounter,* but you could easily persuade me that the letter was much too fulsome.'"

Whereas Lasky believes that he was "insufficiently frank," Galbraith allows that he may have been "too fulsome." It is remarkable what rigorous standards of intellectual honesty the champions of cultural freedom hold themselves up to. Galbraith's urbanity is imperturbable. The letter was "fulsome" indeed. Moreover, it specifically dealt with the Congress for Cultural Freedom, not with *Encounter,* which it does not even mention by name. The letter states that "examination of the record of the Congress, its magazines and its other activities will, we believe, convince the most skeptical that the Congress has had no loyalty except an unswerving commitment to cultural freedom. . . ." Yet one of the signers of this statement was sufficiently skeptical to have "made a mental note" not to attend any more meetings of the Congress! And at the same time that he was assuring the still unsuspecting public of the Congress's unimpeachable independence, he had privately reached the conclusion that it was probably being supported by the CIA. As a further indication of the values that prevail among our more notable intellects, when the *Encounter* affair finally became public, Galbraith's principal concern was that a valuable public enterprise was in danger of being discredited. The whole wretched business seemed inescapably to point to the conclusion that cultural freedom had been consistently confused with American propaganda, and that "cultural freedom," as defined by its leading defenders, was—to put it bluntly—a hoax. Yet at precisely the moment when the dimensions of the hoax were fully revealed, Galbraith joined the Congress's board of directors; and "I intend," he says, "to put some extra effort into its activities. I think this is the right course and I would urge similar effort on behalf of other afflicted but reformed organizations."

What should a "free thinker" do, asks the *Sunday Times* of London, "when he finds out that his free thought has been subsidized by a ruthlessly aggressive intelligence agency as part of the international cold war?" According to the curious values that prevail in American society, he should make a redoubled effort to salvage the reputation of organizations which have been compromised, it would seem, beyond redemption. Far from "reforming" themselves—even assuming that this was possible—*Encounter* and the Congress for Cultural Freedom have vindicated the very men who led them into disaster. At their meeting in Paris in May 1967, officials of the Congress voted to keep Josselson in his post. Lasky was likewise retained by the management of *Encounter*.

Ever since the *New York Times* asserted that *Encounter* had been subsidized by the CIA, the Congress and its defenders have tried to brazen out the crisis by intimidating their critics—the same tactics that worked so well in the days of the Cold War. Arthur Schlesinger leaped into the breach by attacking one of *Encounter*'s principal critics, Conor Cruise O'Brien. Following the *Times*'s initial disclosures, O'Brien delivered a lecture at New York University, subsequently published in *Book Week,* in which he referred to the *Times* story and went on to observe that "the beauty of the [CIA-*Encounter*] operation . . . was that writers of the first rank, who had no interest at all in serving the power structure, were induced to do so unwittingly," while "the writing specifically required by the power structure" could be done by writers of lesser ability, men skilled in public relations and "who were, as the Belgians used to say about Moise Tshombe, *compréhensifs,* that is, they could take a hint." In reply, Schlesinger at first dodged the question of *Encounter*'s relations with the CIA by attacking O'Brien's "apparent inability to conceive any reason for opposition to Communism except bribery by the CIA." When pressed, he said that "so long as I have been a member of the *Encounter* Trust, *Encounter* has not been the beneficiary, direct or indirect, of CIA funds." (The subsidies to *Encounter* are said to have run from 1953 to 1964, although the Congress's connection with the CIA, according to Galbraith, continued until 1966.) Moreover, Schlesinger said, Spender, Lasky, and Kristol had revealed "the past sources of *Encounter*'s support" and documented "its editorial and political independence." They had, of course, done nothing of the kind. The magazine's editorial independence was not to be taken on the editors' word, and the question of its financing was an issue they had studiously avoided. Why did Schlesinger go out of his way to endorse their evasions? Presumably he knew as much about *Encounter*'s relations with the CIA as Galbraith—probably a good deal more. How was cultural freedom served by lending oneself to a deliberate deception?

In its issue of August 1966, *Encounter* published a scurrilous attack on O'Brien by "R" (Goronwy Rees). Karl Miller of the *New Statesman* offered O'Brien space to reply, but when Frank Kermode of *Encounter* (who has since resigned as editor, saying that he knew nothing of Lasky's connections) learned of this, he called Miller and threatened to sue the

New Statesman for libel if O'Brien's piece contained any reference to *Encounter*'s relations with the CIA. O'Brien then sued *Encounter* for libel and won a judgment in Ireland. At this point *Ramparts* broke the story of the CIA's infiltration of NSA, bringing a whole series of other disclosures in its wake, including the CIA's connection with the Congress for Cultural Freedom. The editors of *Encounter*, unable to deny those relations any longer, and threatened with heavy damages, apologized to O'Brien, retracted its aspersions on his integrity (which it now admitted were "without justification"), and agreed to pay his legal expenses.

Throughout this controversy, the editors of *Encounter* have repeatedly pointed to their editorial independence. Spender, Kristol, and Lasky, in their letter to the *Times*, claimed that "We are our own masters and are part of nobody's propaganda." The Galbraith-Schlesinger letter declared that *Encounter* maintained "no loyalty except an unswerving commitment to cultural freedom" and that it had "freely criticized actions and policies of all nations, including the United States." These statements, however, need to be set against Thomas Braden's account of the rules that guided the International Organization Division of the CIA: "Use legitimate, existing organizations; disguise the extent of American interest; protect the integrity of the organization by not requiring it to support every aspect of official American policy."

These rules do more than shed light on the nature and extent of *Encounter*'s editorial freedom. By publishing them at a time when they must surely embarrass the writers concerned, Braden reveals a contempt for their kept intellectuals which the Officers of the CIA cannot conceal. Whatever the intellectuals may have thought of the relationship, the CIA regarded them exactly as the Communist party regarded its fronts in the thirties and forties—as instruments of its own purpose. Most of the beneficiaries of the CIA have been understandably slow to see this point; it is hard to admit that one has been used and that one's sense of freedom and power is an illusion. Norman Thomas, for instance, admits that he should have known where the money for his Institute of International Labor Relations was coming from, but (like

Galbraith, like Thomas Braden himself) what he chiefly
regrets is that a worthwhile work has had to come prema-
turely to an end. The Kaplan Fund, Thomas insists, "never
interfered in any way"—which merely means that he was
never aware of its interference. He does not see that he was
being used, as Stephen Spender puts it in his own case, "for
quite different purposes" from the ones he thought he was
advancing. *He* thought he was working for democratic reform in Latin America, whereas the CIA valued him as a
showpiece, an anticommunist who happened to be a socialist.*

Spender has had the wit to recognize the situation (retro-
spectively) for what it was. "In reality," he writes, the intellectuals employed by the CIA without their knowledge were
"being used for concealed government propaganda." Spender admits that this arrangement made a "mockery" of
intellectual freedom. Michael Wood, formerly of the NSA,
has written even more poignantly of his relations with the
world of power. "Those of us who worked for NSA during
1965–1966, experienced an unusual sense of personal liberation. While actively involved in many of the insurgent
campus and political movements of the day, we were also
able to move freely through the highest echelons of established power." These experiences, Wood says, "gave us a
heady feeling and a sense of power beyond our years." But
"to learn that it had been bought with so terrible a compromise made me realize how impotent we really were."

VIII

What conclusions can be drawn from the history of the
cultural cold war? Some conclusions should be obvious.
Thanks to the revelations of the CIA's secret subsidies, it is
no longer a very novel or startling proposition to say that
American officials have committed themselves to fighting fire
with fire, and that this strategy is self-defeating because the

---

* Braden is under the impression that this sort of thing cut a great deal
of ice in Europe, at which the CIA's cultural program was directed.
"The fact, of course, is that in much of Europe in the 1950s, socialists,
people who called themselves 'left'—the very people whom many
Americans thought no better than Communists—were the only
people who gave a damn about fighting Communism."

means corrupt the end. "In our attempts to fight unscrupulous opponents," asks Arthur J. Moore in *Christianity and Crisis,* "have we ended up debauching ourselves?" The history of the Cold War makes it clear that the question can only be answered with an emphatic affirmative.

These events, if people consider them seriously and try to confront their implications without flinching, will lead many Americans to question (perhaps for the first time) the cant about American "pluralism," the "open society," etc. Andrew Kopkind puts it very well: "The illusion of dissent was maintained: the CIA supported socialist cold warriors, fascist cold warriors, black and white cold warriors. . . . But it was a sham pluralism, and it was utterly corrupting." A society which tolerates an illusory dissent is in greater danger, in some respects, than a society in which uniformity is ruthlessly imposed.

For twenty years Americans have been told that their country is an open society and that communist peoples live in slavery. Now it appears that the very men who were most active in spreading this gospel were themselves the servants ("witty" in some cases, unsuspecting in others) of the secret police. The whole show—the youth congresses, the cultural congresses, the trips abroad, the great glamorous display of American freedom and American civilization and the American standard of living—was all arranged behind the scenes by men who believed, with Thomas Braden, that "the cold war was and is a war, fought with ideas instead of bombs." Men who have never been able to conceive of ideas as anything but instruments of national power were the sponsors of "cultural freedom."

The revelations about the intellectuals and the CIA should also make it easier to understand a point about the relation of intellectuals to power—a point that has been widely misunderstood. In associating themselves with the warmaking and propaganda machinery of the state in the hope of influencing it, intellectuals deprive themselves of the real influence they could have as men who refuse to judge the validity of ideas by the requirements of national power or any other entrenched interest. Time after time in this century it has been shown that the dream of influencing the war machine is a delusion. Instead, the war machine corrupts the intellectuals. The war machine cannot be influenced by the advice of well-meaning intellectuals in the inner councils of government; it can only be resisted. The way to resist it is simply to refuse to put oneself at its service. For intellectuals that does not mean playing at revolution; it does not mean putting on blackface and adopting the speech of the ghetto; it does not mean turning on, tuning in, and dropping out; it does not even mean engaging in desperate acts of conscience which show one's willingness to take risks and to undergo physical danger. Masking as a higher selflessness, these acts become self-serving, having as their object not truth, or even social change, but the promotion of the individual's self-esteem. Moreover they betray, at a deeper level, the same loss of faith which drives others into the service of the men in power—a haunting suspicion that history belongs to men of action, and that men of ideas are powerless in a world that has no use for philosophy. It is precisely this belief that has enabled the same men, in one lifetime, to serve both the Communist party and the CIA in the delusion that they were helping to make history—only to find, in both cases, that all they had made was a lie. But these defeats—the revelation that the man of action, revolutionist or bureaucrat, scorns the philosopher whom he is able to use—have not led the philosopher to conclude that he should not allow himself to be used; they merely reinforce his self-contempt and make him the ready victim of a new political cause.

The despair of intellect is closely related to the despair of democracy. In our time intellectuals are fascinated by conspiracy and intrigue, even as they celebrate the "free marketplace of ideas" (itself an expression that already betrays a tendency to regard ideas as commodities). They long to be on the inside of things; they want to share the secrets ordinary people are not permitted to hear.

In the last twenty years, the elitism of intellectuals has expressed itself as a celebration of American life, and this fact makes it hard to see the continuity between the thirties and forties on the one hand and the fifties and sixties on the other. The hyper-Americanism of the latter period seems to be a reaction against the anti-Americanism of the depression years. Both of these phenomena, however, spring from the same source, the intellectuals' disenchantment with democracy and their alienation from intellect itself. Intellectuals associate themselves with the American war machine not so much because it represents America as because it represents action, power, and conspiracy; and the identification is even easier because the war machine is itself "alienated" from the people it claims to defend. The defense intellectuals, "cool" and "arrogant," pursue their obscure calculations in a little world bounded by the walls of the Pentagon, sealed off from the difficult reality outside which does not always respond to their formulas and which, therefore, has to be ignored in arriving at correct solutions to the "problems" of government. At Langley, Virginia, the CIA turns its back on America and busies itself with its empire abroad. But this empire, which the CIA tries to police, has no relation to the real lives of the people of the world—it is a fantasy of the CIA, in which conspiracy and counterconspiracy, freedom and communist slavery, the forces of light and the forces of darkness, are locked in timeless combat. The concrete embodiments of these abstractions have long since ceased to matter. The processes of government have been intellectualized. Albert D. Biderman, the prophet of "social accounting," speaks for the dominant ethos: "With the growth of the complexity of society, immediate experience with its events plays an increasingly smaller role as a source of information and basis of judgment in contrast to symbolically mediated information about these events. . . . Numerical indexes of phenomena are peculiarly fitted to these needs."[*]

Washington belongs to the "future-planners," men who believe that "social accounting" will solve social "problems." Government is a "think tank," an ivory tower, a community of scholars. A member of the RAND Corporation speaks of its "academic freedom" which "allows you to think about what you want to." A civil servant praises the democratic tolerance, the respect for ideas, that prevail in the Defense Department. Herman Kahn, jolly and avuncular, encourages

[*] See Sol Stein, "The Defense Intellectuals," *Ramparts*, February 1967; Andrew Kopkind, "The Future-Planners," *New Republic*, February 25, 1967.

"intellectual diversity"; on his staff at the Hudson Institute, a center of learning devoted to the science of systematic destruction, he retains a dedicated pacifist who doubtless thinks that he is slowly converting the Hudson Institute to universal brotherhood.

Never before have the ruling classes been so solicitous of cultural freedom; but since this freedom no longer has anything to do with "immediate experience and its events," it exists in a decontaminated, valueless void.

NOTES ON CONTRIBUTORS

Barton J. Bernstein, Assistant Professor of History at Stanford University, is an editor (with Allen J. Matusow) of *The Truman Administration: A Documentary History* and is preparing a history of the Truman years. Born in New York City in 1936, he attended Queens College (B.A., 1957), Washington University (St. Louis), and Harvard University (Ph.D., 1963), where he studied under Professors Frank Freidel and Oscar Handlin. Formerly a member of the Bennington College Faculty and now a Fellow at the Charles Warren Center for American Studies (at Harvard), he is a former Woodrow Wilson Fellow and has received grants from the American Philosophical Society and the American Council of Learned Societies.

Lloyd C. Gardner, Associate Professor of History at Rutgers University, is the author of *Economic Aspects of New Deal Diplomacy* (1964) and the editor of *A Different Frontier: Selected Readings in the Foundation of American Economic Expansion* (1966). Born in Delaware, Ohio, in 1934, a graduate of Ohio Wesleyan University (B.A., 1956) and the University of Wisconsin (Ph.D., 1960), where he studied with Professor William Appleman Williams, Professor Gardner was a Woodrow Wilson Fellow and has held a Social Science Research Council Fellowship for a study of foreign policy of the Progressive Era, which he is completing.

Eugene D. Genovese, Professor of History at Sir George Williams University in Montreal, is the author of *The Political Economy of Slavery: Studies in the Economy and Society of the Slave South* (1965) and is currently working on a series of volumes on the Slave South. Born in Brooklyn, New York, in 1930, he received his education at Brooklyn College (B.A., 1953) and Columbia University (M.A., 1955; Ph.D., 1959). A former member of the faculty at Polytechnic Institute of Brooklyn and at Rutgers University, he is also an editor of the *Journal of Social History* and a founder of the annual Socialist Scholars Conference.

Christopher Lasch, Professor of History at Northwestern University, is the author of *The American Liberals and the Russian Revolution* (1962) and *The New Radicalism in America, 1889–1963: The Intellectual as a Social Type* (1965), and the editor of *The Social Thought of Jane Addams* (1965). Born in Omaha, Nebraska, in 1932, he attended Harvard University (B.A., 1954) and Columbia University (Ph.D., 1961), and has also taught at Williams College, Roosevelt University, and the State University of Iowa. For his research in American Intellectual and Social history, he received the Erb and Gilder Fellowships at Columbia and two grants from the Social Science Research Council.

Michael A. Lebowitz, Assistant Professor of Economics at Simon Fraser University, was born in Newark, New Jersey, in 1937, and attended the New York University School of Commerce (B.S., 1960), during which time he worked as a market research analyst in the electrical products industry. He studied economic history at the University of Wisconsin (M.S., 1964), and is now completing his doctoral dissertation, an examination of banking in developing regions during the Jacksonian period. Recent papers include "In the Absence of Free Banks, What?" (1967) and "The Role of Banks in Developing Regions in the United States in the Nineteenth Century" (1967). He is a former editor of *Studies on the Left.*

Jesse Lemisch, Assistant Professor of History at the University of Chicago, is the editor of *Benjamin Franklin: Autobiography and Other Writings* (1961) and is currently working on a new book entitled *Jack Tar vs. John Bull: Merchant Seamen in the Politics of Revolutionary America.* Born in New York City in 1936, he attended Yale University (B.A., 1957), Columbia University (M.A. 1958), and received his Ph.D. in 1963 from Yale University where he worked with Edmund Morgan. He has had articles published in *The Nation,* the *New-York Historical Society Quarterly* and *William and Mary Quarterly* (in press). He is the recipient of a Fellowship from the American Council of Learned Societies

(1965–1966), a Grant in Aid from the same organization in 1965, and a Willett Faculty Fellowship from the University of Chicago in 1965. He previously taught at Yale.

Staughton Lynd, Assistant Professor of History at Yale University, is the author of *Antifederalism in Dutchess County* (1962), *Class Conflict, Slavery, and the United States Constitution* (1967), and (with Thomas Hayden) *The Other Side* (1967); in 1968 he will publish *Intellectual Origins of American Radicalism*. He is also the editor of *Nonviolence in America: A Documentary History* (1965) and *Reconstruction* (1967). Born in Philadelphia in 1929, he attended Harvard University (B.A., 1951), the University of Chicago, and Columbia University (Ph.D., 1962), where he was an Erb Fellow. He has taught at Spelman College (Atlanta), the Free University of New York, and Yale University, where he also held a Morse Fellowship. A modified version of "Beyond Beard" has appeared as the introductory essay in Lynd's *Class Conflict, Slavery, and the United States Constitution*.

James M. McPherson, Associate Professor of History at Princeton University, is the author of *The Struggle for Equality: Abolitionists and the Negro in the Civil War and Reconstruction* (1964) and the editor of *The Negro's Civil War: How American Negroes Felt and Acted During the War for the Union* (1965). Born in Valley City, North Dakota, in 1936, he graduated from Gustavus Adolphus College (B.A., 1958) and Johns Hopkins University (Ph.D., 1963), where he studied with Professor C. Vann Woodward. A Woodrow Wilson and Danforth Fellow, Professor McPherson has also received a Procter and Gamble Faculty Fellowship at Princeton and fellowships from the National Endowment for the Humanities and the Guggenheim Foundation for his research on Northern liberals and the Negro, 1870–1910.

Robert Freeman Smith, Associate Professor of History at the University of Connecticut, is the author of *The United States and Cuba: Business and Diplomacy, 1917–1960* (1961), and the editor of *What Happened in Cuba? A Documentary History* (1963) and *Background to Revolution: The Development of Modern Cuba* (1966). Born in Little Rock in 1930, he attended the University of Arkansas (B.A., 1952), and the University of Wisconsin (Ph.D., 1958), where he worked with Professor Fred Harvey Harrington. Professor Smith has also taught at the University of Arkansas, Texas Lutheran College, and the University of Rhode Island, and was a visiting professor at the University of Wisconsin (1966–1967).

Stephan Thernstrom, Associate Professor of History at Brandeis University, is the author of *Poverty and Progress: Social Mobility in a Nineteenth Century City* (1964) and is completing a volume on the social history of Boston. Born in Port Huron, Michigan, in 1934, he attended Northwestern University (B.A., 1956), and Harvard University (Ph.D., 1962), where he studied with Professor Oscar Handlin. Recipient of a Woodrow Wilson Fellowship, a Sheldon Traveling Grant, an American Council of Learned Societies Fellowship, and a Samuel Stouffer Fellowship at the MIT-Harvard Joint Center for Urban Studies, he previously taught at Harvard. He is currently on the editorial board of *Dissent*.

Marilyn Blatt Young was born in Brooklyn, New York, in 1937, and attended Vassar College (B.A., 1957) and Harvard University (Ph.D., 1963), where she studied under Professors John King Fairbank and Ernest R. May. She was a Fellow of Harvard's Committee on American Far Eastern Policy Studies for three years, and her research has concentrated on American China policy in the late nineteenth century. Her study of American China policy in the late nineteenth century will be published by Harvard University Press in 1968.

VINTAGE HISTORY—WORLD

A free catalogue of VINTAGE BOOKS *will be sent at your request. Write to* Vintage Books, 457 Madison Avenue, New York, New York 10022.